A CONCISE ENCYCLOPEDIA *of* BUDDHISM

Other books in the same series

A Concise Encyclopedia of Judaism, Dan Cohn-Sherbok, ISBN 1–85168–176–0
A Concise Encyclopedia of Hinduism, Klaus K. Klostermaier, ISBN 1–85168–175–2
A Concise Encyclopedia of Christianity, Geoffrey Parrinder, ISBN 1–85168–174–4
A Concise Encyclopedia of the Bahá'í Faith, Peter Smith, ISBN 1–85168–184–1

Other books on Buddhism published by Oneworld

Buddhism: A Short History, Edward Conze, ISBN 1–85168–221–X
Buddhism: A Short Introduction, Klaus K. Klostermaier, ISBN 1–85168–186–8
Buddhist Texts through the Ages, translated and edited by Edward Conze, I.B. Horner, David Snellgrove and Arthur Waley, ISBN 1–85168–107–8
What Buddhists Believe, Elizabeth J. Harris, ISBN 1–85168–168–X
Buddhism and the Mythology of Evil: A Study in Theraveda Buddhism, Trevor Ling, ISBN 1–85168–132–9
What the Buddha Taught, Walpola Sri Rahula, ISBN 1–85168–142–6

A CONCISE ENCYCLOPEDIA *of* BUDDHISM

JOHN POWERS

ONEWORLD
OXFORD

Dedication
To Mike,
my brother and friend

A CONCISE ENCYCLOPEDIA OF BUDDHISM

Oneworld Publications
(Sales and Editorial)
185 Banbury Road
Oxford OX2 7AR
England
http://www.oneworld-publications.com

Oneworld Publications
(US Marketing Office)
160 N Washington St.
4th Floor, Boston
MA 02114
USA

A CIP record for this title is available
from the British Library

ISBN 1–85168–233–3

Cover design by Design Deluxe
Typeset by LaserScript, Mitcham, UK
Printed and bound in the United Kingdom by Bell & Bain Ltd, Glasgow

Contents

Important Buddhist sites in Asia

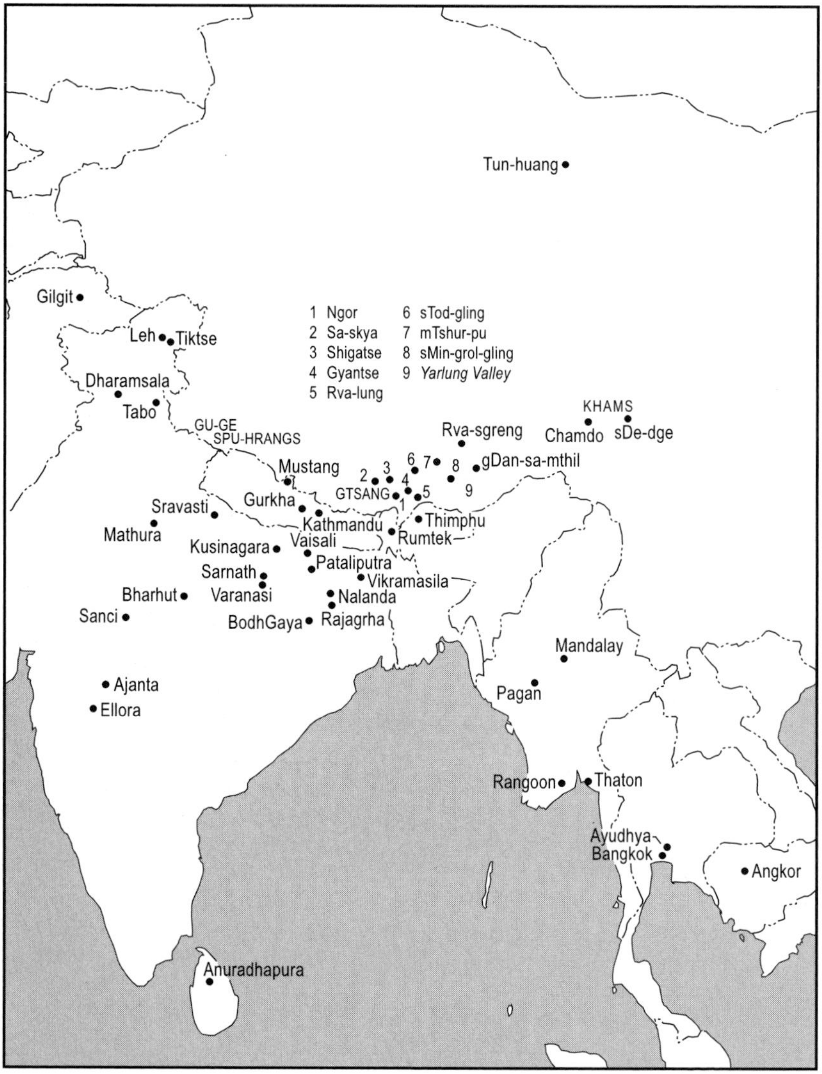

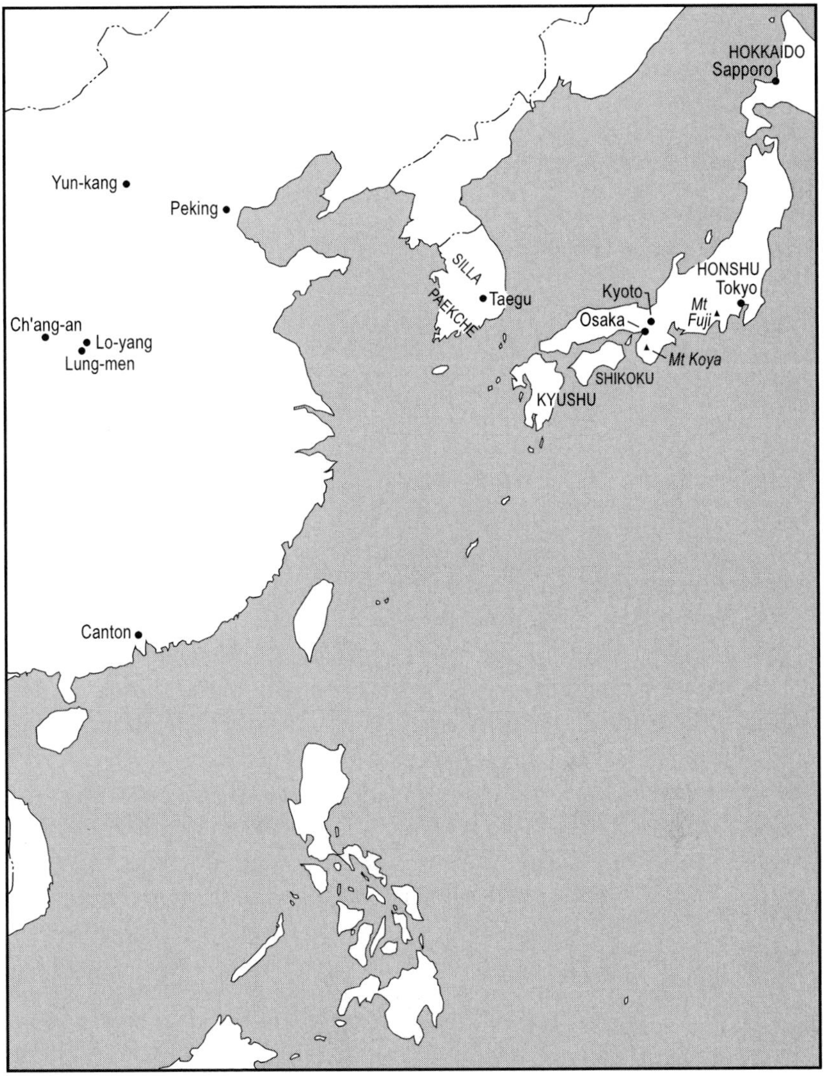

HOKKAIDO
Sapporo
Yun-kang
Peking
SILLA
PAEKCHE
Taegu
Kyoto
HONSHU
Tokyo
Mt
Fuji
Osaka
Mt Koya
SHIKOKU
KYUSHU
Ch'ang-an
Lo-yang
Lung-men
Canton

Preface

Compiling an encyclopedia of Buddhism is a humbling experience. Because of Buddhism's long history and the profusion of its literary sources – as well as its many philosophical and practice traditions – few specialists can claim a comprehensive knowledge of this religion. The compilation of this book required far more work and research than I had initially imagined, and along the way I became aware of the many gaps in my own understanding. Thus this has been a learning experience, which required research and re-evaluation of traditions on which I had previously studied and published, as well as exploration of new areas of which I had previously known little or nothing. Readers of this book will probably have similar experiences, since no matter which parts of Buddhism one knows well, there are many others of which one has little knowledge. Given the long history of Buddhism, this is to be expected, and the richness of the tradition is one of the reasons why so many great minds have been attracted to it through the two and a half millennia of its existence. Given this diversity, it is also to be expected that readers of this book who belong to a particular Buddhist tradition will find many entries that discuss ideas and practices which have little or no resonance with what they identify as "Buddhism."

The primary aim of this book is to provide basic and accurate information on important Buddhist doctrines, practices, figures, and mythological motifs that students might encounter in both introductory and specialist works on the tradition. Since many of these intersect with other entries, readers are pointed to related entries, which are indicated by uppercase letters. The choice of which entries to include was guided by my own evaluations of their relative importance and my goal of providing useful information on a broad range of Buddhist systems, terminology, and figures. The series of which this book is a part has a contemporary orientation, and so I have tried to include information on some of the most influential Buddhists in the modern period from all over the world, as well as entries on historically important figures. Such an endeavor is fraught with difficulties, and undoubtedly readers will question why some entries were included while other important figures and terms were not, but such criticism is inevitable in a work such as this. The choices were guided by my own assessments and by consultation with other specialists, as well as research into traditional sources and modern scholarship.

Because there is little agreement among translators of Buddhist texts regarding English equivalents of technical terms, I decided to give priority to Buddhist canonical languages, such as Sanskrit, Pāli, Chinese, Japanese, Korean, and Tibetan, and to enter terms in accordance with the standard spellings accepted by specialists in the various fields of Buddhist scholarship. Thus Indic technical terms are entered in accordance with the standard Sanskrit or Pāli spellings, and equivalents in other languages are generally provided. In addition, common translation equivalents (and some widely used phonetic spellings) are given in order to direct readers to the relevant entries. Decisions regarding which equivalents to include were based on whether or not a given term is significant in a particular country. Thus some Indic terms have had little impact outside India, and so there seemed to be no reason to mention their equivalents in other languages, while others have had a pervasive influence across the Buddhist world. Similarly, East Asian and Tibetan systems developed distinctive doctrines and practices, some of which reflect Indic origins, while others do not. It is hoped that the overall mix of entries strikes a balance between doctrines, practices, philosophical systems, important figures, mythology, iconography, art, and history. Given the complexity of the subject, it is inevitable that some omissions will occur. A work such as this is not intended as a replacement for the growing corpus of studies on Buddhism, and so a thematic bibliography is provided at the end of the book that should serve as a guide to more substantial studies of some of the entries in this book.

During the process of research and writing, I have received advice and information from a number of people, and wish to thank all of them collectively. Several colleagues provided substantial assistance in proofreading, correcting errors, and providing supplementary information. In particular, I would like to thank David Templeman for his thorough proofreading and the many helpful suggestions he made, Christian Coseru for his insightful comments and corrections, Ben Dorman for his help on Japanese Buddhism, and Ton-That Quyng-Du, who corrected misspellings of Vietnamese terms and provided invaluable information on Vietnamese Buddhism. Finally, I wish to express my gratitude to my wife Cindy for her help and support during this project.

Introduction

During its 2,500 year history, Buddhism has influenced virtually every corner of Asia, and in recent times has also attracted significant numbers of converts and students in other parts of the world. In every country to which it traveled, Buddhism adapted to the languages, customs, and cultural paradigms of the area, with the result that today the term "Buddhism" encompasses a diverse range of practices, doctrines, and terms, as well as different systems, many of which have little or nothing in common with others. For example, one can find within the Buddhist tradition systems that emphasize rational thought and that urge practitioners to use reasoning and debate as means of attaining higher levels of awareness and eventually salvation, but there are also Buddhist traditions that eschew rational thought as antithetical to salvation and instead urge their followers to place their faith humbly in the Buddha (or in other buddhas), in texts or teachers, or in a range of other things. In East Asian Pure Land traditions, for example, people are told that they are incapable of bringing about their own salvations and are advised to rely humbly on Amitābha Buddha. In Japanese traditions that derive from Nichiren, adherents are taught to rely solely on the *Lotus Sūtra* and to chant its title in Japanese in order to access its saving power. In some Tibetan tantric practices, students are supposed to develop uncritical faith in their gurus as embodiments of buddhahood. Other Buddhist schools, such as some Ch'an/Zen/Sŏn lineages, advocate dispensing with Buddhist scriptures and authority figures and engaging in meditation that aims at attaining a direct, intuitive, non-conceptual experience of reality as it truly is. Given the diversity of Buddhism, the task of compiling a concise encyclopedia of the tradition is a daunting one, since there will necessarily be significant omissions and simplifications.

The Buddha and his teaching

According to Buddhist tradition, the dharma (a general term for Buddhist doctrine and practice) is eternal truth that presents a path for liberating oneself and others from the endless round of birth, death, and rebirth in which all beings are trapped. The founder of the tradition, commonly referred to as Śākyamuni Buddha, probably lived sometime around the middle of the first millennium B.C.E. and according to traditional accounts was born in Lumbinī, which is located in present-day Nepal. These accounts relate that he was a prince of the royal family of Kapilavastu, the capital city of the Śākya clan (and thus the epithet Śākyamuni means "Sage of the Śākyas"). His father Śuddhodana was the king of Kapilavastu and the surrounding area, and he reportedly tried to steer his son away from religious pursuits, hoping that he would follow in his footsteps and become a ruler.

Despite his efforts, the prince (who was given the name Siddhārtha, "He whose Aims are Accomplished," at birth) eventually became aware of the harsh realities of life – including sickness, old age, death, loss, and suffering – and subsequently resolved to find a way to transcend these problems. After leaving his family's palace, he wandered for six years as a religious seeker, studying with several teachers, practicing meditation and asceticism in hopes of finding a way out of the sufferings of ordinary existence. After trying a number of unsuccessful methods, he discovered the dharma for himself during a protracted session of meditation. He realized that beings are trapped in the cycle of birth, death, and rebirth (referred to by Buddhists as *saṃsāra*) due to ignorance (*avidyā*), which causes them to cling to impermanent and ultimately unsatisfying things (such as wealth, fame, sex, possessions, power, careers, relationships, etc.). He further perceived that all phenomena are merely collections of parts that are constantly changing (and thus impermanent), that there is no enduring essence or soul, and that because of the constantly shifting nature of phenomena, all beings are prone to suffering.

Traditional accounts report that after realizing these truths, Siddhārtha became a "buddha" – meaning "awakened one" – no longer bound by the ignorance that keeps ordinary beings in the cycle of birth, death, and rebirth, and thus he was free from avoidable suffering (that is, suffering caused by mistaken ideas and afflicted grasping). It should be noted, however, that he is not thought to be the only person to have directly intuited the dharma: according to tradition, there have been many buddhas in the past, and there will be many more in the future. The truth is theoretically accessible to all, but most fail to recognize it because they are so enmeshed in ignorance and its associated activities that they seldom even realize that there is a problem.

Following his awakening experience, the Buddha reportedly feared that his newfound realization was too profound for others to understand. Thus he initially decided to remain in silent contemplation and pass away without teaching, but he was persuaded by the god Brahmā Sahāmpati that there were a few people in the world who had only a small amount of ignorance veiling their awareness and that these people would be able to understand his teaching and attain liberation (*nirvāṇa* or *mokṣa*). The Buddha reportedly agreed to begin instructing those who wished to follow his path, and for the next forty years traveled all over the subcontinent of India, gathering followers wherever he went.

Because he felt that the attainment of liberation requires a complete commitment, he instituted an order of full-time practitioners, whom he called *bhikṣus*, or "mendicants." They renounced home and family, as well as the commitments and obligations of mainstream society, and wandered from place to place, with no fixed abode, subsisting on alms given to them by the laity. As symbols of their rejection of ordinary society, they shaved their heads and dressed in castoff rags that were sewn together as robes and dyed saffron. They were instructed to remain apart from society and to devote their time to meditative practice and study, and also to eliminate as many distractions as possible.

Spread and development of Buddhism

The sole exception to this eremitical ideal was the rainy season retreat, during which monks and nuns lived in small huts. As Buddhism developed, many of these dwellings grew, and monks and nuns began living in them during other times of the year. Eventually large monastic institutions developed, and these required administrators, staff, libraries, living quarters, etc. In addition, as a result of royal patronage and missionizing by Buddhist monastics, the tradition began to attract increasing numbers of lay followers, and it also spread beyond India. The earliest reported Buddhist mission was sponsored by the Mauryan ruler Aśoka (r. 272–236 B.C.E.), whose son Mahinda, a Buddhist monk, traveled to Sri Lanka and converted its king.

Mahinda and the king founded the first Buddhist establishment on the island, and from this base Buddhism subsequently spread throughout Southeast Asia. The tradition that became predominant in the region is the conservative Theravāda school, which bases its teachings and practices on the Pāli canon. Today it is the paramount Buddhist tradition in Sri Lanka, Thailand, Burma, Laos, and Cambodia.

In later centuries, Buddhism spread into Central Asia, and several of the oasis cities along the Silk Roads became centers for the dissemination of Buddhism. Caravans traveling along the northern and southern Silk Roads stopped in these towns, and Buddhist monks followed the routes into China, where they initially founded translation centers, and later monastic establishments. Mahāyāna Buddhism was the dominant tradition in Central Asia, and Mahāyāna lineages, texts, and practices predominated in China. From China Buddhism spread into Japan, Korea, and Vietnam, and in each of these areas its exponents adapted its teachings and practices to local paradigms and languages, with the result that many of the schools that developed in East Asia exhibit significant differences from Indian Buddhism.

Around the eighth century, Indian Buddhist teachers began to travel to Tibet; some of these were scholarly monks who brought the paradigm of the great monastic universities of north India, while others were lay tantrics who viewed monasticism and its structures as being antithetical to Buddhist practice. Both of these remained dominant traditions within Tibetan Buddhism, and even today advocates of both strands are found throughout the Tibetan cultural area. This area includes the whole of modern-day Tibet (which encompasses the "Tibet Autonomous Region" and neighboring culturally Tibetan areas that have been annexed to Chinese provinces such as Qinghai). Tibetan Buddhism also spread throughout the Himalayan region, and today predominates in Sikkim, Bhutan, and Ladakh, areas of northern Nepal and northern India, as well as Mongolia and parts of Russia and some Central Asian republics.

In recent decades, Buddhism has also begun to spread into the West, and today there are several hundred thousand professed Buddhists in North America and Europe, as well as numerous Buddhist centers. As with other places in which Buddhism has become established, Western Buddhism has adapted Asian practices and structures to its new environment.

Buddhist literature

In every area in which it developed, Buddhism produced a substantial literary corpus. Because each region generally has a particular predominant tradition, there are several distinctive Buddhist scriptural collections, as well as numerous non-canonical and paracanonical works. The only Buddhist canon that survives in an Indic language is the Pāli canon of the Theravāda school, which consists of three parts (referred to as the tipiṭaka, or "three baskets"): (1) Sutta-piṭaka, the "Basket of Discourses," which includes teachings attributed to the Buddha (and sometimes his immediate disciples); (2) Vinaya-piṭaka, the "Basket of Monastic Discipline," comprising texts on the life and conduct of Buddhist monks and nuns; and (3) Abhidhamma-piṭaka, "Basket of Higher Doctrine," a collection of scholastic treatises that focus mainly on psychology and epistemology. Other Indian Buddhist schools developed their own canons, but these are extant only in Sanskrit fragments and in Chinese and Tibetan translations.

In Tibet the canon is divided into two parts: (1) bKa' 'gyur (Ganggyur, "Translations of Teachings"), consisting of Mahāyāna sūtras and tantras attributed to the Buddha; and (2) bsTan 'gyur (Dengyur, "Translations of Treatises"), which includes commentaries and philosophical treatises by Indian, Tibetan, and Chinese authors. The suttas of the Theravāda canon were generally not translated into Tibetan (and Theravāda tradition considers the Mahāyāna sūtras to be forgeries), and so aside from the Vinaya sections there is little overlap between these two canons, both of which claim to contain the definitive teachings of Śākyamuni Buddha.

East Asian canonical collections derive from China, which developed a canon that brings together a disparate collection of texts. The dissemination of Buddhism to China took place over many centuries, and there was no systematic movement of texts from India, as happened in Tibet. Thus in China missionary monks and Chinese pilgrims brought texts that they considered important (or that were simply available), and the transmission occurred rather haphazardly. Sometimes a commentary on a text would arrive before the work on which it commented, and some important texts only arrived centuries after they had been widely disseminated in India. As a result, Chinese scholars tended to preserve all of the literature that came to them from India. They created a voluminous canon, which includes a wide variety of Buddhist literature and often has several translations of the same text. This canon has proven to be a treasure trove for modern scholars of Buddhism, since it provides information on texts and traditions that would otherwise be lost and contains evidence on the development of Buddhist doctrines and practices.

Buddhist doctrines

Buddhist doctrines reflect the diversity of the various scriptural collections. Within a few hundred years of the death of the Buddha, different schools began to appear in India, each with its own distinctive doctrines and practices. As Buddhism spread, there was no central ecclesiastical authority, and no person or group was able to dictate what beliefs should be considered orthodox by all Buddhists. There is, however, some agreement on core Buddhist principles, and with some qualification it can be asserted that all Buddhist traditions accept the four "noble truths" (*ārya-satya*: suffering, the arising of suffering, the cessation of suffering, and the path for overcoming suffering), the doctrine of dependent arising (*pratītya-samutpāda*), and the doctrines of selflessness (*anātman*) and impermanence (*anitya*). That being said, there is considerable variation among Buddhist traditions regarding how these should be interpreted, and in some quarters they are acknowledged as authoritative, but have little relevance for practice. Readers of this encyclopedia will encounter a wide variety of doctrines and practices. Inevitably some readers will question the choices made regarding inclusion and exclusion, but it is hoped that a representative selection has been achieved.

Conclusion

In the more than twenty-five centuries of its existence, the fortunes of Buddhism have waxed and waned. During times of royal and lay patronage, Buddhist establishments and literature have flourished, and the tradition has made incalculable contributions to world culture. It has also been the target of a number of organized persecutions, which in some places have severely weakened Buddhism, and in others eradicated it completely. Despite its vicissitudes, Buddhism remains one of the major world religions, with adherents all over the globe. In addition to its huge literary corpus – which includes works in Sanskrit, Pāli, Tibetan, Chinese, Japanese, Korean, Vietnamese, and many other Asian languages, as well as Western languages – Buddhism today has many impressive living exponents, who have immersed themselves in their respective literary and oral traditions and who continue to pass on their insights and learning to successive generations. Those who are interested in exploring the tradition are well advised to seek out both the texts in which core Buddhist ideas are expressed and its contemporary masters, the best of whom embody the living tradition of Buddhism and who express its doctrines and practices both in their teachings and in their daily lives.

Abbreviations

b.	born
B.C.E.	Before the Common Era (i.e., before 0 B.C.)
ca.	circa
C.E.	Common Era (i.e., after 0 B.C.)
Chin.	Chinese
d.	died
fl.	flourished
Jpn.	Japanese
Kor.	Korean
lit.	literally
Mon.	Mongolian
r.	reigned
Skt.	Sanskrit
Tib.	Tibetan
Viet.	Vietnamese

Pronunciation Guide

Since the goal of this encyclopedia is to provide a broad coverage of Buddhism in its various manifestations, it contains terms in a variety of languages, including Sanskrit, Pāli, Tibetan, Mongolian, Japanese, Chinese, Korean, Thai, Sinhala, and Vietnamese. Each of these may be written in various ways, and specialists commonly use diacritical marks to differentiate letters for which there is no clear English equivalent (or for which there may be more than one possible equivalent). For readers unfamiliar with the various languages in which Buddhist ideas have been expressed, these marks are often confusing at first. The purpose of this section is to provide general pronunciation guidelines and to indicate which transcription system has been used for each respective language.

Sanskrit and Pāli

Sanskrit was the *lingua franca* of intellectuals and religious authors in ancient India. The subcontinent had (and still has) a plethora of different language groups and dialects, and so Sanskrit functioned as a common mode of discourse. It is a highly developed linguistic system, capable of expressing philosophical concepts with great subtlety and precision, and it became the main literary medium for Mahāyāna Buddhism. The Buddha is said to have urged his followers not to write or translate texts in Sanskrit, preferring that they use vernaculars that could be widely understood by all classes of people, but after his death Buddhist authors increasingly moved toward Sanskritization, and the majority of influential Mahāyāna works are in Sanskrit (or in what is often referred to by scholars as "Buddhist Hybrid Sanskrit," which combines elements of various dialects). Pāli is a language that appears to be related to north Indian dialects, but contemporary scholars generally believe that it is a Sanskritized literary language which differs from other Indic dialects. It is the language of the Theravāda canon, the only complete Buddhist canon that survives in an Indic language. In the modern period, both Sanskrit and Pāli are often written in the Devanāgarī script, but in ancient India Sanskrit was expressed in many different writing systems. The Sanskrit and Pāli alphabet contains more letters than does English, and so a number of letters are commonly expressed by means of diacritical marks (or by combinations of Roman consonants or vowels). The rules of pronunciation are similar for both Sanskrit and Pāli.

VOWELS AND DIPHTHONGS USED IN THIS BOOK

letter	*pronunciation*
a	uh, as in fun
ā	ah, as in charm
i	ih, as in pin
ī	ee, as in seek
u	oo, as in sue
ū	ooh, as in school
e	ey, as in prey
o	oh, as in phone
ai	aye, as in time
au	ow, as in cow
ṛ	er, as in fur
ḷ	l, as in fulsome

For those interested in correct pronunciation, long vowels should take approximately twice as long to speak as short vowels; thus ā is slightly lengthened and emphasized when pronounced. In addition, it should be noted that emphasis is often different from what English speakers expect, and so *maṇḍala*, for example, is pronounced MUHN duh luh, and not mahn DAH la, as English speakers unfamiliar with Sanskrit often say it. The rules of Sanskrit pronunciation are too complex to explore in this section, but readers who are interested in learning them may consult the opening chapter of William Whitney's *Sanskrit Grammar* (Cambridge, MA: Harvard University Press, 1975).

CONSONANTS

Sanskrit and Pāli have several types of consonants, which are divided into five classes: guttural, palatal, lingual, dental, and labial. These classes are based on where in the mouth the sound is made. Thus gutturals are made in the throat, palatals are made by touching the tongue to the palate, linguals are retroflex sounds made by curling the tongue inside the mouth and touching the bottom of the tip to the palate, dentals are made by touching the tongue to the teeth, and labials are made with the lips. The gutturals are: ka, kha, ga, gha, and ṅa. The palatals are: ca, cha, ja, jha, and ña. The linguals are: ṭa, ṭha, ḍa, ḍha, and ṇa. The labials are: pa, pha, ba, bha, and ma. Other letters that should be mentioned are: (1) the "sibilants" śa and ṣa, both of which are pronounced "sh," as in usher or shine; (2) *anusvāra* ṃ, which is pronounced either as m, as in *saṃsāra*, or as ng, as in *saṃgha*; and (3) *visarga* ḥ, which is silent. V is classified as a "labial semivowel" and is commonly pronounced like English w by modern Indians. Thus "Veda" is pronounced "Wayda." Ca is pronounced cha, as in chair (and so Yogācāra is pronounced "Yogahchahra"). The palatal ña is pronounced nya; other letters are pronounced like their English equivalents.

Chinese

Chinese pronunciation presents a number of significant difficulties, beginning with the fact that Chinese words are written in characters, and not alphabetically. Added to this is the fact that Chinese has a number of sounds that are difficult for speakers of Western languages to approximate. In addition, Classical Chinese has only about four hundred allowable sounds (and four tones), which means that different Chinese terms may be rendered with the same English spelling. To make matters even more problematic, there are two widely used systems of transcribing Chinese sounds into English: (1) the Wade–Giles system; and (2) the Pinyin system. The former was the standard until 1979, when the government of the People's Republic of China (PRC) devised its own system (the Pinyin), which shares many similarities with Wade–Giles, but also has significant differences. Wade–Giles is used in this encyclopedia because although the Pinyin system is becoming progressively more standard among specialists, Wade–Giles is used in many of the most popular introductory works on Chinese Buddhism, and it is also widely used by Chinese Buddhists in Taiwan and other Chinese communities outside the PRC. Both systems are problematic in that those who are not familiar with how transliterations relate to actual speech often arrive at pronunciations that would be unrecognizable by native Chinese speakers. For readers who wish to convert to Pinyin, A. C. Graham provides an excellent guide to equivalents in *Disputers of the Tao* (La Salle, IL: Open Court, 1989), pp. 441–444.

Japanese

The standard way of transcribing Japanese is referred to as the Hepburn system, which is adopted in this book. Most letters used in this system closely approximate their equivalents in the Roman alphabet, with the exception of the long vowels ō and ū, which like Sanskrit long vowels are slightly lengthened and emphasized.

Tibetan

Tibetan presents special problems, the most significant of which relate to the use of unpronounced consonants. Although they are not pronounced, they often affect the pronunciation of other letters. Another difficulty relates to the history of Tibetan Studies in the West: when Western scholars first began studying Tibetan literature, they noted that the Tibetan alphabet was based on a north Indian script, and so they equated Tibetan letters with the Roman letters that were used as equivalents for Indic scripts. The problem with this is that the Tibetan letters are often pronounced very differently from the Indic ones, and so, for example, the Tibetan consonant commonly written as ka is actually pronounced ga, as in English girl (unless a prefixed unpronounced consonant alters how it is spoken). Fortunately, most transliterations of Tibetan letters into English are pronounced similarly to their Roman equivalents. Below is a chart indicating which letters are pronounced differently from their Roman counterparts.

Tibetan letter	*pronounced*
ka	ga, as in girth
ga	ka, as in kilt
nga	nga, as in songbird
ca	ja, as in jar
ja	cha, as in chair
ta	da, as in dole
da	ta, as in tell
pa	ba, as in boy
ba	pa, as in pot
za	sa, as in sell
zha	sha, as in show

In this book, the entries for Tibetan terms are given in accordance with the system developed by Turrell Wylie (see his article, "A Standard System of Tibetan Transcription," *Harvard Journal of Asiatic Studies*, vol. 22, 1959, pp. 261–267), which has become standard among specialists in the field. In light of the fact that most non-specialists generally know Tibetan terms and names in phonetic form, a phonetic pronunciation has been given in parentheses following the Wylie transliteration. The exception to this is the names of contemporary Tibetans who have created phonetic spellings of their own names. In these cases, the Wylie spelling is given in parentheses after the entry. The problems with pronouncing Tibetan are far too numerous to discuss in this section. Readers interested in exploring this topic should consult Joe B. Wilson's *Translating Buddhism from Tibetan* (Ithaca, NY: Snow Lion, 1992).

Korean

Korean language entries in this book follow the standard transcription used by specialists in the field. Most sounds in Hangŭl (the Korean writing system) can be expressed in similar-sounding Roman equivalents. The two main exceptions are: (1) the vowel ŏ, pronounced like o in pot; and (2) the vowel ŭ, pronounced like u in turn.

A

a ni (*ani*)

A colloquial term for a Tibetan Buddhist nun. Because the full monastic ordination for women (Skt. BHIKṢUṆĪ; Tib. *dge slong ma*) was never transmitted to Tibet, nuns only receive the novice (Skt. ŚRĀMAṆERĪ; Tib. *dge tshul ma*) vows.servility and savergy

Abhayagiri

An important early monastery in Sri Lanka, founded by King VAṬṬAGĀMAṆI in Anurādhapura during the first century B.C.E. Its monks formed a separate NIKĀYA (2) that remained intact until the 12th century, when it was ordered to amalgamate with the MAHĀVIHĀRA *nikāya* by King Parākramabāhu I.

abhidharma (Pāli *abhidhamma*; Tib. *chos mngon*; "higher doctrine")

A general term referring to the philosophical and scholastic literature contained in the ABHIDHARMA-PIṬAKAS of Indian Buddhist schools. This is both a distillation and elaboration on the doctrines presented in the SŪTRA (Pāli *sutta*) literature. The discourses reported in the sūtras do not present a consistent philosophical system, and so the aim of the *abhidharma* writers was to codify and systematize their doctrines. *Abhidharma* texts generally rearrange and classify the terms and concepts of the sūtras, focusing particularly on epistemology and psychology. Other important themes include cosmology and meditation theory. According to ERICH FRAUWALLNER, the earliest stratum of this literature was probably a condensation of the doctrines of the sūtras into *mātṛkā*, lists of terms and formulas. This was followed by a period in which scholars brought together concepts from a wide range of texts, but often without a clear pattern of arrangement. The fully developed *abhidharma* consists of voluminous scholastic texts in which doctrines and practices are codified and systematized with great precision and in elaborate detail. As various scholastic traditions developed in INDIAN BUDDHISM, different schools created their own *abhidharmas*. The only complete *abhidharma* that survives in an Indic language is found in the PĀLI CANON of the THERAVĀDA school, but other Indian *abhidharma*s exist in Chinese and Tibetan translations, as well as Sanskrit fragments. In addition to the *abhidharma*s of the schools of NIKĀYA BUDDHISM, there were also *abhidharma* works in MAHĀYĀNA schools, such as ASAṄGA's ABHIDHARMA-SAMUCCAYA.

Abhidharma-kośa (Tib. *Chos mngon pa'i mdzod*; Chin. *A p'i ta mo chü she lun*; Jpn. *Abidatsuma Kusharon*; *Treasury of Higher Doctrine*)

One of the most important works of Buddhist scholasticism, written by VASUBANDHU prior to his conversion to MAHĀYĀNA. The root text is commonly believed to have been written in accordance with the philosophical system of the VAIBHĀṢIKA school (based on the philosophical system of the scholastic treatise MAHĀVIBHĀṢĀ), but his commentary on the text, the *Abhidharmakośa-bhāṣya*, critiques some key elements of the root text from the perspective of the rival SAUTRĀNTIKA school.

Abhidharma-piṭaka (Pāli *Abhidhamma-piṭaka*; Tib. *Chos mngon pa'i sde snod*; "Basket of Higher Doctrine")

Third of the "three baskets" (TRIPIṬAKA) of the Buddhist canon, which contains scholastic treatises that discuss the central doctrines of Buddhism. The primary focus is on philosophy and psychology. Although most of the early Buddhist schools probably developed their own *abhidharmas*, only two complete versions are extant today: (1) the SARVĀSTIVĀDA *abhidharma*, which exists in Chinese and Tibetan; and (2) the THERAVĀDA *abhidharma*, which is preserved in Pāli. (*See also* ABHIDHARMA; SŪTRA-PIṬAKA; VINAYA-PIṬAKA; PĀLI CANON; BUDDHAGHOSA.)

Abhidharma-samuccaya (Tib. *Chos mngon pa kun las btus pa*; *Compendium of Higher Doctrine*)

An important Sanskrit scholastic treatise written by ASAṄGA, which attempts to construct a MAHĀYĀNA ABHIDHARMA. It focuses particularly on the characteristics of DHARMAS, the basic constituents of reality, while also emphasizing their emptiness (ŚŪNYATĀ) of inherent existence (SVABHĀVA). (See also YOGĀCĀRA.)

abhijñā (Pāli *abhiññā*; Tib. *mgon par shes pa*; "higher knowledge")

The six supernatural abilities that are believed in traditional Buddhist meditation theory to result from the practice of meditation: (1) magical powers (*ṛddhi*), such as levitation; (2) the "divine ear," (*divya-śrotra*), or clairaudience; (3) the ability to know others' minds (*paracitta-jñāna*); (4) the "divine eye" (*divya-cakṣus*), or clairvoyance; (5) the ability to recall the details of former lives (*pūrvanivāsānusmṛti*); (6) knowledge of the extinction of defilements (*āśrava-kṣaya-vijñāna*). The first five are classified as mundane abilities, while the sixth is a supramundane ability that results from completion of training in insight meditation (VIPAŚYANĀ).

Abhirati (Tib. *mNgon dga'*; "Very Pleasant")

The heaven of the buddha AKṢOBHYA, located in the eastern quadrant.

abhisamaya (Pāli *abhisamaya*; Tib. *mngon par rtogs pa*; "clear realization")

Direct realization of key Buddhist doctrines. In the THERAVĀDA tradition, it refers to intuitive understanding of the four noble truths (ĀRYA-SATYA). In MAHĀYĀNA meditation theory, it is extended to include a range of non-conceptual (*nirvikalpa*) states of gnosis. In texts that use the term, it implies not only correct understanding of a particular concept, but also a progression from accumulation of merit to intuitive gnosis with respect to core Buddhist doctrines.

Abhisamayālaṃkāra (Tib. *mNgon par rtogs pa'i rgyan*; *Ornament for Clear Realizations*)

Scholastic treatise attributed to MAITREYA (2), which focuses on key doctrines in the "Perfection of Wisdom" (PRAJÑĀ-PĀRAMITĀ) literature. It consists of eight chapters, each of which is referred to as an "ABHISAMAYA," which according to Haribhadra's commentary indicates a non-conceptual (*nirvikalpa*) state of intuitive gnosis.

abhiṣeka (Pāli *abhiseka*; Tib. *dbang*; "initiation")

A ceremony that marks a person's entry into a Buddhist group. In esoteric Buddhism, initiation is generally considered to be essential for anyone wishing to engage in ritual or meditation practice. In tantric practice, initiation often symbolically creates a direct karmic link between the practitioner and the focal deity (Skt. *iṣṭa-devatā*; Tib. YI DAM).

āchān

See AJAHN.

action seal

See KARMA-MUDRĀ.

action tantra

See KRIYĀ-TANTRA.

ādi-buddha (Tib. *dang po'i sangs rgyas, thog ma'i sangs rgyas*; "original buddha")

The primordial BUDDHA, who has always been awakened. In some Buddhist schools, this buddha is associated with SAMANTABHADRA, and in Tibetan tantric Buddhism he is commonly said to be VAJRADHARA. In Japanese esoteric traditions, the *ādi-buddha* is identified with Mahāvairocana (Jpn. Dainichinyorai). (*See also* VAIROCANA.)

afterlife

Since earliest times, Buddhism has asserted that all sentient beings are born, die, and are reborn again in dependence on their past actions (KARMA) in an endless cycle. The question whether or not beings are actually reborn in this way has become a controversial topic among Western Buddhists, many of whom do not accept that the doctrine of rebirth is literally true. The overwhelming majority of Asian Buddhist teachers, however, consider belief in rebirth to be a central tenet of Buddhism, contending that it accords with the teachings of the Buddha as reported in the Buddhist canon. It is also widely thought that the doctrine of rebirth is necessary in order for Buddhist karma theory to make sense, since if there were no rebirth there would be no direct recompense for many actions.

āgama (Pāli *nikāya*; Tib. *lung*; "scriptures")

General name for the texts and teachings of the four main Sanskrit Buddhist collections of discourses attributed to ŚĀKYAMUNI BUDDHA: (1) Dīrgha Āgama (corresponding to the Pāli DĪGHA NIKĀYA), the "Long Discourses"; (2) the Madhyama Āgama (corresponding to the Pāli MAJJHIMA NIKĀYA), the "Middle Length Discourses"; (3) the Saṃyukta Āgama (corresponding to the Pāli SAṂYUTTA NIKĀYA), the "Connected Discourses"; and (4) the Ekottarika Āgama (corresponding to the Pāli AṄGUTTARA NIKĀYA), the "Increased-by-One Discourses." There are also mentions in Buddhist literature of a Kṣudraka Āgama "Lesser Discourses"), but scholars generally believe that this refers to a miscellaneous collection of texts that is not analogous to the Pāli KHUDDAKA NIKĀYA. (*See also* NIKĀYA; PĀLI CANON.)

aggregate

See SKANDHA.

Agonshū

A sect founded by SEIYU KIRIYAMA, which claims to base its doctrines and practices on early Buddhist teachings contained in the ĀGAMAS (collections of texts purport-

Stone stūpa, cave number ten, Ajaṇṭā

edly taught by ŚĀKYAMUNI BUDDHA). Kiriyama claimed that his studies of these texts revealed that most human problems are caused by the malevolent activities of the spirits of the dead, who afflict the living and cause spiritual hindrances and pollution (*tatari*). The goal of Agonshū is to cut the karmic ties to these spirits (*karuma o kiru*), because these ties allow the dead to work their mischief. A tradition with a reputation for aggressive proselytizing, Agonshū is also famous for staging mass ceremonies in which huge bonfires are lit. It is claimed that these rituals serve to cut off massive amounts of karma for many people.

Aitken, Robert

American ZEN *rōshi* who first encountered Japanese culture as a prisoner of war during World War II. In1950 he traveled to Japan and studied Zen with several Japanese masters. In 1974 he was certified as a RŌSHI by Yamada Dōun Rōshi and subsequently settled in Hawaii. He is one of the most influential Western Zen masters and has students all over the world. He has written a number of books, including *Taking the Path of Zen.*

ajahn (also *āchān*; "teacher")

Thai pronunciation of the Sanskrit term *ācārya*, used to refer to a Buddhist meditation master. In lay contexts it can also be used for a senior schoolteacher or college instructor.

Ajaṇṭā

A series of caves excavated in the sixth century C.E. in northwest Hyderabād, India. The complex contains over thirty major structures, mostly monastic residences (VIHĀRA). The cave paintings are among the best-preserved ancient works of Buddhist art, and Ajaṇṭā's surviving inscriptions have given contemporary scholars important insights into the religious lives of Indian Buddhists in this period.

Ajātaśatru (Pāli *Ajātasattu*)

The king of Magadha, who ruled during the last eight years of ŚĀKYAMUNI BUDDHA's life. Son of King BIMBISĀRA, one of the Buddha's major patrons, Ajātaśatru connived in a plot with the Buddha's cousin DEVADATTA. The plot involved killing the Buddha so that Devadatta could lead the monastic community and also killing Bimbisāra so that Ajātaśatru could seize the throne. Both plots failed, but Ajātaśatru subsequently reconciled with the Buddha and his father and ascended the throne with his father's blessing. He later became concerned that his father still presented a threat to his rule and had him imprisoned. Bimbisāra died of starvation in prison. Despite his sometimes adversarial relationship with the Buddha, Ajātaśatru is described as a devout supporter in the PĀLI CANON, and he was involved in the distribution of the Buddha's relics after his cremation.

Akṣobhya Buddha (Tib. *Mi 'khrugs pa*; Chin. *A-chu*; Jpn. *Ashuka Nyorai*; "Imperturbable")

The buddha who resides over the eastern paradise of ABHIRATI. He is generally represented iconographically as having dark blue (and occasionally gold) skin and sometimes as riding on an elephant. He generally holds a VAJRA in his right hand and makes the "earth-touching" gesture (*bhūmi-sparśa-mudrā*) with his left. He is said to have received his name because he kept his vow never to manifest anger toward any being.

ālaya-vijñāna (Tib. *kun gzhi rnam par shes pa*; "basis-consciousness")

An important doctrinal concept that is particularly important in the YOGĀCĀRA tradition. This term is sometimes translated by Western scholars as "storehouse consciousness," since it acts as the repository of the predispositions that one's actions produce. It stores these predispositions until the conditions are right for them to manifest themselves. The Tibetan translators rendered it as "basis-of-all" (*kun gzhi*) because it serves as the basis for all of the phenomena of cyclic existence and *nirvāṇa*, which are said to arise from "stable predispositions" (*brtan pa'i bag chags*; Skt. *dhruva-vāsanā*) within the *ālaya-vijñāna*. Through meditative practice and engaging in meritorious actions, one gradually replaces afflicted seeds with pure ones; when one has completely purified the continuum of the *ālaya-vijñāna*, it is referred to as the "purified consciousness" (*amala-vijñāna*).

Altan Khan (1507–1583)

A descendant of Chinggis Khan and leader of the Tümet Mongols. In 1578 he met with BSOD NAMS RGYA MTSHO (Sönam Gyatso, the third DALAI LAMA) and conferred on him the title "Ta le," or "Ocean," implying that he was an "ocean of wisdom." The title "Dalai Lama" was also retrospectively given to his two predecessors and has become the most common title by which bSod nams rgya mtsho's successors are known.

Amarapura Nikāya

One of the three major orders in the contemporary SAṂGHA in Sri Lanka. Its name derives from Amarapura, the former capital of Burma. It was founded by Ñāṇavimalatissa Thera, who together with five novices and three laymen traveled to Amarapura and received ordination in a ceremony sponsored by King Bodawpaya. In 1803 it split with the SIYAM NIKĀYA.

Ambedkar, Dr. Bhimrao Ramji (1891–1956)

A member of the Māhār (Untouchable) caste, Ambedkar served as the Indian Minister of Law and was one of the drafters of the post-independence constitution. In 1956 he converted to Buddhism in a public ceremony in Nagpur, along with a half million fellow Untouchables. Since then, millions of other Untouchables have followed his lead and converted to Buddhism, which did not adopt Hinduism's caste system.

American Buddhism

In most Asian Buddhist societies, a single tradition of Buddhism – generally one that has existed in the country for centuries – predominates, and so it is relatively easy to sketch the general outlines of Buddhism in these countries. In America, however, the situation is both fluid and diverse. Every major lineage of Buddhism – and most minor ones – are now established in the U.S.A., but Buddhism is still in the process of adapting to this new environment. Moreover, the surge of interest in Buddhism in America is a recent phenomenon, and most American Buddhist centers are less than three decades old. There were certainly instances of interest in Buddhism before this: several of the New England Transcendentalists, for example, read books on Buddhism and incorporated Buddhist ideas into their writings, and Henry David Thoreau (1817–1862) translated Eugène Burnouf's French translation of the *Lotus Sūtra* into English. Despite some examples of interest in Buddhism during the nineteenth century among American intellectuals, however, its first significant movement into the country was due to the influx of Chinese workers in the early nineteenth century, most of whom were manual laborers. The first Buddhist institution in America was a Chinese temple built in 1853 in San Francisco, which was intended to minister to Chinese immigrants. Until the 1950s, Buddhism in America was largely confined to such immigrant communities, but beginning at that time a number of successful Buddhist missionaries arrived in the U.S.A. There was a significant surge of interest during the 1960s and 1970s, during which time a number of centers were founded, many of which are still operating. Several contemporary scholars who study American Buddhism have noted two parallel movements: (1) one mainly involving ethnic Asian communities, which generally establish Buddhist centers on the models of their countries of origin; and (2) mostly Caucasian Americans who have decided to convert to Buddhism (or at least engage in Buddhist practice), who generally train under Asian teachers. According to recently compiled statistics, the latter group is overwhelmingly white, middle class, and well educated. In contrast to the Asian model, lay American Buddhists generally are mainly interested in meditation practice, which in Asia is primarily a monastic activity. Equally significantly, the patriarchal structures that are found in Asian societies have largely been abandoned in the U.S.A., and a number of influential female teachers have emerged. As is true in all countries in which Buddhism has set down roots, in America the religion is adapting to its socio-cultural environment, and Buddhist establishments increasingly reflect American paradigms and values. Thus a number of commentators have noted that American Buddhism tends to be eclectic, and it also has developed a significant element of social activity. One example of this last trend is "engaged Buddhism," a term coined by THICH NHAT HANH to describe Buddhists who attempt to manifest Buddhist ideals through activism on behalf of others. American Buddhist institutions also tend to be democratic, anti-authoritarian, and nonhierarchical. They are often run by boards of directors, which are generally composed of laypeople. A number of Asian teachers have expressed discomfort with such arrangements, since they are effectively employees of the organization and can be dismissed by its membership, a situation that many feel diminishes their traditional authority. Current estimates of the number of American Buddhists vary between 1 and 2 million, but due to the changing nature of the tradition and the shifting affiliations of people associated with Buddhist groups, reliable figures are impossible to obtain.

Amida Butsu

See AMITĀBHA BUDDHA.

Amitābha Buddha

(Tib. *Sangs rgyas 'Od dpag med*; Chin. *A-mi-t'o fo*; Jpn. *Amida Butsu*; Kor. *Amit'a pul*; Viet. *A-Di-Đà Phật*) ("Limitless Light")

A buddha who is said to preside over the western paradise of SUKHĀVATĪ, a realm in which beings born there are assured of attaining buddhahood in that lifetime. The conditions of the paradise are optimal for the practice of Buddhism, in accordance with Amitābha's former vows (in a lifetime during which he was a monk named Dharmākara), in which he declared his intention to create a realm that would be the ideal training ground for beings aspiring to buddhahood. He is the focal buddha of the "Pure Land" (Chin. CH'ING-T'U; Jpn. *Jōdō*; Kor. *Chŏngt'o*; Viet. *Đạo Trang*) tradition in East Asia. This tradition holds that people who speak his name with faith are reborn in Sukhāvatī. In Japan the most important practice for achieving this is recitation of the "NEMBUTSU" (Chin. *nien-fo*; Kor. *yŏmbul*; Viet. *niệm-phật*): "Namu Amida Butsu" (Chin. "Namo A-mi-t'o Fo"; Viet. "Nam-mô A-Di-Đà Phật; "Praise to Amitābha Buddha"). The mythology of this buddha is primarily derived from three Sanskrit texts: (1) the Larger *Sukhāvatī-vyūha-sūtra*; (2) the Smaller *Sukhāvatī-vyūha-sūtra*; and (3) the *Amitāyur-dhyāna-sūtra*. The first of these is the main source for a famous series of vows, the eighteenth of which states that anyone who invokes Amitābha's name ten times (or desires rebirth in Sukhāvatī ten times) will surely be reborn there. This is often referred to as an "easy practice," because it is based on faith and mechanical repetition of the *nembutsu* formula, rather than on difficult meditational practices. (*See also* HŌNEN; JŌDŌ SHINSHŪ; JŌDŌSHŪ; SHINRAN; SUKHĀVATĪ-VYŪHA-SŪTRA.

Amitāyus Buddha (Tib. *Sangs rgyas Tshe dpag med*; "Limitless Life")

An alternative manifestation of AMITĀBHA, who is particularly associated with longevity. In this form, he is the focus of popular "long life" (Tib. *tshe ring*) practices in TIBETAN BUDDHISM. He is generally depicted iconographically with red skin and holding a begging-bowl containing the elixir of immortality.

Amoghasiddhi (Tib. *Don yod grub pa*; "Unfailing Accomplishment")

One of the five Celestial Buddhas of MAHĀYĀNA Buddhism. He is associated with the northern direction, and iconographically he is generally represented as having green skin and with his left hand in his lap, palm up, while his right hand makes the gesture of fearlessness (*abhaya-mudrā*).

An Shih-kao

Kushan monk who traveled to Lo-yang in China in 148 and established the first center for the translation of Buddhist texts. During almost thirty years of activity, he and his associates produced around thirty translations of Indian Buddhist texts, mainly on meditation theory and practice.

anāgamin (Pāli *anāgamin*; Tib. *phyir mi 'ong ba*; "non-returner")

According to NIKĀYA BUDDHISM, a person who has eliminated the first five fetters (*saṃyojana*): clinging to the idea of a self, doubt, clinging to rituals and rules, sexual desire, and resentment. In his or her next life, such a person will be reborn in one of the five "pure abodes" (*śuddhāvāsa*) and will become an ARHAT there.

anagārika ("homeless")

A person who enters the homeless life but without receiving monastic ordination. In modern times this term was used by the Sri Lankan reformer ANAGĀRIKA DHARMAPĀLA, who intended to develop an institution for Buddhists who were committed to religious practice but who did not wish to take monastic vows.

analytical meditation

See VIPAŚYANĀ.

Ānanda (Pāli *Ānanda*; Tib. *Kun dga' bo*; "Bliss")

Śākyamuni Buddha's first cousin and one of his main disciples. Ānanda served as the Buddha's personal attendant during the last twenty-five years of his life. He was instrumental in the creation of an order of nuns after the Buddha initially refused a request by his step-mother Mahāprajāpatī that he allow her and other women to be ordained. Ānanda interceded with the Buddha on her behalf, and the Buddha eventually agreed to institute ordination for women. Ānanda also played a crucial role in the "First Buddhist Council" held at Rājagṛha, at which 500 arhats assembled to recite the discourses of the Buddha from memory. Ānanda had been present at most of these, but he had not yet attained arhathood, and so was initially excluded from the council. He became an arhat on the night before the council, however, and so was able to attend.

T'ang dynasty Chinese statue of Ānanda

Ananda Metteyya (Charles Allen Bennett McGregor, 1872–1923)

Pioneering British *bhikkhu* (bhikṣu) who founded the International Buddhist Society. After reading Sir Edwin Arnold's *The Light of Asia,* he traveled to Sri Lanka and received the novice monk's ordination in Burma in 1901 and became a fully ordained Theravāda monk in the following year. He founded the International Buddhist Society (Buddhasāsana Samāgama) in 1903.

Anāthapiṇḍika ("Feeder of the Destitute")

A wealthy banker from Śrāvastī (Pāli *Sāvatthi*), who bought the Jetavana (1) Grove for Śākyamuni Buddha and his followers. The Buddha spent his last twenty-five rainy-season retreats there. Anāthapiṇḍika is described as the most liberal giver of alms among the Buddha's lay followers, and several of the Buddha's discourses are addressed to him. His generosity was so great that he was reduced to poverty, but he was rewarded with rebirth in Tuṣita (Pāli *Tusita*) heaven. His real name was Sudatta, but he is referred to as Anāthapiṇḍika on account of his philanthropy.

anātman (Pāli *anattā*; Tib. *bdag med*; Chin. *wu-wo*; "no-self")

One of the "three characteristics" (trilakṣaṇa) that the Buddha said apply to all conditioned (saṃskṛta) phenomena (the others being impermanence and unsatisfactoriness or suffering). The doctrine holds that – contrary to the assertions of the brahmanical orthodoxy of the Buddha's time – there is no permanent, partless, substantial "self" or soul. The brahmanical tradition taught that the essence of every individual is an eternal, unchanging essence (called the *ātman*). The Buddha declared that such an essence is merely a conceptual construct and that every individual is in fact composed of a constantly changing collection of "aggregates" (SKANDHA).

Angkor Wat

A major temple complex in central Cambodia built during the reign of King Sūryavarman II (1113–1150). Originally dedicated to the Hindu god Viṣṇu, it became a Buddhist establishment after later Khmer rulers converted to Buddhism. It was abandoned in 1431 and was mostly overrun by jungle until it was rediscovered in the nineteenth century.

Aṅguttara Nikāya ("Increased-by-One Discourses")

The fourth collection in the "Basket of Discourses" (Sutta-piṭaka) of the PĀLI CANON. It contains sermons attributed to the Buddha (and sometimes his disciples) that are arranged according to the number of items contained in the texts. These are numbered from one to eleven.

ani

See A NI.

animal

See TIRYAK.

animitta (Pāli *animitta*; Tib. *mtshan ma med pa*; "signlessness")

The absence of concretely existing characteristics of phenomena (DHARMA). "Signs" include forms, sounds, scents, tastes, and tangible objects, men, women, birth, aging, sickness, death, and so forth. The absence of these is signlessness. *Animitta* is commonly used as an epithet of NIRVĀṆA.

anitya (Pāli *anicca*; Tib. *mi rtag pa*; "impermanence")

One of the "three characteristics" (TRI-LAKṢAṆA) that ŚĀKYAMUNI BUDDHA said distinguish all conditioned (SAṂSKṚTA) phenomena (the others being selflessness and unsatisfactoriness or suffering). According to this doctrine, all conditioned phenomena (i.e., phenomena that come into being due to causes and conditions) are constantly changing, and so there is no possibility of holding onto anything. This is connected with the other two characteristics, since the transitory nature of phenomena leads to inevitable suffering, because beings are inevitably separated from things that they desire. Also, because phenomena are constantly changing, there is no possibility of a permanent and unchanging "self" or soul (*ātman*).

antarābhava

See BAR DO.

anujñā (Tib. *rjes gnang*; "lesser authorization")

Tantric ceremony that authorizes the performance of certain ritual practices associated with a particular tantric cycle, such as recitation of MANTRAS and meditation on a deity. It is not, however, a full initiation, and so a person who receives this empowerment is not allowed to engage in completion stage (SAMPANNA-KRAMA) yogas.

Anurādhapura

The capital of Sri Lanka until the 10th century. It is the site of three important early monasteries: the MAHĀVIHĀRA, JETAVANA (2), and ABHAYAGIRI.

Anuruddha (1) (or Aniruddha)

First cousin of ŚĀKYAMUNI BUDDHA and one of his ten main disciples, said in the PĀLI CANON to be the foremost in the use of the "divine eye" (Pāli *dibba-cakkhu*; Skt. *deva-cakṣus*).

Anuruddha (2) (ca. 10th century)

Influential scholar-monk credited with authoring three important Pāli ABHIDHARMA commentaries: (1) *Compendium of the Meaning of Higher Knowledge* (*Abhidhammattha-saṅgaha*); (2) *Ascertainment of Ultimate Truth* (*Paramattha-vinichaya*); and (3) *Discrimination of Name and Form* (*Nāmaūpa-pariccheda*). According to Sinhalese tradition, he was an elder (*thera*) who lived at the Mūlasoma Vihāra.

anuttara-yoga-tantra (Tib. *bla na med pa'i rnal 'byor*; "highest yoga tantra")

The fourth and highest of the four classes of Buddhist TANTRAS, according to Tibetan doxographical schemas. These texts focus on meditational practices relating to subtle energies called "winds" (Skt. *prāṇa*; Tib. *rlung*) and "drops" (Skt. BINDU; Tib. *thig le*), which move through subtle "channels" (Skt. *nāḍī*; Tib. *rtsa*). The practices of this class of tantra are divided into two main stages: (1) the "generation stage" (Skt. UTPATTI-KRAMA; Tib. *bskyed rim*) and the "completion stage" (SAMPANNA-KRAMA; Tib. *rdzogs rim*). In the first stage the meditator generates a vivid image of a buddha from the wisdom consciousness realizing emptiness (ŚŪNYATĀ), and in the second stage invites the buddha to merge with him or her, so that the practitioner and buddha are viewed as inseparable. (*See also*: CARYĀ-TANTRA; KRIYĀ-TANTRA; YOGA-TANTRA.)

anuyoga (Tib. *rjes su rnal 'byor*; "subsequent yoga")

A class of tantric texts in the RNYING MA PA (Nyingmapa) order of TIBETAN BUDDHISM, which contains teachings referred to as "the trio of Guru, great perfection, and the Great Compassionate One" (*bla rdzogs thugs gsum*). These are teachings attributed to the guru (Tib. BLA MA) PADMASAMBHAVA, the great perfection (RDZOGS CHEN), and AVALOKITEŚVARA, the embodiment of compassion (Tib. *thugs rje*).

apramāṇa

See BRAHMA-VIHĀRA.

araññavāsī ("forest dweller")

General term for THERAVĀDA monks who eschew life in cities or settled monasteries and attempt to recreate the eremitical paradigm of the early Buddhist order. Like the monks of the PĀLI CANON, they wander from place to place – only taking shelter during the rainy season retreat – and subsist solely on alms.

arhat (Pāli *arahant*; Tib. *dgra bcom pa*; Chin. *lo-han*; Jpn. *rakan*; "worthy one")

The ideal of NIKĀYA BUDDHISM; a person who has extinguished all defilements (*āsrava*) and afflictions (KLEŚA) so thoroughly that they will not reappear in the future. At death, the *arhat* enters NIRVĀṆA and will not be reborn again. Although *arhat*s are commonly castigated in MAHĀYĀNA literature for pursuing a "selfish" goal of personal *nirvāṇa*, they are also said to be worthy of respect and to have attained a high level of spiritual development. The figure of the *lo-han* became widely popular in East Asia, particularly in CH'AN (Jpn. ZEN; Kor. SŎN; Viet. THIỀN), which emphasized personal striving for liberation. The earliest known representations of the *arhat* in China date to the seventh century, and the *arhat* motif became widespread in the ninth and tenth centuries. Today groups of 500 *arhat* figures are often seen in Ch'an/Zen/Sŏn monasteries, and some larger complexes have a separate "*arhat* hall." It should also be mentioned that the term *arhat* is also applied to BUDDHAS, because they too have eliminated all defilements and enter *nirvāṇa* at death.

Ariyaratne, A. T.

See SARVODAYA SHRAMADĀNA.

Arnold, Sir Edwin (1832–1904)

Author of an influential poem on Buddhism entitled *The Light of Asia*, which was published in 1879.

art

According to extant records of the earliest Buddhist community, iconographic representation was discouraged by ŚĀKYAMUNI BUDDHA and his followers, who wanted to prevent the development of a cult of personality or a focus on the figure of the Buddha, rather than on the doctrines and practices he taught. In addition, the central focus of the monastic community was introspective meditation, rather than external symbolism.

As Buddhism grew and attracted more followers, artistic representations began to appear. There was, however, an initial reluctance to represent the Buddha directly, and so he was often depicted in aniconic motifs, such as his footprints (*buddha-pāda*) or the Bodhi Tree (BODHI-VṚKṢA). The most widespread aniconic representation of the Buddha was in the form of reliquaries called STŪPAS. These continue to be popular throughout the Buddhist world, and a plethora of styles has developed. In INDIAN BUDDHISM it was commonly thought that they physically represented the Buddha, and some texts indicate that it was widely believed that venerating a *stūpa* was equivalent to venerating the Buddha himself.

Thousand Buddha statues, Taeansa Monastery, South Kyŏngsang, Korea

Stone pillar at Sāñcī depicting the Buddha's attainment of awakening. He is represented iconically by the Tree of Awakening (Bodhi-vṛkṣa)

Iconic representations began to appear on *stūpa*s some time after the reign of AŚOKA (r. 272–236 B.C.E.), and a number of figures are found on *stūpa*s at Bhārhut, SĀÑCĪ, and Amarāvatī. These monuments have carved depictions of various Buddhist motifs, including scenes from the life of the Buddha. The Buddha himself is not directly represented, however, and is only suggested symbolically.

Around the end of the first century C.E., artists began to fashion representations of the Buddha, and the Buddha image continues to be the most widely dispersed symbol in Buddhist art all over the world. The earliest known examples of the Buddha image borrowed motifs from non-Buddhist traditions, since there was at that time no accepted notion regarding how he should be represented. Artists in Mathurā (present-day north central India), for example, adopted imagery from the depiction of YAKṢAS, and in GANDHĀRA (present-day Afghanistan), artists appear to have been influenced by Greek art. As Buddhism spread to other parts of the world this trend continued, and the Buddha image has acquired the characteristics and artistic motifs of the local populations of every Buddhist society.

Despite Buddhism's initial rejection of artistic representation, Buddhist art flourished both in India and throughout Asia. With the development of tantric Buddhism in India, art and imagery became integrated into meditative practice. As tantric Buddhism spread to Tibet, Mongolia, China, Japan, and Korea, elaborate use of imagery became widespread in many quarters.

Ārūpya-dhātu (Pāli *Ārūpa-dhātu*; Tib. *gZugs med khams*; "Formless Realm")

One of the "three worlds" (TRILOKA) of traditional Buddhist cosmology. Beings are born into this realm as a result of successful cultivation of meditative states called the "four formless absorptions" (ĀRŪPYA-SAMĀPATTI), each of which corresponds to a heaven realm within the Formless Realm. In the Formless Realm there is no physicality, and the beings who reside there have lives free from pain and anxiety, but this is seen as unsatisfactory from a Buddhist standpoint, because when their lives in the Formless Realm end they are again reborn in the lower levels of cyclic existence.

ārūpya-samāpatti (Pāli *ārūpa-samāpatti*; Tib. *gzugs med kyi snyoms 'jug;* "formless absorptions")

Four meditative states that correspond to levels within the Formless Realm (ĀRŪPYA-DHĀTU), the highest realm within cyclic existence. One is reborn in one of these levels in dependence upon successfully cultivating the corresponding absorption.

In the absorption of limitless space (*ākāśānantya-samāpatti*), the appearance of forms to the mind completely disappears, and the meditator perceives everything as limitless space, without any obstruction or variety.

In the absorption of limitless consciousness (*vijñānānantya-samāpatti*), the meditator first views the preceding absorption as gross and then views the discrimination that consciousness is limitless as peaceful. This mainly involves stabilizing meditation, and in this absorption the meditator views everything as just limitless, undifferentiated consciousness.

In the absorption of nothingness (*ākiṃcanya-samāpatti*), even viewing everything as limitless consciousness appears as gross, and the meditator cultivates a mental state in which only nothingness appears to the mind. This is more subtle than the preceding absorption, since there is no content at all, only undifferentiated nothingness. In the succeeding absorption, even this is left behind, and there is no coarse discrimination at all, only subtle discrimination. This is generally referred to as the "peak of cyclic existence" (*bhavāgra*), because it leads to rebirth at the highest level of the Formless Realm, a state in which beings have enormously long lifespans characterized by no hint of unpleasantness and only the subtlest of discriminations.

In a Buddhist context, however, this is still unsatisfactory, since one's lifespan eventually ends, and one is again reborn in the lower realms of cyclic existence, where one will again suffer, grow old, and die. Thus for Buddhists the final goal should be a supramundane path, one that leads out of cyclic existence altogether and which results in either the state of buddhahood or at least the more limited NIRVĀṆA of an ARHAT or PRATYEKA-BUDDHA.

ārya (Pāli *ariya*; Tib. *'phags pa*; "superior," "noble," "wise")

A person who has attained the path of seeing (DARŚANA-MĀRGA), the third of the five Buddhist paths (MĀRGA). In MAHĀYĀNA, this means that such a person has had direct experience of emptiness (ŚŪNYATĀ). In NIKĀYA BUDDHISM, *ārya*s are beings who have attained one of the four supramundane paths (ĀRYA-MĀRGA): (1) stream enterer (SROTĀPANNA); (2) once-returner (SAKṚDĀGAMIN); (3) non-returner (ANĀGAMIN); or (4) ARHAT. Everyone below this level of attainment is referred to as an "ordinary being" (PṚTHAG-JANA).

Āryadeva (Tib. *'Phags pa lha*, ca. third century B.C.E.; "Wise God")

One of the main disciples of NĀGĀRJUNA. He was probably born in Sri Lanka, and he is said in some biographical sources to have been blind in one eye. He is one of the major philosophers of the MADHYAMAKA school and the author of the influential work *The Four Hundred* (*Catuḥśataka*). By all accounts he was a fierce polemicist, whose attacks on rival philosophers led to his assassination.

ārya-mārga (Pāli *ariya-magga*; Tib. *'phags pa'i lam;* "supramundane path")

The four paths that lead to the supramundane state of NIRVĀṆA: (1) stream-enterer (SROTĀPANNA); (2) once-returner (SAKṚDĀGAMIN); (3) non-returner (ANĀGAMIN); and (4) ARHAT. (*See also* ĀRYA.)

ārya-satya (Pāli *ariya-sacca*; Tib. *'phags pa'i bden pa*; "noble truths")

Four central tenets of Buddhism: (1) the truth of suffering (DUḤKHA); (2) the truth of the arising of suffering (*samudaya*); (3) the truth of the cessation of suffering (*nirodha*); and (4) the truth of the path (MĀRGA) that leads beyond suffering. The first holds that all existence involves inevitable unsatisfactoriness or suffering. The second asserts that suffering is caused by desire (TṚṢṆĀ). The third claims that suffering can be brought to an end. The fourth is the path that leads to the cessation of suffering, which is completed with the attainment of NIRVĀṆA. In TIBETAN BUDDHISM, each of the four is said to have four attributes. The attributes of the first truth are: (1) impermanence (the fact that possessions, states of happiness, etc. eventually pass away); (2) misery (all ordinary beings and mental states are prone to misery because of being under the influence of afflictions); (3) emptiness (all conditioned phenomena lack inherent existence); and (4) selflessness (there is no enduring self or essence, but ordinary beings cling to the false notion of "self"). The attributes of the second truth are: (1) cause (contaminated actions and afflictions are the causes of suffering); (2) origin (contaminated actions and afflictions are origins because they tend to produce continued suffering); (3) strong production (contaminated actions and afflictions produce suffering with great force); and (4) condition (contaminated actions and afflictions provide cooperative conditions for further suffering). The third truth's attributes are: (1) cessation (suffering can only be overcome through completely extinguishing the roots of suffering); (2) pacification (cultivation of a state in which afflictions are completely abandoned); (3) auspicious improvement (the complete elimination of suffering, said to be the supreme liberation); and (4) definite emergence (completely eliminating suffering and its causes, such that one is fully liberated from cyclic existence). The attributes of the fourth truth are: (1) path (taking meditation on selflessness as the cornerstone of the path to liberation); (2) suitability (meditation on selflessness is suitable as a path to liberation because it serves as an antidote to ignorance); (3) achievement (meditation on selflessness is appropriate as a path to liberation because it correctly intuits the nature of mind); and (4) liberation (direct realization of selflessness leads to final liberation from cyclic existence, after which one transcends all suffering).

āryāṣṭāṅga-mārga (Pāli *ariya-aṭṭhanga-magga*; Tib. *'phags pa'i lam yan lag brgyad*; "eightfold noble path")

Fourth of the four "noble truths" (ĀRYA-SATYA); it involves cultivation of correct views, actions, and meditative practices in order to bring an end to suffering. The eight components of the path are: (1) correct views (*samyag-dṛṣṭi*); (2) correct intention (*samyak-saṃkalpa*); (3) correct speech (*samyag-vāc*); (4) correct actions (*samyak-karmānta*); (5) correct livelihood (*samyag-ājīva*); (6) correct effort (*samyag-vyāyāma*); (7) correct mindfulness (*samyak-smṛti*); and (8) correct concentration (*samyak-samādhi*).

"Correct views" refers to accepting certain key Buddhist concepts such as the four noble truths (*ārya-satya*), dependent arising (PRATĪTYA-SAMUTPĀDA), KARMA, etc., as well as to eliminating wrong views. "Correct intention" involves cultivating a proper orientation, that is, a mental attitude that aims at following the Buddhist path to awakening (BODHI). "Correct speech" involves avoiding harsh, untruthful, or divisive speech and idle chatter, and speaking truthfully, pleasantly, and non-belligerently. "Correct actions" entails adhering to the monastic rules outlined in the PRĀTIMOKṢA, and for laypeople adhering to the five (or ten) lay precepts. "Correct livelihood" requires that one avoid occupations that involve one in negative actions, such as selling slaves, dealing in munitions, butchery, etc. "Correct effort" refers to an attitude of properly orienting the mind toward the desired goal of liberation from cyclic existence and steadily applying oneself to practices that are concordant with it. "Correct mindfulness" involves cultivating a state of mental clarity and alertness in which one is aware of one's mental processes and attitudes and, more importantly, in which one is in control of them. Through continuous self-examination and mental alertness, one can develop the mindfulness that enables one to master one's emotions, thoughts, and feelings and focus them in the direction of awakening (*bodhi*). "Correct concentration" requires the previous steps. Unless one has a concentrated mind that can fix itself calmly and one-pointedly on a single object without being distracted by laxity or excitement, one cannot properly enter into meditation, which requires intense concentration.

aśaikṣa-mārga (Pāli *asekha-magga*; Tib. *mi slob pa'i lam*; "path of no more learning")

Fifth and last of the Buddhist paths (MĀRGA). Following the fourth, the "path of meditation" (BHĀVANĀ-MĀRGA), the meditator overcomes the subtlest traces of afflictions and of the conception of a truly existing self (*ātman*), together with their seeds. A person who completes this path is then referred to as an ARHAT. A Mahāyānist who completes this path becomes a buddha, and according to SARVĀSTIVĀDA at the end of this path one becomes either a *śrāvaka-buddha*, PRATYEKA-BUDDHA, or SAMYAK-SAMBUDDHA.

Āsāḷahā Pūjā

One of the major religious festivals in THERAVĀDA Buddhist countries, which commemorates ŚĀKYAMUNI BUDDHA's preaching of his first sermon.

asaṃskṛta (Pāli *asankhata*; Tib. *'dus ma byas*; "unconditioned")

Whatever DHARMAS lack production, cessation, abiding, and change are "unconditioned." Dharmas are the basic building-blocks of the universe according to ABHIDHARMA literature. Unconditioned dharmas are those which are not produced due to causes and conditions. In the SARVĀSTIVĀDA school, there are three types of unconditioned dharmas: (1) space (*ākāśa*); (2) analytical cessations (*pratisaṃkhyā-nirodha*); and (3) non-analytical cessations (*apratisaṃkhyā-nirodha*). The THERAVĀDA tradition, however, only recognizes one unconditioned dharma, NIRVĀṆA, which is a non-analytical cessation.

Asaṅga (Tib. *Thogs med*, ca. fourth century C.E.; "Unattached")

One of the two main figures of the early Indian YOGĀCĀRA tradition (the other being his brother VASUBANDHU). In traditional biographies, Asaṅga is said to have been a third level (BHŪMI) BODHISATTVA, and TĀRANĀTHA reports that in a previous life his mother had been a Buddhist monk who was a devotee of AVALOKITEŚVARA who had hurt the feelings of another monk while debating with him, and Avalokiteśvara predicted that this would result in repeated births as a woman. During one of these births, as a Buddhist laywoman named Prasannaśīla, she gave birth to Asaṅga, Vasubandhu, and a third son named Viriñcinivatsa, all of whom entered the Buddhist order.

Asaṅga received monastic ordination at an early age and soon demonstrated an unusual memory and great intelligence. He first studied under SARVĀSTIVĀDA teachers, but he found that many of his questions were not being satisfactorily addressed, and so he sought instruction from the future buddha, MAITREYA (1).

After twelve years of meditating in a cave, Asaṅga received a vision of Maitreya, and he later traveled to TUṢITA heaven, where Maitreya instructed him in the doctrines of MAHĀYĀNA Buddhism.

After his sojourn in Tuṣita he returned to India, where he began composing commentaries on Maitreya's works as well as a number of independent treatises (some modern scholars attribute these works to a human master – often referred to as Maitreyanātha to distinguish him from the bodhisattva of the same name – but Buddhist tradition generally assumes them to be the work of the future buddha). Among Asaṅga's most important works are the *Compendium of the Great Vehicle* (*Mahāyāna-saṃgraha*), the *Bodhisattva Levels* (BODHISATTVA-BHŪMI), and the *Compendium of Higher Doctrine* (ABHIDHARMA-SAMUCCAYA). His writings and oral teachings, along with those of his brother Vasubandhu, became the main sources of a new philosophical school, which later came to be known as Yogācāra. His philosophical insights and doctrinal innovations have had a profound impact on Mahāyāna thought and practice, particularly in India, East Asia, and Tibet.

Aśoka (Pāli *Asoka*; Tib. *Chos rgyal Mya ngan med*, r. 272–236 B.C.E.; "Sorrowless")

Third king of the Indian Maurya dynasty. He is widely viewed in Buddhist tradition as the paradigm of the "religious ruler" (Skt. *dharma-rāja*; Pāli *dhamma-rāja*). The grandson of Candragupta Maurya and son of King Bindusara, Aśoka is best remembered for his "rock edicts" that outlined his ruling philosophy and which were placed throughout his realm. According to traditional histories, he was a harsh and ruthless ruler in his early years, but after a bloody war against the neighboring state of Kaliṅga in 260 he renounced armed conquest and became a Buddhist lay disciple in the Vibhajyavāda tradition (described in Rock Edict XIII). Buddhist tradition asserts that he convened the "Third Buddhist Council" at his capital city of PĀṬALIPUTRA under the direction of the monk Moggaliputta Tissa, which was attended by 1,000 monks and which decided that the Vibhajyavāda doctrine should be considered orthodox and that monks adhering to other systems be expelled from the SAṂGHA. His other major contribution to the development of Buddhism was his sponsorship of a mission by his son MAHINDA (a Buddhist monk) to Sri Lanka. This was so successful that the king of Sri Lanka became a Buddhist convert, and subsequently Buddhism became the state religion.

aspiration

See PRAṆIDHĀNA.

Aṣṭa-sāhasrikā-prajñā-pāramitā-sūtra (Tib. *'Phags pa shes rab kyi pha rol tu phyin pa brgyad stong pa'i mdo*; *Eight Thousand Line Perfection of Wisdom Sūtra*)

Widely considered by modern scholars to be the earliest extant text of the "perfection of Wisdom" (PRAJÑĀ-PĀRAMITĀ) literature and the earliest known text of MAHĀYĀNA Buddhism. Probably composed some time around the second century B.C.E., it contains a dialogue purportedly spoken by ŚĀKYAMUNI BUDDHA that discusses many of the key doctrines that later came to characterize Mahāyāna, with a particular focus on "emptiness" (ŚŪNYATĀ).

asura (Pāli *asura*; Tib. *lha ma yin*; "demi-god")

These beings are sometimes considered to be the chief of the evil spirits. They are the opponents of the gods (DEVA), with whom (especially Indra) they wage constant war, primarily motivated by intense envy for the superior fortunes of gods. This is one of the six destinies (GATI) of sentient beings (the others being gods, humans, animals, hungry ghosts, and hell beings).

Aśvaghoṣa (Tib. *rTa dbyangs*, ca. second century C.E.; "Horse Sound")

Author of the BUDDHACARITA, a verse account of the life of ŚĀKYAMUNI BUDDHA. According to Buddhist tradition, he was born a brahman but was converted to Buddhism by a monk named Parśva, who belonged to the VAIBHĀṢIKA school.

Atiśa (Dīpaṃkara Śrījñāna; Tib. *Jo bo rje*, 982–1054)

The leading figure in the "second dissemination" (PHYI DAR) of Buddhism to Tibet. A well-known Bengali scholar resident at the monastic university VIKRAMŚĪLA, Atiśa arrived in Tibet in 1042 in response to an invitation from the rulers of western Tibet. After his arrival he worked to reform and revive Buddhist teachings and practices, and his disciple 'BROM STON (Dromdön, 1008–1064) is credited with founding the first Buddhist order in Tibet, the BKA' GDAMS PA (Kadampa). His most influential work is the *Lamp for the Path to Awakening* (BODHIPATHA-PRADĪPA), in which he outlined a gradual path to buddhahood.

atiyoga

See RDZOGS CHEN.

avaivartika-bhūmi (Tib. *phyir mi ldog pa'i sa*; "irreversible levels")

Stages beyond which a BODHISATTVA is no longer capable of backsliding, generally said to be the eighth through tenth "levels" (BHŪMI).

Avalokiteśvara (Tib. *sPyan ras gzigs dbang phyugs or Chenrezi*; Chin. *Kuan-yin*; Jpn. *Kannon*; Kor. *Kwansom*; Viet. *Quán-âm*; Mon. *Nidubarüsheckchi*; "Lord who Looks Down")

One of the most important BODHISATTVAS in MAHĀYĀNA Buddhism. He is the embodiment of compassion (KARUṆĀ), which along with wisdom (PRAJÑĀ) is one of the two main characteristics of the awakened mind of a BUDDHA. His name literally means "the Lord who Looks Down," implying that he views the sufferings of sentient beings with compassion. He figures prominently in many Mahāyāna sūtras, e.g., several Perfection of Wisdom sūtras, the SUKHĀVATĪ-VYŪHA (in which he is said to be one of the bodhisattvas in the Pure Land of AMITĀBHA), and the SADDHARMA-PUṆḌARĪKA (which has an entire chapter

Thousand-armed Avalokiteśvara, He mis (He mis) Monastery, Ladakh.

[no. 24] in which he is the main figure). In this sūtra, he is described as the savior of beings in trouble. It is said that by merely remembering his name with devotion one can be saved in times of distress. In early East Asian depictions (up to the early Sung Dynasty), he is portrayed as a male, but since at least the tenth century the image of a female in a white robe (Chin. *Pai-i Kuan-yin*) has predominated in East Asia. In Tibet Avalokiteśvara (sPyan ras gzigs dbang phyug) is viewed as the country's patron deity, one of whose physical emanations is the DALAI LAMA incarnational line.

Avataṃsaka-sūtra (Tib. *Sangs rgyas phal po che shin tu rgyas pa chen po'i mdo*; Chin. *Hua-yen ching*; Jpn. *Kegon-kyō*; Viet. *Hoa-nghiêm*; Flower Garland Sūtra)

A voluminous MAHĀYĀNA text that contains a disparate collection of parts. Among its more important sections are the *Sūtra on the Ten Levels* (*Daśabhūmika-sūtra*), which describes the ten BODHISATTVA levels (BHŪMI), and the *Flower Array Sūtra* (*Gaṇḍavyūha-sūtra*) which tells the story of Sudhana's quest to attain buddhahood. The *Avataṃsaka* is the philosophical basis of the Chinese HUA-YEN (Jpn. KEGON; Kor. HWAŎM) school, which particularly emphasizes the sūtra's teachings concerning the interpenetration and connectedness of all phenomena.

avidyā (Pāli *avijjā*; Tib. *ma rig pa*; Chin. *wu-ming*; Jpn. *mu-myō*; "ignorance")

The primary factor that enmeshes beings in the cycle of birth, death, and rebirth. In a technical sense, it refers to lack of understanding of the four noble truths (ĀRYA-SATYA), the effects of actions (KARMA), dependent arising (PRATĪTYA-SAMUTPĀDA), and other key Buddhist doctrines.

avyākṛta (Pāli *avyākata*; Tib. *lung du ma bstan pa*; "indeterminate")

Term relating to metaphysical questions that are posed by several people in dialogues in the PĀLI CANON. In one of these, the wandering ascetic Vacchagotta asks (in the "Aggi-vacchagotta-sutta," *Majjhima-nikāya* 3.72) whether the Buddha teaches that the world is eternal or not; whether the soul (*jīva*) and body are the same or different; and whether TATHĀGATAS exist after death or not. The Buddha refuses to assent to any of the apparently mutually exclusive alternatives, and tells Vacchagotta that asking and answering such questions is a waste of time. They are irrelevant to the present existential situation of sentient beings, who are caught in a cycle of birth, death, and rebirth that involves inevitable suffering and loss. Those who concern themselves with such topics only create greater suffering and perplexity. It should be noted that the Buddha does not state that he does not know the answers to these questions, but rather that there is no benefit in asking or answering them.

awakening

See BODHI.

Awakening of Faith in the Great Vehicle

See TA-SHENG-CH'I-HSIN-LUN.

āyatana (Pāli *āyatana*; Tib. *skye mched*; Chin. *ch'u;* "sense sphere")

The six abodes of perception or sensation: (1) form sense sphere (*rūpa-āyatana*); (2) sound sense sphere (*śabda-āyatana*); (3) scent sense sphere (*gandha-āyatana*); (4) taste sense sphere (*rasa-āyatana*), (5) tangible object sense sphere (*sparśa-āyatana*); and (6) mental sense sphere (*mano-āyatana*) Each sense sphere encompasses the range of potential objects of observation of its respective sense, and the members of each sphere serve as sources of perceptions. For example, a blue form (which is a form sense sphere) gives rise to an eye consciousness perceiving blue. A visible form is called a form sense sphere because it is a cause that gives rise to continued perception of similar type (i.e., later moments of similar eye-consciousnesses).

B

Ba khin, U (Sayaji U Ba Khin, 1889–1970)

Burmese lay Buddhist meditation teacher, who worked for most of his life as an accountant and served as Accountant General of Burma from 1948 to 1953. He developed a method of *vipassanā* (Skt. VIPAŚYANĀ) practice that emphasized intensive meditation retreats and downplayed the importance of theoretical knowledge. His style of meditation has been carried on by a number of his students who themselves became prominent meditation teachers, such as S. N. GOENKA, Ruth Dennison, and Robert Hover.

bala (Pāli *bala*; Tib. *stobs*; "power")

Five abilities developed on the "path of preparation" (PRAYOGA-MĀRGA): (1) faith (ŚRADDHĀ); (2) effort (VĪRYA); (3) mindfulness (SMṚTI); (4) meditative absorption (SAMĀDHI); and (5) wisdom (PRAJÑĀ). In MAHĀYĀNA it is the eighth "perfection" (PĀRAMITĀ) of the tenfold list of perfections that a BODHISATTVA cultivates on the path to buddhahood. It is developed on the eighth bodhisattva level (BHŪMI).

There is also a tenfold list of qualities that in both NIKĀYA BUDDHISM and Mahāyāna are said to be unique to fully awakened buddhas (SAMYAK-SAMBUDDHA): (1) power of knowledge of what is possible and what is impossible (*sthānāsthāna-jñāna-bala*); (2) power of knowledge of the retributions of actions (*karma-vipāka-jñāna-bala*); (3) power of knowledge of the concentrations, liberations, meditative absorptions, and attainments (*dhyāna-vimokṣa-samādhi-samāpatti-jñāna-bala*); (4) power of knowledge of the relative qualities of beings (*indriya-parāpara-jñāna-bala*); (5) power of knowledge of the various intentions of beings (*nānādhimukti-jñāna-bala*); (6) power of knowledge of the various states of beings (*nānādhātu-jñāna-bala*); (7) power of knowledge of the ways in which beings go everywhere (within cyclic existence and *nirvāṇa*) (*sarvatragāminī-pratipajjñāna-bala*); (8) power of knowledge of former abodes (*pūrva-nivāsa-jñāna-bala*); (9) power of knowledge of death and rebirth (*cyutyupapāda-jñāna-bala*); and (10) power of knowledge that the defilements have been extinguished (*āsrava-kṣaya-jñāna-bala*).

Bankei Eitaku (Yōtaku, 1622–1693)

Japanese ZEN master of the RINZAI school who studied under the Chinese master Tao-che Ch'ao-yüan, who gave him the certification of enlightenment (Chin. *yin-k'o*; Jpn. INKA SHŌMEI). After being appointed abbot of Myōshin-ji Monastery in Kyōto in 1672, he was a key figure in the revival of the Rinzai tradition in Japan.

bar do (Skt. *antarābhava*; "intermediate state")

According to TIBETAN BUDDHISM, after death beings enter an "intermediate state" in which they acquire a subtle body that endures until they are reborn. In the intermediate state they experience various intense sounds, sights, etc., which are products of their own minds. This is considered to be a time of great danger, as beings may react to their experiences in ways that cause them to be reborn in lower rebirth situations (GATI). It can also be a time of great opportunity, as beings may make choices that lead them to higher rebirths, or even buddhahood.

There are six *bar do* states, according to the BKA' BRGYUD PA (Kagyüpa) order: (1) *bar do* between birth and death (*skye shi'i bar do*), which refers to the normal waking state between birth and death; (2) dream *bar do* (*rmi lam bar do*), the period between falling asleep and awakening; (3) meditation *bar do* (*bsam gtan bar do*), a state of cessation in which the senses are withdrawn from external objects and the mind is focused on an internal object of observation; (4) *bar do* of becoming (*srid pa bar do*), the period between the moment of death and rebirth; (5) reality *bar do* (*chos nyid bar do*), the time of unconsciousness that beings experience when overwhelmed by death, so called because during this time the mind returns to its primordial nature; and (6) *bar do* of birth (*skye gnas bar do*), which begins at the moment of rebirth into a new lifetime, immediately after the *bar do* of becoming.

Bar do thos grol (*Liberation through Hearing in the Intermediate State*)

A work attributed to PADMASAMBHAVA that contains descriptions of, and rituals for, the intermediate state (BAR DO). Sometimes referred to as the "Tibetan Book of the Dead," it is a "hidden treasure" (GTER MA) that is said to have been concealed until the time was right for its propagation. It was "discovered" in the fourteenth century by Kar ma gling pa (Karma Lingpa).

Bareau, André

French scholar of Buddhism, best known for his work on Indian Buddhist sectarianism and the life of the Buddha. His works include *Recherches sur la biographie du Buddha dans les Sūtrapiṭaka et les Vinayapiṭaka anciens* (Paris, 1963–1995) and *Les sectes bouddhiques du petit véhicule* (Saigon, 1955).

Bassui Zenji (1327–1387)

One of the great Japanese ZEN masters of the RINZAI school, a disciple of Kohō Zenji. He received monastic ordination at the age of twenty-nine but chose not to live in a monastery, shunning comfort in favor of a life of wandering and meditation. At the age of fifty, however, he consented to become abbot of a Zen monastery, where he remained until his death ten years later.

bDud 'joms Rin po che 'Jigs 'bral ye shes rdo rje

See DUDJOM RINPOCHE.

Beal, Samuel (1825–1889)

British scholar who worked at University College, London, best known for preparing some of the earliest translations of important Chinese Buddhist texts. Among his notable publications is a study of the life of HSÜAN-TSANG, entitled *The Life of Hiuen-tsiang, by the Shaman Hwui* (1911).

Bechert, Heinz (b. 1932)

German scholar of Buddhism who specializes in THERAVĀDA Buddhism, whose best-known work is *Buddhismus: Staat und Gesellschaft in den Ländern des Theravāda Buddhismus* (3 vols.: 1966, 1967, 1973).

bhagavan (Pāli *bhagavant*; Tib. *bcom ldan 'das*; "Lord")

An epithet of the Buddha, often translated as "Lord" or "Blessed One." It is derived from the Sanskrit root bhaj, meaning "fortunate," "illustrious," or "venerable." This is the most common form of address for ŚĀKYAMUNI BUDDHA in Buddhist SŪTRAS.

Bhaiṣajyaguru (or Bhaiṣajyarāja; Tib. *sMan gyi bla ma/sMan gyi rgyal po*; Chin. *Yao-shih Fo*; Jpn. *Yakushi Nyorai*; Viet. *Du'oc-su' Phật*; Mon. *Otochi*; "Medicine Teacher"/"Medicine King")

The "Medicine Buddha" who in many MAHĀYĀNA traditions is particularly associated with healing. He is often pictured iconographically as holding healing herbs in one hand and medical treatises in the other. In the *Bhaṣajya-guru-sūtra* he is said to have made twelve vows in a previous life, several of which indicate his desire to focus on healing physical ailments that afflict sentient beings. He is an important figure in China, Japan, and Tibet.

bhava-cakra (Pāli *bhava-cakka*; Tib. *srid pa'i 'khor lo*; Jpn. *rinne*; "wheel of becoming")

A pictorial representation of the cycle of birth, death, and rebirth, which has images of the six destinies (GATI) into which sentient beings may be born: gods, demi-gods, humans, animals, hungry ghosts, and hell beings. In Tibetan versions of this motif, YAMA, the god of death, is often shown with fangs hanging over a wheel divided into six parts. Yama symbolizes the ever-present reality of death, the inevitable end of all beings caught up in cyclic existence

Bhava-cakra, "The Wheel of Time," in the entrance to Rum bteg (Rumtek) Monastery, Sikkim.

(SAṂSĀRA). In the center of the wheel one commonly finds animals representing the forces that perpetuate the cycle: (1) a pig, which represents ignorance; (2) a cock, which represents desire; and (3) a snake, which represents hatred or aversion. The outer rim of the wheel commonly contains representations of the twelve links of the cycle of dependent arising (PRATĪTYA-SAMUTPĀDA).

bhāvanā (Pāli *bhāvanā*; Tib. *sgom pa*) ("meditation," "cultivation")

A term that is widely applied to meditative practice in Buddhism. In general, it can be said to involve familiarization of the mind with an object of observation (*ālambana*), and in meditation treatises it is commonly divided into two main types: (1) stabilizing meditation (ŚAMATHA) – in which a meditator cultivates the ability to focus on the object of observation without losing concentration – and (2) analytical meditation (VIPAŚYANĀ), in which one analyzes the object in order to determine its final mode of subsistence.

Meditating monks, Ŭnahesa Monastery, Korea

Bhāvanākrama (Tib. *sGom pa'i rim pa*; *Stages of Meditative Practice*)

An important treatise on meditation by the Indian monk KAMALAŚĪLA, in which he outlines a gradual program of meditation that progresses through well-defined stages and which culminates in the attainment of buddhahood. This text was purportedly written as a summary of the orthodox MAHĀYĀNA gradualist path to awakening in response to the subitist system of the Chinese CH'AN master HO-SHANG MO-HO-YEN, who, according to Tibetan Buddhist tradition, Kamalaśīla debated in the COUNCIL OF LHASA in 792–794.

bhāvanā-mārga (Pāli *bhāvanā-magga*; Tib. *sgom pa'i lam*; "path of meditation")

Fourth of the five paths to buddhahood, in which the meditator is said to remove the subtlest traces of afflictions so thoroughly that they will never reappear. This prepares one for the next phase, the "path of no more learning" (AŚAIKṢA-MĀRGA), in which one completes the training and becomes a buddha. The meditator also deepens his or her familiarity with meditation on emptiness (ŚŪNYATĀ), which was directly perceived on the previous level, the "path of seeing" (DARŚAṆA-MĀRGA).

Bhāvaviveka

See BHAVYA.

Bhavya (also Bhāvaviveka; Tib. *Legs ldan 'byed*, ca. 490–570)

Indian Buddhist philosopher considered by Tibetan doxographers to be the founder of the "Middle Way Autonomy School" (SVĀTANTRIKA-MADHYAMAKA) because of his use of autonomous (*svatantra*) syllogisms. This is contrasted with the "Middle Way Consequence School" (PRĀSAṄGIKA-MADHYAMAKA), which utilizes *reductio ad absurdum*

(Skt. *prasaṅga*) arguments against its opponents. Born in South India, Bhavya traveled to Magadha, where he studied the philosophy of NĀGĀRJUNA. Bhavya asserted that a Madhyamaka philosopher should be able to formulate a thesis, and not just attack those of rivals. He also asserted that the words of the Buddha are authoritative (*pramāṇa*) and do not need to be verified by reasoning (*yukti*). The purpose of reasoning is to correct misunderstandings of scripture (*āgama*), not to examine its teachings. His system of exposition was opposed to that of his contemporary BUDDHAPĀLITA (ca. 470–540) and CANDRAKĪRTI (ca. seventh century), who are classified by Tibetan doxographers as Prāsaṅgikas. His works include an important text on logic, the *Blaze of Reasoning* (*Tarka-jvālā*) and a commentary on Nāgārjuna's MŪLAMADHYAMAKA-KĀRIKĀ, entitled *Lamp of Wisdom* (*Prajñā-pradīpa*).

bhikṣu (Pāli *bhikkhu*; Tib. *dge slong*; "mendicant," "monk")

The standard term for a Buddhist monk who has received full ordination. Typically men who aspire to become monks first take the "novice" (ŚRĀMAṆERA) ordination and later receive the full ordination. The term *bhikṣu* literally means "beggar," indicating that monks are expected to subsist on alms given to them by the lay community. Those who take full ordination are also expected to observe the rules regarding monastic behavior set out in the VINAYA-PIṬAKA (which number 227 in the THERAVĀDA tradition). During the Buddha's time, monks typically wandered from place to place and had no fixed abode (except during the rainy season), but over time fixed monastic establishments developed, and today most Buddhist monks reside in monasteries.

Chogye monk at Chogyesa Monastery, Seoul, Korea.

bhikṣuṇī (Pāli *bhikkhunī*; Tib. *dge slong ma*; "mendicant," "nun")

A Buddhist nun who has received the full ordination. According to stories in the PĀLI CANON, the first nun was ŚĀKYAMUNI BUDDHA's stepmother, MAHĀPRAJĀPATĪ, who convinced the Buddha's personal attendant ĀNANDA to intercede on her behalf to overcome the Buddha's initial reluctance to allow women to join his order. The Buddha eventually created an order of nuns, who were bound by the 227 rules for monks outlined in the VINAYA-PIṬAKA, as well as eight extra regulations known as "weighty rules" (*guru-dharma*) that clearly relegate nuns to an inferior position in the Buddhist monastic order. The Buddha also is reported to have said that because the order of nuns was established his teaching (DHARMA) would flourish for only 500 years, instead of 1,000. In most Buddhist countries today the full ordination lineage for women has died out, and most Buddhist nuns are thus only able to receive the novice (ŚRĀMAṆERĪ) ordination. The order of nuns probably died out in India around 456 C.E., and the full ordination was probably never transmitted to mainland Southeast Asia. There are, however, full ordination

Nun sweeping in the early morning at Daewŏnsa Monastery, North Cholla, Korea

lineages today in Korea, Taiwan, and Hong Kong, and a number of women from other traditions have received ordination from Chinese preceptors as part of a movement to revive the order of nuns.

bhūmi (Pāli *bhūmi*; Tib. *sa*; "level," "ground")

Sanskrit term referring to stages of development. Each succeeding level represents a further stage of spiritual accomplishment and is accompanied by progressively greater power and wisdom. In MAHĀYĀNA, there are ten levels through which BODHISATTVAS progress on their way to the attainment of buddhahood: (1) the "very joyous" (*pramuditā*), which is attained when a bodhisattva first directly perceives emptiness (ŚŪNYATĀ), and which is simultaneous with the path of seeing (DARŚANA-MĀRGA); bodhisattvas on this level develop the perfection (PĀRAMITĀ) of generosity (DĀNA); (2) the "stainless" (*vimalā*), during which bodhisattvas ripen the perfection of ethics (*śīla*) and overcome all tendencies to engage in negative actions; (3) the "luminous" (*prabhākarī*), when bodhisattvas cultivate the perfection of patience (*kṣānti*); (4) the "radiant" (*arciṣmatī*), when they work at the perfection of effort (VĪRYA); (5) the "difficult to cultivate" (*sudur-jayā*), during which they ripen the perfection of concentration (DHYĀNA); (6) the "manifest" (*abhimukī*), on which they develop the perfection of wisdom (PRAJÑĀ); (7) the "gone afar" (*dūraṃ-gamā*), the stage of perfecting "skill in means" (UPĀYA-KAUŚALYA, the ability skillfully to adapt their teachings to any audience); (8) the "immovable" (*acalā*), during which they work at the perfection of aspiration (PRAṆIDHĀNA; from this point onward they are incapable of backsliding and will inevitably progress steadily toward buddhahood); (9) the "good intelligence" (*sādhumatī*), the level on which they advance the perfection of power (BALA) and fully comprehend all doctrines; (10) the "cloud of doctrine" (*dharma-megha*), during which they eliminate the subtlest traces of remaining afflictions and cultivate the perfection of knowledge (JÑĀNA) and finally attain buddhahood.

Bimbisāra

King of Magadha during ŚĀKYAMUNI BUDDHA's lifetime and one of the major patrons of the early Buddhist order. He is reputed to have given the Buddha the Veṇuvana Ārāma, which was the first dwelling used by the early Buddhist community during the rainy season. At the age of thirty he became a lay disciple and is reported to have been the person who suggested the bi-monthly ceremony called the POṢADHA, during which monks recite the monastic rules and confess any transgressions of them. Bimbisāra died of starvation after being imprisoned by his son AJĀTAŚATRU, who feared that his father might pose a threat to his power.

bindu (Tib. *thig le*; "drop")

The subtle energies that reside in various centers in the body, according to tantric meditation theory. These are a particular focus of highest yoga tantra (ANUTTARA-YOGA-TANTRA), which has meditative practices designed to cause the drops to move through the channels (Skt. *nāḍī*). This process is believed to bring about the actualization of blissful wisdom consciousnesses. The most important of these energies is the "indestructible drop" (Tib. *mi gzhigs pa'i thig le*), which resides in the center of the heart and is comprised of subtle substances deposited by one's father and mother at conception. This remains in the heart until death occurs.

bKa' brgyud pa (Kagyüpa; "Teaching Lineage")

One of the four orders of TIBETAN BUDDHISM. It traces its lineage back to the Indian MAHĀSIDDHA TILOPA (988–1069), who was the teacher of NĀROPA (1016–1100). Nāropa in turn was the teacher of the first major Tibetan exponent of the tradition, MAR PA CHOS KYI BLO GROS (Marpa Chögi Lodrö, 1012–1097). Mar pa's greatest student was the famous yogin and poet MI LA RAS PA (Milarepa, 1040–1123), whose biography is one of the best-known pieces of Tibetan religious literature.

The bKa' brgyud pa tradition is particularly known for its many great non-monastic yogins, but also developed a monastic tradition, beginning with Mi la ras pa's student SGAM PO PA (Gampopa, 1079–1153). The name bKa' brgyud pa literally means "teaching lineage," and its adherents claim that its doctrines and practices are passed down through a succession of awakened teachers, each of whom directly understands the true nature of reality through spontaneous, non-conceptual awareness and then transmits the essence of his/her wisdom to the next generation of disciples. The major practices of the tradition are the "great seal" (MAHĀMUDRĀ) and the "six dharmas of Nāropa" (NĀ RO CHOS DRUG).

The bKa' brgyud pa order is traditionally divided into "the four great and the eight lesser sub-orders." The former derive from sGam po pa and his nephew Dwags po sgom tshul (Takpo Gomtsül, 1116–1169). They are: (1) KAR MA BKA' BRGYUD PA (Karma Kagyüpa), founded by DUS GSUM MKHYEN PA (Tüsum Khyenpa, 1110–1193); (2) mTshal pa bKa' brgyud pa (Tselpa Kagyüpa), founded by Shangs mtshal pa (Shang Tselpa, 1123–1193); (3) 'Ba' ram bKa' brgyud pa (Param Kagyüpa), founded by 'Ba' ram pa Dar ma dbang phyug (Parampa Darma Wangchuk, fl. ca. 12th century); and (4) Phag mo bKa' brgyud pa (Pakmo Kagyüpa), founded by Phag mo gru pa rDo rje rgyal po (Pakmodrupa Dorje Gyelpo, 1110–1170). The eight "lesser sub-orders" are: (1) 'BRI GUNG (Driküng); (2) sTag lung (Taklung); (3) Khro phu (Tropu); (4) 'BRUG PA (Drukpa); (5) dMar (Mar); (6) Yer pa (Yerpa); (7) Shug seb (Shuksep); and (8) g.Yam bzang (Yamsang). Today only the 'Brug pa, 'Bri gung, and sTag lung survive, and the newer lineage of Shangs pa (Shangpa) should be added to the list of bKa' brgyud pa sub-orders. Shangs pa traces itself back to Khyung po rnal 'byor (Khyungpo Nenjor, b. 1286).

bKa' gdams pa (Kadampa; "Oral Instructions School")

The first order of TIBETAN BUDDHISM, founded by 'BROM STON (Dromdön,

1008–1064), the main Tibetan disciple of the Indian master ATIŚA. In 1057 'Brom ston founded Rwa sgrengs (Reting) Monastery, which became the main seat of the order. It declined over the next several centuries, but was revived by TSONG KHA PA (Tsong Khapa, 1357–1419), who called the order he founded the "New bKa' gdams pa." It later came to be most commonly known as DGE LUGS PA (Gelukpa), or "System of Virtue."

bKa' 'gyur (Ganggyur or Kanjur; "Translations of Teachings")

One of the two main scriptural collections of TIBETAN BUDDHISM (the other being the BSTAN 'GYUR). It consists of translations of Indian texts purportedly spoken by ŚĀKYAMUNI BUDDHA and mainly includes MAHĀYĀNA SŪTRAS and TANTRAS. The first compilation of this voluminous collection was reportedly overseen by BU STON (Pudön, 1290–1364), and it was first printed in 1411. It contains thirteen volumes of texts on monastic discipline (VINAYA; Tib. *'Dul ba*), twenty-one volumes of "Perfection of Wisdom" (PRAJÑĀ-PĀRAMITĀ; Tib. *Pha rol tu phyin pa*) texts, six volumes of AVATAṂSAKA (Tib. *Sangs rgyas phal po che shin tu rgyas pa chen po'i mdo*) texts, six volumes of RATNAKUṬA (Tib. *Rin chen brtsegs pa'i mdo*) texts, thirty volumes of sūtras (Tib. *mdo*), and twenty-two volumes of tantras (Tib. *rgyud*).

bKra shis lhun po (Tashilhünpo; "Mount Fortune")

One of the great monasteries of TIBETAN BUDDHISM, located in the town of gZhis ka rtse (Shigatse). It has traditionally been the seat of the PAṆ CHEN BLA MA (Panchen lama), the second most important reincarnate lama (SPRUL SKU) in the DGE LUGS PA (Gelukpa) order after the DALAI LAMA. It was founded by DGE 'DUN GRUB (Gendün Drup, 1391–1474) in 1447 and greatly expanded by the fourth Paṇ chen bLa ma, bLo bzang chos kyi rgyal mtshan (Panchen Losang Chögi Gyeltsen, 1570–1662). Unlike most other Tibetan monasteries, it largely survived the depredations of the Chinese invasion of Tibet and the Cultural Revolution.

bla ma (lama; "religious teacher"; lit. "none higher")

The Tibetan translation of the Sanskrit term GURU. It indicates that a person has been recognized as a spiritual guide. In some orders of TIBETAN BUDDHISM there are formal requirements that must be met before one can receive this designation. In the SA SKYA PA (Sakyapa) order, for example, one must have successfully completed a three-year meditation retreat and be certified by a recognized master. In most orders formal recognition is normally required, but there are numerous examples of people adopting this title without receiving such recognition. The *bla ma* plays a crucial role in Tibetan Buddhism, particularly in terms of transmitting teachings and ritual practices to students.

blo rigs (*lorik*; "knowledge and awareness")

A system of epistemology particularly associated with the DGE LUGS PA (Gelukpa) order of TIBETAN BUDDHISM, derived mainly from the works of DHARMAKĪRTI. Its basic framework consists of definitions (*mtshan nyid*) of key concepts in Buddhist psychology, along with often complex divisions (*dbye ba*) of them and examples (*mtshan gzhi*).

Bodhgayā

A town 90 kilometers south of Patna in the Indian state of Bihār, where ŚĀKYAMUNI BUDDHA is said to have attained awakening (BODHI). It is one of the most important holy sites of Buddhism, and pilgrims travel there from all over the world. According to standard legends of the Buddha's life, after six years of ascetic practices he renounced asceticism and traveled to Bodhgayā, where he resolved to find the key to final release from the sufferings of cyclic existence (SAṂSĀRA). Sitting in meditation under a tree (now referred to Buddhists as the "Tree of Awakening" – BODHI-VṚKṢA), he cultivated progressively deeper meditative states, until at dawn the next day he became fully awakened. From that point on, he is referred to by Buddhists as "Buddha."

bodhi (Pāli *bodhi*; Tib. *byang chub*; Chin. *p'u-t'i*; Jpn. *bodai*; "awakening")

A term that is often translated as "enlightenment" by Western translators, but which literally means "awakening." Like the term BUDDHA, it is derived from the Sanskrit root budh, "to wake up," and in Buddhism it indicates that a person has "awakened" from the sleep of ignorance in which most beings spend their lives. According to Buddhist legend, the Buddha attained *bodhi* in the town of BODHGAYĀ while sitting in meditation under the Bodhi Tree (BODHI-VṚKṢA).

Bodhi, Bhikkhu (Jeffrey Block, b. 1944)

American THERAVĀDA monk who received a Ph.D. in philosophy in 1972 and subsequently traveled to Sri Lanka, where he received the novice vows in 1972 and the full *bhikkhu* ordination in 1973. In 1984 he became the editor of the Buddhist Publication Society, and he now resides at the Forest Hermitage in Kandy. He has written a number of books, including *Nourishing the Roots* and *The Discourse on the All-Embracing Net of Views*.

Bodhi Pūjā

A ritual that focuses on the sacred symbol of the Bodhi Tree (BODHI-VṚKṢA). It was instituted by Ven. Ariyadhamma, a forest-dwelling monk in Sri Lanka, as a Buddhist alternative to increasingly popular rituals derived from Hinduism. It involves making offerings at statues of ŚĀKYAMUNI BUDDHA, recitation of verses from the PĀLI CANON, and veneration of the Bodhi Tree. Like the Hindu rituals it is intended to supplant, it is believed to bring worldly benefits to participants, such as alleviation of sickness, restoration of domestic harmony, etc.

Bodhi Tree

See BODHI-VṚKṢA.

Bodhicaryāvatāra (Tib. *Byang chub sems dpa'i spyod pa la 'jug pa*; *Entry into Bodhisattva Deeds*)

An important MAHĀYĀNA work by ŚĀNTIDEVA (ca. 650–750), which focuses on the career and practices of the BODHISATTVA, the ideal of MAHĀYĀNA Buddhism.

bodhi-citta (Tib. *byang chub kyi sems*; "mind of awakening")

In MAHĀYĀNA Buddhism, this refers to the BODHISATTVA's aspiration to attain buddhahood in order to benefit other sentient beings. The dawning of this orientation represents a profound shift in one's attitudes and marks the beginning of the bodhisattva path. It is often divided into two aspects: (1) the intention to become awakened; and (2) acting on the intention by pursuing the path to awakening (BODHI).

Bodhidharma (Chin. *P'u-t'i ta-mo*; Jpn. *Daruma*; Kor. *Darma Daesa*, ca. 470–543)

The semi-legendary Indian meditation master who is considered by the CH'AN

(Jpn. Zen; Kor. Sŏn; Viet. Thiền) tradition to be its first Chinese patriarch and the twenty-eighth Indian patriarch. According to East Asian legends, he traveled from India to spread the true dharma and is thought to have arrived in the town of Lo-yang in southern China between 516 and 526. The legends report that he traveled to the Shao-lin ssu monastery on Mount Sung, where he meditated facing a wall for nine years. During this time his legs reportedly fell off, and he is also said to have cut off his own eyelids to prevent himself from falling asleep. One legend holds that when he cast his eyelids to the ground a tea plant sprang up, and its ability to ward off sleep due to its caffeine content is thought to be a gift from Bodhidharma to successive generations of meditators. His main disciple was Hui-k'o, who is said to have cut off his own arm as an indication of his sincerity in wishing to be instructed by Bodhidharma. Hui-k'o is considered by the tradition to be its second Chinese patriarch.

Bodhipatha-pradīpa (Tib. *Byang chub lam gyi sgron ma*; *Lamp for the Path to Awakening*)

Treatise by the Indian scholar-monk Atiśa (982–1054), purportedly written for his Tibetan disciples as a guide to the authoritative Indian Mahāyāna tradition regarding the bodhisattva's path to buddhahood. It outlines a gradual approach, arranged in successive stages, each of which requires those that precede it.

bodhisattva (Pāli *bodhisatta*; Tib. *byang chub sems dpa'*; Chin. *bu-sa*; Jpn. *bōsatsu*; Kor. *posal*; Viet. bồ-tát; "awakening-being")

The ideal of Mahāyāna Buddhism. The beginning of the bodhisattva's career is marked by the dawning of the "mind of awakening" (bodhi-citta), which is the resolve to become a buddha in order to benefit others. In Mahāyāna literature, this is commonly followed by a public statement of a vow to attain buddhahood (praṇidhāna) and a prediction of success (*vyākaraṇa*) by a buddha. After that point the bodhisattva pursues the goal of buddhahood by progressively cultivating the six (and sometimes ten) "perfections" (pāramitā): generosity, ethics, patience, effort, concentration, and wisdom. The two primary qualities in which the bodhisattva trains are compassion (karuṇā) and wisdom (prajñā), and when the perfections are fully cultivated and compassion and wisdom developed to their highest level, the bodhisattva becomes a buddha. The bodhisattva path is commonly divided into ten levels (bhūmi). The term "bodhisattva" is not, however, confined solely to Mahāyāna Buddhism: in Theravāda, Śākyamuni Buddha is referred to as "bodhisatta" in the past lives described in the Jātakas, during which he is said to have gradually perfected the good qualities of a buddha. In the Mahāyāna sense, however, the bodhisattva concept is an explicit rejection of Nikāya Buddhism's ideal religious paradigm, the arhat. In Mahāyāna the *arhat* is characterized as limited and selfish, concerned only with personal salvation, in contrast to the bodhisattva, who works for all sentient beings.

Bodhisattva-bhūmi (Tib. *Byang chub sems dpa'i sa*; *Bodhisattva Levels*)

A Sanskrit treatise by Asaṅga, one of the leading figures of the Indian Buddhist Yogācāra tradition. It outlines the path to buddhahood followed by the bodhisattva and describes the practices pertaining to the path. It is the fifteenth section of his voluminous *Levels of Yogic Practice* (*Yogācāra-bhūmi*).

Bodhi-vṛkṣa (Pāli *Bodhirukkha*; Tib. *Byang chub kyi shing*; "Tree of Awakening")

The tree in BODHGAYĀ (classified in botanical terms as *ficus religiosa*) under which SIDDHĀRTHA GAUTAMA, the historical Buddha, is said to have sat in meditation for forty-nine days, during which he completed his quest for buddhahood. The original Bodhi Tree was destroyed in the seventh century, but it remains an important symbol in Buddhism. In the Mahābodhi Temple in Bodhgayā a descendant of the original tree stands today, grown from a shoot sent to Sri Lanka by King AŚOKA in the third century B.C.E.

bōkatsu ("stick and shout")

A Japanese term for a training style common in some ZEN circles, which is said to have been derived from two Chinese CH'AN masters, Te-shan Hsüan-chien (Jpn. Tokusan Senkan, ca. 781–867) and LIN-CHI I-HSÜAN (Jpn. Rinzai Gigen, d. 866). It involves skillful use of blows with a stick (*kyōsaku*, *shippei*) and shouting (*katsu*) by a Zen master, which is believed to bring students to immediate and direct realization of truth if done properly.

Bon (Pön)

A Tibetan tradition that traces its history back to pre-Buddhist practices associated with the cult of the early Tibetan kings. It has absorbed many Buddhist practices and doctrines, but its adherents consider Bon to be distinct from TIBETAN BUDDHISM. According to Bon sources, the tradition came to Tibet from rTag gzigs (Taksik), which appears to refer to roughly the area of Persia. gShen rabs (Shenrap), the mythical founder of Bon, brought the religion from rTag gzigs to the kingdom of Zhang zhung (Shangshung), which was probably an area in western Tibet with Mount Kailash at its center. From there it was disseminated into Tibet.

Borobudur

One of the great monuments of Buddhism, a huge STŪPA built on the island of Java around the ninth century by the rulers of the Śailendra dynasty. It was designed as a giant MAṆḌALA built over a hill and consisting of five square terraces, which are decorated with stone carvings. Surmounting these are three circular platforms and a *stūpa*. Ascending the monument is meant to symbolize the path from the state of ignorance to buddhahood.

bōsatsu

See BODHISATTVA.

brahma-vihāra (Pāli *brahma-vihāra*; Tib. *tshangs pa'i gnas pa*; "divine abodes")

Four meditative states that are said to lead to rebirth in the heaven of Brahmā: (1) immeasurable love (*maitrī-apramāṇa*); (2) immeasurable compassion (*karuṇā-apramāṇa*); (3) immeasurable joy (*muditā-apramāṇa*); and (4) immeasurable equanimity (*upekṣā-apramāṇa*) these are called "immeasurables" (*apramāṇa*) because they arise with respect to an immeasurable field. This field encompasses all sentient beings, whose numbers are limitless. Immeasurable love involves cultivating the attitude of love that one has for someone dear to one and extending it to all beings. It includes the wish to establish other beings in happiness. Immeasurable compassion entails not being able to bear the suffering of others and is caused by observing their pain. Immeasurable compassion has the characteristic of joy and involves absence of envy with respect to others' good fortune. Immeasurable joy is a feeling of joy regarding others' happiness and wishing that they be free from unhappiness. Immeasurable equanimity involves viewing all beings equally, not favoring some and holding others in disfavor.

'Bras spungs (Drebung; "Rice Heap")

Founded in 1416 and located near Lhasa, it became one of the three main monasteries of the dGE LUGS PA (Gelukpa) order of TIBETAN BUDDHISM (the others being dGA' LDAN and SE RA). At one time it was one of the world's largest monasteries, housing around 20,000 monks. It was largely destroyed by the Chinese during the Cultural Revolution, but in recent years much of it has been rebuilt, and a new 'Bras spungs has been built by Tibetan refugees in South India. It contains three main monastic colleges: (1) 'Bras spungs bDe yangs (Drebung Deyang); (2) 'Bras spungs sGo mang (Drebung Gomang); and (3) 'Bras spungs bLo gsal gling (Drebung Loseling).

'Bri gung bKa' brgyud pa (Driküng Kagyüpa)

One of the "eight lesser sub-orders" of the bKA' BRGYUD PA order of TIBETAN BUDDHISM, the headquarters of which was 'Bris gung thil (Driküng Til) Monastery.

British Buddhism

As a result of Britain's contact with Buddhist countries during its colonial period, a number of British scholars began studying Buddhism in its original languages during the 18th century. One of the leading academic organizations devoted to the study of canonical texts was the Asiatic Society of Bengal, founded in Calcutta in 1784 by the pioneering scholar Sir William Jones (1746–1794). In 1881 the PĀLI TEXT SOCIETY was founded by THOMAS W. RHYS DAVIDS (1843–1922), and during the next century it produced translations and critical editions of most of the important works of the PĀLI CANON. SIR EDWIN ARNOLD's influential work *The Light of Asia* generated significant interest in Buddhism, and in 1893 the Sri Lankan Buddhist missionary ANAGĀRIKA DHARMAPĀLA visited England following his participation in the World Parliament of Religions in Chicago. In 1907 the Buddhist Society of Great Britain and Ireland was founded by Rhys Davids. The society was primarily interested in THERAVĀDA Buddhism, and this was reflected in the content of its journal, *The Buddhist Review*. The society was absorbed by the Buddhist lodge of the Theosophical Society, which was founded by TRAVERS CHRISTMAS HUMPHREYS (1901–1983) in 1924. It publishes a journal entitled *The Middle Way*. One of the first Westerners to take Buddhist ordination was Charles Allen Bennett McGregor (1872–1923), who traveled to Sri Lanka after reading *The Light of Asia* sparked in him an interest in Buddhism. He was ordained at Akyab in 1901 and the following year received the *bhikkhu* ordination and took the name ANANDA METTEYYA. In 1907 he founded the Buddhist Society of Great Britain and Ireland with the intention of spreading the DHARMA to the West, but he had little success in this endeavor. The first effective spokesman for Buddhism in England was probably Christmas Humphreys, a barrister who was both a stirring public speaker and a compelling writer. The predominant form of Buddhism in England up until the mid-20th century was Theravāda, but in recent decades other traditions – particularly TIBETAN BUDDHISM and ZEN – have become established in Britain. There are now centers all over the country, but the total number of Buddhists is still a minuscule proportion of the population, probably less than 200,000.

'Brog mi (Drokmi, 993–1077)

A Tibetan who traveled to India and studied at VIKRAMAŚĪLA MONASTIC UNIVERSITY for eight years. Upon his return to Tibet he translated the HEVAJRA-TANTRA into Tibetan; this text became the central TANTRA of the SA SKYA PA (Sakyapa), one of the four main orders of TIBETAN BUDDHISM. He was the teacher of DKON MCHOG RGYAL PO (Gönchok Gyelpo, 1034–1102) of the 'Khon family, who founded Sa skya Monastery in 1073. This monastery subsequently became the main seat of the Sa skya pa order.

'Brom ston rGyal ba'i 'byung gnas (Dromdön Gyelwe Jungne, 1008–1064)

Main Tibetan disciple of ATIŚA (982–1054) and founder of the BKA' GDAMS PA (Kadampa), the first Tibetan Buddhist order.

'Brug pa bKa' brgyud pa (Drukpa Kagyüpa)

One of the "eight lesser sub-orders" of the BKA' BRGYUD PA order of TIBETAN BUDDHISM, which traces itself back to gLing chen ras pa Padma rdo rje (Lingchen Repa Bema Dorje, 1128–1188), who founded Rva lung (Ralung) Monastery around 1180. The monastery was built in an area southeast of rGyal rtse (Gyantse), near the border of Bhutan. The school received its name from an earlier monastery named 'Brug ("Dragon"), purportedly because a dragon appeared in the sky during its construction. It later became the main order of Tibetan Buddhism in Bhutan ('Brug yul, or "Dragon Country," in Tibetan).

bSam yas (Samye; "Expansive Thought")

The first Buddhist monastery in Tibet, which according to Tibetan tradition was built by KHRI SRONG LDE BRTSAN (Trisong Detsen, ca. 740–798), PADMASAMBHAVA, and ŚĀNTARAKṢITA in the eighth century. The central buildings and surrounding monuments are laid out in a MAṆḌALA pattern that reflects traditional Buddhist cosmology. When Buddhism became the state religion, bSam yas was designated as the chapel of the ruling kings. During the eighth to tenth centuries, it played a major role in the establishment of Buddhism in Tibet, but it fell into disrepair after the fall of the YAR LUNG DYNASTY. The temples have suffered from a number of disasters such as fires, and the complex was mostly destroyed by Chinese Red Guards in the 1960s. Despite the destruction, the bottom floor of the main temple remained intact. In recent years it has been restored and is now an important destination for tourists and pilgrims.

bSod nams rgya mtsho (Sönam Gyatso, 1543–1588)

The third DALAI LAMA, best known for his missionary work among the Mongols. In 1578 he accepted an invitation to visit ALTAN KHAN (1507–1583), chief of the Tümet Mongols and the most powerful Mongol leader of his day. Altan conferred on him the title "Ta le," or "Ocean," implying that he was an "ocean of wisdom." The Tibetan version of this designation, "Dalai Lama," was retroactively conferred on his two predecessors (DGE 'DUN GRUB and dGe 'dun rgya mtsho) and is the most common title by which this incarnational lineage is known. According to Mongolian tradition, bSod nams rgya mtsho convinced Altan Khan to ban blood sacrifices and the worship of ancestral images among the Mongols, and due to his missionary activity the Tümet Mongols became adherents of the DGE LUGS PA (Gelukpa) order. The bonds between the Mongols and the dGe lugs pas were further strengthened when the fourth Dalai Lama, YON TAN RGYA MTSHO (Yönden Gyatso, 1589–1617), was discovered in the person of a grandson of Altan Khan.

bsTan 'dzin rgya mtsho

See TENZIN GYATSO.

bsTan 'gyur (Tanjur, Dengyur; "Translations of Treatises")

The second part of the Tibetan recension of the Buddhist canon (the other being the BKA' 'GYUR), containing translations of philosophical treatises and commentaries. The bKa' 'gyur contains works attributed to the historical Buddha, while the bsTan 'gyur contains works by other Buddhist writers, mostly Indians.

Bu ston (Pudön, 1290–1364)

One of the great early scholars of TIBETAN BUDDHISM, who wrote an influential history of Buddhism in India and Tibet, entitled *History of the Dharma* (Tib. *Chos 'byung*). He is also credited with editing the first compilation of the Tibetan Buddhist canon. This is divided into two volumes, BKA' 'GYUR (Ganggyur, "Translations of Teachings") and BSTAN 'GYUR (Dengyur, "Translations of Treatises"). The first comprises 108 volumes of VINAYA texts, Mahāyāna SŪTRAS, and TANTRAS. The second has 225 volumes and includes philosophical treatises and commentaries. A master copy of this compilation was stored in 1334 in Zha lu (Shalu) Monastery, and it became the basis for all later editions of the canon.

buddha (Pāli *buddha*; Tib. *sangs rgyas*; Chin. *fo*; Jpn. *butsu*; "awakened one")

An epithet of those who successfully break the hold of ignorance, liberate themselves from cyclic existence, and teach others the path to liberation.

Stone Buddha statue at Sāñcī.

Derived from the Sanskrit root budh, "to awaken," it refers to someone who attains NIRVĀṆA through meditative practice and the cultivation of such qualities as wisdom, patience, and generosity. Such a person will never again be reborn within cyclic existence, as all the cognitive ties that bind ordinary beings to continued rebirth have been severed. Through their meditative practice, buddhas have eliminated all craving (TṚṢṆĀ) and defilements (*āsrava*). The buddha of the present era is referred to as "ŚĀKYAMUNI" ("Sage of the Śākyas"). He was born SIDDHĀRTHA GAUTAMA, a member of the ŚĀKYA clan.

Buddhabhadra (359–429; "Blessed Buddha")

A Kashmiri monk belonging to the SARVĀSTIVĀDA tradition who traveled to China in 409 and became a translator of Indian Buddhist texts. The most important of his works was a Chinese translation of the AVATAṂSAKA-SŪTRA, the philosophical basis of the HUA-YEN (Jpn. KEGON; Kor. HWAŎM) school.

Buddhacarita (Tib. *Sangs rgyas kyi spyod pa*; *Deeds of the Buddha*)

A poetic work in Sanskrit by AŚVAGHOṢA, which tells the life story of ŚĀKYAMUNI BUDDHA from his birth until his final liberation (PARINIRVĀṆA).

Buddhadāsa Bhikkhu (1906–1993; "Servant of the Buddha")

Influential Thai Buddhist monk who at age twenty-one took ordination, intending to be a monk only during the three month rainy-season retreat. He found that the monastic lifestyle agreed with him, however, and decided to remain in the SAṂGHA. He subsequently spent six years as a forest monk (ARAÑÑAVĀSĪ), during which time he attempted to avoid human contact. In the 1930s he founded a small hermitage called Suan Mokkhabalarama ("Garden of the Power of Liberation"), which was based on three core principles: study, practice, and dharma teaching. He angered the THERAVĀDA establishment by proposing to strip Buddhism of what he considered to be distorting accretions, such as most popular religious practices and the merit-making activities that are the focus of the religious lives of the majority of monks and laypeople. He emphasized such core principles as the four noble truths (ĀRYA-SATYA), the eightfold noble path (ĀRYĀṢṬĀṄGA-MĀRGA), selflessness (ANĀTMAN), and dependent arising (PRATĪTYA-SAMUTPĀDA). Among his more controversial theses is his contention that the doctrine of rebirth is not a core tenet of Buddhism and that Buddhist thought and practice could dispose of it without losing anything essential.

buddha-dharma (Pāli *buddha-dhamma*; Tib. *sangs rgyas kyi chos*; "doctrine of the Buddha")

A common way of referring to the teachings and practices set forth by the Buddha. Among many modern Buddhists (particularly in Western countries), it has been adopted as a non-sectarian way of referring to Buddhism in general, without singling out a particular tradition. In ZEN the Japanese equivalent *buppō* is thought to refer to an essential intuitive grasp of reality that cannot be described in words or doctrines, but rather is understood by awakened masters and passed on to their students by way of mind-to-mind transmission (Chin. *i-hsin-ch'üan-hsin*; Jpn. ISHIN-DENSHIN).

Buddhadhatta

Scholar-monk who was one of the most influential ABHIDHARMA commentators. According to tradition, he met BUDDHAGHOSA and like him resided in the MAHĀVIHĀRA. He is best known for his *Ascertainment of Monastic Discipline* (*Vinaya-vinicchaya*) and *Entry into Higher Knowledge* (*Abhidhammāvatāra*). The first is a commentary on the VINAYA-PIṬAKA, and the second is a commentary on the ABHIDHARMA-PIṬAKA.

Buddhaghosa (ca. 4th–5th century; "Voice of the Buddha")

One of the great scholastic philosophers of Buddhism and the most influential commentator of the THERAVĀDA tradition. According to the MAHĀVAṂSA, he was born into a brahman family but was converted to Buddhism by a monk named Revata. His most productive years were the time of his residence at the MAHĀVIHĀRA in ANURĀDHAPURA in Sri Lanka, during which time he translated Sinhala commentaries into Pāli and wrote some of the most influential commentarial works of Theravāda Buddhism, including the VISUDDHIMAGGA (*Path of Purification*), a monumental treatise on meditation theory and practice.

Buddhapālita (Tib. *Sangs rgyas bskyangs*, ca. 470–540; "Protected by the Buddha")

A contemporary and philosophical rival of BHAVYA who is classified by Tibetan doxographers as an exponent of the Middle Way Consequence School (PRĀSAṄGIKA-MADHYAMAKA), one of the two divisions of Indian MADHYAMAKA. In his *Commentary on [Nāgārjuna's] Fundamental Verses on the Middle Way* (*Mūlamadhyamaka-vṛtti*), Buddhapālita championed the use of prasaṅga (*reductio ad absurdum*) arguments against opponents, in which one draws out the absurd consequences of their positions. Bhavya, by contrast, also utilized autonomous (*svatantra*) syllogisms, and so is regarded in Tibet as the founder of the Middle Way Autonomy School (SVĀTANTRIKA-MADHYAMAKA).

Buddhasāsana Samāgama

See INTERNATIONAL BUDDHIST SOCIETY.

buddhatā (Chin. *fo-hsing*; Jpn. *busshō*; Kor. *pulsŏng*; "buddha-nature")

MAHĀYĀNA Buddhist term that refers to the final, unchanging nature of all reality. This is often equated with emptiness (ŚŪNYATĀ) and defined as simply an absence of any fixed and determinate essence. According to this formulation, because sentient beings have no fixed essence, they are able to change, and thus have the potential to become BUDDHAS. In other Mahāyāna traditions, however (particularly in East Asia), the concept is given a more substantialist formulation and is seen as the fundamental nature of all reality, an eternal essence that all beings possess, and in virtue of which they can all become buddhas. In the Japanese ZEN tradition, for example, it is described as the true self of every individual, and Zen has developed meditation techniques by which practitioners might develop experiential awareness of it. The concept is not found in NIKĀYA BUDDHISM, which does not posit the idea that all beings have the potential to become buddhas. Rather, Nikāya Buddhist traditions hold that only certain exceptional individuals may become buddhas and that others should be content to attain NIRVĀṆA as an ARHAT or PRATYEKA-BUDDHA.

Buddhist Churches of America

One of the largest Buddhist organizations in North America. It began as the Buddhist Mission of North America, founded in 1899. It is now the representative of the JŌDŌ SHINSHŪ ("True Pure Land") tradition in the Western Hemisphere and claims over 100,000 members.

Buddhist Councils

See GANDHĀRA; PĀṬALIPUTRA; RĀJAGṚHA; VAIŚĀLĪ.

Buddhist Peace Fellowship

An organization founded in 1978 by ROBERT AITKEN, Anne Aitken, Nelson Foster, and several other people, which according to its mission statement aims "to bring a Buddhist perspective to the peace movement, and to bring the peace movement to the Buddhist community." It is based on the core principles of nonviolence, protection of all beings, and the promotion of environmental, feminist, and social justice. Its membership includes most of the influential proponents of contemporary "ENGAGED BUDDHISM," and it is active in a range of projects. It publishes a journal called *The Turning Wheel.*

Burmese Buddhism

Because of its position along important land and sea trade routes, Burma has for centuries been influenced by neighboring countries, particularly India. The earliest recorded introduction of Buddhism to Burma was initiated by AŚOKA (r. 272–236 B.C.E.), who sent the monks Soṇa and Uttara as missionaries. They established a Buddhist center in Thaton. Further THERAVĀDA missions came to Burma in the first century C.E., and subsequently SARVĀSTIVĀDA and MAHĀYĀNA lineages arrived. During the tenth and eleventh centuries, an eclectic form of tantric Buddhism became established among people living in the Pagān–Irawaddy River Basin. Early chronicles report that the monks of this sect (who referred to themselves as Ari) rejected the word of the Buddha and taught that esoteric MANTRAS are able effectively to abrogate KARMA. According to the Burmese chronicle *Hmannān mha yazạwintawkyī* (*Glass Palace Chronicle*, begun in 1829), Theravāda Buddhism was decisively established in Burma following the conversion of King Anawrahtā (also referred to as Aniruddha, 1040–1077) by SHIN ARAHAN, a Mon Theravāda monk from Thaton. Subsequently the king requested Pāli texts, relics, and monks from King Manuha (Manohari) of Thaton. The latter's refusal provided the pretext for an invasion, which resulted in the subjugation of the Mons of lower Burma and the eventual ascendancy of Theravāda under Kyanzittha (fl. ca. 1084–1113). In 1287 Pagān was conquered by the Mongols and deserted. The Theravāda tradition survived, but Burma was not united again until 1752. This independence was short-lived, as the British deposed the king in 1886 and annexed Burma to their empire. Burma gained independence in 1948, following which U Nu became prime minister. Buddhist groups, such as the YOUNG MEN'S BUDDHIST ASSOCIATIONS (YMBA), played a significant role in the independence movement, and U Nu continued the trend of mingling Buddhism and politics with what he termed a policy of "Buddhist socialism." In this system, the state would provide for the peoples' material needs, and the SAṂGHA would minister to their spiritual needs. In 1950 he formed the Buddhist Sasana Council to supervise the monks and appointed a minister of religious affairs. In 1960 he initiated a move to make Buddhism the state religion, but this prompted General Ne Win to stage a coup in 1962, which began a period of military dictatorship. The *saṃgha* remains a major force in Burma today, and it is often at odds with the generals of the ruling junta (SLORC). The generals have worked to undermine the popularity of Buddhism, but its broad support among the people has prevented them from having great success in this endeavor. (*See also*: COUNCIL OF RANGOON; MINDON.

busshō

See BUDDHATĀ

butsudan

A shrine or altar found in most Japanese Buddhist monasteries and temples, and in many homes. In Nichiren Buddhist traditions, each member is expected to have a *butsudan*, which serves as the focus of ritual devotions.

C

caitya (Pāli *cetiya*; Tib. *mchod rten*; "sanctuary")

Reliquary monuments that are built to house the remains of a buddha or some other revered personage.

cakra (Pāli *cakka*; Tib. *rtsa 'khor*; "wheel")

The *cakra* is an important symbolic motif in Buddhism, and is used in a number of different contexts. It often represents the doctrine (DHARMA), in which case it is represented as having eight spokes, symbolizing the parts of the "eightfold noble path" (ĀRYĀṢṬĀṄGA-MĀRGA). In other contexts it has twelve spokes, representing the twelve links (*nidāna*) of the cycle of dependent arising (PRATĪTYA-SAMUTPĀDA). In tantric Buddhism, the *cakras* are energy centers, generally seven in number, connected by channels (*nāḍī*). Subtle energies called "winds" (*prāṇa*) and "drops" (BINDU) travel through these channels, and it is believed that through meditation one can control their movements and cause them to remain in the *cakra*s, which leads to the actualization of blissful states of consciousness. The seven *cakra*s are: (1) *mūlādhāra-cakra*, located near the perineum; (2) *svādhiṣṭhāna-cakra*, located at or below the navel; (3) *maṇipūra-cakra*, located near the navel; (4) *anāhata-cakra*, located near the heart; (5) *viśuddha-cakra*, located near the bottom of the throat; (6) *ājñā-cakra*, located between the eyebrows; and (7) *sahasrāra-cakra*, located above the crown of the head.

Cakrasaṃvara (Tib. *'Khor lo sdom pa*; "Wheel Vow")

Tantric buddha who is the central figure of the *Cakrasaṃvara-tantra*. This is classed as a highest yoga tantra (ANUTTARA-YOGA-TANTRA) and is practiced in all orders of Tibetan Buddhism. He is particularly associated with mental purification, and so initiation into practices relating to him is often given to beginning students. Cakrasaṃvara practice is said to be effective in transforming negative situations into opportunities for spiritual progress. Iconographically, he is commonly depicted with blue skin, four heads and eight arms, with a tigerskin draped over his loins, and embracing his consort, Vajravārāhī.

cakra-vartin (Pāli *cakka-vatti*; Tib. *'khor los sgyur ba'i rgyal po*; "wheelturner")

A king whose rule is unbounded, and so the wheels of his chariots can turn anywhere without obstruction. This is also often used as an epithet of the Buddha, whose teaching is said to cover the entire earth.

Cambodian Buddhism

Like its neighbors in Southeast Asia, Cambodia was heavily influenced by Indian culture from an early date. It is located in the Mekong Valley on a trade route between India and China, so a variety of influences passed through the region, and there is evidence that by the fifth century MAHĀYĀNA Buddhism, as well as Brahmanism, had become established in the area. Buddhism appears to have been introduced to the region some time before the sixth century, because in 503 King Jayavarman of Fu-nan sent representatives to China with gifts that included a buddha image, and an inscription by his son Rudravarman mentions the Buddha. The dominant people of Cambodia are the Khmers, who constitute seventy percent of the population. The Khmers developed a great civilization centered in the area of Angkor, and in the following centuries a royal cult developed, which treated the Khmer rulers as "divine kings" (*deva-rāja*) or "buddha-kings" (*buddha-rāja*) identified either with Hindu gods or with buddhas and bodhisattvas, depending on the religious orientation of a particular regime. Thus in the Bayon Temple, constructed by Jayavarman VII (1181–1218), the king is identified with Lokeśvara. In later tradition, he was considered to be an incarnate buddha. The Khmer kings built extensive monuments to themselves, the most famous being ANGKOR WAT, but the enormous cost of financing such huge projects appears to have weakened the monarchy. Several of the kings of Angkor proclaimed themselves to be Mahāyāna Buddhists, but after the abandoning of Angkor in 1431 THERAVĀDA eventually became the dominant form of Buddhism in the area. Theravāda was introduced to the region in the 12th century by a Burmese monk. The first documented Theravāda inscription has been dated to around 1230, during the reign of king Indravarman II, and it appears that the tradition spread rapidly among the masses. King Jayavarman Parameśvara, who ascended the throne in 1327, was a supporter of Theravāda, who replaced Sanskrit with Pāli as the language of religious texts and rituals. Cambodia (along with Vietnam and Laos) was under French colonial rule from 1893 until 1975. In 1975 the colonial period ended when the genocidal Khmer Rouge seized control and began the "killing fields" period, during which most monks and nuns were killed or forced to return to lay life, monasteries were destroyed, and Buddhism mostly disappeared from the country. It was only after the Vietnamese invasion in 1979 that the situation eased somewhat, and in recent decades Buddhism has gradually been making a comeback in Cambodia.

Candrakīrti (Tib. *Zla ba grags pa*, ca. seventh century; "Famous Moon")

Influential MADHYAMAKA philosopher and polemicist, considered by Tibetan doxographers to be the most important commentator of the PRĀSAṄGIKA-MADHYAMAKA tradition. He saw himself as defending the commentarial tradition of BUDDHAPĀLITA against its rivals, most importantly the tradition of BHAVYA and the YOGĀCĀRA tradition, founded by ASAṄGA and VASUBANDHU. His commentary on NĀGĀRJUNA's *Fundamental Verses on the Middle Way* (MŪLAMADHYAMAKA-KĀRIKĀ), entitled *Clear Words* (*Prasanna-padā*), became the definitive interpretation of Nāgārjuna in Tibet.

caryā-tantra (Tib. *spyod rgyud*; "performance tantra")

One of the four sets of TANTRAS, according to Tibetan exegetes. Texts of this class equally emphasize external ritual activities and internal yogas. In these practices one conceives of oneself as a friend or companion of a buddha, and one visualizes the buddha as possessing the qualities that one strives to actualize through meditative practice. (*See also* ANUTTARA-YOGA-TANTRA; KRIYĀ-TANTRA; YOGA-TANTRA.

catur-mudrā (Tib. *phyag rgya bzhi;* "four seals")

The "four seals of correct views" (*lta ba bka' rtags kyi phyag rgya bzhi*), according to Tibetan doxographers, are the central propositions of Buddhism which serve as a way of distinguishing whether or not a particular tenet system is Buddhist or non-Buddhist. At minimum, a Buddhist tenet system must accept that: (1) all conditioned phenomena are impermanent (*'du byas thams cad mi rtag pa*); (2) all afflicted phenomena are prone to suffering (*zag bcas thams cad sdug bsngal ba*); (3) all phenomena are empty and devoid of self (*chos thams cad stong zhing bdag med pa*); and (4) NIRVĀṆA is peace (*mya ngan las 'das pa zhi ba*).

catur-nimitta (Tib. *mtshan ma bzhi*; "four sights")

According to legends about ŚĀKYAMUNI BUDDHA's life, shortly after his birth a fortune-teller predicted that he would become a great king unless he encountered the "four sights": (1) a sick person; (2) an old person; (3) a corpse; and (4) a world renouncer. The first three symbolize the harsh realities of cyclic existence, in which beings become sick, grow old, and die, and the fourth indicates the way to escape this, by renouncing the world and seeking liberation. According to traditional accounts, his father ŚUDDHODANA tried to prevent him from encountering these sights, but was unsuccessful. The young prince went out into the town of KAPILAVASTU on four occasions, and during each of these he was confronted by one of the four sights. He subsequently resolved to leave his father's palace and become a world renouncer.

Central Asian Buddhism

Central Asia was a crucial part of the overland Silk Roads, through which goods and ideas passed between India and China for centuries. It encompasses a wide variety of peoples and cultures, speaking a diverse collection of languages. It is not clear when Buddhism first entered the area, but the earliest reported missionary activity was initiated by AŚOKA (r. 272–236 B.C.E.), who sent Buddhist monks into Bactria during the third century B.C.E. Two Aśokan inscriptions have been found as far north as GANDHĀRA in Afghanistan. The first flowering of Buddhism in Central Asia was during the reign of KANIṢKA I (ca. first–second century C.E.), who is reported in traditional Buddhist histories as a supporter of Buddhism, though there is little actual evidence for this. It is more likely that he promoted religious tolerance and that Buddhism flourished as a result. Another important Buddhist center was Khotan, whose king is said to have converted Kashgar to Buddhism around 100 C.E. Buddhism was established in Kuchā sometime during the first century B.C.E., and was certainly well established by the time of KUMĀRAJĪVA (344–413), whose father was Indian and whose mother was Kuchean. During the early part of the first millennium C.E. Buddhism flourished in a number of Central Asian centers. Several of the most important of these were in East Turkestan, including Khotan, Turfan, TUN-HUANG, and Kocho. Some of the most influential early Buddhist missionaries to China were from Central Asia, including AN SHIH-KAO, a Kushan monk who traveled to Lo-yang in 148 and established the first center for the translation of Buddhist texts in China. Most of the early translations of Buddhist texts into Chinese were reportedly done by monks from western Central Asia, and by the fourth century Buddhism had spread among the Turkic tribes of eastern Central Asia. The Chinese pilgrim HSÜAN-TSANG (596–664) reported that there were a number of flourishing Buddhist centers in the region during the seventh century, but a wave of Arab invasions apparently led to the demise of Buddhism in Central Asia. Following the Arab defeat of the last Sassanian ruler in 642, a series of invaders entered the area, and Islam displaced Buddhism and the other religions that had flourished there. The eradication of Buddhist civilization was so complete that it was not until the nineteenth century that European explorers conducting archeological work in the region began piecing together the story of Buddhism's influence in Central Asia.

Chah, Ajahn (1918–1992)

hai meditation teacher who belonged to the forest monk tradition. Born in a rural village in northeast Thailand, he received *bhikkhu* ordination at the age of twenty, after which he studied meditation with a number of teachers. For several years he pursued an ascetic lifestyle, sleeping in forests, caves, and cremation grounds. Eventually he settled in a forest hermitage near his birthplace, and a large monastery named Wat Pah Pong grew there as he attracted followers. In 1975 it was designated as a special training center for Westerners and named Wat Pah Nanachat, and since that time a number of influential Western Buddhist teachers have studied there. In 1979 the first of several European branch monasteries was established in Sussex, England by his senior Western disciples (among them Ajahn Sumedho, who became the senior monk at Amaravati Buddhist Monastery in England). Today there are branch monasteries in other European countries, as well as in Australia and New Zealand.

Tibetan monk performing 'cham *dance, Spyi dbang (Phyang) Monastery, Ladakh.*

'cham ("dance")

Ritual dances generally performed by Tibetan Buddhist monks in costumes. The participants in the dance represent Buddhist figures and the opponents of Buddhism, and during the dance the antithetical forces are symbolically subdued. These dances are commonly performed before large crowds of lay Buddhists and have both didactic and entertainment functions.

Ch'an (Jpn. *Zen*; Kor. *Sŏn*; Viet. *Thiền*)

A school that developed in East Asia, which emphasized meditation aimed at a non-conceptual, direct understanding of reality. Its name is believed to derive from the Sanskrit term DHYĀNA (meditation). It traces itself back to the Indian monk BODHIDHARMA, who according to tradition traveled to China in the early sixth century. He is considered to be the first Chinese and twenty-eighth Indian patriarch of the tradition. The school's primary emphasis is on meditation, and some schools make use of enigmatic riddles called *kung-an* (Jpn. KŌAN; Kor. KONG'AN; Viet. *công-án*) which are designed to defeat conceptual thinking and aid in direct realization of truth. (*See also* Sŏn; Zen.)

Ch'ang-ch'ing Hui-leng (Jpn. *Chōkei Eryō*, 854–932)

One of the great masters of the Chinese CH'AN tradition, and dharma-successor of Hsüeh-feng I-ts'un (Jpn. Seppō Gison, 822–908).

Chao-chou Ts'ung-shen (Jpn. *Jōshū Jūshin*, 778–897)

One of the major CH'AN masters of the T'ang dynasty, who was the dharma-successor of NAN-CHÜAN P'U-YÜAN (Jpn. Nansen Fugan, 748–835). According to tradition, he had his first awakening experience at the age of eighteen, but continued to deepen his realization during the rest of his life. After the death of his teacher, he wandered around the country until the age of eighty, finally settling down in a small monastery near the town of Chao-chou. He is an important figure in the tradition, and his teachings and activities are described in a number of places in the WU-MEN-KUAN (*Gateless Barrier*) and the PI-YEN-LU (*Blue Cliff Records*).

chao khun ("noble lord")

A title given to senior Thai monks in recognition of their learning and/or meditative accomplishments. Those who receive the title are also given a new honorific name.

Ch'en, Kenneth K. S.

One of the most influential scholars of Chinese Buddhism. Born in Hawaii in 1907, he received a Ph.D. from Harvard University, and subsequently held a number of teaching positions. For many years he taught at Princeton University, and he was the author of *Buddhism in China: A Historical Survey*, which remains one of the most authoritative works on the subject.

Chen-yen (Jpn. *Shingon*; "True Words")

Chinese tradition of esoteric Buddhism. Chen-yen is the Chinese translation of the Sanskrit term "MANTRA," which refers to the spells used in tantric Buddhism. The tradition was brought to China by ŚUBHĀKARASIṂHA (Chin. Shan-wu-wei) during the eighth century and enjoyed a brief period of relative popularity during the T'ang dynasty, but later died out as a separate tradition in China. It was, however, brought to Japan by KŪKAI (774–835), where it continues today as the SHINGON school.

Chenrezi

See AVALOKITEŚVARA.

chien-hsing

See KENSHŌ.

Chih-i (Jpn. *Chisha*, 538–597)

Influential philosopher of the Chinese T'IEN-T'AI (Jpn. TENDAI; Kor. Chŏnt'ae) school who was the main student of Hui-ssu (515–576) and is considered to be the third patriarch of the tradition. In 576 he began a retreat on T'ien-t'ai Mountain and later established the headquarters of the school there. He was influential in establishing the *Lotus*

Sūtra (Skt. SADDHARMA-PUṆḌARĪKA-SŪTRA) – which he viewed as containing the essence of Buddhist doctrine – as a core text of the tradition. Renowned as a meditation master, he wrote a number of influential works on meditative practice, including the *Great Calming and Insight* (*Mo-ho chih-kuan*; Jpn. *Maka-shikan*), which focused on the practices of stabilizing meditation (Chin. *chih*; Jpn. *shi*, *sammai*; Viet. *tam*; Skt. ŚAMATHA) and analytical meditation (Chin. *kuan*; Jpn. *kan*; Viet. *quán*; Skt. VIPAŚYANĀ). After he died he was given the honorary title "Chih-che" ("Master of Wisdom").

chih-kuan (Jpn. *shi-kan*; Kor. *chigwan*; Viet. *tam-quán*; "calming and insight")

Chinese translation of the Sanskrit terms ŚAMATHA and VIPAŚYANĀ. The former refers to stabilizing meditation designed to develop the ability to maintain focus on one's meditative object, and the latter refers to analytical meditation in which one directly perceives the emptiness (Skt. ŚŪNYATĀ) of the object, and by extension all phenomena. This practice is particularly important in the T'IEN-T'AI (Jpn. TENDAI; Kor. *Chŏnt'ae*) school, which was systematized by CHIH-I, who wrote one of the most influential meditation manuals of Chinese Buddhism, the *Great Calming and Insight* (*Mo-ho chih-kuan*), in which he outlined a path of practice that begins with cultivation of morality and leads to perceiving all phenomena directly (Chin. *fa*; Skt. DHARMA) as being empty of inherent existence.

chih-kuan-ta-tso

See SHIKANTAZA.

Chinese Buddhism

Chinese tradition traces the introduction of Buddhism to a dream in which the Han emperor Ming (r. 58–75 C.E.) saw a "golden man," which one of his counselors informed him was a foreign deity called Buddha. He reportedly sent emissaries to northern India, and they returned three years later, accompanied by Buddhist monks. The king subsequently built PAI-MA-SSU ("White Horse Monastery") in Lo-yang to house them. There is no historical evidence to support this story, and the earliest substantiated account of Buddhist influence in China is a royal edict from 65 C.E. indicating that a prince from the area of modern Kiangsu province performed Buddhist sacrifices and entertained Buddhist monks and laypeople.

During the first century C.E., Chinese influence in Central Asia increased. Many of the oasis kingdoms of the region had Buddhist establishments, and missionaries – mainly Parthians, Kushans, Sogdians, and a few Indians – began to arrive in China during that time. In 148 C.E. AN SHIH-KAO, a Kushan monk, settled in Lo-yang, where he established a translation bureau that was staffed by other Central Asians. Others followed, and by the end of the Han dynasty (25–220 C.E.) a significant number of Indian Buddhist texts had been translated into Chinese. Despite these efforts, it appears that Buddhism at this time was viewed as an exotic foreign religion and had little impact among indigenous Chinese. Another important early translator was the Kuchean monk FO T'U-TENG (232–348), who became influential during the later Chao dynasty, serving as a court advisor. Two of his disciples, TAO-AN (312–385) and HUI-YÜAN (334–416), were involved in the translation of a number of important Buddhist texts and supported a small but growing SAṂGHA that included both monks and nuns.

Beginning in the early fourth century, internal weakness allowed non-Chinese invaders to penetrate the Chinese heartland, and in 311 the capital was sacked, forcing the emperor to flee south of the

Siong Lim Temple, Singapore.

Yangtze River. During this time Buddhism appears to have made inroads among both the educated aristocracy and the masses. The former group was attracted by Buddhism's extensive canon, its meditation literature which taught the possibility of cultivating advanced states of consciousness, and its highly developed philosophical systems. The masses were attracted by Buddhism's pantheon of BUDDHAS and BODHISATTVAS, as well as by texts teaching that laypeople could follow the path and attain better rebirths or even final salvation. Many of the "barbarian" rulers found it convenient to patronize Buddhism, which like them was of foreign origin, and which served to counterbalance the power of Confucianism and Taoism. By the fourth century significant numbers of Chinese had adopted Buddhism, and there were a reported 1,700 temples and 80,000 monks and nuns by 400 C.E. in the northern part of the country. During the reign of Emperor Wu of the Liang dynasty (r. 502–549), Buddhism enjoyed royal patronage, and the emperor reportedly took layman's vows, commented on Buddhist scriptures, and banned Taoism. The most significant event of this time for Buddhism was the arrival in China of the Kuchean monk KUMĀRAJĪVA (344–413), who translated a number of influential texts and introduced the Indian MADHYAMAKA tradition to China.

During the next few centuries, a number of schools arose, including the SAN-LUN, founded by Kumārajīva; the Chu-she, founded by PARAMĀRTHA; the FA-HSIANG, founded by HSÜAN-TSANG; the T'IEN-T'AI, founded by Hui-ssü; and the HUA-YEN, founded by TU-SHUN. In addition to these scholastic traditions, the CH'AN school (whose founding is credited to BODHIDHARMA) and the CH'ING-T'U TSUNG (founded by T'AN-LUAN) were established. Despite periods of anti-Buddhist persecution in 452–466 and 574–578, Buddhism experienced steady growth. It reached its apogee during the Sui and T'ang dynasties (589–906), during which it came to permeate every stratum of Chinese society. It was also lavishly patronized by the aristocracy, which led to laxity and corruption within the *saṃgha*. This precipitated a massive persecution of Buddhism in 845, during which more than 40,000 temples were destroyed and 260,500 monks and nuns were forced to return to lay life.

During the Sung (960–1279), Ming (1368–1644), and Ch'ing (1644–1912) dynasties, Confucianism became the dominant intellectual force in the country. Although there was still a large number of Buddhist monks, nuns, and monasteries, it was generally a period of intellectual stagnation in Buddhist circles. The tradition remained strong among the masses, but its practice was mainly confined to rituals and ceremonies. During this time there was a tendency toward syncretism, which resulted in the amalgamation of most Chinese Buddhist traditions into a generic form of Buddhism, which coincided with the development of the notion of the "three traditions" (*san-chiao*), according to which Buddhism, Taoism, and Confucianism are three complementary systems. During the late nineteenth and early twentieth centuries, there were some notable attempts at revival by Buddhist laymen such as T'AI-HSÜ (1899–1947), but their efforts were effectively ended with the ascension to power of Mao Tse-tung and the Communists in 1949. Declaring Buddhism – and all other religions – to be "feudal superstition," the People's Republic of China destroyed religious sites throughout the country and also killed numerous religious professionals or forced them to return to lay life. The persecution was most severe during the "Cultural Revolution" of the 1960s and early 1970s, and beginning in 1979 it eased somewhat, but religion is still tightly restricted today. Religious organizations are under strict government control, and their activities are often confined to the performance of colorful rituals that bring in tourist dollars. While Chinese Buddhism continues to thrive in Taiwan, Hong Kong, and in scattered Chinese communities throughout the world, Buddhism on the Chinese mainland today is only a hollow shell, with little substance, only allowed to continue in a few places and under the constant supervision of a suspicious government.

Chinese Buddhist Association

Organization founded in 1953 by the government of the People's Republic of China, which was conceived as an umbrella organization for all monastic and lay Buddhists. It is dedicated to ensuring that Buddhists are loyal to the Communist Party and that their religious practice contributes to patriotism. Its theoretizers reinterpret Buddhist doctrines in accordance with Marxism–Leninism, and so the Buddha is said to have been a revolutionary engaged in a struggle with heretics and the ruling class of India. Traditional Buddhists are mistaken in their belief that compassion and love are the central guiding tenets of Buddhism; rather, class struggle and conflict are its core concerns and should be embraced by all "patriotic" Buddhists. The organization publishes a monthly magazine called *Hsien-tai fo-hsüeh* (*Modern Buddhism*), which reflects current government policies regarding Buddhism. The organization claims to represent 500,000 monks and 100,000,000 lay Buddhists, but these figures are probably wildly inflated in light of the effects of the government's anti-religious practices.

Ching-te ch'uan-teng-lu (Jpn. *Keitoku-dentō-roku*; *Records of the Transmission of the Lamp for the Ching-te Era*)

One of the most important early CH'AN works, purporting to be a collection of records of the sayings and actions of early Ch'an masters up to Fa-yen Wen-i (Jpn. Hōgen Bun'eki), written by Tao-hsüan (Jpn. Dōsen) in 1004. It contains records of over six hundred Ch'an masters, including biographical details and teachings, and it reports a number of *kung-an* (Jpn. KŌAN) that have been influential in the tradition.

Ch'ing-t'u (Jpn. *Jōdō*; Kor. *Chŏngt'o*; Viet. *Ðạo Trang*; "Pure Land")

The realm of AMITĀBHA BUDDHA, located in the western quadrant. Ch'ing-t'u is the Chinese equivalent of Sanskrit SUKHĀVATĪ, Amitābha's "buddha-realm" (*buddha-kṣetra*), which is described as a place in which there is no suffering, no gender, and in which conditions are optimal for the attainment of buddhahood.

Ch'ing-t'u Tsung (Jpn. *Jōdō Shū*; Viet. *Ðạo Trang*; "Pure Land School")

A Buddhist tradition popular in East Asia, whose adherents strive for rebirth in SUKHĀVATĪ, the "buddha-realm" (*buddha-kṣetra*) of AMITĀBHA BUDDHA. This is regarded by its adherents as an "easy practice," because it does not require the difficult meditations that are considered necessary for the attainment of buddhahood in Indian MAHĀYĀNA Buddhism. Instead, practitioners rely on the "other-power" (Chin. *t'o-li*; Jpn. TARIKI) of Amitābha. This is based on Amitābha's eighteenth vow as reported in the SUKHĀVATĪ-VYŪHA-SŪTRA, in which he promises that those who have faith in him will be reborn in his pure land and attain buddhahood easily. Adherents of this school commonly demonstrate this faith by chanting the *nien-fo* (Jpn. NEMBUTSU; Kor. *Yŏmbul*; Viet. *niệm-phật*), "Namo A-mi-t'o Fo" (Jpn. "Namu Amida Butsu"; Viet. "Nam-mô A-Di-Ðà Phật), "Praise to Amitābha Buddha." The school traces itself back to HUI-YÜAN (344–416), the first Chinese patriarch of the tradition (which claims NĀGĀRJUNA as its first Indian patriarch).

Chinul (1158–1210)

One of the most influential figures in KOREAN BUDDHISM. His teacher was Chonghwi, a SŎN master who belonged to the Hung-chou tradition of CH'AN (Kor. *Sŏn*). According to traditional accounts, he had three major awakening experiences: (1) the first occurred at Ch'ŏngwon-sa in the southwest of the Korean peninsula and was precipitated by his reading of the *Platform Sūtra* of HUI-NENG (LIU-TSU-TA-SHIH FA-PAO-T'AN-CHING); (2) the second occurred at Pomun-sa on Mount Haga in southeastern Korea, as a result of which he decided that Sŏn is fundamentally in agreement with Buddhist scriptures; (3) in 1187, while staying at the remote hermitage of Sangmuju-am on Mount Chiri, he had his final awakening experience after reading a passage by the Chinese Ch'an master Ta-hui P'u-chüeh. He was the first Korean Sŏn master to popularize the practice of *hwadu* (Chin. HUA-T'OU), which involves the use of riddles called KONG'AN (Chin. *kung-an*; Jpn. KŌAN) that are insoluble by logical thought. In his presentation of Sŏn, he developed the idea of "sudden awakening followed by gradual cultivation," which attempted to reconcile the ongoing dispute within the tradition over the question whether awakening is attained suddenly or gradually. This continues to be the dominant paradigm in the Korean Sŏn tradition today. He later settled at Susŏn-sa (formerly named Kilsang-sa) on Mount Songgwan, the name of which was subsequently changed to Mount Chogye, after Ts'ao-ch'i san, the mountain in China on which Hui-neng lived. The modern Korean CHOGYE order, Korea's largest Buddhist sect, traces itself back to Chinul and this monastic community.

After his death he was awarded the posthumous title National Master (Kuksa) Puril Pojo ("Buddha-Sun Shining Everywhere").

Chi-tsang (549–623)

The most influential philosopher of the Chinese San-lun (Jpn. Sanron; Kor. *Sammon*, "Three Treatises") School, so named because it based its teachings on three texts believed to have been written by Indian Buddhist masters of the Madhyamaka tradition, all of which were translated into Chinese by Kumārajīva: (1) Nāgārjuna's *Basic Verses on the Middle Way* (Chin. *Chung-lun*; Skt. Mūlamadhyamaka-kārikā); (2) Āryadeva's *Treatise in 100 Verses* (Chin. *Po-lun*; Skt. *Śata-śāstra*); and (3) the *Twelve Gate Treatise* (Chin. *Shih-erh-men lun*; Skt. *Dvādaśa-dvara-śāstra*, attributed to Nāgārjuna, but only extant in Chinese). This school had a significant impact on Chinese Buddhism, but did not survive for long as a separate tradition after Chi-tsang's death. His best-known work is the *Profound Meaning of the Three Treatises* (*San-lun hsüan-i*). In 625 Chi-tsang's Korean disciple Ekwan established the tradition in Japan, where it became one of the major schools of the Nara period (710–784).

Chogye-chong

The largest Buddhist order in Korea, which controls around ninety percent of Korea's Buddhist temples. It takes its name from Ts'ao-ch'i Mountain in China, where Hui-neng, the sixth Chinese patriarch of Ch'an, is reported to have stayed. Officially a Sŏn order, during the twentieth century Chogye also incorporated temples belonging to other Buddhist sects, with the result that many Chogye temples still adhere to practices other than Sŏn. It traces itself back to Chinul (1158–1210) and the monastic community he founded on Chogye Mountain in the southwest of the Korean peninsula. Despite this claim, however, the connection is considered tenuous by contemporary scholars, and Chogye only seems to have emerged as a distinguishable order in the early twentieth century.

Chogyesa

Headquarters of Chogye-chong, Korea's largest Buddhist order, located in downtown Seoul. It was built in 1910 and became the order's main temple in 1936.

Chōkei Eryō

See Ch'ang-ch'ing Hui-leng.

Chu-she

See Kusha.

chōsan ("morning practice")

Japanese term for the period of sitting meditation practice (zazen) in which Zen monks engage during the early morning.

cintā-maṇi (Pāli *cintā-maṇi*; Tib. *bsam pa'i nor bu*; "wish-fulfilling jewel")

A magical gem that is capable of providing whatever one desires.

circumambulation

See pradakṣiṇa.

citta (Pāli *citta*; Tib. *sems*; "mind")

A term often translated as "mind" or "thought" by Western scholars of Buddhism. It refers to mental processes in general and is commonly said in Indian texts to be synonymous with manas (sentience) and vijñāna (consciousness). In Tibetan Buddhist epistemology, it is said to refer to a "main mind" (*gtso sems*), which is accompanied by "mental factors" (*caitta*).

citta-mātra (Tib. *sems tsam*; Chin. *wei-hsin*; Jpn. *yuishin*; "mind-only")

A term that implies that all of reality is actually a creation of consciousness. It is commonly associated with the YOGĀCĀRA tradition of INDIAN BUDDHISM, although it is only rarely mentioned in Yogācāra works (which generally use the term VIJÑAPTI-MĀTRA, or "cognition-only"). Even though the term is rare in Yogācāra literature, it is used by Tibetan doxographers to designate the tradition, instead of the better-attested term "Yogācāra," or "Practice of Yoga."

cīvara (Pāli *cīvara*; Tib. *chos gos*; "monastic robes")

The robes worn by Buddhist monks. In the early Indian Buddhist order, these were generally colored saffron, as is still the case in contemporary Southeast Asia, but in Tibet monks commonly wear maroon-colored robes. In China and Korea monks wear brown or grey robes, and in Japan monks commonly wear black or grey robes. In the early SAṂGHA, the robes were supposed to be made from cast-off rags sewn together, symbolizing the monk's status as mendicants, but in modern times most robes are made for monks and are often constructed of expensive fabrics.

clear light

See PRABHĀSVARA-CITTA.

compassion

See KARUṆĀ.

completion stage

See SAMPANNA-KRAMA.

consciousness

See VIJÑĀNA.

Conze, Edward (1904–1979)

One of the pioneering European scholars of Buddhism, best known for his ground-breaking work on the "Perfection of Wisdom" (PRAJÑĀ-PĀRAMITĀ) literature.

Council of Lhasa

A public debate reported in several Tibetan and Chinese sources, which purportedly involved the Indian scholar-monk KAMALAŚĪLA and the Chinese meditation master HO-SHANG MO-HO-YEN (Tib. HVA SHANG MA HA YA NA). According to BU STON's account in his *History of the Dharma* (*Chos 'byung*), the debate was arranged by KHRI SRONG LDE BRTSAN (Trisong Detsen) and was held in Lhasa in 792. The central dispute, according to all sources, concerned the proper understanding of the path to awakening. Bu ston indicates that Mo-ho-yen taught that awakening is attained suddenly and is not a result of gradual training. It dawns in a sudden flash of insight, after which all mental afflictions are eliminated. Kamalaśīla, who followed the Indian subitist model of the five paths (MĀRGA) and ten levels (BHŪMI), contended that the process of awakening gradually removes mental afflictions. Because these are deeply rooted and are the result of countless lifetimes of familiarization with negative thoughts and deeds, they cannot be removed all at once. Bu ston reports that the Indian side led by Kamalaśīla won the debate and was declared to be the orthodox Buddhist system, while the Chinese side was defeated and forbidden to propagate its teachings. Mo-ho-yen was reportedly so upset by the result that after his return to China he sent assassins to Tibet, who killed Kamalaśīla by squeezing his kidneys. A Chinese account of the debate, written by a disciple of Mo-ho-yen, reports that he won the debate, but subsequent Tibetan records are unanimous in declaring

Kamalaśīla the victor. Some contemporary Western scholars have raised questions about the historicity of the debate and its details, but it is clear that from that time onward CHINESE BUDDHISM was widely considered in Tibet to be heterodox, and the tradition taught by Kamalaśīla was viewed as authoritative.

Council of Rangoon

Canonical council that was convened from 1954 to 1956 to commemorate the 2,500th year after ŚĀKYAMUNI BUDDHA's death. It was attended by 2,500 monks, who edited and recited the texts of the PĀLI CANON for two years, finishing on the day of the Buddha's death according to Burmese tradition. It was held inside an artificial cave named Mahāpāsāṇaguhā near the World Peace Pagoda in Rangoon. It included monks from all THERAVĀDA countries and is commonly referred to as the "sixth Theravāda council."

Critical Buddhism

See HIHAN BUKKYŌ.

cyclic existence

See SAMSĀRA.

D

Daibutsu ("Great Buddha")

There are several Buddha statues in Japan that are referred to as "Daibutsu," the two most famous being: (1) a huge statue of Birushana (Skt. VAIROCANA) housed in the Tōdaiji Temple in Nara – commissioned by emperor Shōmu (724–748), it was consecrated in 751; and (2) an image of Amida (Skt. AMITĀBHA), which was financed by donations gathered by Jōkō and constructed in 1252. It was originally housed in Kōtokuin Temple, but the building was destroyed by a tidal wave in 1495. The image was left intact, but an earthquake in 1923 damaged its base. Extensive repair work was conducted on it in 1960–1961.

dai-funshi ("great resolve")

This is regarded as one of the "three pillars" of the practice of ZAZEN, according to the Japanese RINZAI tradition. It is defined as an unwavering resolve to overcome the "great doubt" (DAI-GIDAN). The other two pillars are *dai-gidan* and DAI-SHINKON (great basis of faith).

dai-gidan ("great doubt")

A term that is particularly important in the RINZAI order of Japanese ZEN, closely associated with HAKUIN ZENJI (Ekaku) (1686–1769). It is one of the "three pillars" of the practice of ZAZEN, along with DAI-FUNSHI and DAI-SHINKON. Hakuin experienced paralyzing uncertainty and confusion early in his meditative training, but eventually overcame them in an intense moment of awakening (SATORI). In Hakuin's words: "It was as though I was frozen solid in the midst of an ice sheet extending tens of thousands of miles. To all intents and purposes I was out of my mind and the MU KŌAN alone remained." After several days like this, he heard the sound of a temple bell and the ice shattered. All his former doubts vanished. Subsequently he decided that such perplexity is an essential ingredient of the awakening process and that the level of realization is comparable to the intensity of the doubt.

Daijō-kishinron

See TA-SHENG-CH'I-HSIN-LUN.

daimoku ("great title")

The chant recited by members of the Japanese SŌKA GAKKAI sect, "Nam Myōhō Renge-kyō" ("Praise to the *Lotus Sūtra*"). This practice is traced back to NICHIREN (1222–1282), who taught that the *Lotus Sūtra* (Skt. SADDHARMA-PUṆḌARĪKA-SŪTRA) is the only Buddhist scripture that is appropriate to the present degenerate age (Jpn. MAPPŌ). He also felt that its teachings are too profound for most of the beings of this age to comprehend, and so they should content themselves with venerating the text, which he believed has the power magically to confer benefits on those who have faith in it and who chant its title. Members of the Sōka Gakkai believe that their chanting brings immediate and pragmatic benefits and leads to buddhahood in one's present lifetime.

Dainichi Nyorai

See VAIROCANA.

dai-shi ("great death")

The experience of elimination of false notions of "self" that results when one has broken free of the "great doubt" (DAI-GIDAN). This is considered by the Japanese RINZAI tradition of ZEN to be an important component in the practice of ZAZEN, which leads to the "great rebirth" (*dai-gotettei*) of SATORI or awakening.

dai-shinkon ("great basis of faith")

One of the "three pillars" of ZEN, according to the RINZAI tradition, along with DAI-GIDAN ("great doubt") and DAI-FUNSHI ("great resolve"). It is defined as an unwavering conviction in the efficacy of the path, despite the difficulties involved in following it.

Daitoku-ji ("Great Virtue Monastery")

Important ZEN monastery in Kyōto, built in 1319 by Akamatsu Norimura for the master Myōchō, who was also known as Daitō Kokushi (1283–1337). It grew to become one of the major Zen centers in Japan.

ḍākinī (Tib. *mkha' 'gro ma*; "sky-goer")

Female BUDDHAS who are particularly important in Indian and Tibetan VAJRAYĀNA traditions. They are said to frequent cremation grounds, cemeteries, and other fearsome places, and are the keepers of the secret lore of TANTRA, which they pass on to adepts.

Dalai Lama (Tib. *Tā la'i bLa ma*)

The most prominent reincarnate lama (SPRUL SKU) of TIBETAN BUDDHISM, regarded by Tibetan Buddhists as a physical manifestation of AVALOKITEŚVARA (Tib. *sPyan ras gzigs dbang phyug*). The title was first bestowed on the third Dalai Lama, BSOD NAMS RGYA MTSHO (Sönam Gyatso, 1543–1588), by ALTAN KHAN in 1578. It derives from the Mongolian "ta le," or "ocean," and is thought to imply that these men are "oceans of wisdom." It was retroactively applied to bSod nams rgya mtsho's two previous incarnations, DGE 'DUN GRUB (Gendün Drup) and dGe 'dun rgya mtsho (Gendün Gyatso). The fifth Dalai Lama, NGAG DBANG BLO BZANG RGYA MTSHO (Ngawang Losang Gyatso, 1617–1682), became the ruler of the whole of Tibet with the backing of descendants of Altan Khan, and prior to the Chinese invasion and annexation of Tibet in the 1950s the Dalai Lama

Tenzin Gyatso, the fourteenth Dalai Lama.

was the spiritual and temporal leader of Tibet. The Dalai Lama is most often referred to by Tibetans as "rGyal ba rin po che" (Gyelwa Rinpoche, "Precious Lord") or "Kun 'dun" (Kündün, "The Presence").

dāna (Pāli *dāna*; Tib. *sbyin pa*; "generosity," "alms")

In general this refers to an attitude of generosity, and in MAHĀYĀNA it is the first of the six "perfections" (PĀRAMITĀ) that a BODHISATTVA cultivates during the path to buddhahood. It involves developing an attitude of willingness to give away whatever one has in order to benefit sentient beings. It is cultivated on the first bodhisattva level (BHŪMI). In THERAVĀDA Buddhism, it is one of the ten "contemplations" (*anussati*) and the most important of the meritorious activities (PUṆYA). It is seen as a key component in the meditative path, as it serves to overcome selfishness and provides benefits in both the present and future lives. In contemporary Theravāda societies, the practice of giving alms to monks by laypeople is also called *dāna*, and it is one of the most common religious activities for non-monastics in Southeast Asia. Because gifts given to the SAṂGHA are believed to bring greater benefits than giving to other people, monks and nuns are sometimes referred to in Buddhist texts as "fields of merit" (Skt. *puṇya-kṣetra*; Pāli *puñña-kkhetta*).

Đạo Trang

See CH'ING-T'U.

Dar thang sprul sku

See TARTHANG TULKU.

Darma Daesa

See BODHIDHARMA.

darśaṇa-mārga (Tib. *mthong ba'i lam*; "path of seeing")

Third of the Buddhist paths (MĀRGA), attained when one has directly realized emptiness (ŚŪNYATĀ). This also coincides with the first bodhisattva level (BHŪMI). On this path meditators remove the artificial conceptions of inherent existence, that is to say, those that are acquired through study and training in mistaken philosophical systems.

Daruma

See BODHIDHARMA.

dasa silmātā ("ten-precept mothers")

A term that refers to women in Sri Lanka who have adopted ten precepts outlined in the VINAYA for novice nuns. There are two main divisions: lay (*gihi*) and monastic (*pāvidi*). The precepts are the same for both, but the latter group adopts all ten as a single body, and so transgressing one rule is equivalent to breaking all ten precepts. The *pāvidi* is generally considered to be equivalent to a novice ordination (Pāli *sāmaṇerī*; Skt. *śrāmaṇerī*). Like monks, *dasa silmātās* generally shave their heads and wear saffron robes, but because the bhikkhunī (Skt. BHIKṢUṆĪ) lineage died out in THERAVĀDA countries centuries ago, until recently it has not been possible for women to receive the full ordination.

Daśabhūmika-sūtra (Tib. *Sa bcu'i mdo*; Chin. *Shih-ti-ching*; *Sūtra on the Ten Levels*)

One of the most important MAHĀYĀNA texts outlining the ten levels (BHŪMI) through which a BODHISATTVA progresses on the path to buddhahood. It is a section of the voluminous AVATAṂSAKA-SŪTRA.

dauṣṭhulya-bandhana (Pāli *duṭṭulla-bandhana*; Tib. *gnas ngan len gyi bcing ba*; "bonds of assumptions of bad states")

Obstructions of body (*kāyāvaraṇa*) and of mind (*manas-āvaraṇa*). Some Buddhist exegetes also add a third type, obstructions of speech (*vāg-āvaraṇa*). These are said to be caused by influences of past KARMA, in imitation of past activities, and are the subtle traces that remain after the afflictions (KLEŚA) have been destroyed. An example that is commonly given is of an ARHAT – who has eliminated the afflictions – seeing a monkey and jumping up and down while making noises like a monkey.

dbang

See ABHIṢEKA.

deity yoga

See DEVATĀ-YOGA.

demi-god

See ASURA.

den'e ("handing on the robe")

Japanese expression indicating that a ZEN master (RŌSHI) has recognized a particular student as his dharma-successor (HASSU). The passing on of the master's robe symbolizes that the student has grasped the essence of the teaching and is qualified to teach.

Dengyō Daishi

See SAICHŌ.

Denkō-roku (*Records of Transmission*)

Short title of the ZEN classic *Keizan oshō denkō-roko* (*Keizan's Records of the Transmission of the Lamp*), which recounts the transmission of the KŌAN (Chin. *kung-an*; Kor. KONG'AN; Viet. *công-án*) and solutions of fifty-two patriarchs of the tradition from KĀŚYAPA (a disciple of ŚĀKYAMUNI BUDDHA) to DŌGEN ZENJI (1200–1253, the founder of the Japanese SŌTŌ order). Such texts play a key role in the Ch'an/Zen tradition, which has teachings and practices that are at variance with what is described in Indian Buddhist texts. The tradition claims that its doctrines and practices are the true core teachings of the Buddha, which were passed directly by mind-to-mind transmission (Jpn. ISHIN-DENSHIN; Chin. *i-hsin-ch'üan-hsin*) to Kāśyapa and from him through a succession of masters.

dependent arising

See PRATĪTYA-SAMUTPĀDA.

deva (Pāli *deva*; Tib. *lha*; "god")

Beings that inhabit the highest of the six destinies (GATI) within cyclic existence (SAṂSĀRA). They are born into heavenly realms as a reward for their good actions in past lives, and they enjoy great pleasure and long lifespans. The state of gods is seen as unsatisfactory in Buddhism, however, because inevitably their good KARMA is exhausted, and the gods will be reborn in one of the lower realms and experience suffering.

Devadatta

A cousin of the Buddha who is blamed in several Pāli texts for fomenting schism within the monastic order (SAṂGHA). He is said to have plotted with prince AJĀTAŚATRU of Magadha to kill the Buddha. Three assassination attempts are reported in Pāli texts: (1) on the first occasion the two hired assassins to kill the Buddha, but they were so impressed by him that they became his followers; (2) on the second attempt, Devadatta tried to crush the Buddha with a boulder, but through the Buddha's power it stopped before it reached him;

and (3) Devadatta sent a maddened elephant to trample the Buddha, but the Buddha subdued it. Devadatta is credited with causing the first schism within the order when he convinced 500 newly ordained monks to join him in forming a new order based on stricter monastic discipline. He regularly accused the Buddha and his followers of leading lives of leisure, and so he proposed five rules in addition to those instituted by the Buddha: (1) that monks should spend their entire lives in the forest; (2) that they should not accept invitations to meals and only subsist by begging; (3) that they should only wear robes of castoff rags and not accept robes from laypeople; (4) that they should dwell under trees and not under a roof; and (5) that they should never eat fish or meat. The Buddha replied that these rules could be adopted as optional (except for sleeping under a tree during the rainy season), but they would not be required. Although Devadatta succeeded in creating a schism, his followers were later brought back into the order by ŚĀRIPUTRA and MAUDGALYĀYANA. The chronicles also report that after his death Devadatta faced severe karmic retribution for his schismatic activities.

Devānaṃpiya Tissa (r. 247–207 B.C.E.)

The king of Sri Lanka who converted to Buddhism as a result of the mission of MAHINDA, son of king AŚOKA. He invited Mahinda and his companions to the capital, ANURĀDHAPURA, where they established the first Buddhist monastery on the island, the MAHĀVIHĀRA. After this a cutting of the Bodhi Tree was brought to Sri Lanka and planted in the monastic compound, and orders for monks and nuns were instituted. During his reign Buddhism became established in Sri Lanka, and from this base it later spread throughout Southeast Asia. (*See also* SRI LANKAN BUDDHISM.)

Virūdhaka, deva-rāja of the south at Ŭnahesa Monastery, Korea.

deva-rāja (Pāli *deva-rājā*; Tib. *lha'i rgyal po*; Chin. *t'ien-wang*; Jpn. *shitennō*; "god-king")

Often referred to in English as "Celestial Kings." Figures representing these protective deities are found at the entrances of most East Asian Buddhist temples. These fierce-looking beings are believed to live on Mount MERU, and each is associated with one of the four quadrants (north, south, east, and west). Vaiśravana, the guardian of the north, is generally pictured with green skin and holding a banner symbolizing the doctrine (DHARMA). In his right hand is a pagoda or a mongoose. Virūdhaka, the guardian of the south, has blue skin and holds a sword. Dhṛtarāṣṭra, the guardian of the east, has white skin and plays a lute. Virūpākṣa, the guardian of the west, has red skin and holds a NĀGA and a wish-fulfilling jewel (CINTĀ-MAṆI). They are believed to protect Buddhism against its enemies.

devatā-yoga (Tib. *lha'i rnal 'byor*; "deity yoga")

The tantric practice of visualizing oneself as a buddha. This is one of the core practices of TIBETAN BUDDHISM. It is commonly divided into two stages: (1) UTPATTI-KRAMA (Tib. *bskyed rim*), the "generation stage," in which one mentally generates a vivid image of a buddha (generally referred to as a YI DAM); and (2) SAMPANNA-KRAMA (Tib. *rdzogs rim*), the "completion stage," in which one visualizes the buddha entering one's body and completely merging, so that one's body, speech, and mind are perceived as being indistinguishable from those of the buddha, and one visualizes oneself performing the activities of a buddha. This is considered by Tibetan Buddhism to be a particularly rapid path to buddhahood because one directly trains in the result one aims to achieve (i.e., buddhahood), rather than just cultivating qualities that are concordant with it.

dGa' ldan (Ganden; "Joyous")

One of the three largest monasteries of the DGE LUGS PA (Gelukpa) order of TIBETAN BUDDHISM (the other two being SE RA and 'BRAS SPUNGS). Its name is the Tibetan translation of TUṢITA (the heaven realm in which MAITREYA (1), the future buddha, resides). It was founded in 1410, under the direction of DGE 'DUN GRUB (Gendün Drup, the first DALAI LAMA). Prior to the Chinese invasion of Tibet in the 1950s, it was one of the world's largest monasteries, but it was largely destroyed by the People's Liberation Army. It was rebuilt in south India by monks who escaped the invasion, and the original site near Lhasa has been partially restored, although it now only houses a few hundred monks. It has traditionally been the main administrative center of dGe lugs pa order, and the abbot of the monastery, the "Throne Holder of dGa' ldan" (Ganden Tripa; dGa' ldan khri pa), is the head of the order.

dGe 'dun grub (Gendün Drup, 1391–1474)

One of the main disciples of TSONG KHA PA (Tsong Khapa), and later designated as the first DALAI LAMA.

dge bshes (*geshe*; short for *dge ba'i bshes gnyen*; Skt. *kalyāṇa-mitra*; "virtuous friend")

A title awarded to DGE LUGS PA (Gelukpa) monks who successfully complete a series of oral examinations at the culmination of a program of study that commonly takes fifteen to twenty years to complete. During this time, they master a huge range of scholastic material on monastic discipline, logic, epistemology, cosmology, etc.

dGe lugs pa (Gelukpa; "System of Virtue")

The largest order of TIBETAN BUDDHISM, founded by TSONG KHA PA BLO BZANG GRAGS PA (Tsong Khapa Losang Drakpa, 1357–1419). Its name was probably originally DGA' LDAN pa'i lugs ("Ganden System"), derived from the name of its first major monastery. Tsong kha pa saw himself as reviving the BKA' GDAMS PA (Kadampa) tradition founded by 'BROM STON (Dromdön, 1008–1064) the main Tibetan disciple of ATIŚA. From its inception, it emphasized the centrality of extensive study and strict adherence to the rules of monastic discipline (Tib. *'dul ba*; Skt. VINAYA). In the seventeenth century it became the dominant order in Tibet when the fifth DALAI LAMA, NGAG DBANG BLO BZANG RGYA MTSHO (Ngawang Losang Gyatso, 1617–1682), became the ruler of Tibet. The Dalai Lamas, the most influential incarnational lineage in Tibetan Buddhism, are members of this order, a fact that has further enhanced its prestige. They are not, however, the heads of the order; traditionally, this position has fallen to the "Throne Holder of dGa' ldan Monastery" (Ganden Tripa; dGa' ldan khri pa). The dGe lugs pas are commonly referred to as "Yellow Hats" because of the "scholar hats" (*paṇ zhwa*) they often wear during ceremonies, which are modeled on the hats worn by Indian scholars prior to the demise of Buddhism in India.

dgon pa (*gomba*; Skt. *araṇya*; "monastery")

The most common Tibetan term for a monastery.

Dhammapada (*Verses on the Doctrine*)

A text of the KHUDDAKA-NIKĀYA, the fifth portion of the Sutta-piṭaka (SŪTRA-PIṬAKA) section of the PĀLI CANON. It is a collection of 423 verses arranged in 26 sections, and it is one of the most widely influential texts of INDIAN BUDDHISM. Its main focus is ethical conduct and mental training.

Dhammapāla (ca. fifth century)

Regarded by Pāli tradition as the second most influential Abhidhamma commentator after BUDDHAGHOSA. He was born in a Tamil area of South India, and studied at the MAHĀVIHĀRA in ANURĀDHAPURA. He later returned to South India and entered the Badaratittha-vihāra in Nāggapaṭṭana, where he wrote commentaries on seven books of the PĀLI CANON: *Udāna*, *Itivuttaka*, *Vimānavatthu*, *Petavatthu*, THERAGĀTHA, THERĪGĀTHĀ, and *Cariyāpiṭaka*. He is also credited with authoring commentaries on the *Nettippakaraṇa* and *Paramatthamañjūsā*, as well as expositions of the *Aṭṭhakathā*s of the DĪGHA NIKĀYA, MAJJHIMA NIKĀYA, and SAṂYUTTA-NIKĀYA, which are entitled *Līnaṭṭhappakāsinī*.

Dhammayuttika Nikāya

See MONGKUT.

dharma (Pāli *dhamma*; Tib. *chos*; Chin. *fa*; Jpn. *hō*; "doctrine," "truth")

A term derived from the Sanskrit root dhṛ ("to hold," "to bear"), most commonly used to refer to Buddhist doctrine and practice. It is one of the "three jewels" (TRIRATNA) or "three refuges" (TRIŚARAṆA) on which Buddhists rely for the attainment of liberation (the others being the Buddha and the SAṂGHA). It also has other – and quite distinct – meanings in Buddhist literature, including: (1) the basic building-blocks of reality; (2) a law or rule to be followed; (3) good qualities; and (4) truth.

Dharma Publishing

A company with headquarters in Berkeley, California, founded by TARTHANG TULKU after he settled in the United States in 1968. Originally mainly an outlet for his writings, it later expanded its offerings to include works by Western buddhologists and translations by members of the organization. It was responsible for publishing a monumental collection of works belonging to the RNYING MA PA (Nyingmapa) tradition of TIBETAN BUDDHISM in the 1990s, the largest ever compiled.

dharma-cakra (Pāli *dhamma-cakka*; Tib. *chos kyi 'khor lo*; "wheel of doctrine")

A symbol used to designate the Buddha's teaching. Generally pictured as an eight-spoked wheel (each spoke representing an aspect of the "eightfold noble path"), it is found throughout the Buddhist world on monasteries, temples, and art. In the *Sūtra Explaining the Thought* (SAṂDHINIRMOCANA-SŪTRA), the term refers to three cycles of the Buddha's teaching: (1) the doctrines preached in his first sermon in Sārnāth, which center on the four noble

Dharma-cakra, the "wheel of doctrine".

truths; (2) the doctrines of the PRAJÑĀ-PĀRAMITĀ ("perfection of wisdom") literature, which focus on emptiness (ŚŪNYATĀ); and (3) the doctrines of the *Saṃdhinirmocana*, which delineate his fundamental intention. The schema of the "three wheels" has also been utilized by a number of other Buddhist doxographers to differentiate their traditions from others. In a number of esoteric traditions, the first two wheels are designated in the same way, but the third is said to be VAJRAYĀNA.

Dharma-cakra-pravartana-sūtra (Pāli *Dhamma-cakka-pavattana-sutta*; *Discourse of the Turning of the Wheel of Dharma*)

According to Buddhist tradition, this is the first sermon of ŚĀKYAMUNI BUDDHA, preached in the Deer Park in Sārnāth shortly after his awakening. The central themes of the discourse are the "middle way" (MADHYAMA-PRATIPAD), which avoids the extremes of hedonism and asceticism, and the four noble truths (ĀRYA-SATYA).

Dharmaguptaka (Pāli *Dhammaguttika*; Tib. *Chos srung sde*; "Protectors of the Doctrine")

One of the schools of early INDIAN BUDDHISM, which split from the Mahīśāsakas; it is thought by some scholars to be a forerunner of the THERAVĀDA school. Its texts on monastic discipline (VINAYA), translated into Chinese by Buddhayaśas in 105 B.C.E., were widely influential in East Asia.

Statue, at the Deer Park, Sārnāth, of the Buddha delivering his first sermon.

dharma-kāya (Pāli *dhamma-kāya*; Tib. *chos kyi sku*; "truth body")

According to MAHĀYĀNA theory, a BUDDHA has three bodies: (1) emanation bodies (NIRMĀṆA-KĀYA), which are physical manifestations that teach ordinary beings; (2) the enjoyment body (SAṂBHOGA-KĀYA), which resides in heaven realms and is generally considered to be accessible only to advanced practitioners; and (3) the "truth body," which is said to be identical with ultimate reality. After completing the path to awakening, buddhas embody the truth, and this aspect of their awakened personality is doctrinally represented in this concept.

Dharmakīrti (Tib. *Chos kyi grags pa*, ca. 530–600; "Famous Dharma")

One of the great philosophers of MAHĀYĀNA Buddhism and the most influential figure in the Epistemological (PRAMĀṆA) tradition. His best-known work is his *Commentary on [Dignāga's] Compendium of Valid Cognition* (*Pramāṇa-vārttika*). His main concern was the workings of the mind and its relation to the external world. The focus of his system of thought is direct experience and reasoning based on such experience.

dharma-pāla (Tib. *chos skyong*; "protector of the doctrine")

Powerful beings that are particularly important in VAJRAYĀNA Buddhism, in which they are said to serve as protectors of the DHARMA and of its practitioners. They are generally portrayed iconographically as having fearsome demeanors and wearing necklaces of skulls and other terrifying ornaments. An example is MAHĀKĀLA, a wrathful manifestation of AVALOKITEŚVARA. In Tibetan Buddhism, there are two classes of *dharma-pāla*: (1) mundane protectors, who were originally malevolent spirits that were subdued by tantric masters; and (2) supramundane protectors, who are wrathful manifestations of buddhas.

Dharmapāla (530–561; "Protector of the Doctrine")

A student of DIGNĀGA and a teacher of DHARMAKĪRTI, who succeeded Dignāga as abbot of NĀLANDĀ MONASTIC UNIVERSITY. He was one of the most influential expounders of the YOGĀCĀRA tradition, and his *Demonstration of Cognition-Only* (*Vijñaptimātratā-siddhi*, translated into Chinese by HSÜAN-TSANG) had a significant impact in East Asia, where it became the philosophical basis of the FA-HSIANG (Jpn. Hossō; Kor. Pŏpsang) tradition.

Dharmapāla, Anagārika (David Hevāvitārana, 1864–1933)

Sri Lankan Buddhist activist, who founded the MAHĀBODHI SOCIETY. The stated aims of the society were restoration of the Mahābodhi Temple in BODHGAYĀ and wresting it from Hindu control. He adopted the name "anagārika" ("homeless"), a traditional epithet of THERAVĀDA monks, although he was not ordained. He conceived of the *anagārika* as having a position midway between the lifestyles of the laity and the monastic community, but his new paradigm attracted few adherents in Theravāda countries.

dhātu (Pāli *dhātu*; Tib. *khams*; "realm," "element," "sphere")

A term that refers to a number of quite distinct notions in Buddhist philosophy. The three most common divisions of *dhātus* are: (1) a sixfold division of the four elements (*mahābhūta*: earth, water, fire, and air), along with space (*ākāśa*) and consciousness (VIJÑĀNA); (2) an eighteenfold division: the six senses, their six objects, and the six consciousnesses that arise from them; and (3) a threefold division: Form Realm (RŪPA-DHĀTU); Formless Realm (ĀRŪPYA-DHĀTU); and Desire Realm (KĀMA-DHĀTU).

dhyāna (Pāli *jhāna*; Tib. *bsam gtan*; Chin. *ch'an*; Jpn. *zen*; Kor. *sŏn*; Viet. *thiền*; "concentration," "meditative absorption")

In Theravāda meditative literature, this refers to four meditative states that lead to elimination of defilements (*āsava*; Skt. *āsrava*) and that also lead to rebirth in corresponding levels of the Form Realm (RŪPA-DHĀTU). In MAHĀYĀNA, it also refers to the fifth of the "perfections" (PĀRAMITĀ) that a BODHISATTVA cultivates on the path to buddhahood. It involves developing the ability to concentrate for extended periods of time on one's meditative object of observation (*ālambana*) without becoming distracted. It is developed on the fifth bodhisattva "level" (BHŪMI).

Diamond Sūtra

See VAJRACCHEDIKĀ-PRAJÑĀ-PĀRAMITĀ-SŪTRA.

Dīgha Nikāya (Skt. *Dīrghāgama*; "Long Discourses")

The first of the five sections of the PĀLI CANON's Sutta-piṭaka (SŪTRA-PIṬAKA, "Basket of Discourses"), which contains thirty-four long discourses attributed to ŚĀKYAMUNI BUDDHA (and sometimes his immediate disciples). It is mostly the same as the Sanskrit Dīrghāgama, now extant only in Chinese (twenty-seven discourses are common to both).

Dignāga (Tib. *Phyogs glang*, ca. 480–540; "Space Snake")

Considered by Tibetan doxographers to be the founder of the Indian Buddhist Epistemological (PRAMĀṆA) tradition. His *Compendium of Valid Cognition* (*Pramāṇa-samuccaya*) is one of the seminal works of the tradition; it formed the basis of the commentary by his follower DHARMAKĪRTI, the *Commentary on [Dignāga's] Compendium of Valid Cognition* (*Pramāṇa-vārttika*). Dignāga focused primarily on issues of epistemology and logic, and this approach marked a new direction in Indian Buddhist philosophy.

Dil mgo mkhyen brtse Rin po che Rab gsal zla ba gzhan dga' (Dingo Khyentse Rinpoche Rabsel Dawa Shenga, also referred to as Gsal-dga', 1910–1991)

Reincarnate lama (SPRUL SKU) of the RNYING MA PA (Nyingmapa) order of TIBETAN BUDDHISM and one of the most influential RDZOGS CHEN (dzogchen) masters of modern times. Considered to be a mind emanation of 'Jam dbyangs mkhyen brtse dbang po (Jamyang Khyentse Wangpo, 1820–1892), he spent over twenty years in meditative retreat and wrote several influential meditation manuals and commentaries. He is also considered to have been an important "treasure discoverer" (GTER STON).

Dīpaṅkara (Pāli *Dīpankara*; "Light Maker")

According to Indian Buddhist tradition, the present age has seen twenty-four BUDDHAS prior to ŚĀKYAMUNI, the first of whom was Dīpaṅkara. He is said to have lived countless eons ago, and during his lifetime the future Śākyamuni – then a merchant named Sumedha – made a vow in his presence to become a buddha. Dīpaṅkara reportedly confirmed that the promise would be fulfilled.

Dīpavaṃsa (*Island Chronicle*)

An anonymous Pāli chronicle, probably written around the fourth century C.E., that purports to recount the history of

Buddhism in Sri Lanka. Its account begins with the life of ŚĀKYAMUNI BUDDHA and ends with the reign of king Mahāsena (334–361 C.E.).

dKon mchog rgyal po (Könchok Gyelpo, 1034–1102)

Founder of Sa skya (Sakya) monastery in 1073. He was a disciple of the translator 'BROG MI (Drokmi), who traveled to India and studied Sanskrit with Śāntipa. Sa skya later became the chief monastery of the SA SKYA PA (Sakyapa) order of TIBETAN BUDDHISM.

Dōgen Zenji (1200–1253)

Japanese ZEN master who traveled to China in 1223 and studied with T'ien-t'ung Ju-ching (1163–1228) of the TS'AO-TUNG (Jpn. SŌTŌ) tradition. He had an awakening experience after hearing Ju-ching admonish a monk for falling asleep with the words, "One must cast off body and mind." The idea of "casting off body and mind" (Jpn. SHINJIN-DATSURAKU) became the cornerstone of the program of meditative training that he taught to his students after returning to Japan. His most influential work is the *Treasury of Knowledge of the True Dharma* (Shōbōgenzō), a monumental text that covers a wide range of topics relating to the life and meditative practice of a Zen monk. The central practice he taught was SHIKANTAZA ("just sitting"), in which one perceives the act of seated meditation as the actualization of one's innate buddha-nature (Chin. *fo-hsing*; Jpn. *busshō*; Skt. BUDDHATĀ).

dokusan (lit. "going alone to a high person")

Japanese term for the practice of direct meetings between a ZEN master and student, during which the student demonstrates his or her level of understanding. It is mainly found in the Japanese RINZAI tradition and generally focuses on the student's current progress in resolving his or her KŌAN. According to Zen tradition, the practice was initiated by ŚĀKYAMUNI BUDDHA.

dorje

See VAJRA.

Dorje Shukden

See RDO RJE SHUGS LDAN.

Dorjiev, Agvan (1854–1938)

Russian Buddhist who traveled to Tibet and studied at sGo mang (Gomang) College of 'BRAS SPUNGS (Drebung) Monastic University. He distinguished himself in the study of philosophy (Tib. *mtshan nyid*) and debate (Tib. *rtsod pa*) and was awarded the DGE BSHES (*geshe*) degree. He was later appointed as a tutor of the thirteenth Dalai Lama and became one of his main political advisors. Because of his Russian connections, the Dalai Lama sent him on a number of diplomatic missions in an attempt to enlist Russian help against Britain and China. After 1898 he settled in Russia and was a leader in a Buddhist revival among Buryats and Kalmyks. He was arrested in the late 1930s and charged with being a "counter-revolutionary," but he died before his sentence could be carried out.

Dōshō (629–700)

Japanese monk who founded the HOSSŌ (Chin. FA-HSIANG) school. He traveled to China and studied with HSÜAN-TSANG (Jpn. Genjō, 596–664). He also studied CH'AN while in China, and when he returned to his homeland he established the first ZEN meditation hall in Japan.

dPal yul (Beyül or Payül)

One of the major monasteries of the RNYING MA PA (Nyingmapa) order of

TIBETAN BUDDHISM, located in Khams and founded in the seventeenth century by Rig 'dzin kun bzang shes rab (Rikdzin Günsang Sherap).

Drebung

See 'BRAS SPUNGS.

drop

See BINDU.

dṛṣṭi (Pāli *diṭṭhi*; Tib. *lta ba*; "view")

A term that generally refers to "wrong views," that is, attitudes and doctrines that are antithetical to the teachings and practices of Buddhism. In INDIAN BUDDHISM, seven false views are commonly enumerated: belief in a truly existent self (*ātman*); rejection of the workings of cause and effect (KARMA); eternalism (belief that there is a soul that exists after death); annihilationism (belief that the soul perishes at death); adherence to false ethics; perceiving negative actions as good; and doubt regarding the central tenets of Buddhism.

Drukpa

See 'BRUG PA.

Dudjom Rinpoche Jikdrel Yeshe Dorje (bDud 'joms Rin po che 'Jigs 'bral ye shes rdo rje, 1904–1987)

Reincarnate lama (SPRUL SKU) of the RNYING MA PA (Nyingmapa) order of TIBETAN BUDDHISM, recognized as the reincarnation of bDud 'joms gling pa (Dudjom Lingpa, 1835–1904). He belonged to the SMIN GROL GLING (Mindroling) lineage, but studied with many different teachers. He was renowned both as a RDZOGS CHEN (dzogchen, "great perfection") master and as a "treasure-discoverer" (GTER STON). Until his death he was the head of the rNying ma pa order.

duḥkha (Pāli *dukkha*; Tib. *sdug bsngal*; Chin. *k'u*; "suffering," "unsatisfactoriness")

The first of the four "noble truths" (ĀRYA-SATYA) of Buddhism, which holds that cyclic existence is characterized by unsatisfactoriness or suffering. This is related to the idea that since the things of the world are transitory, beings are inevitably separated from what they desire and forced to endure what is unpleasant. The main stated goal of Buddhism from its inception is overcoming *duḥkha*. There are three main types of *duḥkha*: (1) the suffering of misery (*duḥkha-duḥkhatā*), which includes physical and mental sufferings; (2) the suffering of change (*vipariṇāma-duḥkhatā*), which includes all contaminated feelings of happiness (these are called "sufferings" because they are subject to change at any time, which leads to unhappiness); and (3) compositional suffering (*saṃskāra-duḥkhatā*), the suffering endemic to cyclic existence, in which sentient beings are prone to dissatisfaction due to being under the influence of contaminated actions and afflictions.

Dus gsum mkhyen pa (Tüsum Khyenpa, 1110–1193)

Founder of the KAR MA BKA' BRGYUD PA (Karma Kagyüpa) order; he was later recognized as the first RGYAL BA KAR MA PA (Gyelwa Karmapa, one of the major reincarnate lamas [SPRUL SKU] of TIBETAN BUDDHISM).

Duṭṭhagāmaṇi Abhaya (r. 101–77 B.C.E.)

King of Sri Lanka, who according to the DĪPAVAṂSA defeated the Coḷa ruler Eḷāra and expelled the Damiḷas (Tamils) from the island. The chronicle describes this as a "holy war," and although it involved great slaughter the *arahant*s of Sri Lanka reportedly absolved him of any wrongdoing because he fought to secure the island for Buddhism. It further reports that because of his military exploits and his generous donations to the SAṂGHA, he was reborn in TUṢITA and that he will remain there until the birth of the future buddha, MAITREYA (1). He will be the foremost of that buddha's disciples. (*See also* SRI LANKAN BUDDHISM.)

dvātriṃśadvara-lakṣaṇa

(Pāli. *dvattiṃsa-lakkhaṇa*; Tib. *sum bcu gsum pa'i mtshan nyid*; "thirty-two major marks")

These are the physical characteristics that distinguish a "superior person" (Skt. *mahāpuruṣa*; Pāli *mahāpurisa*), i.e., either a BUDDHA or a "wheel-turning king" (CAKRA-VARTIN), which are enumerated in the "Discourse on Characteristics" ("Lakkhaṇa-sutta") of the DĪGHA NIKĀYA: (1) level feet; (2) an impression of a thousand-spoked wheel on the soles of the feet; (3) broad heels; (4) long fingers and toes; (5) soft hands and feet; (6) webbed fingers and toes; (7) raised ankles; (8) legs like an antelope's; (9) arms that reach to his knees; (10) a penis that is covered by a sheath; (11) a bright complexion the color of gold; (12) soft, delicate skin on which dust cannot settle; (13) a separate bodily hair for each pore; (14) bluish-black bodily hairs that grow upward and curl to the right; (15) a straight body; (16) well-rounded shoulders and trunk; (17) the front of his body is like a lion's; (18) there is no hollow between his shoulders; (19) his height is the same as the span of his outstretched arms; (20) rounded bust; (21) his saliva improves the taste of food; (22) jaws like those of a lion; (23) forty teeth; (24) even teeth; (25) no gaps between the teeth; (26) bright canine teeth; (27) long tongue; (28) a voice like the god Brahmā; (29) blue eyes; (30) eyelashes like those of a bull; (31) a white tuft of hair between the eyes (*ūrṇā*); and (32) a protuberance on the top of the head called an UṢṆĪṢA.

dzogchen

See RDZOGS CHEN.

E

effort

See VĪRYA.

eightfold noble path

See ĀRYĀṢṬĀṄGA-MĀRGA.

Eihei-ji ("Monastery of Eternal Peace")

Meditation center founded by DŌGEN ZENJI in 1243, located in the Fukui province of Japan. Today it is one of the two main centers of the SŌTŌ school of ZEN (the other being SŌJI-JI).

Eisai Zenji (Myōan Eisai, 1141–1215)

Japanese monk who traveled to China in 1168 and 1187 and who is credited with being the first successfully to bring ZEN to Japan. He traveled to China to study T'IEN-T'AI (Jpn. TENDAI, the order in which he was ordained), but he also studied CH'AN with Hsü-an Huai-ch'ang (Jpn. Kian Eshō) of the Ōryō lineage of the LIN-CHI (Jpn. RINZAI) order of Ch'an. Hsü-an gave Eisai a certification of awakening (Chin. *yin-k'o*; Jpn. INKA-SHŌMEI), and upon his return to Japan Eisai began instructing students in Ch'an practice. In 1191 he founded the Shōfuku-ji Temple in Kyūshu, but soon came into conflict with local Tendai monks, who resented his statements that Zen is superior to Tendai. To placate them, he began introducing esoteric Tendai rites in his monastery and even wrote a treatise praising Tendai, but steadfastly maintained that Rinzai is "the quintessence of all doctrines and the totality of the Buddha's DHARMA."

ekayāna (Tib. *theg pa gcig*; "one vehicle")

An idea found in a number of MAHĀYĀNA texts, such as the *Lotus Sūtra* (SADDHARMA-PUṆḌARĪKA-SŪTRA), which holds that the three approaches to liberation believed in Mahāyāna literature to have been taught by the Buddha – the hearer vehicle (ŚRĀVAKA-*yāna*) the solitary realizer vehicle (PRATYEKA-BUDDHA-yāna), and the BODHISATTVA vehicle (*bodhisattva-yāna*) – all converge into the one "buddha vehicle" (*buddha-yāna*). This is really the same as the bodhisattva vehicle, which culminates in buddhahood. The other two vehicles are said to be merely expedient teachings for those who would initially be afraid of or uninterested in the path of the bodhisattva.

Ellora

Located in Maharashtra near Aurangabad, Ellora is the site of some of the best-preserved Indian Buddhist cave temples. It also contains Hindu and Jain monuments, including the Kailāsanāṭha temple, dedicated to the Hindu god Śiva.

emptiness

See ŚŪNYATĀ.

Engaged Buddhism

A modern Buddhist movement with representatives all over the world, which seeks to adapt Buddhist principles and practices to contemporary social issues. Some of its most important figures are SULAK SIVARAKSA, the fourteenth Dalai Lama, TENZIN GYATSO, and THICH NHAT HANH. The term "Engaged Buddhism" has been applied to a range of people engaged in many different activities, including social work, anti-poverty and development programs, political activism, human rights agitation, etc. The common unifying component is that people who apply the label to their activities perceive themselves as manifesting Buddhist principles in concrete activities aimed at benefiting others.

Engaku-ji ("Complete Awakening Monastery")

One of the major monasteries of the Japanese RINZAI Zen lineage, built in 1282 by the Chinese Ch'an master Wu-hsüeh Tsu-yüan (Jpn. Mugaku Sogen, 1226–1286) with the financial support of the Shōgun Hōjō Tokimune.

enlightenment

See BODHI.

Ennin (Jikaku Daishi, 794–864)

A student of SAICHŌ and one of the major figures in the early period of the TENDAI (Chin. T'IEN-T'AI) school in Japan. He traveled to China following Saichō's death in 838 and returned nine years later with 559 volumes of sūtras and commentaries. He became the third head priest of the order and played a significant role in increasing its popularity.

ensō ("circle")

An important motif in ZEN art, the empty circle – drawn in a single fluid motion – is particularly associated with the "Ox-herding" pictures (Jpn. JŪGYŪ-NO-ZU), in which it represents the full realization of the true nature of reality.

ethics

See ŚĪLA.

Evaṃ mayā śrutam ekasmin samaye (Pāli *Evaṃ me sutam ekaṃ samayam*; "Thus have I heard at one time")

The standard way of introducing Buddhist SŪTRAS. It serves to authenticate the subsequent teachings as coming from ŚĀKYAMUNI BUDDHA's mouth. According to Buddhist tradition, it was originally used at the first Buddhist council at RĀJAGṚHA, at which 500 ARHATS convened to set down the Buddha's words in writing. They prefaced their recitations with the formula "Thus have I heard at one time" in order to certify their personal acquaintance with a particular teaching.

Evans-Wentz, Walter Yeeling (1878–1965)

Pioneering scholar best known for his work on the Tibetan mortuary text *Liberation through Hearing in the Intermediate State* (BAR DO THOS GROL), which he translated as "The Tibetan Book of the Dead." This text was a collaboration with the Tibetan scholar Kazi Dawa-Samdup, who apparently was mainly responsible for the actual translation, as Evans-Wentz indicates in the preface that he did not read Tibetan. This work has been widely influential in introducing TIBETAN BUDDHISM to Western audiences.

evil

From the earliest period, Buddhist thought has argued that immoral actions are the result of ignorance (AVIDYĀ), which prompts beings to engage in actions (KARMA) that will have negative consequences for them. Thus evil for Buddhism is a second-order problem, which is eliminated when ignorance is overcome. The definition of sin and evil is pragmatic: evil actions are those that result in suffering and whose consequences are perceived as painful for beings who experience them.

exalted wisdom

See JÑĀNA.

F

Fa-hsiang (Skt. *Dharma-lakṣaṇa*; Jpn. *Hossō*; Kor. *Pŏpsang*; "Characteristics of Dharmas")

The Chinese school founded by HSÜAN-TSANG (596–664) and his disciple K'UEI-CHI (632–682). It is based on the writings of ASAṄGA and VASUBANDHU, the main early figures in the Indian YOGĀCĀRA tradition. The main text of the school is Hsüan-tsang's *Establishment of Cognition-Only* (Chin. *Ch'eng wei-shih lun*; Skt. *Vijñaptimātratā-siddhi*), which is said to be based on Vasubandhu's *Thirty Verses* (*Triṃśikā*). Hsüan-tsang emphasizes the doctrine of "cognition-only" (Chin. *wei-shih*; Skt. VIJÑAPTI-MĀTRA), which holds that all the phenomena of existence are simply products of mind and that we never experience anything outside our own cognitions. The school also developed an influential classification of DHARMAS, which divided them into 100 types, subdivided into five categories: (1) consciousness (Skt. VIJÑĀNA); (2) mental factors (*cetasika*); (3) form (*rūpa*); (4) dharmas that are independent of consciousness; (5) unconditioned (ASAṂSKṚTA) dharmas.

Fa-hsien (337–422)

The first Chinese Buddhist pilgrim to travel to India (from 399 to 414) and return to China after his studies. This sort of pilgrimage became popular in later centuries and was one of the main ways in which Indian Buddhist texts made their way to China. Fa-hsien brought back a collection of scriptures, most importantly texts on monastic discipline (VINAYA). Upon his return to China, he and BUDDHABHADRA translated the MAHĀPARINIRVĀṆA-SŪTRA and the VINAYA-PIṬAKA of the MAHĀSĀṂGHIKAS into Chinese. He also wrote an account of his travels, the *Fo-kuo-chi*, which is an important source of information concerning INDIAN BUDDHISM in the early fifth century.

faith

See ŚRADDHĀ.

Fa-tsang (643–712)

A Sogdian monk who traveled to China and studied HUA-YEN under Chih-yen (602–668), the second patriarch of the tradition. He later succeeded him and became the third Hua-yen patriarch, and is generally considered to be its most influential systematizer. (*See also* P'AN-CHIAO.)

festivals

Records of the early Buddhist monastic order indicate that festivals were discouraged, although there were numerous regularly held ceremonies, such as the fortnightly recitation of the VINAYA rules

Villagers at Zanskar celebrating the birth of a child.

in the POṢADHA ceremony. As it became a religion with significant numbers of lay followers, however, regular festivals were developed. In contemporary Buddhism, there are numerous yearly and seasonal festivals, which serve a variety of functions, such as marking important occurrences like the new year or the harvest. Others provide opportunities for merit-making, such as the robe-receiving ceremony (KAṬHINA), held annually in THERAVĀDA countries, or the Tibetan SMON LAM CHEN MO (Mönlam Chenmo) festival. Buddhist festivals also serve the important function of promoting group identity, and they punctuate the year with religiously significant events. The most widely celebrated festival is the date commemorating the birth, awakening, and PARINIRVĀṆA of the Buddha. In Theravāda countries, this is celebrated on the full moon day in May. It is called VESAK in Sri Lanka, and Visākhā Pūjā in Thailand. Other important Sri Lankan festivals include Poson, which commemorates the introduction of Buddhism to the island, and Esala Perahera, in which the Buddha's tooth relic is paraded through the streets of Kandy. In Japan the Hana Matsuri festival (April 8) celebrates Buddha's birth, Nehan (February 15) his awakening, and RŌHATSU (December 8) his death. Another important Japanese festival is Setsubon (early February), which centers on driving away evil spirits. Important Chinese festivals include an annual "hungry ghost" (Skt. PRETA) festival, in which offerings are given to placate these unhappy spirits. (*See also* OBON; RŌHATSU SESSHIN; ULLAMBANA.)

First Buddhist Council

See RĀJAGṚHA.

first dissemination

See SNGA DAR.

first sermon

See DHARMA-CAKRA-PRAVARTANA-SŪTRA.

Fo Kuang Shan

The largest Buddhist temple in Taiwan, founded in 1967 by Venerable Master Hsing Yun. This is the headquarters for an extensive organization which has branch temples all over the world, including the Hsi-lai Temple in Los Angeles. The organization emphasizes social service and operates vocational training centers, educational facilities, and healthcare facilities.

Fo T'u-teng (232–348)

A Central Asian monk who settled in Lo-yang, where he became an advisor to the emperor Shih-lo of the Later Chou. He is reported to have been responsible for establishing the order of Chinese nuns.

Form Realm

See RŪPA-DHĀTU

Formless Realm

See ĀRŪPYA-DHĀTU.

Foundation for the Preservation of the Mahayana Tradition (FPMT)

Tibetan Buddhist organization founded by two DGE LUGS PA (Gelukpa) teachers, LAMA TUPDEN YESHE (bLa ma Thub bstan ye shes, 1935–1984) and LAMA TUPDEN ZOPA Rinpoche (bLa ma Thub bstan bZod pa Rin po che, b. 1946) in 1975. It grew quickly and now claims 110 centers around the world. Its headquarters are at Kopan Monastery in Kathmandu, Nepal. According to Lama Yeshe, it was created "for all mother sentient beings. It aims to help the dharma knowledge-wisdom develop in the human consciousness. This is its only reason to exist."

four noble truths

See ĀRYA-SATYA.

four seals

See CATUR-MUDRĀ.

four sights

See CATUR-NIMITTA.

Fourth Buddhist Council

See GANDHĀRA.

Frauwallner, Erich (1898–1974)

A German scholar who is best known for his ground-breaking work on VINAYA and ABHIDHARMA. He was one of the most revered figures in Buddhist Studies, both for his own work and for the many influential students he trained.

Friends of the Western Buddhist Order (FWBO)

Organization founded in 1967 by Ven. SANGHARAKSHITA, a British monk who studied in India for twenty years. It was conceived as a non-sectarian group in which all traditions of Buddhism are equally respected. After founding the order, Sangharakshita began ordaining men and women on his own authority, but this ordination is not seen as being either monastic or lay. Members of the order typically refer to themselves as *dharmachari* (masculine) and *dharmacharini* (feminine), meaning "one who embraces the dharma."

fugyō-ni-gyō ("actionless action")

ZEN notion of acting spontaneously, without premeditation, considered to be an expression of the mind of an awakened master. Only a person who is unattached to the results of actions is able to act in this way, and it is characterized as perfect freedom of action that responds without hesitation to circumstances.

fukasetsu ("unutterable")

The ZEN notion that the experience of awakening cannot be captured in words. This is connected with the general antinomian orientation of Zen, which is suspicious of the reifying and distorting power of words and concepts.

G

Gampopa

See sGAM PO PA.

Gandan Monastery

The most influential monastery in Mongolia, located in Ulan Bator. It is the seat of the Khambo Lama, who is the spiritual head of MONGOLIAN BUDDHISM. The current Khambo Lama is also the president of the Asian Buddhists' Conference for Peace.

Gaṇḍavyūha-sūtra (Tib. *sDong po bskod pa'i mdo*; Chin. *Ju fa-chieh p'in*; "*Flower Array Sūtra*")

A part of the voluminous AVATAṂSAKA-SŪTRA, which purports to be a discourse given by ŚĀKYAMUNI BUDDHA in Śrāvastī that tells the story of Sudhana's quest for buddhahood. His quest begins after he hears a sermon by the bodhisattva MAÑJUŚRĪ, during which he generates the aspiration to attain buddhahood for the sake of other sentient beings (BODHI-CITTA). Following this he travels to various mythical realms and meets fifty-three buddhas. His quest culminates with his attainment of awakening (BODHI) following his meeting with the buddha SAMANTABHADRA.

Ganden Monastery

See DGA' LDAN.

Gandhāra

Area in northwest India where according to Buddhist tradition the "Fourth Buddhist Council" was held some time near the end of the first century C.E. It was sponsored by KANIṢKA I, third king of the Kuṣāṇa dynasty and attended by 499 monks, including AŚVAGHOṢA. The monk Vasumitra was chosen as the council's president. One of its important outcomes was the production of the *Great Book of Alternatives* (MAHĀVIBHĀṢĀ), which expounds the philosophy of the SARVĀSTIVĀDA tradition. Gandhāra is also famous as a center for Buddhist art. Artists in this area produced some of the greatest early Buddhist sculptures, whose style is commonly referred to as "Greco-Buddhist" because it shows signs of influence from the Greeks who had conquered neighboring areas. The Buddha figures produced there are among the earliest known iconic representations of the Buddha (the earliest dating to somewhere around the second century B.C.E.). (*See also* ART.)

gandharva (Pāli *gandhabba*; Tib. *dri za*; lit. "scent eater")

In Indian Buddhist mythology, these are the celestial musicians whose king is named Dhṛtarāṣṭra. They live in the region of the air and the heavenly waters and are especially associated with the

Cāturmahārājika realm. Their special duty is to guard the heavenly *soma* (an intoxicating drink that is important in Vedic rituals), which the gods obtain through their intervention.

garuḍa (Pāli *garuḍā, garuḷā*; Tib. *nam mkha' lding*; lit. "devourer")

Golden winged birds, the vehicles of Viṣṇu, lords of the winged race and natural enemies of NĀGAS.

garu-dhamma (Skt. *guru-dharma*; "weighty rules")

Pāli term for the eight additional rules imposed on Buddhist nuns by ŚĀKYAMUNI BUDDHA when he agreed to allow his stepmother MAHĀPRAJĀPATĪ (Pāli Mahāpajāpatī) and other women to receive monastic ordination. These rules clearly place women in an inferior position within the Buddhist monastic order. The tenth section (*khandhaka*) of the *Cullavagga* lists them as follows: (1) a nun (*bhikkhunī*) of even 100 years standing should rise, greet respectfully, and bow down before a monk (*bhikkhu*), even if he was only ordained that day; (2) a nun should not spend the rainy-season retreat (*vassa*) in a place in which there are no monks; (3) every fortnight a nun should ask the assembly of monks (*bhikkhu-saṅgha*) to set the time for observing the *uposatha* (Skt. POṢADHA) ceremony and to send a monk to lead it; (4) after the rainy-season retreat a nun should conduct a recounting before both the assemblies of monks and nuns regarding what has been seen, heard, or suspected; (5) a nun who has committed a serious offense must undergo a public expiation before both assemblies; (6) after a nun has trained for two years in the six probationary (*sikkhamānā*) rules for nuns, she should request ordination from both assemblies; (7) a nun must never deride or insult a monk; and (8) nuns must never publicly admonish monks, but public admonishment of nuns by monks is not forbidden. These rules show that the Buddha was a product of his times who accepted his society's gender hierarchy.

gati (Pāli *gati*; Tib. *'gro ba*; "destiny")

This Sanskrit term refers to the six (and sometimes five) possible types of birth for sentient beings, according to traditional Buddhist philosophy: (1) gods (DEVA); (2) demi-gods (ASURA); (3) humans (MANUṢYA); (4) animals (TIRYAK); (5) hungry ghosts (PRETA); and (6) hell beings (NĀRAKA). The first three are said to be "fortunate destinies," while the latter three are said to be "unfortunate destinies" because of the amount of suffering that such beings endure.

gcod

See MA GCIG LAB KYI SGRON MA.

Ge sar of gLing (Gesar of Ling)

A mythical Tibetan king whose epic saga is one of the best-known literatures in Tibet. There are different Ge sar legends in different parts of the Tibetan cultural area (referred to collectively as *gLing sgrung*, "Stories of gLing"), but most share the notion that Ge sar was an incarnation of AVALOKITEŚVARA (Tib. sPyan ras gzigs dbang phyugs) who ruled the kingdom of gLing and battled against the enemies of Buddhism, particularly proponents of BON.

gedatsu ("liberation")

Japanese term for the attainment of the liberation of NIRVĀṆA, which is the goal of Buddhist meditative practice. It is often equated with the practice of seated meditation (ZAZEN), which is the actualization of the state of liberation.

Gelukpa

See DGE LUGS PA.

Ladakhis performing a dance from the Ge sar epic at the annual Leh Festival.

generation stage

See UTPATTI-KRAMA.

generosity

See DĀNA.

Genjō-kōan (*Presence of Things as They Are*)

A work by DŌGEN ZENJI (1200–1253), a portion of his monumental SHŌBŌ-GENZŌ, which focuses on the relation between formal meditation practice (ZAZEN) and awakening. The technique advocated by Dōgen involves allowing phenomena to manifest themselves without becoming involved in evaluation or categorization.

Genshin (942–1017)

The first Japanese advocate of the "Pure Land" (Jpn. JŌDŌ SHŪ) tradition, which emphasizes practices designed to lead to rebirth in SUKHĀVATĪ, the paradise of AMITĀBHA BUDDHA, rather than buddhahood. Unlike later figures of the tradition, he taught that mere recitation of Amitābha's name is not sufficient and that this practice must be accompanied by a sincere attitude and concentrated meditation. His most influential work was the *Compendium of the Essentials of Rebirth* (*ōjōyōshū*).

geshe

See DGE BSHES.

giving

See DĀNA.

giving and taking

See GTONG LEN.

gLang dar ma (Lang Darma, r. 838–842)

Last king of the YAR LUNG dynasty of Tibet, who came to power following the assassination of RAL PA CAN (Relbachen, r. 815–836). In traditional Tibetan histories he is said to have orchestrated a persecution of Buddhism, but records of the period suggest that his anti-Buddhist activities may have been mainly confined to such measures as closing monasteries and nunneries, forcing monks and nuns to return to lay life, and cutting off government subsidies for Buddhism, rather than active persecution. His assassination by the Buddhist monk dPal gyi rdo rje (Belgi Dorje) is still regularly re-enacted today in the "Black Hat Dance." Following his death, the Yar lung dynasty came to an end.

gNas chung Chos rje (Nechung Chöje)

The main protector deity of the Tibetan government, who during certain ceremonies possesses the state oracle, who resides at gNas chung Monastery. In Tibet this was located near 'BRAS SPUNGS (Drebung) Monastery, and the Tibetan exile community has rebuilt the monastery in Dharamsala. While in trance the oracle utters prophetic (and generally enigmatic) statements in response to questions. He is consulted about all important affairs of state and often predicts events that will occur in the future. gNas chung is regarded as one of the "five protector kings" (*rgyal po sku lnga*). He is said to be related to Pe har, the main "dharma-protector" (Tib. *chos skyong*) of TIBETAN BUDDHISM, who according to tradition was appointed to this position by PADMASAMBHAVA. gNas chung is also often identified with rDo rje grags ldan (Dorje Drakden), another of the five protector kings.

gods

Although Buddhism denies the existence of a supreme being, there are numerous mentions of gods (DEVA) in Buddhist literature. According to Buddhism, they are merely sentient beings whose good deeds in past lives result in their being born as gods. They have long and pleasant lifespans and great power, but the state of a god is considered to be ultimately unsatisfactory from a Buddhist standpoint, since eventually their past good KARMA will be exhausted and they will return to one of the lower destinies (GATI) of cyclic existence. Various gods appear in Buddhist texts, both in the PĀLI CANON and in MAHĀYĀNA literature. An example is the story of Brahmā Sahāmpati appearing to ŚĀKYAMUNI BUDDHA as he sat under the Bodhi Tree following his awakening. The Buddha had decided that his realization was too profound for ordinary beings to comprehend, and so he resolved to pass into NIRVĀṆA without teaching anyone, but Brahmā Sahāmpati convinced him to embark on a teaching career for the benefit of the few people who could profit from his DHARMA. In Mahāyāna sūtras a multitude of gods appear. As in the Pāli texts, they are subservient to the Buddha and commonly bow down before him,

Tolharubang (Grandfather Stone) statue representing a deified ancestor who has become a village protector, Sŏguipo, Chejudo, Korea.

touching their crowns to his feet while proclaiming his superiority. This was probably at least partly polemical in intent, as the gods who prostrate before the Buddha and beg his teachings are some of the most popular deities of the Hindu pantheon.

Goenka, Satya Narayan (b. 1924)

A lay Indian meditation teacher, born in Burma to a Hindu family, who began studying *vipassanā* (Skt. VIPAŚYANĀ) with the Burmese lay teacher U BA KHIN (who belonged to the tradition of the 18th-century Burmese master Ledi Sayādaw), hoping to find relief for migraines. He spent the next fourteen years studying meditation. Upon his return to India in 1969, he began teaching *vipassanā* courses, and in 1976 he founded the Vipassanā International Academy in Igatpuri, Maharashtra. In 1982 he founded the Vipassanā Meditation Center in Shelburne Falls, MA, U.S.A. Goenka's method is a combination of mindfulness of breathing combined with investigation of the "three signs" (Pāli *ti-lakkhaṇa*): selflessness, impermanence, and suffering.

gohonzon

The scroll inscribed by NICHIREN (1222–1282), which contains his rendering of the Chinese characters of the DAIMOKU: "Nam Myōhō Renge-Kyō" ("Praise to the *Lotus Sūtra*"). This chant is central to the traditions inspired by Nichiren, particularly NICHIREN SHŌSHŪ and SŌKA GAKKAI, both of whose members use copies of the *gohonzon* as a focal point of their daily worship.

go-i (Jpn. *hen-chū-shō*; "five levels of awakening")

A scheme for classifying levels of spiritual attainment in the CH'AN (Jpn. ZEN; Kor. SŎN) tradition, which is said to have been developed by the Chinese TS'AO-TUNG-TSUNG (Jpn. SŌTŌ-SHŪ) master TUNG-SHAN LIANG-CHIEH (Jpn. Tōzan Ryōkai, 807–869): (1) *sho-chu-hen*, "conventional reality within the ultimate"; (2) *hen-chu-sho*, "ultimate reality within the conventional"; (3) *sho-chu-rai*, "the ultimate by itself"; (4) *ken-chu-shi*, "the conventional by itself"; and (5) *ken-chu-to*, "reaching the balance of both."

goke-shichishū ("five houses, seven schools")

A term used in ZEN Buddhism to designate the main divisions of the CH'AN tradition in T'ang dynasty China. The schema was first articulated by Fa-yen Wen-i (Jpn. Hōgen Bun'eki, 885–958). The "five houses" are: (1) LIN-CHI (Jpn. RINZAI), founded by LIN-CHI I-HSÜAN (Jpn. Rinzai Gigen, d. 866); (2) Kuei-yang (Jpn. Igyō), founded by KUEI-SHAN LING-YU (Jpn. Isan Reiyū, 771–853) and YANG-SHAN HUI-CHI (Jpn. Kyōzan Ejaku, 807–883); (3) TS'AO-TUNG-TSUNG (Jpn. SŌTŌ), founded by TUNG-SHAN LIANG-CHIEH (Jpn. Tōzan Ryōkai, 807–869) and Ts'ao-shan Pen-chi (Jpn. Sōzan Honjaku, 840–901); (4) Yün-men (Jpn. Ummon), founded by YÜN-MEN WEN-YEN (Jpn. Ummon Bun'en, 864–949); and (5) Fa-yen (Jpn. Hōgen), founded by Fa-yen Wen-i (Jpn. Hōgen Bun'eki, 885–958). The "seven houses" include these five, plus two branches of Lin-chi: Yang-ch'i (Jpn. *Yōgi*), founded by Yang-ch'i Fang-hui (Jpn. Yōgi Hōe, 992–1049); and Huang-lung (Jpn. ŌRYŌ), founded by Huang-jung Hui-nan (Jpn. Ōryō E'nan, 1001–1069).

Goldstein, Joseph

American *vipassanā* teacher who trained with S. N. GOENKA in India and subsequently helped to found the Insight Meditation Society in Barre, MA,

U.S.A. He has written a number of books, including *The Experience of Insight.*

Gombrich, Richard F.

Eminent scholar of THERAVĀDA Buddhism, Boden Professor of Sanskrit at Oxford University. He has published a number of highly influential books, including *Buddhism Transformed: Religious Change in Sri Lanka* and *Precept and Practice: Traditional Buddhism in the Rural Highlands of Ceylon.*

Gosan-Bungaku ("Five Mountain Literature")

General Japanese term for writings of ZEN masters of the five most important monasteries (Jpn. *gosan*) of Kyōto during the Ashikaga period (1338–1573). The concept is believed to have been first developed by the Chinese master I-shan I-ning (Jpn. Issan Ichinei, 1247–1317), who arrived in Japan in 1299, and his Japanese student Sesson Yūbai (1288–1346).

goseki ("trace of awakening")

A term used in Japanese ZEN for someone who has had an initial awakening experience, whose superior behavior is noticed and admired by others. This is seen as undesirable, and when a person progresses further, the traces are eliminated and the awakened master appears as an ordinary person to the masses.

Govinda, Lama Anagarika (E. L. Hoffmann, 1898–1985)

German Buddhist who received ANAGĀRIKA ordination in Burma in 1929. In 1931 he traveled to Darjeeling, where he became interested in TIBETAN BUDDHISM and received initiation in the 'BRUG PA BKA' BRGYUD PA (Drukpa Kagyüpa) order. His own approach toward Tibetan Buddhism was eclectic, and he saw himself as belonging to the "Non-Sectarian" (RIS MED) tradition. His many writings had a wide influence on Western audiences, particularly *The Foundations of Tibetan Mysticism* and his autobiographical work *Way of the White Clouds.*

Gṛdhrakūṭa (Pāli *Gijjakūṭā*; "Vulture Peak")

A mountain near RĀJAGṚHA in India, on which ŚĀKYAMUNI BUDDHA is said to have delivered a number of sermons, including the *Lotus Sūtra* (SADDHARMA-PUṆḌARĪKA-SŪTRA). It is reported to have received its name after MĀRA took the form of a vulture in an attempt to distract ĀNANDA from his meditation.

great seal

See MAHĀMUDRĀ.

Great Vehicle

See MAHĀYĀNA.

gsar ma (*sarma*, "new schools")

The three most recently formed orders of TIBETAN BUDDHISM, collectively referred to as the "new schools" because they favor the translations of TANTRAS prepared according to the rules of the "new translation" (*gsar skad bcad*) style, in contrast to the "Old Translation School" (RNYING MA PA), which relies on the translations prepared during the "first dissemination" (SNGA DAR) of Buddhism to Tibet. They are: BKA' BRGYUD PA (Kagyüpa), SA SKYA PA (Sakyapa), and DGE LUGS PA (Gelukpa).

gsang ba'i rang rnam (*sangwai rangnam*; "secret autobiography")

A genre of Tibetan Buddhist literature that focuses on events that are particularly religiously important to the writer, such as visions, meditative attainments and experiences, and memories of past lives.

gter ma (*terma*; "hidden treasures")

A general term for relics and texts purportedly hidden by PADMASAMBHAVA and his disciples during the eighth century and later discovered at a time preordained by them. Particularly associated with the RNYING MA PA (Nyingmapa) order of TIBETAN BUDDHISM, these "treasures" are believed to have special "time-lock" spells which ensure that they will only be discovered at the appropriate time and by the appropriate "treasure discoverer" (GTER STON). Although often dismissed as forgeries by some Tibetans, these "treasures," particularly revealed texts, have had an enormous impact on all schools of Tibetan Buddhism. (*See also* 'JIGS MED GLING PA.)

gter ston (*tertön*; "treasure discoverer")

The Tibetan Buddhist yogins and visionaries who "discover" texts and relics purportedly hidden by PADMASAMBHAVA and his disciples during the eighth century. Such people are believed to be preordained as the discoverers of the "treasures" (GTER MA), but in order to be able to fulfill this role they must become adept at the sexual yogas of highest yoga tantra (ANUTTARA-YOGA-TANTRA) and be able to communicate directly with ḌĀKINĪS (female BUDDHAS who are believed to safeguard the "treasures"). The first *gter ston* was Sangs rgyas bla ma (Sangye Lama, 1000–1090), and the tradition has included a number of influential figures, such as 'JIGS MED GLING PA (Jikme Lingpa, 1730–1798) and O rgyan gling pa (Orgyen Lingpa, 1323–1360).

gtong len (*tonglen*; "giving and taking")

Tibetan Buddhist practice that is generally undertaken in order to prepare the mind for attainment of BODHI-CITTA (Tib. *byang chub kyi sems*). It involves imagining that one gives away all of one's possessions – even one's own body and the positive consequences of one's actions – to benefit others. At the same time, one imagines that one is taking on all of their negative emotions, suffering, pain, etc. This practice is said to undermine grasping and selfishness and to develop compassion for others.

gTsang smyon He ru ka (Tsangnyön Heruka, 1452–1507; "Madman of gTsang")

Author of the most popular biography of MI LA RAS PA (*Mi la'i rnam thar*). He was one of the eccentric saints of TIBETAN BUDDHISM called "madmen" (*smyon pa*), lay tantric practitioners who live outside the monastic establishment. gTsang nyon considered the monastic lifestyle to be stultifying and an obstacle to meditative practice, and he spent most of his life wandering and meditating in remote places. He traced his lineage back to Ras chung rdo rje grags pa (Rechung Dorje Drakpa, 1084–1161), Mi la ras pa's lay yogin disciple, rather than SGAM PO PA (Gampopa, 1079–1153), who founded a monastic order within the BKA' BRGYUD PA (Kagyüpa) order. gTsang nyon claimed to adhere to the oral instruction lineage (*snyan rgyud*) of Mi la ras pa. He is regarded by later tradition as a reincarnation of Mi la ras pa, but there is no evidence that he supported this identification.

gtum mo (*dumo*; Skt. *caṇḍālī*; "heat yoga")

First of the "six dharmas of NĀROPA" (NĀ RO CHOS DRUG), which involves developing the ability to increase and channel inner heat, generally involving the visualization of the sun in various places of the meditator's body. The technique requires that the meditator become aware of subtle energies that move through energy channels (Skt. *nāḍī*; Tib. *rtsa*). Through manipulating and directing these energies, the meditator learns to concentrate them in particular places.

Guenther, Herbert V. (b. 1917)

German buddhologist who has published a number of influential studies of Tibetan Buddhism. He received Ph.D.s from Münich University and the University of Vienna, after which he took up an appointment teaching Sanskrit and Buddhist Studies at the Sanskrit University in Sārnāth, India. In 1954 he became head of the department of Far Eastern Studies at University of Saskatchewan, where he spent most of his academic career. He developed a unique translation style that uses terminology from continental philosophy to render Buddhist technical terms. This approach is admired by some scholars and criticized by others. He has published a plethora of books and articles, including *Kindly Bent to Ease us* and *Ecstatic Spontaneity*.

Guhyasamāja-tantra (Skt. *Gsang ba 'dus pa'i rgyud*; *Secret Assembly Tantra*)

One of the most important TANTRAS for TIBETAN BUDDHISM, divided into two sections: (1) a "root tantra" (*mūla-tantra*) of seventeen parts; and (2) a section called "higher tantra" (*uttara-tantra*). It is generally classified as belonging to the "highest yoga tantra" (ANUTTARA-YOGA-TANTRA) class and is particularly important for the DGE LUGS PA (Gelukpa) order, which bases its tantric system on it. The main buddha is Guhyasamāja, who is visualized as being dark blue in color and as having three faces and six arms. He is accompanied by four female bodhisattvas: Māmakī; Locanā, Pāṇḍarā, and TĀRĀ.

guru (Pāli *garu*; Tib. *bla ma*; lit. "heavy")

A Sanskrit term for a religious teacher. The main role of the guru in Buddhism is to instruct students on the doctrines and practices that constitute the Buddhist path to awakening. For this reason, it is desirable that the guru be one who has attained a high level of realization.

Guru Rinpoche

See PADMASAMBHAVA.

guru yoga (Tib. *bla ma'i rnal 'byor*)

One of the central practices of Tibetan Buddhist tantric systems, which involves purifying one's awareness by visualizing one's GURU (Tib. BLA MA) as a buddha. One imagines the guru as embodying all the good qualities of all the buddhas, and one simultaneously cultivates an attitude of perceiving oneself and the guru as being empty of inherent existence. By also visualizing oneself and the guru as being inseparable in nature, one is able to attain buddhahood quickly by becoming familiar with having actualized the attributes of buddhahood.

Gyatso, Geshe Kelsang

See NEW KADAMPA TRADITION.

Gyōgi (668–749)

Japanese monk of the Nara period who belonged to the *hijiri* tradition (monks who generally avoided the mainstream orders and often worked among the peasants), best known for his work among the peasants of the rural countryside. A civil engineer by training, he is credited with building bridges and with a number of irrigation projects. Originally ordained in the scholastic HOSSŌ tradition, he later became a missionary preacher and was one of the first monks to attempt to spread Buddhism beyond the aristocracy. He and other *hijiri* were influential in making JAPANESE BUDDHISM a religion of the masses, whereas the Nara period was mostly dominated by six scholastic traditions that appealed almost exclusively to the aristocratic elite.

gzhan stong (*shendong*; "other-emptiness")

Doctrine particularly associated with certain lineages within the BKA' BRGYUD PA (Kagyüpa) and RNYING MA PA (Nyingmapa) orders of TIBETAN BUDDHISM. It was articulated by the JO NANG PA sect, which postulated a positive, self-existent entity of TATHĀGATA-GARBHA (Tib. *de bzing gshegs pa'i snying po*, "embryo of the TATHĀGATA"), conceived as an inherent buddha-nature that is made manifest by meditative practice. It is not, however, newly developed, but rather is the basic nature of mind. *Tathāgata-garbha* is said to exist truly, and it is characterized as subtle, ineffable, permanent, and beyond the grasp of conceptual thought. It is said to be the luminous essence of mind, which is primordially untainted by afflictions. It is often compared to the sky, which remains the same at all times, although it may be temporarily obscured by clouds. Similarly, the nature of mind is obscured by adventitious (Tib. *glo bur*) afflictions, but these never affect its basic nature. This position was attacked by the DGE LUGS PA (Gelukpa) school, and the fifth Dalai Lama suppressed the Jo nang pas and ordered their books burnt. Despite such opposition, *gzhan stong* continues to be a popular doctrine among many contemporary lineages, particularly those associated with the RIS MED (Rime, "Non-Sectarian") movement. (*See also* RANG STONG.)

H

Haeinsa ("Reflection on a Calm Sea Temple")

One of Korea's major temples, founded in 803 by the monks Sunyong and Yijong. It is located on Kaya-san in Southern Kyongsang province and is best known for the Korean canon on 81,340 carved wood blocks housed in one of its buildings. These were commissioned by King Kojong (r. 1213–1259) and carved on Kanghwado Island. The stated purpose of the project was to generate merit that would protect the nation, but ironically the need for a new canon arose as a result of a Mongol invasion, during which an earlier set of wood blocks was destroyed. Their carving, which took sixteen years to complete, was finished in 1252. Haeinsa is one of Korea's "Three Jewels Temples," and represents the DHARMA (the others are TONGDOSA, representing the Buddha, and SONGGWANGSA, representing the SAṂGHA). It was founded as the seat of the HWAŎM (Chin. HUA-YEN) tradition in Korea, and its name derives from a meditative state called the *haein* (calm sea) *samādhi* that is mentioned in the AVATAṂSAKA-SŪTRA.

haibutsu-kishaku ("eradicate the buddhas and destroy Śākyamuni")

Slogan of an anti-Buddhist campaign sponsored by the Meiji government of Japan, which began with the promulgation of a new constitution in 1889. The anti-Buddhist measures were part of the government's program to establish Shintō as the state religion and to restore the emperor's place as a semi-divine ruler descended from Amaterasu Ōmikami. In Japan there is a great deal of mutual borrowing between Buddhism and Shintō, and it is common for Shintō shrines to house images of buddhas. One goal of the government's program was to "purify" the shrines by eliminating all Buddhist symbols.

Hakuin Zenji (also Hakuin Ekaku, 1689–1769)

One of the great masters of the Japanese RINZAI (Chin. LIN-CHI) tradition, who revitalized the use of KŌAN and emphasized the centrality of ZAZEN practice. According to his autobiographical writings, he was first drawn to Buddhism after hearing a temple priest describe the tortures of the eight hot hells and resolved to become a Buddhist monk in order to escape such fates by attaining buddhahood. He had his first awakening (KENSHŌ) experience at the age of twenty-two after hearing a passage from a Buddhist scripture, but he realized that he still had not attained final peace of mind (ANJIN), and subsequently he worked even more diligently at his practice. During this period, however, his doubt and mental anguish increased.

His great awakening experience occurred at a point at which he felt physically paralyzed by doubt. He wrote: "It was as though I was frozen solid in the midst of an ice sheet extending tens of thousands of miles. To all intents and purposes I was out of my mind and the MU KŌAN alone remained." After several days in this state, he heard the sound of a temple bell, and he felt as though the ice had shattered and he was free. He took his own experiences as being paradigmatic for ZEN practice and later declared that three things are required for awakening: (1) "great basis of faith" (DAI-SHINKON); (2) "great doubt" (DAI-GIDAN); and (3) "great resolve" (DAI-FUNSHI). He later became the abbot of several Zen monasteries, including Ryūtaku-ji. He stressed the importance of physical work as a component of Zen training and was instrumental in establishing the centrality of *kōan* practice in the Rinzai tradition. One of his best-known sayings is a *kōan* he developed himself, "What is the sound of one hand clapping?"

hannya ("intuitive insight")

Japanese translation of the Sanskrit term PRAJÑĀ, meaning "wisdom" or "insight." In INDIAN BUDDHISM it is commonly held that this results from the attainment of meditative concentration (SAMĀDHI), but HUI-NENG taught that the two are identical and that both are inherent in every moment of thought. This notion has subsequently been accepted by most ZEN traditions.

Han-shan (Jpn. *Kanzan*, ca. seventh century; "Cold Mountain")

Chinese Buddhist layman who lived during the T'ang dynasty on Han-shan, a peak in the T'ien-t'ai mountain range. His real name is unknown, but a collection of his poetry (entitled *Poems from Cold Mountain*; Chin. *Han-shan-shih*) survives. He later became a symbol of the enlightened lay CH'AN master, living entirely on his own devices, owing no allegiance to any particular school or tradition.

hara (also kikai-tanden; "belly," "gut")

Japanese term often used in ZEN literature to refer to a person's "spiritual center." It is physically located in the lower abdomen, and students are commonly encouraged to focus their mindfulness of breathing in this area.

Harada Rōshi Daiun Sōgaku (1870–1961)

One of the most prominent ZEN masters of modern Japan, whose teachings became widely influential in the West due to the efforts of his student and dharma-successor (HASSU), Hakuun Ryōko Yasutani.

hassu ("dharma-successor")

Japanese term for the recognized spiritual successor of a ZEN master. Such a person must first receive INKA-SHŌMEI (Chin. *yin-k'o*; Kor. *inga*), official recognition of having attained awakening (KENSHŌ or SATORI). This designation is important in Zen, which sees itself as maintaining a mind-to-mind transmission (Chin. *i-hsin-ch'üan-hsin*; Jpn. ISHIN-DENSHIN) that is independent of doctrines and scriptures. The conferral of succession is a certification that the student has fully grasped the essence of the teaching and is thus empowered to pass it on to others.

Hayagrīva (Tib. *rTa mgrin*; Jpn. *Batō Kannon*; "Horse Neck")

A wrathful meditation deity (Skt. *iṣṭa-devatā*; Tib. YI DAM), generally red in color and with a horse's head. He is an important figure in the tantric system of the RNYING MA PA (Nyingmapa) order of TIBETAN BUDDHISM, in which he is

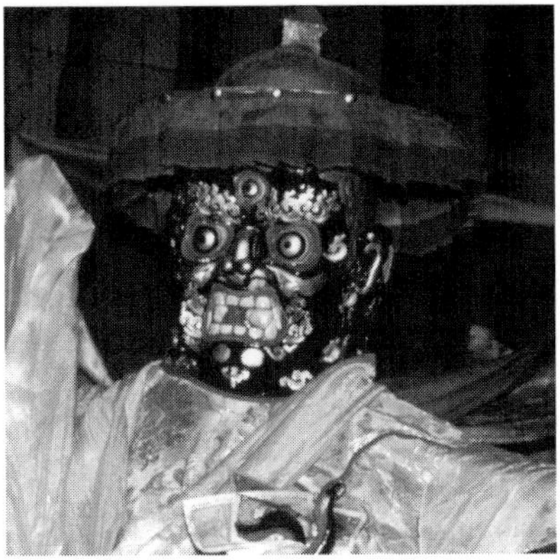

A statue of Hayagrīva in the Potala, Lhasa.

considered to be a wrathful manifestation of AVALOKITEŚVARA. He is a protector of SE RA rje (Seraje) college and is also found alongside Acala as a protector in Tibetan temples. In Japan he is believed to be a protector of horses and other animals.

Hayes, Richard Philip (b. 1945)

American-born scholar of Buddhism, who has published on a wide range of subjects, including the Epistemological tradition and MADHYAMAKA, and who has also become a prominent commentator on the emerging field of Western Buddhism. In 1991 he co-founded (with James Cocks) an electronic forum named Buddha-l, which was originally intended as a venue in which professional buddhologists could discuss matters of common concern and interest. Within a few years, however, it had almost eight hundred subscribers, the vast majority of whom were not academics. Among Hayes' most influential works are *Dignāga on Interpretation* (1988) and *Land of No Buddha* (1999).

Heart Sūtra

See PRAJÑĀ-PĀRAMITĀ-HṚDAYA-SŪTRA.

heaven

Buddhist literature contains a plethora of descriptions of realms in which beings are reborn as a consequence of performing good actions (KARMA), but there is considerable disagreement within Buddhism concerning the number of such realms, their locations, etc. The ABHIDHARMA-KOŚA divides heavens into two types, six belonging to the "Desire Realm" (KĀMA-DHĀTU) and seventeen belonging to the "Form Realm" (RŪPA-DHĀTU). The beings born into these heavens are referred to as "gods" (Skt. DEVA) and are said to live long and blissful lives. Rebirth as a god, however, is seen as undesirable in Buddhism, because gods inevitably exhaust their good karma and are reborn in one of the lower realms of existence, where they again become subject to suffering. Thus the final goal of religious practice should be to transcend the cycle of rebirth altogether. In MAHĀYĀNA Buddhism there was an expansion of the number of heavens, which included a number of new "buddha-lands" (*buddha-kṣetra*), paradises created by BUDDHAS as ideal training grounds. The most famous of these is SUKHĀVATĪ, the realm of AMITĀBHA BUDDHA.

Hekigan-roku

See PI-YEN-LU.

hell (Pāli *niraya*; Skt. *naraka*)

Buddhist cosmology includes numerous realms in which beings experience the results of their negative deeds. Hell-beings (NĀRAKA) are subjected to physical and psychological suffering in direct proportion to the negative actions they performed in past lives. The best-known hells are the eight hot hells and the eight cold hells, each of which is surrounded by sixteen subsidiary hells. Hell beings are subjected to a range of tortures, including being flayed alive, burned,

Mural depicting the tortures of hell, Haedongsa Monastery, North Kyŏngsang, Korea.

frozen, and tortured by demons. The lowest level of hell is called Avīci, whose denizens experience uninterrupted torment.

hell being

See NĀRAKA.

Herrigel, Eugen (1884–1955)

German author who traveled to Japan and studied archery (*kyūdō*). He subsequently wrote a book entitled *Zen and the Art of Archery*. He later returned to Germany and reportedly became an enthusiastic member of the Nazi Party.

Heruka (Tib. *Khrag 'thung dpa' bo*; "Blood Drinker")

A general term in Tibetan tantric Buddhism for a wrathful meditational deity (Skt. *iṣṭa-devatā*; Tib. YI DAM). It is particularly applied to the buddha CAKRASAṂVARA.

Hevajra-tantra (Tib. *Kye rdo rje rgyud*)

An important tantric text that exists in Sanskrit, Tibetan, and Chinese versions. It is classified in Tibet as belonging to the "highest yoga tantra" (ANUTTARA-YOGA-TANTRA) class of tantras. Its main buddha is Hevajra, and it is particularly important in the SA SKYA PA (Sakyapa) order of TIBETAN BUDDHISM, in which it is the basis of its "path and result" (LAM 'BRAS) system of meditative training. The central teaching of the TANTRA is the "inseparability of cyclic existence and *nirvāṇa*" (Skt. *saṃsāra-nirvāṇa-abheda*; Tib. *'khor 'das dbyer med*).

Hieizan

The mountain near Kyōto where SAICHŌ (767–822) built a monastery that became the headquarters of the Japanese TENDAI (Chin. T'IEN-T'AI) school, one of the most influential traditions of medieval JAPANESE BUDDHISM.

highest yoga tantra

See ANUTTARA-YOGA-TANTRA.

Hihan Bukkyō ("Critical Buddhism")

Recent movement in academic Buddhist Studies in Japan, led by Noriaki Hakamaya and Shirō Matsumoto, both of Komazawa University. The movement investigates developments within East Asian Buddhism in light of the core doctrines of Indian Pāli literature and early Mahāyāna texts, and its exponents have concluded that many of the most widespread doctrines of East Asian Buddhist traditions are fundamentally incompatible with the central tenets of INDIAN BUDDHISM. They have generated heated controversy with such provocative statements as "ZEN is not Buddhism" and "TATHĀGATA-GARBHA (Jpn. *nyoraizō*) thought is not Buddhism." They label such substantialist notions as *tathāgata-garbha* and "original awakening" (HONGAKU) as attempts to introduce into Buddhism a doctrine advocating a truly existent self (Skt. *ātma-vāda*), which is explicitly rejected in early Indian sources.

Hīnayāna (Tib. *Theg dman*; Chin. *Hsiao-ch'eng*; Jpn. *Shōjō*; "Lesser Vehicle")

A term coined by Mahāyānists to describe their opponents, whose path they characterized as selfish and inferior to their own. Traditionally the term is said to encompass eighteen schools of INDIAN BUDDHISM (although Indian Buddhist literature mentions many more schools) which were based on the discourses attributed to ŚĀKYAMUNI BUDDHA that were collected in the SŪTRA-PIṬAKA (Pāli *Sutta-piṭaka*). Many of these schools developed their own ABHIDHARMA literatures and VINAYAS, but the extant versions of these collections indicate that they shared a great deal in common, particularly a realistic worldview and an emphasis on a group of core concepts, such as the four truths (ĀRYA-SATYA) dependent arising (PRATĪTYA-SAMUTPĀDA), and the ideal of individual liberation (NIRVĀṆA). The only "Hīnayāna" school that survives today is THERAVĀDA, whose members reject the label "Lesser Vehicle." (*See also* NIKĀYA BUDDHISM.)

Hirakawa, Akira (b. 1915)

Influential Japanese scholar of Buddhism, best known for his encyclopedic studies of Indian Buddhism and Vinaya literature. These include *Bukkyō kenkyū no shomondai* (1987) and *A History of Indian Buddhism: From Śākyamuni to Mahāyāna* (1990).

hishiryō ("without thinking")

A term that is particularly important in the thought of DŌGEN ZENJI, which refers to a state of mind in which one no longer clings to thoughts, but rather allows them to flow freely. It is said to be a pre-reflective and non-conceptual mode of consciousness, in which one is open to the full range of experience, without selecting out certain thoughts and focusing on them.

hoguk pulgyo ("state-protection Buddhism")

A Korean term that first developed during the "Three Kingdoms" period in Korea (late fourth century–668 C.E.). As in Japan, KOREAN BUDDHISM was associated with thaumaturgical and magical practices, and Buddhist monks commonly chanted texts and performed ceremonies for the protection of the country. The rulers in turn sponsored the building of temples and the support of monks, in the belief that the merit derived from such activities would lead to security and prosperity.

Hōnen (1133–1212)

Patriarch of the Japanese "Pure Land" (Jōdō Shū) tradition. He was ordained in the TENDAI school and soon gained a reputation for his erudition, but at the age of forty-three became dissatisfied with Tendai and its scholastic approach. His main concern was that no one seemed to be attaining buddhahood through its methods, and he decided to adopt practices of the Pure Land teachers SHAN-TAO and GENSHIN, which he believed constituted a certain path to liberation. This path involved the practice of chanting the name of AMITĀBHA BUDDHA (Jpn. NEMBUTSU) in order to be reborn in his "Pure Land" of SUKHĀVATĪ, in which conditions are optimal for the attainment of buddhahood. In his *Senchakushū*, he argued that calling on Amitābha is the highest of all religious practices and that recitation of Amitābha's name constitutes an "easy path" particularly appropriate for laypeople in the present age, which he believed to be the last period of the degeneration of Buddhism (Jpn. MAPPŌ). He taught that this practice should not be viewed as an "insurance policy" in case one is unable to attain liberation through the more difficult practice of meditation, but rather should be undertaken wholeheartedly as one's sole path. Because he publicly proclaimed that the Pure Land tradition alone is effective during the time of *mappō*, he ran afoul of other Buddhist orders and was sent into exile at the age of seventy-four. He was allowed to return five years later, but died one year after that. (*See also* CH'ING-T'U; JŌDŌ SHINSHŪ; SHINRAN; SUKHĀVATĪ-VYŪHA-SŪTRA.

hongaku ("original awakening")

Japanese term particularly associated with KŪKAI and the SHINGON school, which implies that all beings possess the "buddha-nature" (*busshō*; Skt. BUDDHATĀ) and so are already awakened. This fact, however, is obscured by ignorance.

honrai-no-memoku ("original face")

An important term in ZEN Buddhism, which refers to one's buddha-nature (*busshō*; Skt. BUDDHATĀ), the fundamental reality that is obscured by attachment to conceptual thought and language. The term is used in one of the best-known KŌANS, "What is your original face before your parents were born?"

Hopkins, P. Jeffrey (b. 1940)

American scholar of Buddhism who has written a number of influential books on the DGE LUGS PA (Gelukpa) order of TIBETAN BUDDHISM. He served as the main English interpreter for the Dalai Lama for over a decade and founded a graduate program in Buddhist Studies at the University of Virginia. His books include *Meditation on Emptiness* (1983) and *Emptiness in the Mind-only School of Buddhism* (1999).

Horner, Isabelle Blew (1896–1981)

British Pāli scholar, who was one of the leading figures of the Pāli Text Society. She served as president of the society and was also vice-president of the Buddhist Society. She published a number of influential translations of Pāli texts, as well as independent scholarly studies, including *Women under Primitive Buddhism* and *Gotama the Buddha*.

hossen ("dharma contest")

Japanese term particularly associated with ZEN, referring to an encounter between two practitioners, the goal of which is to demonstrate directly one's understanding of truth, without recourse to conceptual ideas or terminology. It is not a debate or a competitive exercise, but rather an opportunity for the participants to deepen their respective understandings.

Hossō (Skt. *Dharma-lakṣaṇa*; Chin. *Fa-hsiang*; Kor. *Pŏpsang*; "Characteristics of Dharmas")

The Japanese order derived from the Chinese FA-HSIANG school, which in turn traces itself back to the Indian YOGĀCĀRA tradition. It was first brought to Japan by DŌSHŌ (629–700), who traveled to China in 653 and studied with HSÜAN-TSANG. It became one of the six main Buddhist schools of the Nara period (710–784; the others were KUSHA, SANRON, JŌJITSU, RITSU, and KEGON).

Hsüan-hua

Buddhist monk from Hong Kong referred to as "Tripitaka Master Hsüan Hua" by his disciples. He founded the Sino-American Buddhist Association in San Francisco in 1968. Since 1971 the association's headquarters has been the Golden Mountain Dhyana Monastery. He has attracted a number of Western followers, and his center emphasizes monastic discipline and study of traditional Chinese Buddhist texts with his explanations.

Hsüan-tsang (Jpn. *Genjō*, 596–664)

One of the most influential figures of CHINESE BUDDHISM, who spent sixteen years in India (629–645), during which he traveled all over the subcontinent. He later chronicled his travels and observations in his *Records of the Western Regions* (*Ta-t'ang Hsi-yü-chi*), which is a valuable source of information about INDIAN BUDDHISM during this period. While in India, he went to NĀLANDĀ MONASTIC UNIVERSITY, where he studied YOGĀCĀRA philosophy with Śīlabhadra. When he returned to China, he and his student K'UEI-CHI (632–682) established a Chinese Yogācāra school, called FA-HSIANG. He was one of the great translators of Chinese Buddhism and is credited with seventy-five translations, in addition to his original writings. His most important work was the monumental *Establishment of Cognition-only* (Chin. *Cheng-wei-shih lun*; Skt. *Vijñaptimātratā-siddhi*), said to be a commentary on VASUBANDHU's *Thirty Verses* (*Triṃśikā*).

Hsü-yün (1840–1959)

One of the leading Chinese CH'AN masters of the modern period. Born in Fukien Province, he received monastic ordination at the age of twenty from Miao Lien, following which he trained on Mount Ku for four years. From 1868 to 1871 he lived in the wilderness, subsisting by foraging, and later went on several pilgrimages. At the age of fifty-six he had an awakening experience at Kao Min Monastery in Yang Chou. He later moved to Ts'ao-ch'i, the temple of HUI-NENG, which he restored. He was one of the outstanding figures of the revival of Chinese Buddhism in the early part of the twentieth century. His biography has been translated by Charles Luk under the title *Empty Cloud*.

hua-t'ou (Jpn. *wato*; Kor. *hwadu*; "main [topic] of speech")

The stories from which *kung-an* (Jpn. KŌAN; Kor. *kong'an*; Viet. *công-án*) are derived, used as a topic of meditation in the CH'AN (Jpn. ZEN, Kor. SŎN; Viet. THIỀN) tradition. The stories are thought to get to the very essence of truth and to encapsulate the moment at which speech exhausts itself, leading to non-conceptual, direct realization of reality.

Hua-yen (Skt. *Avataṃsaka*; Jpn. *Kegon*; Kor. *Hwaŏm*)

Chinese Buddhist tradition founded by TU-SHUN (557–640), which is based on the *Flower Garland Sūtra* (*Avataṃsaka-sūtra*), translated into Chinese by BUDDHABHADRA. Its most influential exponent was FA-TSANG (643–712), who is credited with reorganizing the school and composing some of its most important works. The main doctrine of Hua-yen is the interdependence and interpenetration of all phenomena, expressed in the metaphor of "Indra's net," in which there is a gem at every interstice. Each gem reflects all the others, while simultaneously being reflected in them. Hua-yen contends that all the phenomena of the universe spontaneously arose from the "sphere of reality" (Skt. *dharma-dhātu*) and that all phenomena are empty. They are conceived in two aspects, dynamic and static. The former refers to the sphere of reality, which is immutable and always remains the same, and the latter refers to the interpenetration and mutual causation of phenomena.

Hui-k'o (Jpn. *Eka*, 487–593)

The second Chinese CH'AN patriarch, who is said to have demonstrated the sincerity of his desire to study with BODHIDHARMA by cutting off his own arm and offering it to him. After six years of practicing meditation, he was designated by Bodhidharma as his dharma-successor.

Hui-neng (Jpn. *E'nō*, 638–713)

The sixth Chinese patriarch of the CH'AN tradition, who was the dharma-successor of HUNG-JEN (Jpn. Gunin or Kōnin, 601–674), the fifth patriarch. In the *Sūtra [Spoken] from the Platform of the Dharma Treasure* (LIU-TSU-TA-SHIH FA-PAO-T'AN-CHING, commonly referred to as the "*Platform Sūtra*," *T'an-ching*), he reports that he was born into a poor family, received little formal schooling, and had to support himself and his mother by selling firewood. One day he heard someone reciting a verse of the *Diamond Sūtra*, "Let the mind flow freely without fixating on anything," which precipitated an awakening experience. Following this he traveled to the monastery of Hung-jen, but was not immediately accepted as a student. Instead, he was put to work doing menial tasks, but his status changed when he composed a poem expressing his understanding of the DHARMA. Hung-jen had asked his students to submit verses to determine who was best suited to be his dharma-successor, and his main student, SHEN-HSIU,

Mural of Hung-jen bequeathing his robe and bowl to Hui-neng, symbolizing that he was his dharma-heir. Sudoam Hermitage, South Kyŏngsang.

responded by writing the following verses on a wall of the monastery:

The body is the Bodhi Tree;
The mind is like a clear mirror.
One must polish it constantly and earnestly;
One must not let any dust settle on it.

Hui-neng responded with his own verses:

From the beginning awakening has no tree
And the bright mirror has no stand.
Buddha-nature is always pure –
Where could dust settle?

When he heard of the two sets of verses, Hung-jen decided to make Hui-neng his successor, which he certified by handing him his robe and bowl. The succession was challenged by Shen-hsiu, who is considered to be the founder of the "Northern School" (Pei-tsung) of Ch'an, which stressed a gradual path to awakening, while Hui-neng is said to be the founder of the "Southern School" (NAN-TSUNG) which emphasized "sudden awakening," in which one directly understands truth in a flash of intuitive insight. The Northern School died out within a few generations, but the Southern School became the dominant tradition in Ch'an, and contemporary ZEN and SŎN lineages trace themselves back to Hui-neng. With his death, the institution of the patriarchate came to an end, since he did not name a successor.

Hui-yüan (334–416)

Considered by the Pure Land (Chin. CH'ING-T'U; Jpn. JŌDŌ SHŪ) tradition to be its first Chinese patriarch. In 402 he gathered a group of 123 followers in front of an image of AMITĀBHA BUDDHA, and they all vowed to be reborn in Amitābha's "Pure Land" of SUKHĀVATĪ. The group was named the "White Lotus Society" (Chin. PAI-LIEN-TSUNG), and it was conceived as a mutual help society, with the idea that those who succeeded in being reborn in the Pure Land would work to bring the others there.

human

See MANUṢYA.

Humphreys, Travers Christmas (1901–1983)

British barrister involved in a number of prominent murder trials, who became a Buddhist in his late teens. He founded the Buddhist Lodge of the Theosophical Society in 1924. In 1943 the name was changed to the Buddhist Society. The Society publishes *The Middle Way*, one of the longest-running Buddhist journals in the West.

Hung-jen (Jpn. *Gunin* or *Kōnin*, 601–674)

Fifth Chinese patriarch of CH'AN, dharma-successor of Tao-hsin (Jpn. Dōshin) and teacher of HUI-NENG (Jpn. E'nō).

hungry ghost

See PRETA.

Hva shang Ma ha ya na

See MO-HO-YEN, HO-SHANG.

Hwaŏm (Skt. *Avataṃsaka*; Chin. *Hua-yen*; Jpn. *Kegon*)

The Korean branch of the HUA-YEN tradition, which rose to popularity during the Unified Silla period (668–918). It was founded by ŬISANG (625–702), who traveled to China and studied with the second Chinese patriarch of the tradition, Chih-yen (602–669). His major work was entitled *Chart of the Avataṃsaka One-Vehicle Dharmadhātu* (*Hwaŏm ilsŭng pŏpkye to*), which was written in 661. In 670 he returned to Korea and in 676 founded Pusŏk-sa, which became the main temple of the Hwaŏm order.

I

icchantika (Tib. *'dod chen po*; lit. "great desire")

A class of beings who have cut off all their "virtuous roots" (*kuśala-mūla*) and so have no hope of attaining buddhahood. The status of *icchantika*s was an important topic of debate in East Asian Buddhism, with some groups claiming that they are utterly unable to attain liberation, while others asserted that all beings, including *icchantika*s, have the buddha-nature, and so the virtuous roots may be re-established.

I-ching (635–713)

One of the early Chinese pilgrims, who traveled to India in 671 by sea and spent more than twenty years there. At NĀLANDĀ MONASTIC UNIVERSITY he studied a range of Buddhist subjects, and he returned to China in 695 with over four hundred Buddhist texts. Together with Śikṣānanda, he began translating the Indian texts into Chinese. He is credited with translating 56 texts in 230 volumes, including the AVATAṂSAKA-SŪTRA and the MŪLASARVĀSTIVĀDA VINAYA.

ignorance

See AVIDYĀ.

i-hsin-ch'üan-hsin

See ISHIN-DENSHIN.

Ikeda, Daisaku (b. 1928)

Third president of SŌKA GAKKAI, one of the largest Buddhist organizations in Japan. He first encountered the organization in 1947 and became a passionate adherent soon after. Following the death of the organization's second president, JŌSEI TODA (1900–1958), he succeeded him and began a program of expanding the membership of the organization. Today it claims several million followers in Japan, but the membership has split in recent years as a result of conflict between the lay Sōka Gakkai and the priests of NICHIREN SHŌSHŪ over the leadership and direction of the organization. Under Ikeda's leadership it has also expanded its activities overseas and today has many thousands of members in Europe and the U.S.A.

Ikkyū Sōjun (1394–1481)

One of the most famous Japanese ZEN masters, particularly renowned for his unorthodox lifestyle and his poems extolling the virtues of wine and sex. Though he belonged to the RINZAI tradition, he often castigated its leaders for their dogmatic adherence to form and tradition. It is reported that he was so disturbed by the ossification of Zen that he tore up the certificate of awakening (INKA-SHŌMEI) given to him by his master, and he refused to name a dharma-successor.

impermanence

See ANITYA.

Indian Buddhism

Although Buddhism originated in India, today the tradition mainly flourishes in other countries. There are, of course, long-established Buddhist cultures at the northern fringes of the subcontinent, in Ladakh, Sikkim, and Bhutan, and since 1959 several hundred thousand Tibetan refugees have swelled the ranks of Buddhists in India. The largest group of Buddhists in India, however, consists of former Untouchables who, prompted by the example of Dr. B. R. AMBEDKAR, converted to Buddhism in order to escape the Hindu caste system.

Indian Buddhism begins with the life of ŚĀKYAMUNI BUDDHA (ca. fifth century B.C.E.), who according to tradition was born into a royal family in what is now southern Nepal. After leaving his father's kingdom in order to find liberation from cyclic existence (SAṂSĀRA), he is said to have attained "awakening" (BODHI), after which he began to teach others the path he had discovered. Early on in his teaching career, he instituted a monastic order (SAṂGHA), which in later centuries spread all over the subcontinent, and also to other countries in Asia. The Buddha is said to have traveled widely in India, attracting followers wherever he went, and by the end of his forty-year ministry the tradition was well established. Shortly after his death, traditional histories report that a council (*saṃgīti* or *saṃghāyanā*) was convened in RĀJAGṚHA, during which a canon was compiled. This included the Buddha's sermons (collected in the SŪTRA-PIṬAKA) and rules for monastic discipline (compiled in the VINAYA-PIṬAKA).

The accounts all agree that at this time the Buddhist community was unified, but the beginnings of sectarianism began to manifest soon afterward, and within a century early histories report that a second council was convened at VAIŚĀLĪ to adjudicate a dispute between monks of that area and another monk named Yaśas, who believed that some of

The exterior of the Aurangabad Caves Vihāra, Mahārāṣṭra, India.

their practices contravened the *vinaya*. Whether or not this was a historical event, it points to the fact that fissures were beginning to form within the previously unified community, and probably at least by the time of AŚOKA (r. 272–236 B.C.E.) divergent philosophical and disciplinary traditions had developed. Under the Mauryan dynasty (322–185 B.C.E.), Buddhism enjoyed a period of significant growth due to royal patronage, and during the reign of Aśoka (the third Mauryan monarch) it began to spread beyond the subcontinent, initially due to missions sponsored by him.

The first persecution of Buddhism was initiated by Puṣyamitra Śuṅga (r. ca. 187–151 B.C.E.), but the Śuṅga dynasty (185–73 B.C.E.) was also generally a time of prosperity for Buddhism, during which some of its greatest monuments were constructed (including SĀÑCĪ, Bhārhut, and Amarāvatī). The Śuṅga dynasty came to an end as a result of foreign invasions from Central Asia, and this marked the beginning of a long period of foreign military incursions into India. The invaders included Greeks, Parthians, Kushans, and Scythians (Śaka). Some of the foreign rulers supported Buddhism; for example, the Kushan king KANIṢKA I (ca. first–second century C.E.) is reported to have been a patron of Buddhism and is also said to have convened the fourth Buddhist council in GANDHĀRA.

Despite continuing political uncertainty, Buddhism continued to flourish for several centuries, which saw significant doctrinal development, most notably the rise of the MAHĀYĀNA ("Great Vehicle"), which appears to have begun as a reaction against an overemphasis on scholasticism and monasticism. The new movement developed a greater role for the laity and significantly altered the paradigm of the Buddha. No longer was he viewed as a merely human teacher, but was invested with miraculous powers, as well as such exalted qualities as omniscience (*sarvajñātā*). The movement produced new texts, which, like the discourses of the early canons, were called SŪTRAS, but which were significantly different in form and content from the earlier discourses.

Some time around the seventh century, another radically new movement arose in India, which like the Mahāyāna before it produced new scriptures that it claimed had been spoken by the Buddha, although he had been dead for over a millennium. These texts were called TANTRAS, and they contained new paradigms and practices, particularly meditations involving rituals and visualizations. This strand of Buddhism is commonly referred to as VAJRAYĀNA ("Vajra Vehicle").

Despite the growth and development of Buddhist thought and literature, records of the first millennium indicate that it was probably never a very widespread movement, and by the seventh century its most vital centers were mainly large monastic universities (most notably NĀLANDĀ, founded by Kumāra Gupta I, 414–455). It later grew to be the major center of learning in the Buddhist world. During the seventh century Buddhism enjoyed the patronage of king Harṣa, and during the Pala dynasty (ca. 650–950) several of its rulers patronized major Buddhist centers of learning, such as VIKRAMAŚĪLA (founded ca. 800) and Odantapurī (founded ca. 760). Vikramaśīla later eclipsed Nālandā as Buddhism's greatest center of learning, but both were eventually destroyed as a result of the Muslim invasions that entered India in waves during the eleventh–thirteenth centuries. Before this time, Buddhist philosophy enjoyed a last notable flowering due to the MADHYAMAKA philosophers ŚĀNTARAKṢITA (ca. 680–740) and KAMALAŚĪLA (ca. 700–750), both of whom reportedly played significant roles in the dissemination of Buddhism into Tibet.

Although Buddhism had apparently been in decline for centuries, its final death knell was sounded by the invasions of the Turkic general Mahmud Shabuddin Ghorī, who sacked Nālandā in 1197 and Vikramaśīla in 1203. Despite these attacks, Buddhism continued for some time in isolated pockets, and when the Tibetan pilgrim Dharmasvāmin (1197–1264) visited Nālandā in 1235 he encountered a few monks with a small group of students. During his visit, however, another raiding-party arrived and they had to flee. Because its strength was concentrated in the large northern monasteries in areas that bore the brunt of the Muslim attacks, once these were destroyed the tradition was unable to survive. Buddhism effectively vanished from the subcontinent and was only revived in the nineteenth and twentieth centuries, as Buddhists from other countries came to India either as pilgrims or as refugees and began to re-establish the tradition in the land of its origin.

inherent existence

See SVABHĀVA.

initiation

See ABHIṢEKA.

inka shōmei (Chin. *yin-k'o*; Kor. *inga*; "seal of authentication")

The certification of awakening (KENSHŌ, SATORI) given by a ZEN master to a student, which indicates that the master is satisfied with the student's progress. It also confers authority to teach, but does not indicate that the student has reached the highest level of understanding. This system is important in Zen, which claims to be a mind-to-mind transmission (Chin. *i-hsin-ch'üan-hsin*; Jpn. ISHIN-DENSHIN) of non-conceptual direct understanding, which began when ŚĀKYAMUNI BUDDHA passed the dharma to his student KĀŚYAPA. The *inka-shōmei* serves as a quality-control device by which Zen masters can ensure that a particular person's teachings and practices accord with those accepted in the tradition.

insight meditation

See VIPAŚYANĀ.

intermediate state

See BAR DO.

International Buddhist Society (Buddhasāsana Samāgama)

Organization founded by the British monk ANANDA METTEYYA in 1903. Its first headquarters were in Rangoon, Burma, and it later opened a branch in England.

International Network of Engaged Buddhists (INEB)

Organization founded by the Thai lay activist SULAK SIVARAKSA. It first met in 1989 and quickly grew into an important international organization devoted to promoting peace and non-violence, working for human rights and environmental protection, and improving the lives of poor women. Its symbol is the "wheel of *dhamma*" (Skt. DHARMACAKRA), and it is intended as a non-hierarchical and non-authoritarian organization based on core Buddhist principles. It aims "to encourage all involved groups to understand linkages between their own concerns and those of other groups and help them to avoid narrow single-issue stances in favor of a holistic understanding" (from the draft statement of the Progressive Buddhists Conference, February, 1989).

Ippen (1239–1289)

Japanese Pure Land (Jpn. Jōdō; Chin. Ch'ing-t'u) teacher, best known for creating the practice of "dancing *nembutsu*," in which he and his followers would dance for joy while chanting the nembutsu ("Namu Amida Butsu," "Praise to Amitābha Buddha"). He said that the practice was intended to demonstrate his joy and gratitude toward Amitābha, because he was certain that he was already saved by him. Ippen also initiated the practice of giving people small amulets called *ofuda* inscribed with the *nembutsu*. During his lifetime he and his followers handed out over 600,000 *ofuda*, telling people that just touching one would create a karmic connection with Amitābha which would enable him to use his saving power to bring them to salvation, even if they had performed evil deeds (and even if they had no faith at all in the practice or in Amitābha).

ishin-denshin (Chin. *i-hsin-ch'üan-hsin* "mind-to-mind transmission")

According to Zen tradition, its teachings are passed on directly from the mind of the master to that of the disciple, without recourse to words and concepts. This requires that students demonstrate their direct experience of truth to their teachers, who serve as the arbiters who authenticate the experience.

Ivolginsky Monastery

One of the major Buddhist monasteries in Russia, constructed in 1948 about 25 miles from Ulan-Ude. It is the seat of the Hambo Lama, one of the most influential reincarnational lineages (Mon. *khubilgan*; Tib. sprul sku) among the Mongols living in Russia. The two main Buddhist Mongol groups in Russia are the Kalmyks and the Buryats, who follow Buddhist traditions imported from Tibet.

J

'ja' lus ("rainbow body")

Tibetan term for the final state of attainment in some traditions of TIBETAN BUDDHISM, in which a fully awakened master dissolves the physical body into multicolored light and re-emerges in a new body composed of subtle energy, rather than coarse matter.

'Jam dbyangs mkhyen brtse chos kyi blo gros (Jamyang Khyentse Chögi Lodrö, 1896–1969)

One of the leading masters of the RIS MED (Rime) movement in eastern Tibet, recognized as the activity reincarnation of 'Jam dbyangs mkhyen brtse dbang po (Jamyang Khyentse Wangpo, 1820–1892). Many of the leading Tibetan lamas of the twentieth century were his students, including Dingo Khyentse Rinpoche (DIL MGO MKHYEN BRTSE RIN PO CHE), KALU RINPOCHE (Ka lu Rin po che), and SOGYAL RINPOCHE (bSod nams rgyal mtshan Rin po che).

'Jam mgon kong sprul blo gros mtha' yas (Jamgön Kongtrül Lodrö Taye, 1811–1899)

One of the most influential figures of nineteenth-century TIBETAN BUDDHISM, who was instrumental in establishing the "Non-Sectarian" (RIS MED) movement, which sought to overcome the paralyzing sectarianism that pervaded Tibetan Buddhism at the time. He was born into a Bon po family, and after taking monastic ordination he studied with, and received initiations from, a wide variety of teachers from different traditions. He witnessed first hand the negative effects of the prevailing sectarianism of the time and sought to combat it by emphasizing the harmony of different Buddhist traditions. He wrote a number of important works, including his *Encyclopedia of All Knowledge* (*Shes bya kun khyab*) and an eclectic collection of tantric texts entitled *Treasury of Secret Mantra* (*gDams ngag mdzod*). (*See also* BON.)

Jambudvīpa (Pāli Jambudīpa; Tib. Dzam bu'i gling)

The southernmost of the four great land masses (Skt. *catur-dvīpa*) of traditional Buddhist cosmology. It is said to be named after the Jambu tree that grows there. It measures 2,000 YOJANAS on three sides, and its fourth side is only three-and-a-half *yojana*s long.

Japanese Buddhism

When Buddhism first entered Japan in the sixth century, it was a foreign religion that differed significantly from the unorganized indigenous cults and practices that would later develop into Shintō. In the succeeding centuries, however, it gradually adapted to its

The Golden Temple, Kyoto.

new environment, and distinctively Japanese forms of Buddhism arose, which melded elements of Japanese culture with Buddhist traditions that were imported largely from China and Korea. According to the *Nihonshoki*, Buddhism was first imported to Japan in 552 from Paekche, a Korean kingdom that was at war with the neighboring state of Silla. The king of Paekche sent Buddhist statues and texts as gifts to enlist the military support of Japan, but did not send anyone who could explain their significance. Thus although this is traditionally viewed as the first introduction of Buddhism to Japan, it had little impact at the time.

The first recorded adoption of Buddhism in Japan was initiated by the Soga clan, which viewed the Buddha as a god (Jpn. *kami*) of the powerful culture of China. Some Sogas wanted to adopt Buddhism as a clan cult in hopes of gaining access to the magical powers that were widely thought to belong to Buddhist monks and artefacts. When the Sogas later managed to defeat their main rivals, they apparently credited the Buddha with playing a role in their success and began to propagate Buddhism. It is clear from records of the time, however, that they had little or no knowledge of Buddhist philosophy and practice and conceived of it in terms of indigenous religious paradigms.

During the seventh century Buddhism began to attract converts, and by 624 there were reportedly 816 monks and 569 nuns in Japan. In this early period, Buddhism was mainly viewed as a means to cure illness and harness magical power. Ordinations were thought to generate merit, and this was believed to result in worldly benefits, such as health, protection of the country, etc. As was true of other countries in which Buddhism became established, state patronage played a crucial role in propagating the new religion. The first Japanese ruler to accept Buddhism was Yōmei (r. 585–598). His son SHŌTOKU (574–622) was by all accounts an enthusiastic supporter of Buddhism, who wrote a constitution based on Buddhist and Confucian principles and built numerous temples. He also sponsored monks and nuns to travel to China for study, and he conceived of Buddhism as a national religion (before this it had mainly been a clan cult).

After Shōtoku's death, the imperial capital moved to Nara, and several emperors increased royal patronage of Buddhism. In 741 the emperor Shōmu (r. 724–749) issued a decree mandating that a network of temples (*kokubunji*) be built to protect the country (*chingo kokka*), and in each province at least one was constructed to house twenty or more monks. One of their primary duties was chanting the *Sūtra of Golden Light* (Skt. *Suvarṇa-prabhāsa-sūtra*; Jpn. *Konkōmyō-kyō*), which promises that the four celestial kings (Skt. DEVA-RĀJA; Jpn. *shitennō*) will protect any ruler who sponsors chanting of the text. During

Todaiji Temple.

the Nara period (710–784), interest in Buddhism increased among the intelligentsia, and six schools developed, all of which were imported from China: (1) RITSU (Skt. VINAYA; Chin. Lu); (2) KEGON (Chin. HUA-YEN); (3) KUSHA (Chin. Chu-she); (4) HOSSŌ (Chin. FA-HSIANG); (5) JŌJITSU (Skt. Satyasiddhi; Chin. Ch'eng-shih); and (6) SANRON (Chin. SAN-LUN). Three of these still exist today: Hossō, which has its headquarters at Kōfukuji and Yakushiji; Ritsu, whose main temple is Tōshōdaiji; and Kegon, which is based at Tōdaiji. The three are mainly confined to these temples, however, and are only minor traditions with little lay support. During the Nara period, interest in Buddhism was mainly confined to the aristocracy, but there were some Buddhists who began to proselytize among the masses. Among these were the *hijiri*, monks who were often self-ordained and who generally kept apart from the major orders. The most famous of these was GYŌGI (668–749), who had a background in civil engineering that he put to use in projects for rural peasants.

The establishment of a new capital in Heiankyō (modern day Kyōto) in 794 marked the beginning of the Heian period (794–1185), during which imperial power waned as feudal chieftains gained greater autonomy. At the same time, many Buddhist orders became large landholders, which often allied themselves with local hegemons. During this period, some new schools were imported from China, most notably SHINGON, founded by KŪKAI (774–835), and TENDAI, founded by SAICHŌ (767–822). One of the most significant developments of this time was a move toward syncretism. Buddhist traditions borrowed rituals and practices from each other, and Buddhism as a whole increasingly incorporated native Shintō deities and practices. During this period eclectic temples called *jingūji* were constructed, in which Buddhist rituals were performed in what were otherwise Shintō shrines. At the same time, Buddhists increasingly identified figures in the Buddhist pantheon (buddhas and bodhisattvas) with indigenous *kami*.

Saichō's tomb, Mount Hiei.

The late Heian period was characterized by a growing sense of pessimism, probably due in part to the increasingly unstable political situation. This continued into the Kamakura period (1185–1333), during which military leaders seized power from the aristocracy and developed a feudal system that lasted until 1868. During this time it was widely believed that the world had entered the "age of final dharma" (Jpn. MAPPŌ) that was foretold in some Indian Buddhist texts. According to this idea, the time of ŚĀKYAMUNI BUDDHA was the "true dharma age," during which people had superior capacities, enabling them to practice effectively and attain liberation. During the next period, the "counterfeit dharma age," practice would decline, and during *mappō* there would be continued degeneration until Buddhism disappeared altogether. Estimates regarding the timing of the three periods varied widely, but during the Kamakura period it was generally accepted that the third age had begun, and the schools that arose in Japan at that time developed strategies for coping with decline. Despite the political uncertainty, however, this was generally a time of growth for Buddhism, and three new schools appeared: ZEN, JŌDŌ SHŪ (Pure Land), and Nichiren-shū. Zen was first brought to Japan by EISAI ZENJI (1141–1215), who traveled to China in 1168 and 1187 and subsequently introduced the RINZAI (Chin. LIN-CHI) lineage. The SŌTŌ (Chin. TS'AO-TUNG) tradition was first propagated in Japan by DŌGEN ZENJI (1200–1253), who traveled to China in 1223. Zen's general response to *mappō* was to emphasize the importance of intensive meditative practice, which was believed to be the only way to overcome the negative influences of the age. By contrast, both Jōdō Shū and Nichiren-shū contended that the beings of *mappō* are too depraved and weak-willed to have any hope of securing salvation through their own efforts, and so they should rely on others to save them. For Jōdō Shū, this involves placing one's faith in Amida (Skt. AMITĀBHA) Buddha, while NICHIREN taught his followers to rely solely on the *Lotus Sūtra* (Skt. SADDHARMA-PUṆḌARĪKA-SŪTRA; Jpn. *Myōhō-renge-kyō*).

The Kamakura period is often viewed as the apogee of the development of Buddhism in Japan, since by its end all of the major classical Buddhist traditions had been established. The Tokugawa period (1600–1867) was a time of unprecedented power for Buddhism in Japan, but its success at the political level led to stagnation and apathy. When the warlord Tokugawa Ieyasu (1542–1616) seized power in 1600, he initiated a violent persecution of Christianity, which had made significant numbers of converts in Japan. Viewing this as the thin end of the wedge of Western colonialism, he issued an edict requiring all Japanese to become officially affiliated with a Buddhist temple, and people were issued certificates (*tera-uke*) to this effect. Buddhist temples became part of the government bureaucracy and were required to keep records of births and deaths and also to aid the government's efforts to eradicate Christianity. This system, called *danka-seido*, was abolished in the Meiji period (1868–1912, during which Shintō became the state religion), but the bonds forged by the old system continue to maintain a sense of connection between many Japanese and their family temples.

During the Tokugawa period, the number of Buddhist temples increased, as did the revenues from parishioners who were eager to avoid being suspected of harboring Christian sympathies. But this very success led to a situation in which the priesthood became lazy and corrupt, since there was no need for them to actively work to interest people in Buddhism. The Meiji restoration revived the old imperial cult, which identified the emperor as a living *kami*, and a nationalistic form of Shintō became the state ideology. At the same time, Buddhism was suppressed, and because its public support had eroded due to its ossification and corruption, there was a general decline, which persisted through World War II. Since the post-war Restoration period, Japan has made freedom of religion a part of the legal system, but the traditional schools of Buddhism have generated little enthusiasm among the masses of Japanese. For most Japanese today, institutional Buddhism is primarily associated with the performance of rituals for the dead, and many Japanese only come into contact with Buddhism when someone in the family dies and they go to the ancestral temple for the mortuary rites. A nationwide survey conducted by the Sōtō school found that even among Japanese who identify themselves as Buddhists, only ten percent could even name their sect's main temple or founder. Government surveys consistently reveal that only about thirty percent of the population embraces any religious belief, while sixty-five percent are indifferent to religion. What vitality there is in Japanese religions is mainly found in the so-called "New Religions" (SHIN-SHŪKYŌ, such as AGONSHŪ and SŌKA GAKKAI), which generally have charismatic founders and make a direct emotional appeal to their followers. Aside from the fervor of the "New Religions," however, there is little interest in religion among most Japanese. Although many Japanese consider themselves to be affiliated with a Buddhist sect, this often means little in terms of actual belief or practice.

Jātaka (Pāli *Jātaka*; Tib. *sKyes rabs*; "Birth Stories")

Pāli term for a collection of 547 stories of the previous lives of ŚĀKYAMUNI BUDDHA, which focus on how he cultivated the various good qualities that characterize a BUDDHA, such as generosity, morality, wisdom, etc. These are part of the THERAVĀDA canon and are contained in the KHUDDAKA NIKĀYA of the Sutta-piṭaka (SŪTRA-PIṬAKA). They are very popular in Buddhist countries because they are mostly easily understood stories extolling key Buddhist virtues. Each Jātaka concludes with a verse indicating the Buddhist moral of the story (technically speaking, the verses are the only part of the stories that are considered canonical).

jenang

See ANUJÑĀ.

Jetavana (1)

Indian Buddhist monastery located at Śrāvastī. The site was donated by ANĀTHAPIṆḌIKA, a wealthy lay follower of the Buddha. The site was selected by ŚĀRIPUTRA, who spent the last twenty-five rainy season retreats of his life there. It was also the Buddha's favorite retreat, and he spent nineteen rainy season retreats at Jetavana.

Jetavana (2)

A monastery in Sri Lanka built by king Mahāsena (r. 334–362) for Mahāyāna monks. It maintained a separate NIKĀYA (2) until the twelfth century, when king Parākramabāhu I ordered it to amalgamate with the MAHĀVIHĀRA *nikāya.*

'Jigs med gling pa (Jikme Lingpa, 1730–1798)

Famed visionary and discoverer (GTER STON) of "hidden treasures" (GTER MA), most importantly the *Heart Sphere of the Great Expanse* (KLONG CHEN SNYING THIG), which has been widely influential in the RNYING MA PA (Nyingmapa) school of TIBETAN BUDDHISM.

Jina (Pāli *Jina*; Tib. *rGyal ba*; "Conqueror")

One of the most common epithets of the Buddha, which indicates that he has triumphed over the factors that bind ordinary beings to continued rebirth, such as anger, desire, and obscuration.

jiriki (Chin. *t'zu-li*; "own-power")

Japanese term referring to Buddhist practices that rely on one's own effort. This is generally contrasted with TARIKI ("other-power"), which encompasses approaches in which one relies on a buddha's help for salvation. The former type includes ZEN training in which liberation is attained through intense meditative practice. The latter type includes Pure Land (Chin. CH'ING-T'U; Jpn. JŌDŌ SHINSHŪ) traditions, in which one prays to AMITĀBHA BUDDHA to be reborn in his "Pure Land" of SUKHĀVATĪ.

Jizō

See KṢITIGARBHA.

jñāna (Pāli *ñāṇa*; Tib. *ye shes*; "knowledge")

In general, this term refers to knowledge. It is derived from the Sanskrit root jñā, "to know." In MAHĀYĀNA, it is also the tenth in the tenfold list of "perfections" (PĀRAMITĀ) that a BODHISATTVA cultivates on the path to buddhahood. It is developed on the tenth "bodhisattva level" (BHŪMI) and is said to refer to the expansive wisdom that is perfected with the attainment of buddhahood.

Jñānagarbha (Tib. *Ye shes snying po*, fl. ca. eighth century; "Knowledge Womb")

Influential MADHYAMAKA philosopher belonging to the tradition of BHAVYA, who is said by the Tibetan historian Sum pa mkhan po to have been the teacher of ŚĀNTARAKṢITA. He is commonly classified by Tibetan doxographers as a SVĀTANTRIKA-MADHYAMIKA, and he is the author of several important works, including *Differentiation of the Two Truths* (*Satya-dvaya-vibhaṅga*).

Jo nang pa (Jonangpa)

An order of TIBETAN BUDDHISM that produced a number of influential scholars, but was suppressed by the fifth Dalai Lama, NGAG DBANG BLO BZANG RGYA MTSHO (Ngawang Losang Gyatso, 1617–1682) in the seventeenth century. Its most notable figure was Shes rab rgyal mtshan of Dol po (Dolpopa Sherap Gyeltsen, 1296–1361), and the lineage also included 'Ba ra ba rGyal mtshan dpal bzang (Barawa Gyeltsen Belsang, 1310–1391), Thang stong rgyal po (Tangdong Gyelpo, 1385–1464), and TĀRANĀTHA (1575–1634). It was best known for its positive interpretation of the doctrine of TATHĀGATA-GARBHA (Tib. *de bzhin gshegs pa'i snying po*), which conceived of it as a positive essence that is actualized through meditative practice. This view is commonly referred to as "other-emptiness" (Tib. GZHAN STONG), and it is said to be based on the KĀLACAKRA-TANTRA. The Dalai Lama considered this to be a thinly disguised version of the brahmanical notion of an unchanging, primordially undefiled "self" (Skt. *ātman*), and he issued a decree that Jo nang pa monasteries be destroyed or forced to convert to the DGE LUGS PA (Gelukpa) order, and their books burned. Some contemporary scholars suspect that the reasons behind the suppression had as much to do with politics as doctrine, since the Jo nang pas had been aligned with the KAR MA BKA' BRGYUD PA (Karma Kagyüpa) hierarchs, who had fought against (and lost to) the Dalai Lama for political control of Tibet. Despite this persecution, many of the order's works survived, and the *gzhan stong* teachings remain influential in Tibetan Buddhism, particularly in the RIS MED (Rime, "Non-Sectarian") movement.

Jōdō

See CH'ING-T'U.

Jōdō Shinshū ("True Pure Land School")

The Japanese tradition founded by SHINRAN (1173–1262) and later reorganized by Rennyo (1414–1499). Shinran claimed to be following the teachings of HŌNEN (1133–1212) and, like Hōnen, he taught his followers to rely exclusively on the saving power of AMITĀBHA BUDDHA (Jpn. Amida Butsu). The tradition is based on the *Sukhāvatī-vyūha*, and particularly on the forty-eight vows taken by Amitābha in a past life. The most important of these for Jōdō shinshū is the eighteenth vow, in which Amitābha promised that anyone who calls on him with faith ten times (or wishes rebirth in his Pure Land ten times) will surely be reborn there. Once in the Pure Land, one is assured of attaining buddhahood in that lifetime. Shinran taught that this practice is the only one appropriate to the present "final dharma age" (Jpn. MAPPŌ) and that one should dedicate oneself to it wholeheartedly. The central practice is chanting the NEMBUTSU, "Namo Amida Butsu" ("Praise to Amitābha Buddha"), but this is not conceived as a way of making merit; rather, one chants the *nembutsu* as an act of gratitude to Amitābha because one is already assured of being saved. Shinran emphasized that Amitābha's power is so great that he can save even the most depraved sinner; all that is required is that one have a single moment of "believing mind" (*shinjin*), after which one is assured of being reborn in the Pure Land. Because one relies on Amitābha and not on one's own effort, this practice is referred to in Japanese as TARIKI ("other-power"), in contrast to traditions like ZEN, which assert that one must attain salvation through one's own power (JIRIKI). Shinran is generally credited with establishing a married priesthood in Japan, and today there is no monastic element in Jōdō Shinshū. Its temples are run by lay priests, and the priesthood is hereditary. The tradition has two main divisions: Ōtani and Honganji, both of which have their main centers in Kyōto.

Jōdō Shū (Chin. *Ch'ing-t'u-tsung*; Kor. *Chŏngt'o-chong*; Viet. *Đạo Trang*; "Pure Land School")

Japanese tradition founded by HŌNEN (1133–1212). It was first brought to Japan by ENNIN (794–864), who studied in China. Hōnen developed it into a distinctive school, emphasizing the centrality of the NEMBUTSU, "Namo Amida Butsu" ("Praise to AMITĀBHA BUDDHA"). Though originally trained in the scholastic TENDAI tradition, Hōnen later encountered the writings of SHAN-TAO and GENSHIN and subsequently decided that the "difficult path" of traditional Buddhism – involving study and meditative practice in order to attain liberation – was not feasible for the people of the "final dharma age" (Jpn. MAPPŌ). He taught that in the present degenerate age the only hope for salvation lies in total reliance on the saving power of Amitābha. This he termed the "easy path," because it is open to all, and salvation is assured for those who recite the *nembutsu* with sincere faith. The doctrinal basis for his school is found in four Indian texts: the Larger and Smaller SUKHĀVATĪ-VYŪHA-SŪTRA, the *Amitāyur-dhyāna-sūtra*, and the *Amitābha-sūtra*.

Jōjitsu (Skt. *Satyasiddhi*; Chin. *Ch'eng-shih*; "Establishment of Truth")

A scholastic tradition brought to Japan by the Korean monk Ekwan in 625. The doctrines of the school are based on the *Establishment of Truth* (*Satyasiddhi*) by the fourth-century Indian Buddhist scholar Harivarman. Although it was a distinct school in China, in Japan it was considered to be a part of the SANRON (Chin. SAN-LUN) tradition. During the Nara period (710–784), it became one of the six main schools of Japanese Buddhism (the others were KUSHA, HOSSŌ, SANRON, RITSU, and KEGON)

Jōshū Jūshin

See CHAO-CHOU TS'UNG-SHEN.

Journal of Buddhist Ethics

Electronic journal founded by CHARLES PREBISH and Damien Keown, first published in 1994. It has become one of the most influential periodicals in the field of Buddhist Studies. Its focus is on contemporary issues, such as human rights, gender issues, the environment, etc.

Journal of the International Association of Buddhist Studies

The premier academic journal for Buddhist Studies. It is published by the International Association of Buddhist Studies, an organization of academic buddhologists which was founded in 1976.

jūgyū-no-zu ("ten ox-herding pictures")

One of the most widespread sets of images of the CH'AN (Jpn. ZEN; Kor. SŎN) tradition. They depict the levels of increasing realization of a student of Ch'an. The most famous set comes from the Chinese master K'uo-an Chih-yüan (Jpn. Kakuan Shien, fl. twelfth century): (1) looking for the ox; (2) spotting its tracks; (3) first sight of the ox; (4) catching the ox; (5) taming the ox; (6) riding the ox; (7) leaving the ox behind; (8) leaving one's self behind; (9) returning to the source; and (10) entering the marketplace. In some depictions, the ox is black at the beginning, becomes gradually whiter, and then becomes pure white. After this the ox disappears. The sequence symbolizes the student's gradual mastery of meditation practice, in which the mind is progressively brought under control and trained. Eventually the training is left behind, and one is able to function in the world with a changed perspective.

jukai ("ten precepts")

Japanese term for formal acceptance of the ten precepts for lay Buddhists: (1) not killing; (2) not stealing; (3) avoiding sexual misconduct; (4) not lying; (5) not selling or buying alcohol; (6) not gossiping about others' misdeeds; (7) not praising oneself and denigrating others; (8) avoiding miserliness with respect to the dharma; (9) avoiding aggression; and (10) not slandering. Adopting these is generally accompanied by formal declaration of one's faith in the "three jewels" (Jpn. *sambō*; Skt. TRIRATNA): Buddha, DHARMA, and SAṂGHA.

K

Kabilsingh, Chatsumarn (b. 1944)

A professor at Thammasat University who has become one of the leading advocates for women's issues in Thailand. Her mother, Voramai Kabilsingh (Bhikkhunī Ta Tao, b. 1908), was the first Thai woman to take the full *bhikkhunī* ordination, which died out centuries ago in THERAVĀDA countries. In order to receive it, she traveled to Taiwan, where she was given the ordination name Ta Tao. In 1957 she established the first monastery in Thailand for women, called Wat Songdharma Kalyani. Both mother and daughter have been instrumental in working to establish full ordination for women in Thailand.

Kagyüpa

See BKA' BRGYUD PA.

Kailāsa (also Kailāsh; Tib. *Gangs rin po che, Gangs ti se*)

Sacred mountain in the western Himālayas believed to be the abode of the god Śiva by Hindus and of CAKRASAṂVARA by Tibetan Buddhists. It is one of the most important pilgrimage spots for Tibetan Buddhists.

kaimyō ("precept name")

Honorific title given to Japanese Buddhist monks at their initiation. In contemporary Japan, many temples sell these as honorific names for deceased lay people, generally for a large sum of money.

Kakushin (also known as Shinichi Kakushin, 1207–1298)

Japanese monk who was ordained at Tōdaiji and studied in the SHINGON school before traveling to China in 1249. While there he became a student of the greatest CH'AN master of the day, WU-MEN HUI-K'AI (Jpn. Mumon Ekai, 1183–1260), who belonged to the Yang-ch'i (Jpn. Yōgi) school of LIN-CHI (Jpn. RINZAI). Wu-men conferred the certificate of awakening (Chin. *yin-k'o*; Jpn. INKA-SHŌMEI) on him and named him as his dharma-successor. He also gave him a handwritten copy of a work containing his teachings, entitled WU-MEN-KUAN (Jpn. *Mumonkan*), which was to become one of the most important works of Japanese ZEN. After his return to Japan Kakushin became an influential Zen master. His eclectic teachings emphasized KŌAN practice, but he also incorporated elements of Shingon and Fuke-shū (Chin. *P'u-hua-tsung*, one of the secondary traditions of Chinese Ch'an).

Kālacakra-tantra (Tib. *Dus kyi 'khor lo'i rgyud*; *Wheel of Time Tantra*)

One of the most important Indian tantric texts for TIBETAN BUDDHISM. It consists of three parts: inner, outer, and other. The first part discusses the external world. The second part focuses on the psycho-physical world of sentient beings, particularly the mystical physiology of subtle energies called "winds" (Skt. *prāṇa*; Tib. *rlung*) and "drops" (Skt. BINDU; Tib. *thig le*), which move through subtle "energy channels" (Skt. *nāḍī*; Tib. *rtsa*). The third section is concerned with visualization practices. The *Kālacakra* was probably one of the latest TANTRAS produced in South Asia (some scholars believe that it was probably composed in or near Sogdiana ca. tenth century), and it was not transmitted to Tibet until 1027. The text says that it was spoken on the fifteenth day of the third month after ŚĀKYAMUNI BUDDHA's awakening. At that time he appeared on the Vulture Peak dressed in monk's robes and preached the *Perfection of Wisdom Sūtra in 100,000 Lines*, and he simultaneously manifested at Dhanyakataka in South India as the buddha Kālacakra, in which form he taught the *Kālacakra-tantra*. The tantra is said to have been spoken at the request of Sucandra, king of ŚAMBHALA and an emanation of the buddha VAJRAPĀṆI, who compiled the tantra in its long form (said to be 12,000 verses, but no longer extant). Its central practice is a six-session yoga: (1) individual withdrawal (of winds); (2) concentration; (3) stopping vitality; (4) retention; (5) subsequent mindfulness; and (6) meditative absorption. The initial stages are techniques for withdrawing the winds into the central channel (Skt. *avadhūti*; Tib. *rtsa dbu ma*). In the sixth branch one actualizes immutable bliss, which is the object of Kālacakra practice. In Tibet the tantra forms the basis of the traditional astrological calendar and the medical system. Yearly Kālacakra initiation ceremonies given by the Dalai Lama are among the most popular events of Tibetan Buddhism today, because it is widely believed that receiving the Kālacakra empowerment ensures rebirth in Śambhala.

kalpa (Pāli *kappa*; Tib. *bskal pa*; "eon")

An immeasurably long period of time, based on the Buddhist cosmological notion (shared with Hinduism) that the world comes into being, develops, degenerates, and is destroyed. Following its destruction, there is a period of chaos, after which the cycle begins again. The cycle is said to be beginningless and endless. The traditional metaphor for the duration of a *kalpa* tells of a bird who flies over the Himālayas once every hundred years, trailing a thin scarf that gently touches the rocks. A *kalpa* is the amount of time required for this action to wear down the mountains.

Kalu Rinpoche (Ka lu Rin po che Kar ma rang 'byung kun khyab phrin las, 1905–1989)

Reincarnate lama (SPRUL SKU) of the KAR MA BKA' BRGYUD PA (Karma Kagyüpa) lineage of TIBETAN BUDDHISM, recognized as an "activity emanation" of 'JAM MGON KONG SPRUL (Jamgön Kongtrül; an activity emanation is said to be generated by the activity of the deceased lama; a reincarnating lama may have up to four emanations, the others being body, speech, and mind emanations). He was ordained at age thirteen by the eleventh Si tu Rin po che, Kar ma rang 'byung kun khyab (Situ Rinpoche Karma Rangjung Günkyab). Three years later he began a three-year, three-month, and three-day retreat, and for the next thirteen years after that engaged in yogic practice. His fame as a meditator grew, and he was appointed meditation teacher at dPal spungs (Pelpung) Monastery. In 1962 he left Tibet and settled in Sonada in West Bengal. From 1971 to 1981 he traveled widely, and established meditation centers in the U.S.A., Canada, and Europe. He was the first Tibetan teacher to lead a group of Western students in the traditional three-year retreat (in France from 1976 to 1980).

kalyāṇa-mitra (Pāli *kalyāṇa-mitta*; Tib. *dge ba'i bshes gnyen*; Jpn. *zenjishiki*; "spiritual friend")

A term that refers to people who help one on the path. Specifically, this generally refers to one's preceptor – and may include other religious teachers – but it can also refer to anyone who provides useful help and advice on the path. Because Buddhist practice is difficult and fraught with pitfalls, the choice of spiritual friends is considered to be of crucial importance. In the PĀLI CANON, the Buddha is reported to have said that the best choice is a buddha, the next best is an ARHAT, but that anyone who is knowledgeable and sincerely committed to DHARMA practice may be suitable. (*See also* DGE BSHES.)

kāma (Pāli *kāma*; Tib. *'dod*; "desire")

Specifically refers to sexual desire, but in many contexts is used to encompass desire in general. It is considered to be one of the major hindrances to the Buddhist path.

Kāma-dhātu (Pāli *Kāma-dhātu*; Tib. *'Dod khams*; "Desire Realm")

The lowest of the three realms of existence (the other two being RŪPA-DHĀTU and ĀRŪPYA-DHĀTU). It is the realm in which humans live, and it receives its name because desire is the dominant motivation for its inhabitants.

Kamalaśīla (Tib. *Ka ma la shi la*, ca. 700–750; "Lotus Ethics")

One of the great Indian Buddhist masters of the eighth century, author of an influential meditation text entitled *Stages of Meditative Practice* (*Bhāvanākrama*), which according to Tibetan tradition was written as a response to the quietist and antinomian teachings of HO-SHANG MO-HO-YEN (Tib. *Hva shang Ma ha ya na*). BU STON reports that the two met at the "COUNCIL OF LHASA," during which Kamalaśīla championed Indian gradualist paradigms of meditation, while Mo-ho-yen advocated a form of CH'AN practice. Kamalaśīla was declared victorious, but the defeated Mo-ho-yen sent some Chinese assassins to Tibet, and they killed Kamalaśīla by squeezing his kidneys.

Kaniṣka I (ca. first–second century C.E.)

Third ruler of the Kuṣāṇa dynasty, reported to have been a patron of Buddhism, particularly the SARVĀSTIVĀDA school. He also reportedly convened the Council of GANDHĀRA around 100 B.C.E., which was headed by the monk Vasumitra and attended by 499 monks. One significant outcome of the council was the production of an important scholastic treatise, the *Great Book of Alternatives* (MAHĀVIBHĀṢĀ), which is considered to be the standard reference for the doctrines of the Sarvāstivādins.

Kanjur

See BKA' 'GYUR.

Kannon

See AVALOKITEŚVARA.

Kapilavaddho (William Purfurst, 1906–1971)

British Buddhist who worked as a photographer during World War II and began studying meditation with U Thittila after the war. He traveled to Thailand in 1954, where he received the bhikkhu ordination, and after returning to London founded the English Sangha Trust. In 1957 he gave back his vows, changed his name to Richard Randall, and married. In 1967 he again received ordination and became the director of Wat Dhammapadipa. He gave back his vows again in 1971 and married.

Kapilavastu (Pāli *Kapilavatthu*)

The home of SIDDHĀRTHA GAUTAMA, where he lived until his decision to pursue awakening (BODHI). It was the capital city of the ŚĀKYA clan, whose king was ŚUDDHODANA, Siddhārtha's father. It is located in the foothills of the Himālayas, in present-day Nepal.

Kapleau, Philip (b. 1912)

American ZEN master (RŌSHI) who founded the Zen Center in Rochester, New York (in 1966), and who is the author of the influential book *The Three Pillars of Zen*. From 1953 to 1966 he trained at various Zen centers in Japan. His main teachers were HARADA RŌSHI, YASUTANI RŌSHI, and NAKAGAWA SŌEN RŌSHI. In 1956 he experienced KENSHŌ, and in 1966 was certified by Yasutani Rōshi as a teacher. He subsequently began teaching Zen in the U.S.A. He founded a number of Zen centers in North America, South America, and Europe, and regularly visits them to lead meditation retreats.

Kar ma bKa' brgyud pa (Karma Kagyüpa)

One of the "four major sub-orders" of the BKA' BRGYUD PA order of TIBETAN BUDDHISM, founded by DUS GSUM MKHYEN PA (Tüsum Khyenpa, 1110–1193, who was later recognized as the first RGYAL BA KAR MA PA). They are commonly known as the "Black Hats" because of the ceremonial hat (*zhwa nag*) worn by the rGyal ba Kar ma pas. The rGyal ba Kar ma pa places it on his head in certain ceremonies, and it is believed that when the hat is on his head he manifests the essence of the buddha AVALOKITEŚVARA (of whom he is considered to be a manifestation). The main seat of the school is MTSHUR PHU (Tsurpu) Monastery in Tibet. The sixteenth rGyal ba Kar ma pa, Rang 'byung rigs pa'i rdo rje (RANGJUNG RIKBE DORJE, 1924–1981), left Tibet for India following the Chinese invasion, and in 1966 established Rum bteg (Rumtek) Monastery in Sikkim, which is presently the headquarters of the order. The Kar ma bKa' brgyud pa has a number of other important incarnational lineages in addition to the rGyal ba Kar ma pas, including the ZHWA DMAR RIN PO CHE (Shamar Rinpoche), rGyal tshab Rin po che (Gyeltsap Rinpoche), and TA'I SI TU RIN PO CHE (Tai Situ Rinpoche).

Entrance to Rum bteg (Rumtek) Monastery, Sikkim.

Kar ma pa

See rGyal ba Kar ma pa.

karma (Pāli *kamma*; Tib. *las*; Jpn. *gō*; "actions")

Buddhist ethical theory is primarily concerned with volitional actions, that is, those actions that result from deliberate choice. Such actions set in motion a series of events that inevitably produce concordant results. These results may be either pleasant or unpleasant, depending on the original volition. In some cases the results of actions are experienced immediately, and in others they are only manifested at a later time. Some karmic results do not accrue until a future life.

karma-mudrā (Tib. *las kyi phyag rgya*; "action seal")

A female tantric consort. In some highest yoga tantra (anuttara-yoga-tantra) practices, yogas involving sexual union (Tib. *sbyor*) are used, and in some traditions of Tibetan Buddhism (e.g. dGe lugs pa) it is said that it is impossible to attain buddhahood without engaging in these practices. The consort must be a person with a high level of attainment and should also have a high level of control over the manipulation of the subtle energies called "winds" (Skt. prāṇa).

karuma o kiru

See Kiriyama, Seiyu; Agonshū.

karuṇā (Pāli *karuṇā*; Tib. *snying rje*; "compassion")

Refers to an attitude of active concern for the sufferings of other sentient beings. It is one of the most important qualities of buddhas and is the motivation behind their pursuit of awakening (bodhi). In Theravāda, it is one of the four "immeasurables" (apramāṇa). It involves developing a feeling of sympathy for countless sentient beings. In Mahāyāna, however, this attitude is viewed as insufficient, and is said to be inferior to the "great compassion" (Skt. *mahākaruṇā*) of bodhisattvas, which extends to *all* sentient beings. In Mahāyāna, buddhas are said to train in both wisdom (prajñā) and compassion, with each balancing and enhancing the other. In Mahāyāna traditions, Avalokiteśvara is said to be the embodiment of the compassion of all buddhas. (*See also* brahma-vihāra.)

kasiṇa ("complete field")

Pāli term for a category of meditative objects used in the Theravāda meditative tradition as bases for developing the ability to enter into meditative absorptions (Pāli *jhāna*; Skt. dhyāna). The ten *kasiṇa* as enumerated in the Pāli canon are: earth, water, fire, wind, blue, yellow, red, white, space (Pāli *ākāsa*; Skt. *ākāśa*), and consciousness (Pāli *viññāna*; Skt. vijñāna). The meditator concentrates one-pointedly on a particular external object as the preparatory image (*parikamma-nimitta*) until it appears even when the eyes are closed (at which point it is called an "acquired image," *uggaha-nimitta*). When one is able to concentrate single-mindedly on the meditative object, one enters into the first *jhāna*.

Kāśyapa (Pāli *Kassapa*; also referred to as Mahākāśyapa)

One of the ten main disciples of Śākyamuni Buddha, said in the Pāli canon to have excelled in ascetic practices and moral uprightness. He was the convenor of the "First Buddhist Council" held at Rājagṛha, at which 500 arhats are said to have recited from memory the teachings of the Buddha. He is also revered in East Asia as the first Indian patriarch of the Ch'an (Jpn. Zen; Kor. Sŏn; Viet. Thiền) tradition. This is based on a story in which the Buddha stood in front of his assembled disciples as if to give a discourse, but instead merely held out a single flower. Most of the audience was perplexed, but Kāśyapa smiled, and the Buddha declared that he had grasped the true import of his teaching, which involves direct experience of truth and is not dependent on words or concepts. This event became paradigmatic for Ch'an, which claims to have inherited this same teaching, passed on directly from mind to mind (Chin. *i-hsin-ch'üan-hsin*; Jpn. ISHIN-DENSHIN) through a succession of masters. The flower incident is reported in a Chinese text entitled *Ta-fan-t'ien-wang-wen-fo-chüeh-i-ching* (Jpn. *Dai-bontennōmombutsu-ketsugi-kyō*) and is referred to in Japanese Zen as *nenge-mishō* (Viet. *niêm-hoa vi-tiếu*, "smiling and twirling a flower"). The story is also example 6 in the WU-MEN-KUAN (Jpn. *Mumonkan*).

Katagiri Rōshi, Dainin (b. 1928)

Japanese ZEN master of the EIHEI-JI lineage of SŌTŌ, who in 1963 moved to the U.S.A. to teach at Zenshu-ji Soto Zen Mission in Los Angeles. He later helped to establish the SAN FRANCISCO ZEN CENTER and Tassajara Mountain Center in California. He has been one of the most influential Zen masters in the West and has trained a number of students who later became teachers themselves.

kaṭhina ("robe offering")

Ceremony performed in THERAVĀDA countries at the end of the rainy-season retreat (mid-October), during which lay-people give new robes to Buddhist monks. This is one of the major opportunities for the laity to earn merit from generous actions (DĀNA). It takes place during the month immediately following the full moon *uposatha* (Skt. POṢADHA) ceremony in October. It generally lasts between one and three days and involves gifts of food, clothing, and other necessities to the SAṂGHA. The highlight of the festival is the actual presentation of robes, in which the laity often form a procession of people carrying gifts, sometimes accompanied by music and other entertainment.

katsu (Chin. *ho*; "shout")

The shout often used by ZEN (Chin. CH'AN) masters to shock their students into direct experience of reality (KENSHŌ or SATORI). According to the tradition, it was first used by MA-TSU TAO-I (Jpn. *Baso Dōitsu*, 709–788). It is mainly associated with RINZAI (Chin. LIN-CHI), a tradition that is famous for its abrupt and confrontational methods, which also include blows with sticks (Jpn. KYOSAKU). It is believed that an awakened master is able to perceive that a student is close to *kenshō* and that the veils of ignorance can be wiped away quickly with the skillful use of such techniques.

Kegon (Chin. *Hua-yen*; Kor. *Hwaŏm*)

Japanese lineage of the Chinese HUA-YEN school, which bases its teachings on the AVATAṂSAKA-SŪTRA. It was introduced to Japan by the Chinese monk Shen-hsiang (Jpn. *Shinshō*) around 740 and was patronized by the emperor SHŌMU (724–748). It became one of the six main Buddhist schools of the Nara period (710–784; the others were: KUSHA, HOSSŌ, JŌJITSU, RITSU, and SANRON). Its main monastery is the Tōdai-ji in Nara.

Keizan Jōkin Zenji (1268–1325)

Founder of Sōji-ji Monastery; he is regarded in the Japanese SŌTŌ tradition as its most important master after DŌGEN ZENJI. He is also the fourth Japanese patriarch (*soshigata*) of Sōtō, and is best known for his *Records of the Transmission of the Lamp* (DENKŌ-

ROKU), which chronicles the transmission of the tradition from KĀŚYAPA to Dōgen.

Kennett Rōshi, Jiyu (Peggy Theresa Kennett, b. 1924)

British-born SŌTŌ Zen master who studied at SŌJI-JI in Japan under Chisan Koho Zenji. In 1970 she became the abbot of Shasta Abbey, and she has taught at the University of California at Berkeley, as well as numerous Zen centers. She is the founder of the Order of Buddhist Contemplatives and author of a number of books, including *The Book of Life* and *How a Zen Buddhist Prepares for Death.*

kenshō (Chin. *chien-hsing*; "awakening," "realization," "enlightenment")

One of the terms used in ZEN (Chin. CH'AN) for direct apprehension of truth. It literally means "seeing nature," and is said to be awareness of one's true nature in an insight that transcends words and conceptual thought. It is equated with SATORI in some contexts, but in others *kenshō* is described as an initial awakening that must be developed through further training, while *satori* is associated with the awakening of BUDDHAS and the patriarchs (*soshigata*) of Zen.

Khema, Ayya (Ilse Ledermann, 1923–1997)

German-born Jewish nun who wrote a number of books on Buddhism, the most popular of which was *Being Nobody, Going Nowhere*, which received the Christmas Humphreys Memorial Award. She was one of the most influential Western meditation teachers, and taught courses in the U.S.A., Australia, and Asia. In 1978 she became the assistant to Ven. Khantipalo at Wat Buddhadhamma in New South Wales.

Khensur Rinpoche

See MKHAN ZUR RIN PO CHE.

Khri Srong lde brtsan (Trisong Detsen, ca. 740–798)

Regarded by the Tibetan Buddhist tradition as the second of the three "religious kings" (*chos rgyal*) of the YAR LUNG DYNASTY who worked to establish Buddhism in Tibet. He is said to have been a physical emanation of MAÑJUŚRĪ and is credited with inviting the Indian scholar-monk ŚĀNTARAKṢITA and the tantric master PADMASAMBHAVA to Tibet. The three established the first monastery in Tibet, called BSAM YAS (Samye).

khubilgan

See SPRUL SKU.

Khuddaka-nikāya ("Lesser Discourses")

The fifth part of the Pāli Sutta-piṭaka (Skt. SŪTRA-PIṬAKA), comprising fifteen sections. It contains a number of important works, including the DHAMMAPADA, the *Udāna*, the *Sutta-nipāta*, the THERAGĀTHĀ, the THERĪGĀTHĀ, and the JĀTAKA.

kiṃnara (Pāli *kinnara*; Tib. *mi 'am ci*; lit. "what sort of man?")

The musicians of Kubera, with human bodies and horses' heads (or horses' bodies and human heads), described as being human and yet not human.

kinhin ("walking meditation")

Japanese term for the walking meditation used in ZEN. After a session of seated meditation (ZAZEN), practitioners commonly walk in a line, with heads down, looking at the ground. This practice is said to refresh the body while maintaining the mind's concentration on meditation.

Kiriyama, Seiyu (b. 1921)

Founder of AGONSHŪ, a Japanese Buddhist sect that claims to have revived pure and original Buddhism as taught in its earliest texts. Kiriyama asserts that he received a vision of Kannon (Skt. AVALOKITEŚVARA) in 1970, during which he was told that the problems of most people (including himself) are caused by the malicious actions of the dead, who plague the living unless the karmic ties that allow them to do so are cut off (referred to in Agonshū as *karuma o kiru*). Subsequent to this vision, he founded a new movement that emphasized worship of Kannon. His followers also commonly engage in ascetic practices designed to cut off KARMA, as well as meditation, reciting Buddhist texts, and standing under waterfalls in order to cleanse themselves. In 1978 he began calling his organization Agonshū, claiming that its doctrines and practices derive from the ĀGAMAS.

kleśa (Pāli *kilesa*; Tib. *nyon mongs*; Chin. *fan-nao*; "affliction," "defilement")

Negative mental factors that lead beings to engage in non-virtuous (*akuśala*) actions, which produce karmic results leading to rebirth in cyclic existence (SAṂSĀRA). In Buddhist meditation literature there is a sixfold and a tenfold list. The six are: (1) desire (*rāga*); (2) anger (*pratigha*) (3) boastful pride (*māna*); (4) ignorance (AVIDYĀ); (5) doubt (*vicikitsā*); and (6) wrong views (DṚṢṬI). The tenfold list has similar elements, and it adds: obscuration (*moha*); laxity (*styāna*); excitement (*auddhatya*); shamelessness (*ahrīka*); and lack of conscience (*anapatrāpya*). They are weakened through meditative practice, and are completely eliminated by ARHATS.

kLong chen rab 'byams pa (Longchen Rabjampa, 1308–1364)

One of the most influential masters of the RNYING MA PA (Nyingmapa) order of TIBETAN BUDDHISM, particularly important in the RDZOGS CHEN (*dzogchen*, "great perfection") tradition. Among his best-known works are the *Seven Treasuries* (*mDzod bdun*) and the *Fourfold Innermost Essence* (*sNying thig ya bzhi*).

kLong chen snying thig (*Longchen Nyingtig*; *Heart Sphere of the Great Expanse*)

An important two-volume collection of "treasure texts" (GTER MA) "discovered" by the 18th century Tibetan "treasure discoverer" (GTER STON) 'JIGS MED GLING PA (Jigme Lingpa, 1730–1798), which have been widely influential in the RNYING MA PA (Nyingmapa) order.

knowledge and awareness

See BLO RIGS.

kōan (Chin. *kung-an*; Kor. *kong'an*; Viet. *công-án*; "public case")

Japanese term for enigmatic cases whose purport cannot be discerned by conceptual and analytical thinking. Their solution requires that students directly and intuitively perceive the true nature of reality. They are commonly used in the ZEN (Chin. CH'AN; Kor. SŎN) tradition and are particularly important in the RINZAI (Chin. LIN-CHI; Kor. *Imje*) school. They are generally derived from a story or phrase attributed to a Zen master whose meaning the student must discern and explain without recourse to discursive thought. The most famous of these – commonly used at the beginning of Zen training – is the MU KŌAN, in which the Chinese master CHAO-CHOU (Jpn. *Jōshū*) is asked whether or not a dog has the buddha-nature, to which he replies, "Mu!"

Kōbō Daishi

See KŪKAI.

ko-i ("matching concepts")

A translation style adopted for early Chinese renderings of Buddhist texts, which involved using indigenous Chinese terms for Sanskrit words. Most commonly Taoist concepts were equated with Sanskrit technical terms that were thought to have similar connotations. Since the two traditions were very different, this method led to inexact translations, and the conflation of Buddhist and Taoist concepts helped to introduce a number of Taoist notions into CHINESE BUDDHISM. The reason for adopting the *ko-i* method was to aid in the assimilation of the foreign ideas and practices of Buddhism in China. According to Chinese tradition, it was invented by Chu Fa-yen (ca. fourth century). It was used by a number of translators, such as HUI-YÜAN (334–416) and KUMĀRAJĪVA (344–413), but strongly condemned by TAO-AN (312–385), who favored a translation system based on more precise terminology.

Kōmeitō ("Clean Government Party")

Japanese political party associated with the SŌKA GAKKAI, which traces itself back to NICHIREN (1222–1282). Ironically, despite its name and stated intention of bringing ethical conduct into Japanese politics, it has been involved in a number of high-profile scandals.

Könchok Gyelpo

See DKON MCHOG RGYAL PO.

kong'an (Chin. *kung-an*; Jpn. KŌAN; Viet. *công-án*; "public case")

Korean term for problem cases derived from stories and phrases of great CH'AN masters (Kor. *hwadu*; Chin. HUA-T'OU), which cannot be solved by rational and discursive thought. In Korean SŎN, unlike most of Japanese ZEN, it is widely believed that "all *kong'an* are contained in one," and so it is common for a student to remain with one *hwadu* throughout his or her life, rather than (as is common in Japan) progressing through a series of supposedly deeper *kong'an*. The one *kong'an* is most often CH'AO-CHOU'S "MU KŌAN," from a *hwadu* in which he is asked whether or not a dog has the buddha-nature, to which he replies, "Mu!"

Korean Buddhism

According to traditional Korean accounts, Buddhism was introduced to the Korean Peninsula in 372, when the emperor Fu-chien of the Former Ch'in dynasty (r. 351–394) sent a delegation to Koguryŏ (earliest of the "Three Kingdoms," the other two being Paekche and Silla). This was led by the monk Shun-tao (Kor. *Sundo*), who met directly with Sosurim (r. 371–384), the Koguryŏ king. He brought Buddhist images and texts. Shortly thereafter, the Serindian monk Mālānanda (Kor. *Maranant'a*) traveled to Paekche and was successful in interesting the royal court in Buddhism. After these two missions, Buddhism quickly grew in Korea, and the rulers of Koguryŏ and Paekche had temples built and supported the propagation of Buddhism among their subjects. Buddhism was introduced to Silla in the early sixth century, and largely due to the influence of the aristocracy of the newly conquered states of Koguryŏ and Paekche, its influence grew rapidly.

During the Three Kingdoms period (late fourth century–668), imported Chinese schools dominated in intellectual circles, and a number of Korean monks traveled to China to study. Korea also was a major Buddhist center in its own right, and according to traditional

Memorial carvings commemorating a deceased general and a nun from Buguisa Monastery, North Kyŏngsang. The inscription on the nun's memorial indicates that she has led a long and happy life, and has no fear of her impending death.

sources Buddhism was first introduced to Japan by representatives of Paekche in 552. During this period, both in Japan and Korea, Buddhism was widely seen as being a force for protection of the state, an idea referred to as *hoguk pulgyo* ("state-protection Buddhism").

During the Unified Silla period (668–918), Buddhism became widely established throughout Korea. Originally the smallest and weakest of the three kingdoms, with the help of T'ang China Silla managed to consolidate power over the whole Korean peninsula. The Unified Silla period was a time of intellectual productivity in Buddhist circles, and some of Korea's great early figures – for instance WŎNHYO (617–686), ŬISANG (625–702) and Chajang (fl. seventh century) – were among the leaders of this intellectual ferment. The first established Buddhist schools were mainly scholastic in character and thus appealed primarily to the educated elite, but during this period a number of Buddhist monks began to spread the DHARMA among the common people. Particularly important in this regard were Wŏnhyo, Hyesuk, and Hyegong. Through their efforts, Buddhism spread to the masses and developed a broad base.

After King T'aejo (r. 918–943) initiated the Koryŏ period (918–1392) following the collapse of Silla, SŎN became the dominant Buddhist school in Korea after being designated the state religion. Government support of Buddhism was generous during his reign and continued with his descendants, but at times became so excessive that it depleted the treasury and fostered corruption within the monastic order. This situation precipitated an anti-Buddhist movement, led by neo-Confucians, which resulted in persecutions of Buddhism in the succeeding Chosŏn period (1392–1909). During this time Buddhism's fortunes declined noticeably. Numbers of monks and nuns were reduced, and at one point there were only thirty-six operating temples in the whole country (at the end of the Koryŏ there had been several hundred). Buddhist establishments were forbidden in the cities, and monks and nuns were chased deep into the mountains. A turning-point in public perceptions of Buddhism came in the late sixteenth century, when armies of "righteous monks" (*ŭisa*) formed the vanguard of Korean resistance to the invasions of the Japanese general Hideyoshi Toyotomi (from 1592 to 1598). Led by the monk Sŏsan Hyujŏng (1520–1604), they waged a successful guerrilla war against the invaders.

Buddhism's travails continued during the Japanese occupation of Korea from 1910 to 1945. The Japanese authorities lifted the restrictions preventing the monastic order from operating in the cities, and indigenous traditions came into competition with missionaries of Japanese Buddhist traditions. During this time the Japanese practice of married Buddhist clergy was introduced to Korea, but this has been generally rejected in recent decades (though only after a great deal of controversy and violence). In the intervening decades, Sŏn has consolidated its position as the dominant Buddhist tradition in Korea. Its largest order is CHOGYE, which controls around ninety percent of Korea's operating monasteries. During the twentieth century, Buddhism has also come into direct competition with aggressive Christian proselytizing. After a long period of decline, however, Korean Buddhism today is on the rebound, and according to government estimates twenty-five percent of the Korean population consider themselves to be Buddhists (twenty-five percent identify themselves as Christians, and the remaining fifty percent state that they are indifferent to religion).

Kornfield, Jack

American lay *vipassanā* teacher who trained with AJAHN CHAH and S. N. GOENKA. CHÖGYAM TRUNGPA invited him to teach THERAVĀDA meditation at NAROPA INSTITUTE in the early 1970s, and for several years after that he taught meditation in a variety of places all over the world. He co-founded the Insight Meditation Society in Barre, MA, U.S.A., where he is one of the main teachers. He has published a number of books, including *Living Buddhist Masters* and *Dharma Talks* (with JOSEPH GOLDSTEIN).

Körösi, Csoma Sándor (1784–1842)

Transylvanian scholar who traveled to Ladakh in search of the origins of the Hungarian people. He believed that these origins lay in Central Asia among the Uighurs (and thought that their language was related to Hungarian). In order to trace Hungarian origins, he traveled throughout Central Asia and the Himalayan region, and he conducted research in Leh for almost two years. Although he never found records relating to Hungarians, during his studies he produced a seminal Tibetan–English dictionary and grammar. He also brought a wealth of information about Tibetan culture to Europe, and is widely regarded as the father of Tibetan Studies in the West.

kriyā-tantra (Tib. *bya ba'i rgyud*; "action tantra")

One of the four divisions of TANTRA texts, according to Tibetan doxographers. Action tantras are said to have been taught for meditators who require external activities. The practices of this type of tantra emphasize purification and external ritual activities of worship, rather than internal yogas. (*See also* CARYĀ-TANTRA; YOGA-TANTRA; ANUTTARA-YOGA-TANTRA.)

kṣānti (Pāli *khanti*; Tib. *bzod pa*; "patience")

A general term for an attitude of forebearance. In MAHĀYĀNA it is the third of the "perfections" (PĀRAMITĀ) that a BODHISATTVA cultivates on the path to buddhahood. It is developed on the third "bodhisattva level" (BHŪMI), and involves deepening an attitude of equanimity that is able to endure insults and hardships without becoming discouraged.

Kṣitigarbha (Tib. *Sa'i snying po*; Chin. *Ti-ts'ung*; Jpn. *Jizō*; Viet. *Địa-tạng*; "Earth Womb")

An important figure in MAHĀYĀNA Buddhism, a BODHISATTVA who is said to have been entrusted by ŚĀKYAMUNI BUDDHA with the task of helping all the beings in the six destinies (GATI) until the birth of the next buddha. In contemporary Japan he is seen as the protector of children who have met untimely deaths, including aborted fetuses. In Japanese cemeteries for fetuses there is generally a statue of Kṣitigarbha (Jpn. *Jizō*), who is depicted as a monk with a staff in his right hand and a jewel in his left, and wearing a bib under his neck.

Kuan-yin

See AVALOKITEŚVARA.

K'uei-chi (632–682)

The main student of HSÜAN-TSANG, who is credited with founding the FA-HSIANG school. Fa-hsiang was widely influential during the lifetimes of Hsüan-tsang and K'uei-chi, but later waned, mainly as a result of the anti-Buddhist persecution that began in 845.

Kuei-shan Ling-yu (771–853)

Chinese CH'AN master, dharma-successor of PAI-CHANG HUAI-HAI (Jpn. *Hyakujō Ekai*, 720–814), who together with his student YANG-SHAN HUI-CHI (Jpn. *Kyōzan Ejaku*, 807–883) co-founded the Kuei-yang (Jpn. *Igyō*) school, one of the "five houses" of Ch'an.

Kūkai (Kōbō Daishi, 774–835)

Founder of the Japanese SHINGON (Chin. CHEN-YEN) school, the most influential tradition of esoteric Buddhism (Jpn. *mikkyō*; Chin. MI-TSUNG) in Japan. He traveled to China with SAICHŌ in 804 and studied Chen-yen (the Chinese tantric tradition) with Hui-kuo (Jpn. *Keika*). Upon his return to Japan in 805 he established himself as a teacher of esoteric Buddhism. He founded a monastery on Mount Kōya in 810, which remains the headquarters of Shingon today.

kuksa ("national master")

A title instituted during the Koryŏ dynasty (937–1382) and awarded to the most prominent members of the Korean Buddhist monastic order.

Kumārajīva (Jpn. Rajū, 334–413; "Soul Prince")

Influential teacher and translator of Indian Buddhist texts into Chinese. Son of a royal family from Kucha, he traveled to Ch'ang-an in 401 and became the leader of a team of translators. Together they translated a number of important Buddhist Sanskrit texts. He is also credited with establishing the SAN-LUN school, which is derived from the Indian MADHYAMAKA tradition.

kung-an

See KŌAN; KONG'AN.

Kusan Sunim (1909–1981)

Korean SŎN monk, born in Namwon to a farming family. At the age of twenty-six he chanted Buddhist MANTRAS during a period of illness, and when he was cured decided to become a monk. He studied under Hyobong Sunin at SONGGWANGSA, and at the age of thirty-one received monastic ordination at TONGDOSA. From 1962 to 1966 he served as abbot of Tonghwasa, and in 1967 he founded the Bul-il International Meditation Center at Songgwangsa as a place for foreigners to practice meditation. He was one of the most influential Sŏn masters of the twentieth century, and had a significant impact on the CHOGYE order. He is particularly known for emphasizing the centrality of meditative practice and considering study of scriptures to be of secondary importance. His books include *The Way of Korean Zen* and *Nine Mountains*.

Kusha (Chin. *Chu-she*)

Japanese Buddhist school whose doctrines are based on VASUBANDHU's *Treasury of Higher Doctrine* (ABHIDHARMA-KOŚA), which was translated into Chinese by PARAMĀRTHA and HSÜAN-TSANG. In China it only existed as a separate school during the T'ang dynasty. It was brought to Japan in the seventh and eighth centuries. It is a realistic school that conceives of phenomena as being composed of subtle elements called DHARMAS, and much of the school's philosophy is devoted to categorization of them.

Kuśinagara (Pāli *Kusinārā*)

According to Buddhist tradition, the town in northern India where ŚĀKYAMUNI BUDDHA died. Today it is one of the major pilgrimage sites of Buddhism.

kyabgön

See SKYABS MGON.

kyabje

See SKYABS RJE.

Kyojong ("Textual School")

During the reign of King Sejong (r. 1418–1450), fourth ruler of the Chosŏn dynasty, the number of Buddhist schools in Korea was reduced to two. The Kyojong school brought together elements of the HWAŎM (Chin. HUA-YEN), Pŏpsang (Chin. FA-HSIANG), and Sammon (Chin. SAN-LUN) traditions. The other major school was SŎNJONG ("Meditation School"), which combined the Kyeyul (Chin. LÜ-TSUNG; Skt. VINAYA), Chŏnt'ae (Chin. T'IEN-T'AI), and SŎN (Chin. CH'AN) traditions. These two remained the only official schools of Buddhism in Korea until 1935.

kyosaku ("wake-up stick")

A flat stick about one meter in length, used in ZEN monasteries to help students maintain alertness during periods of sitting meditation (ZAZEN). Although the stick is commonly applied vigorously to the backs of students who drift off, it is not conceived as punishment, but rather as an aid to concentration. A monitor who patrols the meditation room looks for students who lean slightly forward, indicating that their attention is wandering, and he taps them on the shoulder, after which they bend forward and are given three sharp raps on the back.

Kyŏmik (fl. fifth century)

A Korean monk of the Paekche kingdom who traveled to India, where he studied Sanskrit and concentrated on the study of monastic discipline (Skt. VINAYA; Kor. *kyeyul*). He returned to Paekche in 526, along with the Indian monk DEVADATTA (Kor. *Paedalta*) and several recensions of the *vinaya* and some ABHIDHARMA texts. Together with a team of monks, he translated the texts into Korean, and is widely credited with establishing the Vinaya tradition (Kyeyul chong) in Korea.

L

la Vallée Poussin, Louis de (1869–1929)

Belgian scholar of Buddhism, best known for his monumental translation of the Chinese version of VASUBANDHU's ABHIDHARMA-KOŚA. He also published a number of other influential translations and thematic studies. He spent most of his career at the University of Ghent, and in 1921 founded the Société Belge d'Études orientales.

Lalitavistara (Tib. *rGya cher rol pa'i mdo*; *Extensive Sport*)

Sanskrit text believed by scholars to have originated in the SARVĀSTIVĀDA tradition, but later revised with the addition of MAHĀYĀNA elements. It purports to tell the story of ŚĀKYAMUNI BUDDHA's two most recent lives, his decision to be reborn in India and attain buddhahood, and the story of his final life up to the event of his first sermon.

lam 'bras (*lamdre*; "path and result")

Tibetan term for a meditative system that forms the basis of the training of the SA SKYA PA (Sakyapa) order of TIBETAN BUDDHISM. It is a comprehensive vision of Buddhist practice, based on the HEVAJRA-TANTRA. In this system, path and result are viewed as being inseparably linked: the result subsumes the path – since the latter leads to the former – and the path subsumes the result – since it is the means by which it is attained. The practice is traced back to the Indian MAHĀSIDDDHA Virūpa, whose *Vajra Verses* (Skt. *Vajra-gāthā*; Tib. *rDo rje tshig rkang*) is considered one of its seminal texts. The main outlines of the system were developed by Sa chen Kun dga' snying po (Sachen Günga Nyingpo, 1092–1158).

lam rim (Skt. *paṭha-krama*; "stages of the path")

Tibetan term for a genre of literature found in all orders of TIBETAN BUDDHISM, the oldest example of which is SGAM PO PA's (Gampopa, 1079–1153) *Jewel Ornament of Liberation* (*Thar pa rin po che'i rgyan*). *Lam rim* is also central to the meditative system of the DGE LUGS PA (Gelukpa) order. The *lam rim* tradition conceives of the path to buddhahood in hierarchically ordered stages, and trainees are expected to master each stage before moving on. The meditative training involves progressively eliminating negative mental states and tendencies while simultaneously engaging in virtuous actions and training in concordant attitudes. TSONG KHA PA (Tsong Khapa, 1357–1419), the founder of dGe lugs pa, wrote several works of this type, the most comprehensive being his *Great Exposition of the Stages of the Path* (*Lam rim chen mo*).

lama

See BLA MA.

Lamaism

Term coined by Western scholars to describe the prevalent form of Buddhism in Tibet and the Himalayan region. The designation is generally rejected by the practitioners of the tradition, however, because a common implication of the term is the notion that TIBETAN BUDDHISM is not "true Buddhism," but rather a debased aberration in which human clerics (BLA MA) are worshiped and the austere meditative practices of early Buddhism have been replaced by idolatry, superstition, and magic. It is rarely seen in recent publications on Tibetan Buddhism.

Lamaist Buddhist Monastery of North America

The first Tibetan Buddhist monastery in North America, founded by the Kalmyk Mongolian DGE LUGS PA (Gelukpa) dGe bshes dBang rgyal (GESHE WANGYAL, 1901–1983) in Freewood Acres, NJ.

Lamayuru (Tib. *bLa ma g.Yung drung dgon pa*)

The oldest Buddhist monastery in the Ladakh and Zanskar region of the Indian Himālayas. According to legend, NĀROPA (ca. 1016–1100) selected the site and magically drained a lake that filled the valley. It is a 'BRUG PA BKA' BRGYUD PA (Drukpa Kagyüpa) monastery, which houses several hundred monks.

lamdre

See LAM 'BRAS.

Lamotte, Étienne (1903–1983)

Belgian scholar of Buddhism who spent most of his academic career at the Université de Louvain and who produced some of the most influential studies and translations of Indian Buddhism, including a monumental translation of the *Mahāprajñāpāramitā-śāstra*, attributed to Nāgārjuna, and his *Histoire du Bouddhisme Indien.*

Lâm-tê̂ (Chin. *Lin-chi*)

Vietnamese lineage of the LIN-CHI tradition of CH'AN. It was brought to Vietnam in the seventeenth century by

bLa ma g. yung drung (Lamayuru) Monastery, Ladakh.

Nguyên-Thiều (d. 1712). In contemporary Vietnam, it is the largest Buddhist order.

Lang Darma

See GLANG DAR MA.

Laṅkāvatāra-sūtra (Tib. *Lang kar gshegs pa'i mdo*; Chin. *Ju-leng-chia ching*; Jpn. *Ryōga-kyō*; Viet. *Lăng-già*; *Descent into Lanka Sūtra*)

Indian MAHĀYĀNA text that purports to be a discourse by ŚĀKYAMUNI BUDDHA in response to questions by the bodhisattva Mahāmati. It discusses a wide range of doctrines, including a number of teachings associated with the YOGĀCĀRA school (though it does not seem to have been particularly influential in Yogācāra). Among these is the theory of eight consciousnesses, the most basic of which is the ĀLAYA-VIJÑĀNA ("basis-consciousness"), which is comprised of the "seeds" (*bīja*) of volitional activities. The text is particularly important in TATHĀGATA-GARBHA ("embryo of the *tathāgata*") thought because of its assertion that all sentient beings already possess the essence of buddhahood, which is merely uncovered through meditative practice. This text was highly influential in East Asia, particularly in the CH'AN and ZEN traditions.

Laotian Buddhism

Laos is a small, landlocked country east of the Mekong River, surrounded by larger neighbors (China, Thailand, Burma, Cambodia, and Vietnam), which has periodically been overrun as a consequence of the region's frequent conflicts. During its early period, it was the center of the Nan-chao kingdom, which by 800 had conquered areas of Burma and established contacts with India. Later, however, it was taken over by the Khmers, who probably introduced Buddhism and Brahmanism to the region. The first Laotian state was established in the fourteenth century with the help of the Khmers. Lao chronicles report that king Jayavarman Parmesvara (1327–1353) helped Phi Fa and Fa Ngum in establishing the independent kingdom of Lān Chāng and that Buddhism was adopted as the state religion. There are inscriptions at Wat Keo in Lua Prabang stating that three Sinhala monks traveled to Lān Chāng as missionaries, bringing THERAVĀDA Buddhism. From the fourteenth century onward, the region came under Thai control, and subsequently the Thai form of Theravāda was introduced to Laos. It remains the dominant religion in the country. Thai hegemony lasted until the late nineteenth century, when the French annexed the area to their colonial empire. In 1975 the communist Pathet Lao took power, which prompted many monks to flee the country. A substantial number remained, however, and the SAṂGHA has largely managed to reach accommodation with the government. The future of Lao Buddhism is unclear, but since 1994 the country's improving economy has led to increasing prosperity for the *saṃgha*.

Laughing Buddha

See PU-TAI.

lCang skya Khutukhtu

(Janggya Hutukhtu)

The major reincarnate lama (SPRUL SKU) of Inner Mongolia. The first was Ngag dbang blo bzang chos ldan (Ngawang Losang Chöden, 1642–1714). His recognized reincarnation, Rol pa'i rdo rje (Rolbe Dorje, 1717–1786), studied in Tibet and became one of the most influential DGE LUGS PA (Gelukpa) scholars of the time.

Lesser Vehicle

See HĪNAYĀNA.

liberation

See NIRVĀṆA.

Lin-chi (Jpn. *Rinzai*; Kor. *Imje*; Viet. Lâm-tế)

Tradition of Chinese CH'AN founded by LIN-CHI I-HSÜAN (d. 866), which emphasises the use of *kung-an* (Jpn. KŌAN) and abrupt methods such as shouting at students or hitting them in order to shock them into awareness of their true nature. It was one of the traditional "five houses of Ch'an," and was widely influential in China. It was brought to Japan by EISAI ZENJI (1141–1215), and today the RINZAI is one of the two traditions of ZEN still operating as a distinctive school in Japan (the other being SŌTŌ).

Lin-chi I-hsüan (Jpn. *Rinzai Gigen*, d. 866)

Chinese CH'AN master, founder of the LIN-CHI school and dharma-successor of Huang-po Hsi-yun (Jpn. *Ōbaku Kiun*, d. 850).

Lindtner, Christian

Danish scholar of Buddhism, best known for his influential work on Madhyamaka and the Epistemological tradition. His books include *Nāgārjuniana* (1982) and *Miscellanea Buddhica* (1985).

Liu-tsu-ta-shih fa-pao-t'an-ching (Jpn. *Rokuso daishi hōbōdangyō*; *Platform Sūtra of the Sixth Patriarch*)

Commonly referred to as the "*Platform Sūtra*" (Chin. *T'an-ching*; Jpn. *Dangyō*), this is one of the most influential works of the Ch'an/Zen tradition. It purports to be a discourse delivered by the sixth patriarch of Ch'an, HUI-NENG (638–713), at the Ta-fan Temple. It is divided into two parts: the first describes his life, and the second contains his teachings on CH'AN practice and doctrine.

lo-han

See ARHAT.

Lokakṣema (ca. second century C.E.)

Scythian monk who traveled to China in the second century C.E. and became an important translator of Buddhist texts. He worked with AN SHIH-KAO in Loyang for twenty years. One of his most important works was a partial translation of the *Eight Thousand Line Perfection of Wisdom Sūtra* (AṢṬASĀHASRIKĀ-PRAJÑĀ-PĀRAMITĀ-SŪTRA).

Lokamitra, Dharmachari (Jeremy Goody)

British Buddhist and member of the FRIENDS OF THE WESTERN BUDDHIST ORDER (FWBO) who was one of the founding members of the TRAILOKYA BAUDDHA MAHASANGHA SAHAYAKA GANA (TBSMG), an organization based in India that works among the former Untouchables who followed B. R. AMBEDKAR in converting to Buddhism.

Longchen Nyingtig

See KLONG CHEN SNYING THIG.

Longchen Rabjampa

See KLONG CHEN RAB 'BYAMS PA.

lotus

See PADMA.

lotus position

See PADMĀSANA.

Lotus Sūtra

See SADDHARMA-PUṆḌARĪKA-SŪTRA.

Lumbinī

The grove located between KAPILAVASTU and Devadaha where ŚĀKYAMUNI BUDDHA was born. According to legend, his mother, MĀYĀ, decided to travel to her parents' house to give birth to her son, but when she arrived at Lumbinī she went into labor. In hagiographical accounts of the Buddha's life, it is said that she gave birth standing up, with her arm against a tree, and the future Buddha stepped out of her side. Today it is an important Buddhist pilgrimage site.

Lung-men

A group of grottos near Lo-yang in the Hunan province of China, the construction of which began in 494, near the beginning of the Northern Wei dynasty. The massive complex has 2,100 caves, 750 niches, 40 stone pagodas, and around 100,000 statues.

Lü-tsung (Jpn. RITSU-SHŪ; Kor. *Kyeyul-chong*; "Monastic Discipline School")

Chinese tradition founded by Tao-hsüan (596–667), which focused on monastic discipline (VINAYA). It was based on the DHARMAGUPTAKA Vinaya, which was translated into Chinese by Buddhayaśas and Chu Fo-nien in 412 and referred to in China as "the *vinaya* in four parts" (*ssu-fen lü*). This *vinaya* contains 250 rules for monks and 348 for nuns. Although the DHARMAGUPTAKAS were considered to be a "HĪNAYĀNA" school in East Asia, this *vinaya* became the standard code of monastic discipline in China, Korea, Japan, and Tibet.

M

Ma gcig lab kyi sgron ma (Machik Lapgi Drönma, 1055–1145)

A student of Pha dam pa sangs rgyas (Padampa Sangye, ca. eleventh–twelfth century) who is best known for developing the practice of *gcod* (*chö*, "cutting off"). This is based on the doctrines of the "Perfection of Wisdom" (PRAJÑĀ-PĀRAMITĀ) sūtras and involves practices designed to destroy attachment to the notion of "self." Central to the system of *gcod* are visualizations in which one imagines that one's body is cut up and devoured by demons, which is believed to illustrate its impermanence graphically and to lead to a sense of detachment from physical things. According to traditional biographies, Ma gcig was born an Indian brahman male near Vārāṇasī. He converted to Buddhism, but after a debate with other brahmans he was urged to flee the country by a ḌĀKINĪ. He separated his consciousness from his body and transferred it into a female body in Tibet, who was named Ma gcig lab kyi sgron ma. She married a tantric yogin and later gave birth to three sons and two daughters. After receiving tantric instructions from Pha dam pa and his student sKyo ston bsod nams bla ma (Gyodön Sönam Lama), she built a hermitage, where she spent the rest of her life. She died at the age of ninety-five.

Madhyamaka (Tib. dBu ma pa'i lugs; "Middle Way School")

Indian MAHĀYĀNA Buddhist school whose doctrines are based on the notion that all phenomena are empty (*śūnya*) of inherent existence (SVABHĀVA). It developed the doctrines of the "Perfection of Wisdom" (PRAJÑĀ-PĀRAMITĀ) literature. NĀGĀRJUNA (ca. second century C.E.) is considered to be the founder of the tradition, and his *Fundamental Verses on the Middle Way* (MŪLAMADHYAMAKA-KĀRIKĀ) is its most influential text. (*See also* BHAVYA; BUDDHAPĀLITA; CANDRAKĪRTI; PRĀSAṄGIKA-MADHYAMAKA; SVĀTANTRIKA-MADHYAMAKA.)

madhyama-pratipad (Pāli *majjhima-paṭipadā*; Tib. *dbu ma'i lam*; "middle way")

The doctrine attributed to ŚĀKYAMUNI BUDDHA that rejects the extremes of hedonistic self-indulgence on the one hand and extreme asceticism on the other. The Buddha taught that one should follow a middle path between these two. In later Buddhist traditions, it was extended to other areas, including philosophical views.

mae chī (or *chī phā khāw*)

Term for Thai female renunciants who take the eight (or ten) precepts for lay Buddhists but also observe many of the rules for novice nuns outlined in the VINAYA. The term is derived from the Pāli word *pabbajitā*, "one who has gone forth (from the home life into homelessness)." Their position in Thai society is ambiguous, as they are not recognized as nuns either by the SAṂGHA or by most of the laity and are not able to take full monastic ordination because the *bhikkhunī* lineage disappeared in THERAVĀDA countries centuries ago. They generally wear white robes and shave their heads and eyebrows, and like monks they avoid eating after noon and do not wear perfume or jewelry.

Māgha Pūjā

Festival celebrated in THERAVĀDA countries, which commemorates the Buddha's miraculous gathering of 1,250 disciples at Veluvana Mahāvihāra in RĀJAGṚHA.

Mahābodhi Society

Organization founded in 1881 by the Sri Lankan Buddhist activist ANAGĀRIKA DHARMAPĀLA (1864–1933), the original aim of which was to re-establish Buddhist control over BODHGAYĀ. The organization is still active today and has branches all over the world.

Mahākāla (Tib. *Nag po chen po*; Chin. *Ta-hei wang*; Jpn. *Daikoku*; Mon. *Yeke gara*; "Great Black One")

Wrathful aspect of AVALOKITEŚVARA. He is considered by Mongolians to be the country's patron buddha, and in Tibet is viewed as a "dharma-protector" (Tib. *chos skyong*; Skt. DHARMA-PĀLA) and as a tutelary deity (Tib. YI DAM; Skt. *iṣṭa-devatā*). In Japan he is associated with good luck. Iconographically, in Tibetan and Mongolian representations he is shown with black skin, a buffalo head, and six arms, and is often surrounded by fire.

Mahākāśyapa

See KĀŚYAPA.

Mahāmāyā

See MĀYĀ.

mahāmudrā (Tib. *phyag rgya chen po*; "great seal")

Meditation system found in all orders of TIBETAN BUDDHISM, but particularly associated with the BKA' BRGYUD PA (Kagyüpa), in which it is considered to be the quintessence of all Buddhist teachings and practices. It is not found in books or words, but rather in direct, personal realization of truth. Its central focus is direct apprehension of the luminous and empty nature of mind, which leads to the realization that all phenomena are creations of mind. In the language of the system, one recognizes the undifferentiability of appearance (Tib. *snang ba*; Skt. *ābhāsa*) and emptiness (Tib. *stong pa nyid*; Skt. ŚŪNYATĀ).

Mahāparinibbāna-sutta (*Discourse of the Great Final Release*)

Pāli text that purports to recount ŚĀKYAMUNI BUDDHA's last days and final entry into NIRVĀṆA (*parinibbāna*), as well as the immediate aftermath, including the cremation of his body and the distribution of relics. It is included in the DĪGHA-NIKĀYA and presents a vision of the Buddha as a human teacher who lived a human lifespan, unlike the MAHĀYĀNA text MAHĀPARINIRVĀṆA-SŪTRA, which is very different in tone and content.

Mahāparinirvāṇa-sūtra (Tib. *Yongs su mya ngan las 'das pa chen po'i mdo*; Chin. *Ta-pan-nieh-p'an-ching*; Jpn. *Nehangyō*; Viet. *Niết-bàn*; *Discourse of the Great Final Release*)

Sanskrit title of a MAHĀYĀNA text that is extant only in Chinese and Tibetan, which is very different from the Pāli MAHĀPARINIBBĀNA-SUTTA in tone and content. The Mahāyāna text, purportedly spoken on the occasion of ŚĀKYAMUNI's death, is an important source in East Asia for the notion that the buddha-nature is present in all beings.

Mahāprajāpatī (Pāli *Mahāpajapatī*)

ŚĀKYAMUNI BUDDHA's stepmother, who married his father ŚUDDHODANA and raised him after his mother MĀYĀ (Mahāprajāpatī's sister) died seven days after his birth. According to the *Cullavagga* of the VINAYA-PIṬAKA, she was responsible for convincing the Buddha to start an ordination lineage for women, and herself became the first Buddhist nun (Pāli *bhikkhunī*; Skt. *bhikṣuṇī*).

Mahāsāṃghika (Tib. *dGe 'dun phal chen po'i sde*; "Great Assembly School")

A group of monks who are thought to have been involved in the first sectarian schism in the Buddhist community, some time after the "second Buddhist council," held at VAIŚĀLĪ. They apparently propounded more liberal doctrines than their main rival group, the STHAVIRAS ("Elders"), who took a conservative approach to monastic discipline and doctrinal interpretation. The Mahāsāṃghikas apparently conceived of the Buddha as a supramundane being, while the Sthaviras emphasized that he was only a human being (though an exceptional one). Some scholars believe that the Mahāsāṃghikas may have been a proto-MAHĀYĀNA school, because they adopted some doctrines that later became associated with MAHĀYĀNA, such as the idea that a BODHISATTVA may voluntarily choose to be reborn in lower realms of existence in order to benefit others. This school later split into a number of sub-sects, including the Ekavyāvahārikas, Gokullikas, Bahuśrutīyas, Lokkotaravādins, Caitikas, and Prajñāptivādins.

Mahāsena (r. 334–362)

King of Sri Lanka who patronized MAHĀYĀNA monks and who is reported to have razed the THERAVĀDA stronghold MAHĀVIHĀRA and built a new Mahāyāna monastery called JETAVANA (2) on the site. His son Śrīmeghavaṇṇa, however, decided to restore the Mahāvihāra and to reinstate Theravāda as the dominant form of Buddhism on the island.

Mahāsi Sayādaw (1904–1982)

Burmese monk and meditation teacher whose approach diverged from the traditional meditative program in THERAVĀDA Buddhism by dispensing with the standard preliminaries of *appanā samādhi* and *samatha* (Skt. ŚAMATHA) and instead teaching his students to practice insight meditation (*vipassanā*; Skt. VIPAŚYANĀ) intensively during extended periods of meditative retreat. In his system, meditators learn to label their immediate experiences carefully and cultivate "momentary concentration" (*khaṇika samādhi*), in which they become aware of the arising of momentary phenomena. He also differed from mainstream Theravāda by de-emphasizing ritual, merit-making, and other popular aspects of Theravāda Buddhism, and by encouraging laypeople to practice meditation.

mahāsiddha (Tib. *grub thob chen po*; "great adept")

Tantric masters who are particularly important in VAJRAYĀNA traditions, renowned for the magical abilities (SIDDHI) they develop through their meditative practice. The best known are a group of eighty-four, who are said to have come from all social classes and walks of life (as well as both genders). One important thing that distinguishes them is that most were not monastics, and they are often depicted with long hair, wearing strange ornaments, and as living unconventional lives. The tradition began some time around the eighth century, and it continues to be influential today in Himalayan Buddhism.

Mahāsthāmaprāpta (Tib. *mThu chen thob*; Chin. *Ta-shih-chih*; Jpn. *Seishi Bosatsu*, *Dai-seishi*; Viet. *Đại-thếchí*; "Holder of Great Power")

Bodhisattva of Indian origin whose image is found throughout East Asia, where he is commonly depicted alongside AVALOKITEŚVARA as a companion of AMITĀBHA BUDDHA. Iconographically, he is generally recognizable by the pagoda in his hair, and is commonly thought to welcome beings into Amitābha's "pure land" of SUKHĀVATĪ.

mahāthera ("great elder")

Title given to THERAVĀDA monks who have been ordained for at least twenty years. In Thailand they must have passed a high-level examination in Pāli. Those who have been given the title generally refer to themselves as "Thera" ("Elder").

Mahāvairocana

See VAIROCANA.

Mahāvaṃsa (*Great Chronicle*)

A chronicle of the history of the island of Sri Lanka up to the fourth century C.E., focusing on the introduction of Buddhism and its subsequent fortunes.

Mahāvastu (*Great Account*)

A text written in a hybrid Sanskrit that contains stories of some of ŚĀKYAMUNI BUDDHA's previous lives, as well as information about his final lifetime, stories about his chief disciples, and some discourses. It is attributed to the Lokottaravāda school (one of the subsects of the MAHĀSĀṂGHIKA), and its earliest parts are believed to date from the second century B.C.E.

Mahāvibhāṣā (*Great Book of Alternatives*)

ABHIDHARMA treatise of the SARVĀSTIVĀDA school of INDIAN BUDDHISM, purportedly composed at the "Council of GANDHĀRA," which was sponsored by king KANIṢKA I (ca. first–second century C.E.). It is said to be a commentary on the *Jñāna-prasthāna*. The Sanskrit text is no longer extant (though there are numerous references to it in Indian Buddhist literature), but it does exist in two Chinese versions. It is an important source of information concerning Buddhism during that period, as it recounts many differing philosophical positions of a number of schools.

Mahāvihāra ("Great Monastery")

The monastery built in the Sri Lankan capital of ANURĀDHAPURA by King DEVĀNAṂPIYA TISSA (247–207 B.C.E.) after the successful mission of the monk MAHINDA, son of King AŚOKA. It became the seat of THERAVĀDA orthodoxy on the island for centuries afterward. For centuries it competed with the NIKĀYAS (2) of ABHAYAGIRI and JETAVANA (2), but in the twelfth century the other two were ordered to amalgamate with it, and the Mahāvihāra nikāya was declared to be orthodox.

Mahāyāna (Tib. Theg pa chen po; Chin. Ta-sheng; Jpn. Daijō; Viet. Bắc-Tông; "Greater Vehicle")

One of the two main strands of INDIAN BUDDHISM (the other being NIKĀYA BUDDHISM, referred to by Mahāyāna as "HĪNAYĀNA" or "Lesser Vehicle"). It emphasizes the ideal of the BODHISATTVA, which it contrasts with the

ARHAT ("worthy one"), the ideal of the "Hīnayāna." It considers the *arhat* to be selfish because the *arhat* path leads to NIRVĀṆA for oneself alone, while the bodhisattva strives to bring all sentient beings to salvation. The Mahāyāna movement began some time around 200 B.C.E. in India, and it appears to have been a reaction against the scholastic traditions, which it perceived as being overly concerned with texts and philosophical disputation, while ignoring meditation and concern for others. It emphasized the two interrelated virtues of KARUṆĀ (compassion) and PRAJÑĀ (wisdom), in which the bodhisattva trains on the path to buddhahood. The two main early philosophical schools of Indian Mahāyāna were MADHYAMAKA and YOGĀCĀRA, and some time around the seventh century another significant movement, the VAJRAYĀNA, or tantric tradition, developed. (*See also* ASAṄGA; NĀGA; NĀGĀRJUNA; PRAJÑĀ; VASUBANDHU.)

The Katbaui, an image of Maitreya carved from solid rock dating to the Unified Silla period.

Mahāyāna-śraddhotpāda-śāstra

See TA-SHENG-CH'I-HSIN-LUN.

Mahinda (fl. ca. 250 B.C.E.)

Son of King AŚOKA, who became a monk and later led a successful mission to Sri Lanka. He converted king DEVĀNAṂPIYA TISSA and helped him to establish the first Buddhist monastery on the island, which later grew into the MAHĀVIHĀRA.

mahoraga (Tib. *lto 'phye chen po*)

Large-bellied creatures shaped like boas who are said to be lords of the soil. They are mentioned among the audience of a number of Mahāyāna sūtras.

Maitreya (1) (Pāli *Metteyya*; Tib. *Byams pa*; Chin. *Mi-lo-fo*; Jpn. *Miroku*; Kor. *Mi-rug*; Viet. *Di-lặc*; Mon. *Maijdari*; "Love")

The future BUDDHA, who presently resides in the paradise of TUṢITA in preparation for his last rebirth, in which he will be born as the last buddha of the present age. The cult of Maitreya is found throughout the Buddhist world; it commonly involves practices and prayers designed to lead to rebirth at the time of his appearance on earth, believed to be about 30,000 years in the future. (*See also* PU-TAI.)

Maitreya (2)

An enigmatic figure in the YOGĀCĀRA tradition (often referred to as "Maitreyanātha" by contemporary scholars), who probably lived during the fourth–fifth centuries and who is credited with the authorship of five important treatises. According to the Yogācāra tradition, this author is actually the future buddha Maitreya, with whom ASAṄGA is said to have met on a number of occasions.

Majjhima Nikāya ("Middle Length Discourses")

Second section of the Pāli Sutta-piṭaka ("Basket of Discourses"), corresponding to the Sanskrit Madhyama-āgama. It contains 152 sermons, most of which are attributed to ŚĀKYAMUNI BUDDHA.

Makiguchi, Tsunesaburō (1871–1944)

Founder of the Sōka Kyoiko Gakkai ("Value Creation Society"), which later developed into SŌKA GAKKAI. The school bases itself on the teachings and practices of NICHIREN (1222–1282).

makyō ("evil phenomena")

Japanese term that refers to supernatural phenomena which are said to be side-effects of ZAZEN, such as levitation, clairvoyance, and other magical abilities, as well as hallucinations. They are considered to be distractions, and so meditators are taught to ignore them as much as possible and to concentrate on meditative practice.

manas (Pāli *mano*; Tib. *sems*; "sentience")

Sanskrit term for sentience, commonly equated with the terms CITTA (mind) and VIJÑĀNA (consciousness). It is derived from the Sanskrit root man, "to think, believe, imagine, suppose," and is associated with the intellectual activity of consciousness and with the process of reasoning. It is listed as one of the twelve "sense spheres" (ĀYATANA), which include the six senses and their objects. *Manas* refers to the mental sense, the object of which is thoughts.

maṇḍala (Pāli *maṇḍala*; Tib. *dkyil 'khor*; Chin. *man-t'o-lo*; Jpn. *mandara*; "circle")

Refers both to sacred areas, such as the spot underneath the Bodhi Tree (BODHI-VṚKṢA) where ŚĀKYAMUNI BUDDHA sat in meditation (referred to as *Bodhi-maṇḍa*) as well as to circular diagrams used for symbolic representations that are objects for meditation. These diagrams symbolize aspects of Buddhist iconography and soteriology and depict the palace or "buddha-land" (*buddha-*

Monks from rNam rgyal (Namgyel) Monastery creating a sand maṇḍala in Oneonta, New York.

kṣetra) of a particular buddha. They occur in both two- and three-dimensional forms, and the central buddha is placed at the center, often surrounded by symbols associated with him/her and with a retinue of other buddhas, bodhisattvas, and attendants. *Maṇḍalas* are particularly important in Vajrayāna, where they serve as the focus of meditative visualizations. Tantric practitioners generally are authorized to engage in a particular practice after being initiated into the *maṇḍala* of the central buddha.

Mañjuśrī (Tib. *'Jam dpal dbyangs*; Chin. *Wen-shu*; Jpn. *Monju*; Viet. *Văn-thù*; "Soft Glory")

One of the most important figures in the pantheon of Mahāyāna Buddhism, considered to be the embodiment of wisdom (prajñā) and also associated with "inspired courage" (*pratibhāna*). He is sometimes referred to as "Soft Voice" (Mañjughoṣa), "Lord of Speech" (Vāgīśvara), and "Crown Prince" (Kumārabhūta). He is closely associated with the "Perfection of Wisdom" (Prajñā-pāramitā) sūtras and is often a main interlocutor in them, generally asking the Buddha about the ramifications of the perfection of wisdom. He is often depicted iconographically holding in one hand a flaming "sword of wisdom" that cuts through false views and a Perfection of Wisdom text in the other. A number of Tibetan masters (for example Tsong kha pa) are regarded as physical manifestations of Mañjuśrī. (*See also* Yamāntaka.)

Carving of the mantra of Avalokiteśvara, "Oṃ maṇi padme hūṃ," on a rock along the circumambulation path around the Dalai Lama's residence in Dharamsala

mantra (Pāli *manta*; Tib. *sngags*; "prayer," "spell")

A spell or prayer, commonly a syllable or phrase, believed to have magical powers. Derived from the Sanskrit root man, "to think," mantras are designed as tools for focusing the mind through repetition. The use of the mantra "Namo Amida Butsu" ("Praise to Amitābha Buddha") is central to East Asian Pure Land (Chin. ch'ing-t'u; Jpn. Jōdō; Kor. Chŏngt'o) practice, and mantras are also widely used in Vajrayāna traditions. They commonly invoke the power of a particular buddha, and are used both as a meditative aid (to concentrate the mind on the qualities of a buddha that is the focus of one's visualization practice) and as magical spells that are believed to provide protection and worldly benefits.

manuṣya (Pāli *manussa*; Tib. *mi*; "human")

One of the six "destinies" (gati) within cyclic existence (saṃsāra) into which beings may be born. It is considered by Buddhists to be ideal for the attainment of liberation, because humans are not plagued by the constant sufferings of beings of the lower three destinies (hell beings, hungry ghosts, and animals), and they also do not have the great power and happy lives of gods and demi-gods. Thus they experience enough suffering to become aware of its pervasive nature, and they have enough leisure to be able to pursue the path to liberation.

mappō (Chin. *mo fa*; "final dharma age")

Japanese term for the last days of Buddhism's existence in the world, during which practice and adherence to monastic rules will gradually decline, until even the external symbols of Buddhism disappear. The idea became widely popular during the Kamakura period (1192–1338), and a number of schools developed "easy practices" that they claimed to be more effective during the period of degeneration than the "difficult practices" (such as meditation) of earlier times. Among these were the Pure Land (Chin. CH'ING-T'U; Jpn. *Jōdō*; Kor. *Chŏngt'o*) schools, which maintained that the most appropriate practice for *mappō* is chanting the name of AMITĀBHA BUDDHA in order to be reborn in his "Pure Land" of SUKHĀVATĪ, in which the conditions will be optimal for attaining buddhahood in one's next lifetime. The notion of *mappō* was used to justify a number of significant innovations, such as the institution of married monks, since it was asserted that it is impossible for the degenerate people of *mappō* to adhere to the rules of the VINAYA.

Mar pa Chos kyi blo gros (Marpa Chögi Lodrö, 1012–1097)

First Tibetan master of the BKA' BRGYUD PA (Kagyüpa) tradition, who made three visits to India, where he studied Sanskrit and received tantric initiations from several Indian masters, including NĀROPA (Nāḍapāda, 1016–1100). Nāropa gave him a number of initiations and teaching lineages, including the ritual and meditative practices of CAKRASAṂVARA (the main tutelary deity of the bKa' brgyud pa order), MAHĀMUDRĀ (Tib. *phyag rgya chen po*), and the "six dharmas of Nāropa" (NĀ RO CHOS DRUG). Upon his return to Tibet he became a noted translator (*lo tsā ba*), married a woman named bDag med ma (Dakmema), and raised several sons, while also establishing himself as a lay tantric practitioner (*sngags pa*). Mar pa is one of the most widely revered figures in TIBETAN BUDDHISM, and in bKa' brgyud pa is considered to have attained a level of awakening equivalent to that of the buddha VAJRADHARA. He eschewed the monastic lifestyle, adopting instead the outward appearance of an ordinary householder and local hegemon, although he had completely transcended all attachments to worldly affairs. His best-known disciple was MI LA RAS PA (Milarepa), whose biography tells of a series of arduous tasks ordered by Mar pa to overcome his negative karma and prepare him for meditative training.

Māra (Pāli *Māra*; Tib. *bDud*; "Death," "Demon")

Demonic figure who attempts to turn beings away from Buddhist practice and thus prevent them from escaping cyclic existence. In traditional stories of ŚĀKYAMUNI BUDDHA's life, Māra appears to SIDDHĀRTHA GAUTAMA as he sits under the Bodhi Tree and tries to prevent him from attaining buddhahood, and when he is unsuccessful in this tries to keep him from teaching others. According to Buddhist mythology, there are many *māras*, whose goal is to tempt people into ignorance. They are portrayed as taking on the appearances of ARHATS, BODHISATTVAS, and even buddhas in order to teach false doctrines to gullible people. There are four main types of *māra*: (1) the *māras* of the aggregates (*skandha-māra*); (2) the

Mural at Hwagaesa Monastery, Seoul, depicting Māra's temptation of Śākyamuni Buddha during the night he attained awakening.

*māra*s of the Lord of Death (*mṛtyu-māra*); (3) the *māra*s of the afflictions (*kleśa-māra*); and (4) the *māra*s who are sons of gods (*devaputra-māra*).

mārga (Pāli *magga*; Tib. *lam*; "path")

A general term for Buddhist practice that leads to liberation from cyclic existence. There are a number of divisions of paths, the two most common of which are: (1) the "eightfold noble path" (ĀRYĀṢṬĀṄGA-MĀRGA: correct views, intention, speech, actions, livelihood, effort, mindfulness, and concentration); and (2) a fivefold enumeration: (a) SAṂBHĀRA-MĀRGA (path of accumulation); (b) PRAYOGA MĀRGA (path of preparation); (c) DARŚAṆA-MĀRGA (path of seeing); (d) BHĀVANĀ-MĀRGA (path of meditation); and (e) AŚAIKṢA-MĀRGA (path of no more learning).

marriage

There are no canonical Buddhist marriage ceremonies, and Buddhist monks have traditionally avoided participation in the process of marriage, which is not surprising in light of the fact that the Buddha's emphasis was on a monastic community whose members were expected to dissociate themselves from worldly life and its concerns. Marriage is generally seen in Buddhism as part of a process that leads to birth, aging, and death, and the household life is commonly characterized in Buddhist texts as involving people in a web of entanglements that inevitably lead to suffering. Moreover, the PRĀTIMOKṢA contains a passage stating: "If one of this SAṂGHA acts as an intermediary, bringing a man and a woman together – whether for the purpose of marriage or for a single act of intercourse – this person should be suspended." Despite this, it is common for monks in THERAVĀDA countries to be invited to wedding ceremonies, where they commonly chant selected Buddhist texts (for example the *Maṅgala-sutta* and the *Mettā-sutta*). They do not, however, play any role in the ritual joining of the bride and groom in marriage. The participation of monks in any capacity appears to be a modern phenomenon, and traditionally Buddhist monks have avoided marriage ceremonies, perceiving them as affairs of the lay community. The actual marriage in Theravāda countries is performed by laypeople, and the role of the monks is to chant texts for the general well-being of the participants. The same is true of most Tibetan Buddhist communities, in which marriage is also seen as a secular affair. Marriage rituals are performed by laypeople, but monks are often invited to provide a blessing. In modern times there are at least two examples of Tibetan Buddhist wedding rituals, one developed by 'JAM MGON KONG SPRUL (Jamgön Kongtrül) and another by bDud 'joms Rin po che (DUDJOM RINPOCHE). A number of Western Buddhist centers have also created wedding rituals in order to meet a perceived need for such ceremonies on the part of their members. Despite these recent innovations, however, most Buddhist monks tend to see participation in weddings as inappropriate for monks and as a violation of the rules of the VINAYA.

Ma-tsu Tao-i (Jpn. *Baso Dōitsu*, 709–788)

Chinese CH'AN master, dharma-successor of Nan-yüeh Huai-jang (Jpn. *Nangaku Ejō*, 677–744) and teacher of PAI-CHANG HUAI-HAI (Jpn. *Hyakujō Ekai*, 720–814). He is best known for his use of abrupt methods, such as shouting at his students, striking them with a stick, or twisting their noses sharply in order to shock them into direct realization of their true natures.

Maudgalyāyana (Pāli *Moggallāna*)

One of ŚĀKYAMUNI BUDDHA's ten main disciples, said by the Buddha to be the foremost in attainment of miraculous powers (Skt. *ṛddhi-pāda*; Pāli *iddhi-pāda*).

Māyā (Mahāmāyā; Pāli *Māyā*)

Mother of ŚĀKYAMUNI BUDDHA, who died seven days after giving birth to him. His father, King ŚUDDHODANA, then married Māyā's sister MAHĀPRAJĀPATĪ.

meat eating

In light of the Buddhist precept prohibiting killing, one might expect that Buddhism would also enjoin vegetarianism. In the PĀLI CANON, however, there are several places in which the subject is raised, and in all of them the Buddha explicitly refuses to require that monks abstain from meat. As mendicants, the monks subsisted on alms food, and the VINAYA consistently indicates that they are to eat whatever is given to them, viewing it only as a means to sustain life. Refusing alms food deprives the donor of an opportunity for making merit, and it also leads to negative feelings toward the SAṂGHA from people whose offerings are refused. There are, however, some restrictions. Certain types of meat are forbidden, including human flesh, as well as meat from dogs, snakes, elephants, horses, and carnivores. The Vinaya-piṭaka (IV.237) states that monks can only eat meat that is "pure in three respects," which means that they must not have seen, heard, or suspected that an animal was killed for them. The Vinaya commentary explains that if a monk is suspicious of the origin of meat, he should inquire how it was obtained. Reasons for suspicion include evidence of hunting, absence of a butcher nearby, or the bad character of a donor. If these conditions are met, however, the monk is "blameless." If a donor kills (or causes someone else to kill) an animal to feed monks, this results in negative karma for the giver. The Pāli canon also reports that the Buddha's cousin DEVADATTA specifically asked him to make vegetarianism compulsory, but he refused to do so, only allowing that it was acceptable as an optional ascetic practice. These examples indicate that the Buddha and his followers would have frequently eaten meat on their begging rounds, and the MAHĀPARINIBBĀNA-SUTTA states that he died after eating pork.

This does not mean, however, that the killing of animals is condoned. Occupations that involve killing, such as butchery, are condemned as examples of "wrong livelihood," and in Buddhist countries today these tasks are commonly performed by non-Buddhists. Those who perform them are often treated as being karmically polluted. In THERAVĀDA countries, vegetarianism is widely admired, but seldom practiced. Most laypeople eat meat, but there are certain observance days during which many people avoid it. In these countries, it is generally thought that is better to eat less intelligent animals, such as fish, and to eat small animals, rather than large ones. In Tibet the prevailing philosophy is just the opposite: Tibetans generally believe that it is better to eat larger animals, since a single large animal yields more meat, and so fewer animals need to be killed overall.

There are, however, a number of MAHĀYĀNA texts that argue against eating meat, emphasizing that it is incompatible with the BODHISATTVA practices of generating compassion toward all sentient beings and viewing them as one's former mothers. The MAHĀPARINIRVĀṆA-SŪTRA, for example, states that meat-eating "extinguishes the seed of great compassion," and in it the Buddha orders his followers to adopt a vegetarian diet. The LAṄKĀVATĀRA-SŪTRA has a chapter in which the Buddha directly contradicts his earlier statements in the Vinaya and gives a series of reasons why bodhisattvas should never eat meat. These include the idea that all beings in past lives were one's mothers, relatives, and friends; that the smell of carnivores frightens beings and leads to a bad reputation; that eating meat interferes with meditative practice; that eating meat leads to bad dreams and anxiety; that it leads to bad rebirths; and that even if one only eats meat that was not explicitly killed for oneself, one still participates in the process of killing and thus promotes the suffering of sentient beings. The sūtra concludes that, contrary to statements in earlier texts, the Buddha never ate meat.

These sūtras were widely popular in East Asia, and this may partly account for the fact that most monasteries in China and Korea are strictly vegetarian. In Japan, vegetarianism is often viewed as admirable by Buddhists, and is formally practiced in most ZEN monasteries. Vegetarianism is also enjoined in the supplementary monastic code known as the *Brahma-jāla-sūtra*, which is widely influential in East Asia. An early East Asian example of this attitude is the proclamation by Emperor Wu in 511 prohibiting meat eating and hunting. Vegetarianism is practiced by some pious laypeople in East Asia and is often seen as being entailed by the precept prohibiting killing. In Tibetan and Mongolian Buddhism, however, vegetarianism is seldom practiced. The Dalai Lama has urged Tibetans to eat less meat (and to eat larger animals in order to reduce the number of deaths), but is not a vegetarian himself. In the harsh environment of Tibet, vegetarianism was not feasible, since the soil and climate could not support large-scale agriculture, but only a few lamas have adopted a vegetarian diet in exile. The question of how they can reconcile teachings enjoining students to view all sentient beings as their mothers with eating their flesh is often raised by Western students, but most lamas either avoid the subject or advise students to chant MANTRAS to help the animals achieve a better rebirth. There is considerable uneasiness concerning this subject among Tibetan Buddhist teachers, most of whom would clearly prefer to avoid it altogether. As the remarks above indicate, there is no unanimity among Buddhists regarding the eating of meat, and there is a wide variety of opinions in Buddhist canonical literature.

Medicine Buddha

See BHAIṢAJYAGURU.

meditation

See BHĀVANĀ.

menpeki (Chin. *mien-pi*; "facing a wall")

Japanese term for the sort of meditation in which BODHIDHARMA reportedly engaged at SHAO-LIN Monastery for nine years upon his arrival in China (referred to as *menpeki-kunen*). This practice is still common in Japanese SŌTŌ monasteries, in which younger monks generally practice ZAZEN facing a wall, while in RINZAI monasteries meditators generally face the center of the meditation hall (ZENDŌ).

Meru (Pāli *Sineru*; Tib. *Ri rab or Lhun po*)

Also called Sumeru, this is the *axis mundi* of traditional Buddhist cosmology, said to be an enormous mountain in the center of the world surrounded by four continents oriented toward the cardinal directions and eight sub-continents.

Mi la ras pa (Milarepa, 1040–1123; "Cotton Clad Mi la")

One of the great figures of TIBETAN BUDDHISM, particularly revered as an example of an ordinary person who attained awakening in one human lifetime, despite being burdened by negative karma. According to his biography, he and his family were dispossessed of their inheritance by his greedy aunt and uncle, following which his mother coerced him into learning black magic. He cast a spell that killed many people (but ironically left the aunt and uncle unharmed), and then, concerned that his actions would doom him to terrible suffering in his next lifetime, sought a teacher (BLA MA) who could help him. He eventually found MAR PA CHOS KYI BLO GROS, who made him perform a series of painful and dispiriting tasks, which cleansed his karma and provided a basis for his practice. After this Mar pa taught him MAHĀMUDRĀ and the "six dharmas of NĀROPA" (NĀ RO CHOS DRUG). His biography and ecstatic songs (Tib. *mgur*; Skt. *dohā*) are among the most widely known pieces of Buddhist literature throughout the Himalayan region.

middle way

See MADHYAMA-PRATIPAD.

mikkyō

See MI-TSUNG.

Milarepa

See MI LA RAS PA.

Milindapañha ("*Questions of King Milinda*")

Important non-canonical THERAVĀDA text, purporting to be a dialogue between the Buddhist monk Nāgasena and the Bactrian king Menander (first century C.E.), who conquered a large part of northern India stretching from Patna to Peshawar. It focuses on the central doctrines of Buddhism and contains particularly illuminating discussions of selflessness (ANĀTMAN), the problem of how rebirth is possible without a soul, and karma. According to Theravāda tradition, following the dialogue with Nāgasena, Menander abdicated the throne and became a Buddhist monk.

mind

See CITTA; MANAS; VIJÑĀNA.

mind of clear light

See PRABHĀSVARA-CITTA.

Mind-Only

See YOGĀCĀRA.

mindfulness

See SMṚTI.

Mindon (1853–1878)

Burmese king who worked to revive Buddhism in Burma. In 1871 he sponsored the "Fifth Buddhist Council," which was held in Mandalay. The council was convened in order to revise the PĀLI CANON, and after this task was finished the texts were engraved on 729 marble tablets and stored in the Kuthodaw Pagoda in Mandalay.

mi-tsung (Jpn. *mikkyō*; "secret teaching")

General term for esoteric Buddhism (VAJRAYĀNA) as practiced in China. Its teachings and practices are derived from Indian TANTRAS, texts that emphasize ritual and visualization, along with extensive use of symbolism and imagery. It was brought to China in the eighth century by three Indian masters: Vajrabodhi (Chin. *Chin-kang-chih*, 663–723), Amoghavajra (Chin. *Pu-k'ung chin-kang*, 705–774), and Śubhākarasiṃha (Chin. *Shan-wu-wei*, 637–735). Śubhākarasiṃha translated the main text of the tradition, the *Mahāvairocana-sūtra* (Chin. *Ta-jih-ching*; Jpn. *Dainichi-kyō*), into Chinese, and Amoghavajra translated the *dhāraṇī* (magical formulas) that accompany it. The tradition was brought to Japan by SAICHŌ (767–822) and KŪKAI (774–835). The former made tantric practices a part of the TENDAI school, and the latter established esoteric Buddhism as a separate tradition known as SHINGON.

mKhan zur Rin po che (Khensur Rinpoche; "Precious Former Abbot")

Tibetan term for someone who has retired as abbot of a monastery.

Mo-ho-yen, Ho-shang (Tib. *Hva shang Ma ha ya na*, fl. ca. eighth century)

Chinese CH'AN master who, according to Tibetan tradition, debated with KAMALAŚĪLA in the "COUNCIL OF LHASA," held during the reign of KHRI SRONG LDE BRTSAN (Trisong Detsen, ca. 740–798). He reportedly taught that awakening is attained all at once, in a flash of insight, following which all afflictions are eliminated. BU STON (Pudön) reports that he was defeated and that Kamalaśīla's gradualist position – reflecting mainstream Indian MAHĀYĀNA paradigms of practice and doctrine – was declared to be orthodox DHARMA. Following this, Mo-ho-yen reportedly went back to China, but was so upset with his defeat that he sent a team of Chinese assassins to Tibet, who killed Kamalaśīla by squeezing his kidneys.

monastery

See DGON PA; VIHĀRA; WAT.

mondō (Chin. *wen-ta*; "question and answer")

The dialogues between a CH'AN/ZEN master and student, or between two masters, which are thought to demonstrate their respective levels of understanding. They are not debates, but rather spontaneous expressions and responses. The focus is generally a Buddhist doctrine or doctrinal issue, and the answer is supposed to get to the essence of the issue without recourse to conceptual or dialectical thought.

Mongkut (Rāma IV, r. 1851–1868)

Thai king who was a Buddhist monk from 1824 to 1868, during which time he founded the Thammayut sect. As the name Thammayut (Pāli *Dhammayuttika*, "Adhering to the Dhamma") implies, this is a reformist group, which emphasizes strict adherence to the rules of monastic conduct (VINAYA) as well as study of the scriptures. During his reign, he worked to purify the Thai SAṂGHA, both the Thammayut and its main rival, the Mahānikāya. (*See also* THAI BUDDHISM.)

Mongolian Buddhism

The earliest Mongolian contacts with Buddhism probably occurred during the fourth century C.E. when Chinese monks began missionizing in border areas. By the seventh century, Buddhist influence had spread as far as the Yenisei region, and the Mongols also came into contact with Buddhism through the cultural influence of the Buddhist oasis states along the Silk Route. These early contacts seem to have had no lasting influence, however, and the first substantial influx of Buddhism among the Mongols was initiated by the visit of the SA SKYA PA (Sakyapa) hierarch SA SKYA PAṆḌITA (Sakya Pandita, 1182–1251) to the court of Godan Khan in 1244. This was intended as a formal accession of Tibet to Mongol hegemony, but according to traditional chronicles the khan was so impressed by Sa skya Paṇḍita that he converted to Buddhism and appointed him as court chaplain. The reality, however, was probably somewhat different, and records of the time indicate that Sa skya Paṇḍita's appointment as regent (Mon. *darugachi*) of Tibet, along with the khan's request that he remain at the court, may really have been intended to keep him as a hostage in order to prevent rebellion in Tibet. Sa skya pa rule over Tibet was passed on to Sa skya Paṇḍita's nephew and successor 'PHAGS PA BLO GROS (Pakpa Lodrö, 1235–1289), who by all accounts played a major role in converting the Mongols to Buddhism. He is considered to have converted Khubilai Khan (r. 1260–1294) and his consort Chamui to Buddhism, and together with the khan he developed the "patron–priest" (Tib. *yon mchod*) relationship. This involved the Sa skya pa hierarchs serving as spiritual preceptors to the Mongol court, and the khan in turn pledged to protect Tibet and the Sa skya pas. In 1269 'Phags pa devised a block script (Mon. *Dörbeljin*) that led to the translation of a large number of Buddhist texts into Mongolian, mostly from existing Uighur translations.

Despite these efforts, it appears that at this time Buddhism was mainly confined to the aristocracy, and when Mongol rule over China ended in 1369 the Mongols returned to indigenous shamanism. In the sixteenth century a second phase of Buddhism's dissemination to Mongolia began as a consequence of military conquests in eastern border regions of Tibet by ALTAN KHAN (1507–1583), which again brought contacts with Tibetan Buddhists. The third DALAI LAMA, BSOD NAMS RGYA MTSHO (Sönam Gyatso, 1543–1588), visited Altan Khan's palace in Köke Khota (Chin. *Kuei-hua ch'eng*) in 1578, and after this a number of Buddhist missionaries traveled to Mongolia. Among these were Neyichi Toyin (1557–1653), who converted the eastern Mongols, and Zaya Paṇḍita (fl. seventeenth century), who converted the western and northern Mongols. With the help of royal patronage, Tibetan Buddhism quickly spread among the Mongolian masses. The process continued among the northern Mongols as a result of the efforts of Abadai Khan of the Khalkha, who also visited the third Dalai Lama during his stay in Mongolia and in 1586 built the Erdini J̌uu monastery to house images that bSod nams rgya mtsho gave him. As a sign of their commitment to Buddhism, Mongol rulers promulgated a number of Buddhist laws, including the banning of live sacrifices and hunting. In addition, many of the practices of shamanism were proscribed, talismans were outlawed, and every *yurt* was required to have an image of MAHĀKĀLA (Mon. Yeke gara). The process of translation was also restarted, and within a few decades a substantial corpus of Tibetan Buddhist works had been rendered into Mongolian. Tibetan became the *lingua franca* of Buddhist monks and scholars.

During the Ch'ing dynasty in China (1644–1911), several of the Manchu rulers patronized Tibetan Buddhism, and with the financial support of Emperor K'ang-hsi (1661–1722) a revised edition of the Mongolian BKA' 'GYUR (Ganggyur, "Translations of Teachings") was printed from 1718 to 1720. A translation of the BSTAN 'GYUR (Dengyur, "Translations of Treatises") was initiated by Emperor Ch'ien-lung (1736–1795) and finished in 1749. Copies of the complete canon were then printed in Beijing and distributed throughout Mongolia. In the eighteenth and nineteenth centuries, Buddhism spread rapidly, and during the nineteenth century there were over 1,200 monasteries and temples in Inner Mongolia and over 700 in Outer Mongolia. In addition, there were 243 reincarnate lamas (Mon. *khubilgan*; Tib. SPRUL SKU) among the Mongols. Even more significantly, a reported one-third of the adult male population were monks.

In modern times Mongolia has been split into two parts. Inner Mongolia is a part of China, and Buddhism there has suffered much the same fate as in Tibet. Outer Mongolia (the area of the present-day Mongolian Peoples' Republic) established itself as an independent republic in the 1920s with Russian help, and although the socialist government was initially hostile to Buddhism, in recent decades religious tolerance has increased. There are signs of religious revival in Mongolia, and when the Dalai Lama performed the YAMĀNTAKA initiation ceremony there in 1982 for 140 lamas, a crowd of 200,000 reportedly gathered outside. With the recent relaxing of government restrictions in Inner Mongolia, the number of monks is increasing, and some reincarnate lamas have returned to their monastic seats. (*See also* GANDAN MONASTERY; LCANG SKYA KHUTUKHTU; RJE BTSUN DAM PA KHUTUKHTU.)

monk

See BHIKṢU.

morality

See ŚĪLA.

moxa (*mokusa*; "burning herbs")

Japanese Buddhist practice (also found in Chinese Buddhism) of burning small scars on the forehead of a newly ordained monk or nun with a cone of incense. The practice is said to have begun in China. The number of scars varies between three and twelve.

mTshur phu dGon pa (Tsurpu Gompa)

Seat of the KAR MA BKA' BRGYUD PA (Karma Kagyüpa) order of TIBETAN BUDDHISM, located in the upper Stod lung (Tölung) Valley northwest of Lhasa. The monastery was badly damaged during the Cultural Revolution, but much of it has been rebuilt.

mu kōan

Often the first KŌAN presented to a student of ZEN Buddhism, based on a story in which the Chinese master CHAO-CHOU TS'UNG-SHEN (Jpn. *Jōshū Jūshin*, 778–897) is asked, "Does a dog have the buddha-nature?" He responds by saying "Wu!" "(Jpn. *mu*). "Wu" literally means "nothing" or "not," but in this context indicates a refusal to provide an answer that is based on conceptual thought or ordinary language. The problem of the *kōan* is that according to Ch'an/Zen tradition all beings have the buddha-nature, and so dogs would naturally be included. But if Chao-chou responds to the question affirmatively, he falls into the trap of dogmatically following tradition and authority. On the other hand, if he responds negatively, he puts himself at odds with the received wisdom of the patriarchs of the tradition. Thus his response indicates that the answer to the question lies beyond words and doctrines and must be grasped directly and intuitively. When a student understands the purport of Chao-chou's answer, it is said that a spontaneous flash of insight dawns.

mudrā (Pāli *muddā*; Tib. *phyag rgya*; Chin. *yin*; Jpn. *inzō*; "seal")

Hand gestures found in Buddhist iconography that symbolize aspects of Buddhist doctrine, as well as such activities as teaching, protection, etc. They are particularly important in VAJRAYĀNA traditions, in which they are used in connection with ritual and meditation.

Mūlamadhyamaka-kārikā (Tib. *dBu ma rtsa ba'i tshig le'ur byas pa*; *Fundamental Verses on the Middle Way*)

Philosophical text in twenty-seven sections by the Indian master NĀGĀRJUNA (ca. 150–250 C.E.), which became the central text of the MADHYAMAKA tradition. It focuses on the doctrine of emptiness (ŚŪNYATĀ), according to which all conditioned phenomena (SAṂSKṚTA) are empty of inherent existence (SVABHĀVA), come into being in dependence upon causes and conditions, and are thus impermanent (ANITYA). Nāgārjuna draws out the implications of this doctrine, applying it to such commonly accepted notions as motion and rest and causation, and he also subjects the doctrines of rival schools to critical analysis using a *reductio ad absurdum* (*prasaṅga*) method of argumentation. In this method he uses the assumptions of his opponents in order to draw out their absurd unintended consequences.

Mūlasarvāstivāda (Tib. *Thams cad yod par smra ba*; "Basic School Asserting that Everything Exists")

Indian Buddhist school whose VINAYA became the standard in Tibet. (*See also* SARVĀSTIVĀDA; MAHĀVIBHĀṢĀ.)

Mumonkan

See WU-MEN-KUAN.

Myōan Eisai

See EISAI ZENJI.

N

nā ro chos drug ("six dharmas of Nāropa")

Tantric practices taught to MAR PA CHOS KYI BLO GROS (Marpa Chögi Lodrö, 1012–1097) by NĀROPA (Nāḍapāda, 1016–1100) and brought to Tibet by him. They are particularly important in the BKA' BRGYUD PA (Kagyüpa) order. The six are: (1) heat (Skt. *caṇḍālī*; Tib. GTUM MO); (2) illusory body (Skt. *māyā-deha*; Tib. *sgyu lus*); (3) dream (Skt. *svapna*; Tib. *rmi lam*); (4) clear light (Skt. *prabhāsvara*; Tib. *'od gsal*); (5) intermediate state (Skt. *antarābhava*; Tib. BAR DO); and (6) transference of consciousness (Skt. *saṃkrama*; Tib. *'pho ba*). The first involves increasing and channeling inner heat through visualizing fire and the sun in various places of the meditator's body. Illusory body is a practice in which one mentally generates an image of a subtle body composed of subtle energies and endowed with the ideal qualities of a buddha, such as the six perfections (PĀRAMITĀ). This is eventually transformed into the "*vajra* body" (Skt. *vajra-kāya*; Tib. *rdo rje'i sku*), symbolizing the state of buddhahood. Dream yoga trains the meditator to take control of and manipulate the process of dreams. The yoga of clear light is based on the tantric notion that the mind is of the nature of clear light, and this practice involves learning to perceive all appearances as manifestations of mind and as representing the interplay of luminosity and emptiness. Intermediate state yoga trains the meditator for the state between birth and death, in which one has a subtle body, which is subjected to disorienting and frightening sights, sounds, and other sensory phenomena. A person who is adept in this yoga is able to understand that these are all creations of mind, and this realization enables one to take control of the process, which is said to present numerous opportunities for meditative progress if properly understood and handled. Transference of consciousness yoga develops the ability to project one's consciousness into another body or to a buddha-land (Skt. *buddha-kṣetra*; Tib. *sangs rgyas kyi shing*) at the time of death. One who fully masters the technique can transmute the pure light of the mind into the body of a buddha at the time of death.

nāga (Pāli *nāga*; Tib. *klu*)

Serpent-like beings with bodies of snakes and human heads, said to inhabit the waters or the city of Bhoga-vatī under the water. Their king is named Virūpākṣa. They are said to be endowed with miraculous powers and to have capricious natures. According to MAHĀYĀNA mythology, they played a key role in the transmission of the "Perfection of Wisdom" (PRAJÑĀ-PĀRA-

MITĀ) texts. Fearing that they would be misunderstood, the Buddha reportedly gave the texts to the *nāgas* for safekeeping until the birth of someone who was able to interpret them correctly. This was NĀGĀRJUNA (ca. 150–250 C.E.), who is said to have magically flown to the *nāgas*' city and retrieved the hidden books. The story is apparently intended to explain the chronological discrepancy between the death of the Buddha and the appearance of these texts, but it is doubtful that it actually convinced anyone except the faithful.

Nāgārjuna (Tib. *kLu sgrub*; Chin. *Lung-sheng*; Jpn. *Ryūju*, ca. 150–250 C.E.; "White Snake," "Snake Bush")

Indian Buddhist philosopher, credited with founding the MADHYAMAKA school. Although a plethora of works are attributed to him by Buddhist tradition, only a handful are thought by contemporary scholars to have actually been composed by him. The most important of these is the *Fundamental Verses on the Middle Way* (MŪLAMADHYAMAKA-KĀRIKĀ), in which he extends the logic of the doctrine of emptiness (ŚŪNYATĀ) to an analysis of phenomena and to a critical evaluation of the positions of opponents. (*See also* BHAVYA; BUDDHAPĀLITA; CANDRAKĪRTI; NĀGA; PRĀSAṄGIKA-MADHYAMAKA; SVĀTANTRIKA-MADHYAMAKA.)

Nagatomi, Masatoshi

Eminent scholar of Buddhist Studies who spent most of his career at Harvard University's Yenching Institute. Best known for his work on Buddhist epistemology, he is also renowned in the field for his extensive knowledge of the whole of Indian Buddhism, and is responsible for training a number of prominent scholars.

Nakagawa Sōen Rōshi (1908–1983)

Japanese master of the RINZAI tradition, dharma-successor (HASSU) of Yamamoto Gempo Rōshi 1865–1901), who was influential in both Japanese and Western ZEN. He made his first visit to the U.S.A. in 1949, which led to the founding of the Zen Studies Society in New York in 1965.

Nakamura, Hajime (1912–1999)

One of the leading figures in Buddhist Studies in Japan, best known for his *Indian Buddhism: A Survey with Bibliographical Notes*, which covers an impressive range of studies in the field by Japanese and Western scholars.

Nālandā Monastic University

One of the greatest centers of Buddhist learning in ancient India, founded in Bihār some time around the second century by King Śakrāditya of Magadha. It was probably named after a local spirit and was originally a small institution, but beginning with Kumāra Gupta I (414–455) it began to receive royal support from the Gupta rulers of North India. In its heyday, it attracted some of the greatest scholars of MAHĀYĀNA Buddhism in India, both as teachers and students, and pilgrims from all over the Buddhist world traveled there to study. The Chinese pilgrims I-CHING (635–713) and HSÜAN-TSANG (596–664) studied there during their visits to India, and it later became one of the principal sources for the transmission of Buddhism to Tibet. It was destroyed by Muslim invaders in the twelfth century.

Nam Myōhō Renge-kyō

See DAIMOKU.

nāma-rūpa (Pāli *nāma-rūpa*; Tib. *ming gzugs*; "name and form")

The fifth part of the twelvefold process of dependent arising (PRATĪTYA-SAMUTPĀDA). It refers to the psycho-physical personality, and is said to be conditioned by consciousness. *Nāma* encompasses the four "aggregates" (SKANDHA) of feelings (*vedanā*), discriminations (*saṃjñā*), consciousness (VIJÑĀNA), and compositional factors (SAṂSKĀRA), while *rūpa* refers to physical form or matter.

namthar

See RNAM THAR.

Namu Amida Butsu

See NEMBUTSU.

Nanamoli Bhikkhu (Osbert Moore, 1905–1960)

British Theravāda monk who was ordained in 1950 in Sri Lanka. He translated a number of important Pāli works into English, including BUDDHAGHOSA's VISUDDHIMAGGA (*Path of Purification*) and the *Netti-pakaraṇa* (*The Guide*).

Nan-chüan P'u-yüan (Jpn. *Nansen Fugan*, 748–835)

Teacher of the great CH'AN master CHAO-CHOU TS'UNG-SHEN (Jōshū Jūshin, 778–897) and dharma-successor of MA-TSU TAO-I (Jpn. *Baso Dōitsu*, 709–788). He was one of the most influential Ch'an masters of the T'ang period in China.

Nan-tsung-ch'an (Jpn. *Nanshō-zen*; "Southern School of Ch'an")

According to CH'AN tradition, this is the tradition that derives from the sixth patriarch, HUI-NENG. It is contrasted with the "Northern School" (Pei-tsung), founded by Hui-neng's rival SHEN-HSIU, which received its designation because most of its exponents lived in northern China. While the Northern School emphasized study of the scriptures and the notion that awakening is attained through a gradual process, the Southern School generally downplayed the value of study and valorized the idea of "sudden awakening." The Northern School died out within a few generations of Shen-hsiu, and all major lineages of modern Ch'an/Zen/Sŏn trace themselves to the Southern School. The Southern School is also often referred to as "Patriarch Ch'an" (Chin. Tsu-chih-ch'an; Jpn. Soshi-zen) because it claims descent from Hui-neng.

nāraka (Pāli *niraya*; Tib. *dmyal ba*; "hell beings")

One of the six destinies (GATI) of beings within cyclic existence (SAṂSĀRA) according to traditional Buddhist cosmology (the others being gods, demigods, humans, animals, and hungry ghosts). Hell beings are born into one of a number of HELLS (the main ones being eight hot hells and eight cold hells), in which they are subjected to various tortures in accordance with their past evil deeds.

Nāropa (Nāḍapāda, 1016–1100)

Indian Buddhist tantric master, student of TILOPA and teacher of MAR PA CHOS KYI: BLO GROS. According to legends about his life, he was a renowned scholar at NĀLANDĀ MONASTIC UNIVERSITY, but left his position after an experience in which a hideously ugly woman appeared before him and demanded that he explain the essence of the dharma. He was unable to do so, and was informed that her ugliness was a reflection of his own pride and other negative emotions. She instructed him to seek out Tilopa, who only agreed to teach him after subjecting him to a series of painful (and bizarre) tests, such as crushing his penis between two rocks. After mastering the practices taught to him by Tilopa, he passed them on to Mar pa, who in turn brought them to Tibet, where this lineage developed into the BKA' BRGYUD PA (Kagyüpa) order. (*See also* NĀ RO CHOS DRUG; MAHĀMUDRĀ.)

Naropa Institute

The first accredited Buddhist university in the U.S.A., founded in 1974 by Chögyam Trungpa (Chos kyi rgya mtsho drung pa Rin po che, 1940–1987), a reincarnate lama (SPRUL SKU) of the BKA' BRGYUD PA (Kagyüpa) order of TIBETAN BUDDHISM. The goal of the Institute is to combine Buddhist contemplative practices and Western academic subjects; Trungpa claimed that he was trying to follow the model of NĀLANDĀ MONASTIC UNIVERSITY.

Nechung

See GNAS CHUNG CHOS RJE.

nembutsu (Chin. *nien-fo*; Kor. *yŏmbul*; Viet. *niệm-phật*)

Japanese term that refers to the MANTRA "Namu Amida Butsu" (Chin. "*Na mo A-mi-t'o-fo*"; Viet. "*Nam-mô A-Di-Đà Phật*"; "Praise to AMITĀBHA BUDDHA"), which is chanted in East Asian Pure Land (Chin. CH'ING-T'U; Jpn. *Jōdō*; Kor. *Chŏngt'o*; Viet. *Đạo Trang*) traditions. It is an expression of faith in Amitābha, who is believed to have the power to bring people to his "pure land" of SUKHĀVATĪ after they die. Once reborn there, they will inevitably progress toward buddhahood because the conditions in Sukhāvatī are optimal for Buddhist practice. Adherents of the tradition commonly claim that chanting the *nembutsu* with sincere faith is the only effective religious practice for the present "final dharma age" (Jpn. MAPPŌ), in which people are unable to follow the "path of the sages," that is, the practices taught by ŚĀKYAMUNI BUDDHA to his followers, which require personal effort (JIRIKI). In the present age, the spiritual capacities of humans have degenerated to such an extent that they must rely on the "other-power" (TARIKI) of Amitābha for their salvation.

New Kadampa Tradition (NKT)

International organization founded by dGe bshes bsKal bzang rgya mtsho (Geshe Kelsang Gyatso, b. 1931), headquartered in England. The group has been at odds with the Tibetan government-in-exile and the Dalai Lama, primarily due to its insistence on continuing the propitiation and worship of the protector deity RDO RJE SHUGS LDAN (Dorje Shukden), who according to Tibetan Buddhist mythology is a wrathful dharma-protector (Tib. *chos skyong*; Skt. *dharma-pāla*) who is dedicated to defending the DGE LUGS PA (Gelukpa) order against its enemies. The Dalai Lama has proscribed practices related to rDo rje shugs ldan because the protector is associated with sectarianism, but the NKT claims that this ban infringes on its members' religious freedom. The choice of the name "New Kadampa Tradition" indicates that the group sees itself as continuing the lineage of ATIŚA and TSONG KHA PA. The NKT has been characterized as a fundamentalist movement because it believes that the dGe lugs pa order as a whole has strayed from the teachings of Tsong kha pa, and it claims to be maintaining a pure form of the tradition. The group has a publishing company named Tharpa Publications, which publishes books by Kelsang Gyatso.

Ngag dbang blo bzang rgya mtsho (Ngawang Losang Gyatso, 1617–1682)

The fifth Dalai Lama, referred to by Tibetans as the "Great Fifth" because of his accomplishments as a scholar, meditator, and ruler. With the help of Mongol forces he came to power in 1642, and during the next few decades united the three provinces of Tibet (the Central, South, and West) under a single ruler for the first time since the assassination of king gLANG DAR MA (Lang Darma) in 842. During his reign construction of the POTALA palace was initiated, but he died before it could be finished. His chief minister (*sde srid*), Sangs rgyas rgya mtsho (Sangye Gyatso), fearing that news of his death would halt the construction, concealed it for several years, claiming that the Dalai Lama was in meditative retreat. Subsequent Dalai Lamas were also rulers of Tibet until the invasion by China in the 1950s forced the fourteenth Dalai Lama to flee into exile.

ngakpa

See SNGAGS PA.

ngöndro

See SNGON 'GRO.

Ngor pa Sa skya pa (Ngorpa Sakyapa)

One of the two main branches of the SA SKYA PA order of TIBETAN BUDDHISM (the other being the TSHAR PA). Its headquarters is Ngor E wam chos ldan (Ngor Ewam Chöden) Monastery, founded by the LAM 'BRAS (*lamdre*) master Ngor chen Kun dga' bzang po (Ngorchen Günga Sangpo, 1382–1457).

Nguyên, Thiều (d. 1712)

Chinese monk who received ordination at the age of nineteen, and in 1665 fled to Vietnam following the Manchu conquest of China. He settled in Bính-Định province and founded the Thập-Tháp Di-Đa Temple. He subsequently founded a number of other temples. At the request of King Anh-Tôn (r. 1687–1691), he traveled to China, and subsequently returned with Buddhist images, sūtras, and records of Zen patriarchs. According to the *Lịch-Truyền Trõ-Đồ* (*Biographies of Zen Patriarchs*), he belonged to the sixty-ninth generation after ŚĀKYAMUNI BUDDHA and the thirty-third one following LIN-CHI I-HSÜAN. He is viewed by Vietnamese tradition as the founder of the Nguyên Thiều school of Thiền (Chin. CH'AN; Jpn. ZEN), a LÂM-TẾ (Chin. LIN-CHI; Jpn. RINZAI) tradition that today is the largest Buddhist order in the country.

Nhat Hanh, Thich (Thích Nhất Hạnh, b. 1926)

Vietnamese ZEN (Viet. *Thiền*) monk who was ordained in 1942, and during the 1950s and 1960s helped found the ENGAGED BUDDHISM movement. He is also credited with coining the term "Engaged Buddhism," and has been one of its most influential theoreticians. Following study at Princeton University and a teaching stint at Columbia University, he returned to Vietnam to engage in anti-war agitation following the fall of the Diem regime. He was one of the leaders of a non-violent protest movement based on Gandhian principles. In 1964, he founded the School of Youth for Social Service, which sent teams of people into the countryside to help war victims, establish schools and health clinics, and later rebuild villages that had been bombed. By the fall of Saigon, the organization had over 10,000 volunteers, including monks, nuns, and laypeople. Because of his anti-war activities, he was forced into exile by the Vietnamese government, and now lives in the West. In 1967 Martin Luther King, Jr. was so impressed by his efforts on behalf of peace that he nominated him for the Nobel Peace Prize. In 1982, he founded Plum Village, a monastery and retreat center in southwestern France, which now is his main residence. He has authored more than seventy-five books, mainly on Buddhist topics and peace, in Vietnamese, French, and English, including the best-selling *Being Peace.*

Ni gu ma (Niguma, ca. eleventh century)

Sister (or consort) of NĀROPA (ca. 1016–1100). She is best known for developing a set of tantric practices referred to as the "six dharmas of Ni gu ma" (*ni gu chos drug*). These have the same names and the same general outlines as the "six dharmas of Nāropa" (NĀ RO CHOS DRUG), but her explanations differ on a number of points.

Nichiren (1222–1282)

Japanese priest, son of a fisherman who was ordained at the age of fifteen and subsequently studied in the TENDAI tradition on Mount Hiei. He later became dissatisfied with Tendai and began preaching that in the present degenerate age (Jpn. MAPPŌ) the only valid text is the *Lotus Sūtra* (Skt. SADDHARMA-PUṆḌARĪKA-SŪTRA; Jpn. *Myōhō-renge-kyō*). He considered the doctrines of the text to be too profound for most people, however, and so he urged his followers to chant "Namu *Myōhō-renge-kyō*" ("Praise to the *Lotus Sūtra*") while facing a GOHONZON (a scroll with the Chinese characters of the sūtra's title – referred to as the DAIMOKU – inscribed on it). He trenchantly criticized other Buddhist schools, accusing them of propounding heretical teachings that he believed would lead to disaster for Japan, and he wrote several missives to the emperor urging that all other forms of Buddhism be suppressed. Not surprisingly, this led to some animosity, and there was even an attempt on his life. He miraculously escaped, and credited his survival with the power of the *Lotus Sūtra*. He was subsequently exiled to the remote island of Sado. Despite this setback, he managed to attract a sizeable number of followers. His persecutions convinced him that he was the incarnation of a bodhisattva mentioned in the sūtra, and he thought that he was living the predictions of the text. Today there are two main schools claiming descent from Nichiren: the lay SŌKA GAKKAI and the NICHIREN SHŌSHŪ priesthood. The two are engaged in a bitter rivalry, with the latter claiming that its priesthood has sole authority for administering the tradition, while the former is a lay organization that has formally severed its connection with the priesthood. The Nichiren Shōshū keeps the original *gohonzon* inscribed by Nichiren at its headquarters Taiseki-ji, at the foot of Mount Fuji, and maintains that this is the only authentic one. The priesthood further claims that members of Sōka Gakkai are using false *gohonzon*s and will derive no benefit from practices using them. The Sōka Gakkai began to distribute to its members copies of a *gohonzon* originally inscribed by Nichikan, the twenty-sixth high priest of Nichiren Shōshū, after the current dispute erupted.

Nichiren Shōshū ("True School of Nichiren")

One of the two main contemporary organizations (along with SŌKA GAKKAI) that trace themselves back to NICHIREN (1222–1282). The Nichiren Shōshū Sōkagakkai ("Nichiren Value Creation Society") was founded in 1930 by TSUNESABURŌ MAKIGUCHI and further expanded by his disciple Jōsei Toda (1900–1958). It was formally incorporated in 1937, and in 1951 adopted the name Nichiren Shōshū Sōkagakkai. In its early years it enjoyed phenomenal growth, largely due to its aggressive (and controversial) recruitment practices. One of the most effective of these was SHAKUBUKU, which involved pressuring potential converts in order to wear them down. This practice has been de-emphasized in recent years. After an acrimonious battle between the priesthood and the lay leadership, in 1991 the high priest of Nichiren Shōshū, Nikken Abe, officially excommunicated the lay Sōka Gakkai organization. He declared that only the priesthood of the Nichiren Shōshū represented the true tradition of Nichiren, and further claimed that only its GOHONZON (a scroll inscribed by Nichiren with the Chinese characters of the DAIMOKU) is an authentic basis for chanting and worship. The priests of the Nichiren Shōshū assert that the practice of chanting the *daimoku* ("Namu *Myōhō-renge-kyō*," "Praise to the *Lotus Sūtra*") requires that the practitioner perform it in front of an authentic *gohonzon* and that those used by the Sōka Gakkai are ineffective for worship.

nien-fo

See NEMBUTSU.

nikāya (1) ("scripture collection")

Pāli and Sanskrit term that refers to collections of scriptures. In the THERAVĀDA canon, there are five *nikāya*s in the Sutta-piṭaka (SŪTRA-PIṬAKA, "Basket of Discourses"): (1) Dīgha nikāya ("Long Discourses"); (2) MAJJHIMA NIKĀYA ("Middle Length Discourses"); (2) SAṂYUTTA NIKĀYA ("Connected Discourses"); (3) AṄGUTTARA NIKĀYA ("Increased-by-One Discourses"); and (5) KHUDDAKA NIKĀYA ("Lesser Discourses"). (*See also* ĀGAMA.)

nikāya (2)

An individual school. In this sense, it refers to a group of monks who choose to share a common textual tradition and who engage in the same communal rituals. Often the key factor distinguishing one *nikāya* from another is its interpretation and practice of VINAYA rules. A separate *nikāya* is formed when a group of monks can no longer agree on the performance of *vinaya* rules (*vinaya-karma*) or on matters of doctrine. The result is a "splitting of the SAṂGHA" (Skt. *saṃgha-bheda*). Although such schisms have occurred often in Buddhist history, they are considered to be a serious breach of the *vinaya*. (*See also* SIYAM NIKĀYA; THERAVĀDA NIKĀYA.)

Nikāya Buddhism

In this encyclopedia, those Buddhist traditions that base themselves on the discourses contained in the five NIKĀYAS (1) (Skt. ĀGAMA) are referred to as "Nikāya Buddhism," in preference to the common (but pejorative) term "HĪNAYĀNA," meaning "Lesser Vehicle." The choice of "Nikāya Buddhism" as a designator was made in view of the fact that the adherents of these schools have rejected the notion that they are inferior to their rivals (who refer to themselves as "MAHĀYĀNA," or "Greater Vehicle"), and despite their widely varying doctrines and practices, all agree on the authoritativeness of the *nikāya*s. Traditionally the number of these schools was said to be eighteen, but in fact many more are mentioned in Indian Buddhist literature. The only Nikāya Buddhist tradition that continues today is THERAVĀDA.

nirmāṇa-kāya (Tib. *sprul sku*; "emanation body")

One of the three bodies of a BUDDHA, according to MAHĀYĀNA buddhology (the other two are enjoyment body and truth body). Although conceived as human in early Buddhism, in Mahāyāna buddhas are credited with a variety of supernatural powers, including the ability to create "emanation bodies," physical manifestations that are produced in order to benefit sentient beings. These may be human or animal forms, or may even be bridges or other physical objects that provide benefit. The most important type of emanation body is the physical form of a buddha, such as ŚĀKYAMUNI, who according to Mahāyāna was a manifestation that can be perceived by ordinary beings. Enjoyment bodies, by contrast, reside in "pure lands" and can only be seen by advanced practitioners. In TIBETAN BUDDHISM the term "emanation body" (Tib. SPRUL SKU) is used to refer to lamas (BLA MA) who are believed to be the physical manifestations of buddhas or BODHISATTVAS or the reincarnations of deceased masters (these are not, of course, mutually exclusive). (*See also* DHARMA-KĀYA; SAṂBHOGA-KĀYA.)

nirvāṇa (Pāli *nibbāna*; Tib. *mya ngan las 'das pa*; Jpn. *nehan*; "cessation")

Liberation from cyclic existence (SAṂSĀRA), which is the final goal of Buddhist practice. The term is a combination of the Sanskrit prefix *nir* plus the verbal root vā, and literally means "blow out" or "extinguish." It is attained when the afflictions – such as anger, desire, and obscuration – have been eliminated and one has brought to a halt the effects of compositional factors (SAṂSKĀRA). At this point the energies that lead to rebirth within cyclic existence have been eliminated, and so one is released from the round of birth, death, and rebirth. *Nirvāṇa* is described in both negative and positive terms in Buddhist literature: it is said to be the cessation of suffering (DUḤKHA), and it is also said to be a peaceful and supramundane (*lokottara*) state. With the development of the BODHISATTVA ideal in MAHĀYĀNA, the concept was revaluated, and it was said that bodhisattvas, due to their great compassion, forgo their own *nirvāṇa*s in order to lead others to liberation. A number of Mahāyāna texts further declare that the "HĪNAYĀNA" understanding of *nirvāṇa* (viewed as one's own individual liberation) is based on a category mistake, since there is fundamentally no real difference between *saṃsāra* and *nirvāṇa* – the state in which one lives is a result of one's perceptions, which reflect one's level of spiritual development.

noble truths

See ĀRYA-SATYA.

no-mind

See WU-NIEN.

no-self

See ANĀTMAN.

non-Buddhist

See TĪRTHIKA.

non-returner

See ANĀGAMIN.

Non-Sectarian

See RIS MED.

Nor bu gling ka (Norbulingka; "Jewel Park")

Summer residence of the DALAI LAMAS prior to the Chinese invasion and annexation of Tibet in the 1950s. It was constructed in the eighteenth century and is located outside Lhasa.

Northern School of Ch'an

See NAN-TSUNG-CH'AN; SHEN-HSIU.

novice

See ŚRĀMAṆERA.

nun

See BHIKṢUṆĪ.

The Nor bu gling ka ("Jewel Park"), former summer residence of the Dalai Lamas.

Nyānatiloka (Anton Walter Florus Gueth, 1878–1957)

German violin virtuoso who converted to Buddhism after traveling to India, Sri Lanka, and Burma. He was ordained as a Theravāda monk in Burma in 1903, and in 1911 he returned to Sri Lanka, where he founded a hermitage. He wrote a number of books, including *Guide through the Abhidhamma Piṭaka* and *Path to Deliverance.*

Nyingmapa

See RNYING MA PA.

O

Ōbaku

The smallest of the surviving lineages of Japanese Zen (the other two are Sōtō and Rinzai), founded by the Chinese Ch'an master Yun-yüan Lung-ch'i (Jpn. Ingen Ryūki, d. 1673). He traveled to Japan in 1654 and founded the school's main temple, Ōbakusan Mampuku-ji, in Kyōto. Today it is the smallest of the three Zen lineages, and has only a handful of operating temples.

Obon (Skt. *Ullambana*; Chin. *Yu-lan*; Viet. *An-cư*)

Yearly Japanese festival in which people make offerings to the spirits of the dead. The practice goes back to a story in the PĀLI CANON, in which MAUDGALYĀYANA realized through his psychic power that his mother had been reborn as a hungry ghost (Pāli *peta*; Skt. PRETA). By making offerings and performing rituals for her, he was able to free her from her suffering. The festival began in China in the sixth century and was later introduced to Japan, where it incorporated elements of local folk religion. It is celebrated during July 13–16, and sometimes in August. (*See also* ULLAMBANA.)

Olcott, Col. Henry Steele (1832–1907)

American who co-founded the Theosophical Society with Helena Blavatsky. He took Buddhist refuge vows in Sri Lanka in 1880 and was involved in a number of Buddhist causes. He is perhaps best known for developing a "Buddhist flag" and a "Buddhist catechism."

Oldenberg, Hermann (1854–1920)

Eminent German buddhologist, best known for his work on Pāli canonical texts and his influential book *The Buddha, his Life, his Doctrine, his Community*. He also translated the DĪPAVAṂSA and edited the five volumes of the VINAYA-PIṬAKA.

oṃ

Sanskrit syllable that is often found at the beginning of Buddhist MANTRAS. It was inherited from Hinduism, and there are various explanations of its meaning. One common notion found in MAHĀYĀNA literature is that it symbolizes the funda-

mental nature of reality, i.e., emptiness (ŚŪNYATĀ).

Oṃ maṇi padme hūṃ ("*Oṃ* Jewel Lotus *hūṃ*")

The MANTRA of AVALOKITEŚVARA, who in MAHĀYĀNA is said to be the embodiment of compassion (KARUṆĀ). It is the most commonly chanted mantra in TIBETAN BUDDHISM, probably due to the fact that Avalokiteśvara is widely viewed as being particularly closely associated with Tibet and its history. Several of the most prominent lineages of reincarnating lamas (Tib. SPRUL SKU) – including the DALAI LAMAS and the RGYAL BA KAR MA PAS – are believed to be physical manifestations of Avalokiteśvara. The meaning of the mantra has been debated by contemporary scholars. Some read "*padme*" (lotus) as a Sanskrit locative, in which case it would be translated as "*Oṃ* Jewel in the Lotus *hūṃ*." Others interpret *padme* as a vocative feminine, and thus translate it as "*Oṃ* Jewel-Lotus *hūṃ*." Both readings are, however, problematic: in the first interpretation the mantra would be ungrammatical (which is not uncommon with Buddhist Sanskrit mantras); and the second interpretation faces the problem of why a male buddha would be referred to with a feminine vocative.

once-returner

See SAKṚDĀGAMIN.

one vehicle

See EKAYĀNA.

ordinary being

See PṚTHAG-JANA.

ordination

In order to enter the Buddhist monastic community (SAṂGHA), a formal initiation procedure is required, in which the ordinand takes certain vows with respect to lifestyle and conduct. In the THERAVĀDA tradition (and in other traditions that follow the MŪLASARVĀSTIVĀDA VINAYA), there are two main types of ordination: novice ordination and full monastic ordination. The novice ordination (ŚRĀMAṆERA for males, ŚRĀMAṆERĪ for females) involves formally "taking refuge" (in the "three refuges" [ŚARAṆA]: Buddha, DHARMA, *saṃgha*) and acceptance of ten rules of conduct (*daśa-śīla*). The ordinand is required to follow the code of conduct outlined in the PRĀTIMOKṢA (a set of rules for monks and nuns) and is assigned two teachers: (1) an *ācārya* ("instructor"); and (2) an *upādhyāya* ("preceptor"). The novice's head is shaved, and he/she is presented with three robes (*tricīvara*) and a begging-bowl. This ordination is referred to as *pravrajyā* ("going forth" from the home life into homelessness). The full ordination is called *upasampadā*, and through this a person becomes a full-fledged adult member of the *saṃgha* (BHIKṢU for males, BHIKṢUṆĪ for females). Both types of ordination require a quorum of properly ordained members of the *saṃgha* (generally either five or ten). Buddhist ordination is a voluntary act, and the ordinand may at any time decide to leave the monastic community and return to lay life.

Ōryō-ha (Chin. *Huang-lung p'ai*)

The first school of ZEN (Chin. CH'AN) in Japan, a RINZAI (Chin. LIN-CHI) tradition brought from China by EISAI ZENJI (1141–1215). It was founded by Huang-lung Hui-nan (Jpn. *Ōryō E'nan*, 1001–1069) and is counted among the "seven schools" (Jpn. GOKE-SHICHISHŪ) of Ch'an. It died out in China during the Sung dynasty and in Japan several generations after Eisai.

padma (Pāli *paduma*; Tib. *padma*; "lotus")

Water lily (*nelumbo nucifera, nelumbium speciosum*), widely used as a symbol of awakening (BODHI) in Buddhism. In Buddhist iconography – particularly in VAJRAYĀNA traditions – buddhas are often depicted sitting on huge lotus thrones.

Padma Nor bu Rin po che Thub bstan legs bshad (Penor Rinpoche Thupden Lekshe, b. 1932)

Head of the rNYING MA PA (Nyingmapa) order of TIBETAN BUDDHISM, eleventh throne holder (*khri 'dzin*) of the dPAL YUL (Beyül) lineage. He studied with and received initiations from many of the leading lamas of his time and holds all of the main lineages of the rNying ma pa. In 1959 he fled to Nepal following the Chinese invasion of Tibet and eventually re-established the dPal yul lineage in Bylakuppe, South India.

Padmasambhava (Tib. *Padma 'byung gnas, Gu ru Rin po che*, ca. eighth century; "Lotus Born")

Tantric master from Oḍḍiyāna (Tib. U rgyan, which some scholars believe was modern-day Swāt, but others think may have been near Ghazni) who according to later Tibetan chronicles traveled to Tibet at the behest of KHRI SRONG LDE BRTSAN (Trisong Detsen, ca. 740–798). Upon his arrival he encountered fierce opposition from the demons of Tibet and from adherents of the indigenous religion of BON, but through his magical powers was able to defeat them all. Following this, Padmasambhava, Khri srong lDe brtsan, and ŚĀNTARAKṢITA established the first Buddhist monastery in Tibet, named BSAM YAS (Samye), in 775. He is considered by the RNYING MA PA (Nyingmapa) order of TIBETAN BUDDHISM to be its founder, and is revered within the tradition as a physical emanation of AMITĀBHA BUDDHA. Along with his disciple and consort, YE SHES MTSHO RGYAL (Yeshe Tsogyel), he is credited with composing a huge corpus of texts called "hidden treasures" (Tib. GTER MA), which were concealed by them. The concealment was safeguarded by spells which ensured that only their respective ordained "treasure-discoverers" (GTER STON) would be able to find and reveal them. In light of the importance assigned to Padmasambhava by later Tibetan tradition, it is interesting to note that there is not a single mention of him in any sources composed during his purported lifetime, a fact that has led some contemporary scholars to question his historicity.

padmāsana (Pāli *padumāsana*; Tib. *padma'i gnas mal*; Jpn. *kekka-fusa*; "lotus position")

One of the most common positions for seated meditation, in which one crosses both legs, placing the feet on the inside of the thighs, soles facing upward. The palms rest in the lap, facing upward, with right on top of left and the tips of the thumbs touching.

pagoda

Architectural style that became popular in East Asian Buddhism, believed to have been derived from the Indian Buddhist STŪPA. There is also speculation that the term "pagoda" may have derived from the Sri Lankan term for *stūpa*, *dägaba*. The pagoda style is attested in China as early as the fifth century. The basic design consists of a central axis with three or more eaves, which become gradually smaller from bottom to top. Pagodas, like *stūpas*, are often built to house the remains of deceased Buddhist masters. The style is also used for small votive objects which are found throughout East Asia.

Pagoda at Nan Tien Temple, Woolongong, New South Wales, Australia.

Pai-chang Huai-hai (Jpn. *Hyakujō Ekai*, 720–814)

Dharma-successor of MA-TSU TAO-I (Jpn. *Baso Dōitsu*, 709–788) and one of the most influential Chinese CH'AN masters. He is best known for his rules for the conduct of monks in Ch'an monasteries, the *Pure Rule of Pai-chang* (*Pai-chang ch'ing-kuei*). His rules emphasize the importance of both daily sitting meditation (Chin. *tso-ch'an*; Jpn. ZAZEN) and manual work. He is credited with first enunciating the famous Ch'an/Zen dictum, "A day without work is a day without food." With this emphasis on self-sufficiency, Ch'an monks no longer followed the Indian paradigm of relying primarily on alms received by begging. Pai-chang retained the alms round (Jpn. *takuhatsu*), however, as an exercise in humility.

Pai-lien-tsung ("White Lotus Society")

Group founded in the twelfth century by Mao Tzu-yüan, a T'IEN-T'AI monk who became interested in the teachings of HUI-YÜAN (334–416) and the CH'ING-T'U tradition. The society included monks, nuns, and laypeople, whose collective goal was to be reborn in AMITĀBHA's "Pure Land" of SUKHĀVATĪ. Its members engaged in a daily recitation of penance and performed good works in order to accumulate the karma necessary for rebirth in Sukhāvatī. They followed a strict vegetarian diet, and also avoided wine, milk, and onions. They were accused of worshiping demons and banned, but the group survived, becoming a secret society.

Pai-ma-ssu ("White Horse Monastery")

The oldest Buddhist monastery in China, said to have been built on the model of the Indian JETAVANA (1) retreat some time around the first century C.E.

Pāli canon

Scriptural collection of the THERAVĀDA NIKĀYA, consisting of "Three Baskets" (*tipiṭaka*; Skt. TRIPIṬAKA) of texts: (1) Sutta-piṭaka (Skt. SŪTRA-PIṬAKA, "Basket of Discourses"), containing sermons believed to have been spoken by ŚĀKYAMUNI BUDDHA or his immediate disciples; (2) VINAYA-PIṬAKA, "Basket of Discipline"), which includes texts outlining the rules and expected conduct for Buddhist monks and nuns; and (3) ABHIDHAMMA-PIṬAKA (Skt. ABHIDHARMA-PIṬAKA, "Basket of Higher Doctrine"), consisting of scholastic treatises that codify and explain the doctrines of the first "Basket." Pāli is an Indian language that is structurally and grammatically similar to SANSKRIT, but appears to be different from any other dialect so far attested. Contemporary scholars generally believe that it is a hybrid dialect which exhibits features of dialects spoken in northwestern India. Theravāda orthodoxy maintains that the Pāli canon contains the actual words of the Buddha and that it was definitively redacted and sealed shortly after his death at the "First Buddhist Council" at RĀJAGṚHA, but modern scholarship has shown that it consists of materials evidencing different styles and authors, and that it was probably redacted and altered over the course of centuries before being written down.

Pāli Text Society

Academic organization founded by THOMAS W. RHYS DAVIDS in 1881 with the stated purpose of translating and editing the texts of the PĀLI CANON. It brought together most of the leading scholars in the field, and it has succeeded in producing Romanized edited transliterations and English translations of most of the canon.

Paṇ chen bLa ma (Panchen Lama)

The second most influential reincarnate lama (SPRUL SKU) of the DGE LUGS PA (Gelukpa) order of TIBETAN BUDDHISM, believed to be a physical manifestation of AMITĀBHA BUDDHA. The seat of the Paṇ chen bLa mas is BKRA SHIS LHUN PO (Tashilhünpo) Monastery, located in the town of gZhis ka rtse (Shigatse) in Tibet. The title "Paṇ chen," or "Great Scholar," was first given to dGe 'dun grub (Gendün Drüp, 1391–1475), the abbot of bKra shis lhun po. It was later inherited by successive abbots of the monastery. In the seventeenth century, the fifth Dalai Lama conferred the title "Paṇ chen bLa ma" on his teacher, bLo bzang chos kyi rgyal mtshan (Losang Chögi Gyeltsen, 1567–1662). He further announced that bLo bzang chos kyi rgyal mtshan would reincarnate in the form of a recognizable child-successor. The title "Paṇ chen bla ma" was retroactively conferred on his two previous incarnations. There is an ongoing dispute between the DALAI LAMA and the People's Republic of China (PRC) regarding the identity of the eleventh Paṇ chen bLa ma. The Dalai Lama officially recognized a Tibetan boy named dGe 'dun chos kyi nyi ma (Gendün Chögi Nyima) as the reincarnation of the tenth Paṇ chen bLa ma, but the PRC has rejected both his choice and his authority to recognize reincarnations (despite the fact that he is the spiritual leader of Tibetan Buddhism and official PRC doctrine denounces the institution of reincarnation as a "feudal superstition"). The PRC has even gone so far as to install its own candidate, but the absurdity of non-Buddhist Communist Party officials choosing reincarnations has made it necessary for the PRC to use force and imprisonment to coerce Tibetans to accept its choice.

pañca-mahābhaya (Pāli *pañca-mahābhaya*; Tib. *'jigs pa chen po lnga*) ("five great fears")

The main fears of beginners on the BODHISATTVA path: (1) fear concerning livelihood (*ājīvikā-bhaya*); (2) fear of disapproval (*aśloka-bhaya or akīrti-bhaya*); (3) fear of death (*maraṇa-bhaya*); (4) fear of bad transmigrations (*durgati-bhaya*); and (5) fear that is timidity when addressing assemblies (*pariṣacchāradya-bhaya*). They are said to be overcome when one attains the level of the "unusual attitude" (*adhyāśaya*; this is a feeling of genuine concern for the sufferings of sentient beings, which precedes BODHI-CITTA).

pañca-śīla ("five precepts")

Rules of conduct for Buddhist lay practitioners, generally conferred in a formal ceremony that involves first chanting the Buddhist refuge formula and then taking a vow to avoid: (1) killing living beings; (2) taking what is not given; (3) sexual misconduct; (4) harmful and false speech; and (5) intoxicants. In contemporary Buddhist societies, it is common for lay practitioners to take only one or several of the precepts if they believe that they will be unable to observe all five.

Panchen Lama

See PAṆ CHEN BLA MA.

p'an-chiao ("classification of teachings")

Chinese practice of classifying Buddhist doctrines and schools hierarchically. It was a response to the plethora of doctrines and texts that arrived in China from India and Central Asia, which contained a range of ideas and systems, many of them claiming to be the supreme teaching (but often contradicting others also claiming to be the supreme teaching). There are a number of such classification schemes in CHINESE BUDDHISM, and not surprisingly each ranks Buddhist schools in such a way that its own system comes out on top. The two most influential classification schema were those of Hui-kuang (468–537) and FA-TSANG (643–712). Hui-kuang divided Buddhist teachings into four main doctrines (Chin. TSUNG): (1) that phenomena arise in dependence upon pre-existing causes and conditions (*yin-yüan-tsung*); (2) that phenomena are mere names (*chia-ming-tsung*) and do not exist independently from causes and conditions; (3) that names are also empty and do not refer to any truly existent phenomena (*k'uang-hsiang-tsung*); and (4) the HUA-YEN doctrine that the buddha-nature (Chin. *fo-hsing*; Skt. BUDDHATĀ) is all-pervasive and is the ultimate reality (*ch'ang-tsung*). The first position is identified with certain ABHIDHARMA traditions (mainly SARVĀSTIVĀDA), which considered phenomena (Chin. *fa*; Skt. DHARMA) to be truly existent in the past, present, and future. The second position is associated with the SATYASIDDHI (Chin. CH'ENG-SHIH) school, and the third is held by the SAN-LUN school.

Fa-tsang divided Buddhist teachings into five categories: (1) the teachings of ŚRĀVAKAS; (2) basic MAHĀYĀNA teachings; (3) definitive Mahāyāna teachings; (4) the abrupt teachings of Mahāyāna; and (5) the round or complete teachings of Mahāyāna. The first refers to doctrines associated with the ĀGAMAS, which deny the existence of the individual but assert the true existence of its component parts (*dharma*). The second includes Mahāyāna doctrines that assert the emptiness (ŚŪNYATĀ) of all things, which are said to come into being as a result of causes and conditions, and so they lack own-being (SVABHĀVA). This category includes San-lun and FA-HSIANG. The third category comprises systems that assert the conventional existence of conditioned phenomena, while also asserting that all phenomena are empty. An example is T'IEN-T'AI. The third category refers to doctrines that teach that awakening is attained all at once, in a sudden flash of insight. It includes CH'AN and the VIMALAKĪRTI-NIRDEŚA-SŪTRA. The final category is represented by Hua-yen, and refers to the notion that all phenomena interpenetrate and derive from the "sphere of reality" (Skt. *dharma-dhātu*), which is said to be the immutable and unchanging nature of all reality.

Paramārtha (Chin. *Chen-ti*, 499–569; "Ultimate Truth")

Indian Buddhist monk who traveled to China in 546 and became a noted translator, particularly of YOGĀCĀRA texts, including ASAṄGA's *Compendium of the Great Vehicle* (*Mahāyāna-saṃgraha*) and VASUBANDHU's *Twenty Verses* (*Viṃśatikā*) and *Treasury of Higher Doctrine* (ABHIDHARMA-KOŚA). In all he is credited with translating 64 works in 278 volumes.

paramārtha[-satya] (Pāli *paramatta*[*-sacca*]; Tib. *don dam pa*[*'i bden pa*]; "ultimate [truth]")

Refers to the final nature of reality, which is unconditioned (*asaṃskṛta*) and which neither is produced nor ceases. It is equated with emptiness (ŚŪNYATĀ) and truth body (DHARMA-KĀYA) and is contrasted with conventional truths (SAṂVṚTI-SATYA), which are produced by causes and conditions and impermanence (ANITYA).

pāramitā (Tib. *pha rol tu phyin pa*; "perfection")

The six (and sometimes ten) qualities that BODHISATTVAS cultivate on the path to buddhahood: (1) generosity (DĀNA); (2) ethics (ŚĪLA); (3) patience (KṢĀNTI); (4) effort (VĪRYA); (5) concentration (DHYĀNA); and (6) wisdom (PRAJÑĀ). An additional four are often presented in texts that correlate their cultivation with attainment of the ten bodhisattva "levels" (BHŪMI): (7) skill in means (UPĀYA-KAUŚALYA); (8) aspiration (PRAṆIDHĀNA); (9) power (BALA); and wisdom (JÑĀNA).

parinirvāṇa (Pāli *parinibbāna*; Tib. *yongs su mya ngan las 'das pa*; "final *nirvāṇa*")

Originally this term referred to the passing of ŚĀKYAMUNI BUDDHA, whose death marked the end of the cycle of birth, death, and rebirth for him. It indicates that he successfully brought to an end all of the conditions that might lead to further rebirth within cyclic existence.

paritta (or *pirit*; "protection")

Pāli term for a common practice in THERAVĀDA countries, which involves chanting Buddhist texts as a way of generating merit. Often laypeople make donations to monks who do the chanting, believing that this activity makes merit both by supporting the monks and by causing the texts to be chanted. It is believed that this activity helps those who engage in it to accrue merit, which is conducive to a better rebirth, and it is also thought to bring benefits in the present life. The most common form of *paritta* involves a group of monks who chant a set of texts during the course of a night.

Pāṭaliputra

Ancient Indian city corresponding to modern-day Patna. It was the capital of the Mauryan dynasty, and under the sponsorship of King AŚOKA was the site of the "Third Buddhist Council." The council (*saṃgīti* or *saṃghāyanā*) occurred some time around 250 B.C.E. and was headed by the monk Moggaliputta Tissa. A thousand monks were convened at the council to debate various theories that had developed since the death of ŚĀKYAMUNI BUDDHA. These viewpoints were later collected in an ABHIDHARMA text entitled *Points of Controversy* (*Kathāvatthu*). The views of the Vibhajyavāda sect – a precursor of Theravāda – were reportedly declared to be orthodox.

path of accumulation

See SAṂBHĀRA-MĀRGA.

path of meditation

See BHĀVANĀ-MĀRGA.

path of no more learning

See AŚAIKṢA-MĀRGA.

path of preparation

See PRAYOGA-MĀRGA.

path of seeing

See DARŚANA-MĀRGA.

patience

See KṢĀNTI.

Payül

See DPAL YUL.

Pei-tsung-ch'an

See SHEN-HSIU; NAN-TSUNG-CH'AN.

Penor Rinpoche

See PADMA NOR BU RIN PO CHE.

perfection of wisdom

See PRAJÑĀ-PĀRAMITĀ.

perfections

See PĀRAMITĀ.

performance tantra

See CARYĀ-TANTRA.

'Phags pa blo gros, Chos rgyal (Chögyel Pakpa Lodrö, 1235–1289)

Nephew of SA SKYA PAṆḌITA (Sakya Pandita, 1182–1251), who succeeded him as regent of Tibet and chaplain to the Mongol court. The requirement that the SA SKYA PA (Sakya̮pa) hierarch remain there was probably originally intended to keep him as a hostage in order to ensure that Tibet remained compliant, but 'Phags pa used it as an opportunity for missionizing, and reportedly converted Khubilai Khan (r. 1260–1294) and his consort Chamui to Buddhism. He was appointed to the posts of "royal preceptor" (*ti-shih*) and "preceptor of the state" (*kuo-shih*). 'Phags pa and Khubilai developed the "patron–priest" (Tib. *yon mchod*) relationship, which stipulated that the khan would protect Tibet and the Sa skya pa hierarchs, and that they would serve as the spiritual preceptors to the royal court. (*See also* MONGOLIAN BUDDHISM.)

phra ("elder")

The Thai equivalent of the Pāli term *thera*, given to monks who have been ordained at least twenty years and who have passed a standard examination in Pāli.

phur ba (Skt. *kīla*; "dagger")

Ritual dagger used in Tibetan tantric ceremonies. It commonly has a shaft with three blades and a VAJRA at the end of the handle. It is often used in ceremonies in which evil forces are subdued, and is commonly plunged into an effigy representing these forces.

phyi dar (*chidar*; "second dissemination")

With the demise of the YAR LUNG DYNASTY following the assassination of King GLANG DAR MA (Lang Darma, r. 838–842), TIBETAN BUDDHISM began a period of decline. The tradition was revived by ATIŚA (982–1054) after his arrival in Tibet in 1042. Under his influence, the MAHĀYĀNA Buddhism of the great North Indian monasteries of NĀLANDĀ and VIKRAMAŚĪLA was established as the orthodox tradition of Tibet. During the second dissemination there was also a coordinated effort to translate the Indian Buddhist canon, and to this end groups of translators (Tib. *lo tsā ba*) were formed, and standard lexicons were developed. The "new orders" (Tib. GSAR MA) of Tibetan Buddhism – SA SKYA PA, BKA' BRGYUD PA, and DGE LUGS PA – all rely on translations of tantric texts prepared during this period, while the RNYING MA PA order favors the translations of the "first dissemination" (SNGA DAR), which began with the arrival of PADMASAMBHAVA.

piṇḍa-pāta ("alms-giving")

The daily alms round of monks in THERAVĀDA countries, which constitutes one of the major opportunities for merit-making on the part of the laity. In the morning, monks walk in a line, carrying their begging-bowls in their hands, and laypeople place food in the bowls.

pirit

See PARITTA.

Pi-yen-lu (Jpn. *Hekigan-roku*; *Blue Cliff Records*)

Oldest collection of *kung-an* (Jpn. KŌAN), the earliest stratum of which was compiled by the Chinese Ch'an master Hsüeh-tou Ch'ung-hsien (Jpn. *Setchō Jūken*, 980–1052) and developed into its present form by Yüan-wu K'o-ch'in (Jpn. *Engo Kokugon*, 1063–1135). He added an introduction to the 100 *kung-an*s of the earlier text, along with poetic explanations that are considered masterpieces of classical Chinese poetry. Along with the WU-MEN-KUAN, it is one of the two most influential collections of *kung-an*.

Platform Sūtra

See LIU-TSU-TA-SHIH FA-PAO-T'AN-CHING.

poṣadha (Pāli *uposatha*; Tib. *gso sbyong*; "fasting")

The bi-monthly ceremony held alternately on full-moon and new-moon days. It is required of monks and nuns according to the rules of the VINAYA. The central practice is a recitation of the monastic rules as contained in the *Prātimokṣa-sūtra*, followed by public confession of any transgressions of them. According to the rules of the *vinaya*, it should be performed by all the monks of a particular area and should occur within an established boundary (*sīmā*) and according to a prescribed formula (Skt. *karma-vācanā*; Pāli *kamma-vācā*). It is still observed today in THERAVĀDA countries, and the laity often mark the occasion by visiting local monasteries, where monks commonly give dharma instructions.

Potala

The winter palace of the DALAI LAMAS in Lhasa, the construction of which was begun during the life of the fifth Dalai Lama, NGAG DBANG BLO BZANG RGYA MTSHO (Ngawang Losang Gyatso, 1617–1682) and completed after his death. The name is derived from an island named Potalaka in the Indian Ocean, believed by tradition to be an abode of AVALOKITEŚVARA. Prior to the Chinese invasion and annexation of Tibet in the 1950s, it was the seat of the Tibetan government and housed the Dalai Lama's personal monastery, rNam rgyal (Namgyel). After the flight of the fourteenth Dalai Lama into exile in 1959, it was turned into a propaganda museum and tourist attraction by the People's Republic of China.

power

See BALA.

prabhāsvara-citta (Pāli *pabhassara-citta*; Tib. *'od gsal sems*; "mind of clear light")

According to TIBETAN BUDDHISM, this is the most fundamental level of mind, in relation to which all other minds are adventitious (Tib. *glo bur*; Skt. *agantuka*). During the process of death, the coarser levels of mind progressively pass away, until the mind of clear light dawns. This is said to be the moment of death according to tantric medical theory. The term is also found in the *Aṅguttara-nikāya*. (*See also* ANUTTARA-YOGA-TANTRA; BAR DO.)

pradakṣiṇa (Pāli *padakkhiṇa*; Tib. *skor ba*; "circumambulation")

One of the most common merit-making activities throughout the Buddhist world, popular among both monastics

The Potala, former winter residence of the Dalai Lamas in Lhasa.

and laypeople. It takes different forms, but its central practice is walking a circular route around a holy place in a clockwise direction (an exception to this is the non-Buddhist Tibetan Bon po tradition, whose members circumambulate in a counter-clockwise direction). The probable reason for the clockwise orientation for Buddhists is the Indian notion that the left hand is ritually impure.

prajñā (Pāli *paññā*; Tib. *shes rab*; Jpn. *hannya*; "wisdom")

In general, this refers to the development of intuitive understanding of key Buddhist concepts. In MAHĀYĀNA, the "perfection of wisdom" is the sixth of the "perfections" (PĀRAMITĀ) that a BODHISATTVA cultivates on the path to buddhahood. In Mahāyāna it is associated with direct perception of emptiness (ŚŪNYATĀ) and is attained on the sixth bodhisattva "level" (BHŪMI). Along with KARUṆĀ (compassion), it is one of the two main qualities that bodhisattvas cultivate in pursuit of buddhahood.

Prajñā-pāramitā sūtras (Tib. *Shes rab kyi pha rol tu phyin pa'i mdo*; Chin. *Pan-jo ching*; Jpn. *Hannagyō*; Viet. *Bát-nhã*; "Perfection of Wisdom sūtras")

A collection of texts that share a number of similar themes, the central one being a focus on the "perfection of wisdom" and its implications. The earliest stratum of this literature is probably found in the early parts of the *Eight Thousand Line Perfection of Wisdom Sūtra* (AṢṬASĀHASRIKĀ-PRAJÑĀ-PĀRAMITĀ-SŪTRA), which was probably composed around the first century B.C.E. From this basic text several much larger variations developed, the larger size mostly being due to elaborations of lists. Thus there are versions in 18,000, 25,000, and 100,000 verses. According to EDWARD CONZE, the period of increasing size was followed by a period in which the texts were condensed, which resulted in such influential sūtras as the PRAJÑĀ-PĀRAMITĀ-HṚDAYA-SŪTRA and the VAJRACCHEDIKĀ-PRAJÑĀ-PĀRAMITĀ-SŪTRA. In structure, they differ markedly from the discourses of the PĀLI CANON, though some important features are maintained. Like the earlier discourses, they begin with the formula, "Thus have I heard at one time . . ." (EVAṂ MAYĀ ŚRUTAM EKASMIN SAMAYE), and the setting is generally one of the places in which the Pāli discourses were reported, but the audience is greatly expanded. Many of the sūtras are discourses between the Buddha and his immediate disciples (for instance SUBHŪTI and ŚĀRIPUTRA), but other participants – and the doctrinal content – are distinctively MAHĀYĀNA, with a focus on the BODHISATTVA path, the implications of meditation on emptiness (ŚŪNYATĀ), etc.

Prajñā-pāramitā-hṛdaya-sūtra (Tib. *Shes rab kyi pha rol tu phyin pa'i snying po'i mdo*; Chin. *Po-jo hsin ching*; Jpn. *Maka Hannyaharamita shingyō*; *Heart of the Perfection of Wisdom Sūtra*)

One of the most widely influential texts of MAHĀYĀNA Buddhism, which is thought to contain the condensed essence of the voluminous "perfection of wisdom" literature. It is about one page in English translation, and it consists of a dialogue between ŚĀKYAMUNI BUDDHA and AVALOKITEŚVARA, focusing on "emptiness" (ŚŪNYATĀ). One of its most famous statements is: "Form is emptiness, and emptiness is form." It is also famous for the enigmatic MANTRA at its conclusion: "Gone, gone beyond, gone completely beyond, hail awakening!" (Skt. "*Gate gate paragate parasaṃgate bodhi svāha*").

Pramāṇa-vāda (Tib. *Tshad ma'i lugs*; "Epistemology")

Tradition of Buddhist philosophy whose founder is generally considered to be DIGNĀGA (ca. 480–540) and whose most celebrated exponent was his disciple DHARMAKĪRTI (ca. 530–600). The philosophers of this school developed a widely influential system of logic and epistemology, the elaboration of which owed a great deal to their debates with the Nyāya tradition of Indian philosophy. Dignāga and Dharmakīrti, as well as later exponents of the tradition such as Prajñākaragupta (ca. 850), ŚĀNTARAKṢITA (ca. eighth century), KAMALAŚĪLA (ca. eighth century), and Ratnakīrti (ca. eleventh century), were primarily concerned with reasoned proofs based on empirical evidence, rather than uncritical acceptance of scripture. The seminal texts of the school are Dignāga's *Compendium of Valid Cognition* (*Pramāṇa-samuccaya*) and Dharmakīrti's *Commentary on [Dignāga's] Compendium of Valid Cognition* (*Pramāṇa-vārttika*).

praṇidhāna (Pāli *paṇidhāna*; Tib. *smon lam*; "aspiration")

In general, this refers to the fulfillment of religious vows and developing a correct attitude toward religious practice. In MAHĀYĀNA, it is the ninth in the tenfold list of "perfections" (PĀRAMITĀ) that a BODHISATTVA cultivates during the path to buddhahood. It is developed on the ninth bodhisattva "level" (BHŪMI). In a Mahāyāna context, it mainly involves being motivated to attain buddhahood in order to benefit sentient beings.

Prāsaṅgika-madhyamaka (Tib. *dBu ma thal 'gyur pa'i lugs*; "Middle Way Consequence School")

One of the two divisions of MADHYAMAKA, according to Tibetan doxographers (the other is Svātantrika). The founder of this branch is said to be BUDDHAPĀLITA (ca. 470–540), who was the philosophical rival of BHAVYA, the founder of SVĀTANTRIKA-MADHYAMAKA. Buddhapālita championed the use of *reductio ad absurdum* (*prasaṅga*) argumentation. His position was later elaborated and defended by Candrakīrti (ca. seventh century), and through his efforts this tradition became the dominant school of Madhyamaka in India, and it was later brought to Tibet by ATIŚA and others.

prātimokṣa (Pāli *pāṭimokkha*; Tib. *so sor thar pa*; "individual liberation")

The list of rules for monks and nuns contained in the *Prātimokṣa-sūtra*, a text of the VINAYA-PIṬAKA. There are separate versions for monks and nuns, and both groups are enjoined by the Vinaya to recite their respective *prātimokṣa*s twice each month during the POṢADHA (Pāli *uposatha*) gathering. Different schools have different *prātimokṣa*s, and the number of rules for monks varies between 218 and 263 (the THERAVĀDA version has 227), and the number for nuns ranges from 279 to 380 (348 in the Theravāda canon). Following the recitation, those who have transgressed a rule are required to confess in front of the community, and the punishment varies in accordance with the severity of the offense. There are seven categories of offenses, arranged in order of severity: (1) transgression of the "most serious rules" (*pārājika-dharma*) leads to expulsion from the SAṂGHA; (2) "rules permitting continued association with the *saṃgha*" (*saṃghāvaśeṣa-dharma*) relate to offenses that lead to temporary expulsion, after which the offender may return; (3) "undetermined rules" (*aniyata-dharma*) relate to offenses involving sexual misconduct; they are called "undetermined" because punishment depends on circumstances; (4) "rules relating to forfeiture and falling (to lower realms of existence)" (*naiḥsargika-pāyantika-dharma*) concern offenses requiring expiation that lead to negative consequences if one does not confess them; (5) "rules relating to falling (to lower realms of existence)" (*pāyantika-dharma*) refer to offenses that may also be addressed by expiation; (6) "rules requiring confession" (*pratideśanīya-dharma*) is a miscellaneous category; and (7) "rules of etiquette" (*śaikṣa-dharma*) concern offenses relating to matters of conduct within the community.

pratītya-samutpāda (Pāli *paṭicca-samuppāda*; Tib. *rten cing 'brel bar 'byung ba*; "dependent arising," "dependent origination")

Doctrine that phenomena arise and pass away in dependence upon causes and conditions. Dependent arising refers to cause and effect, and the operation of this process is one of the key realizations attained by ŚĀKYAMUNI BUDDHA during the final night of his awakening (BODHI). He is said in traditional biographies to have become fully aware of the interconnected dynamics of causality, and he fully understood that all conditioned phenomena (SAṂSKṚTA) are subject to causes and conditions. Every conditioned phenomenon is a dependent arising because it comes into being in dependence upon causes and conditions, abides because of causes and conditions, and disintegrates because of causes and conditions. In Buddhist literature there are two standard lists of the process, one that diagnoses it in a forward direction, and another that looks at the process in reverse. In the former schema the twelve "links" (*nidāna*) in the process are enumerated as follows: (1) AVIDYĀ (ignorance); (2) SAṂSKĀRA (compositional factors); (3) VIJÑĀNA (consciousness); (4) NĀMA-RŪPA (name and form); (5) *ṣaḍāyatana* (six sense spheres); (6) *sparśa* (contact); (7) *vedanā* (feelings); (8) TṚṢṆĀ (thirst, craving); (9) *upādāna* (appropriation); (10) *bhava* (becoming); (11) *jāti* (birth); and (12) *jarā-maraṇa* (old age and death). In MAHĀYĀNA this schema is connected with the doctrine of emptiness (ŚŪNYATĀ) in the sense that since phenomena are dependent on other factors for their arising, subsistence, and cessation there is no underlying substance or essence.

pratyeka-buddha (Pāli *pacceka-buddha*; Tib. *rang sangs rgyas*; "solitary realizer")

A Buddhist practitioner who has attained a personal NIRVĀṆA without depending on a teacher. In Buddhist literature the *pratyeka-buddha* is said to be "solitary like the horns of a rhinoceros" because of not belonging to a community and attaining liberation through individual effort. In NIKĀYA BUDDHISM it is said that *pratyeka-buddhas* can only exist during a time and place in which there is no BUDDHA, and there are several stories of *pratyeka-buddhas* who committed suicide when ŚĀKYAMUNI BUDDHA was born, since they could no longer continue to live in a world that would soon have a fully awakened buddha. They are said to be superior to ARHATS in terms of meditative attainment and wisdom, but inferior to buddhas. The path of the *pratyeka-buddha* is said in MAHĀYĀNA to be one of the three possible paths to salvation taught by the Buddha, along with the path of the arhat and that of the BODHISATTVA.

prayoga-mārga (Tib. *sbyor ba'i lam*; "path of preparation")

Second of the five paths (*mārga*) to buddhahood, which begins when a meditator attains the level of "union of calming and higher insight" (*śamatha-vipaśyanā-yuganaddha*). It is prefatory because the meditator is preparing for the first supramundane path, the "path of seeing" (DARŚAṆA-MĀRGA), which begins with direct perception of emptiness (ŚŪNYATĀ). There are four levels of the path of preparation: (1) heat (*uṣma-gata*); (2) peak (*mūrdhan*); (3) patience (*kṣānti*); and (4) supreme mundane qualities (*laukikāgra-dharma*). In the first stage the meditator has a direct, non-conceptual awareness of suchness (TATHATĀ), which is said to burn away false conceptuality. "Peak" marks a point at which the "virtuous roots" (*kuśala-mūla*) that one previously cultivated will not decrease or be lost, and one progresses in understanding of suchness. At the level of "patience" the meditator becomes increasingly familiar with the concept of emptiness and overcomes fear with respect to it. From this point onward one will never again be reborn in the lower destinies (GATI) of hell beings, hungry ghosts, or animals due to the force of afflicted actions and attitudes. Supreme mundane qualities refers to the fact that the meditator actualizes the highest qualities that are possible within cyclic existence, and at the same time prepares for direct realization of emptiness, which is a supramundane attainment.

Prebish, Charles S. (b. 1944)

American scholar of Buddhism, best known for his work on Buddhist monasticism. He has also been at the forefront of scholarship in the new field of studies on American Buddhism. He received his Ph.D. from University of Wisconsin-Madison in 1971 and has spent most of his academic career at University of Pennsylvania. Together with Damien Keown, he founded the JOURNAL OF BUDDHIST ETHICS, a highly successful electronic academic publication. He has published a number of influential books and articles, including *A Survey of Vinaya Literature* (1994) and *Luminous Passage: The Practice and Study of Buddhism in America* (1999).

preliminary practices

See SNGON 'GRO.

preta (Pāli *peta*; Tib. *yi dwags*; Jpn. *gaki*; "hungry ghost")

One of the six possible destinies (GATI) in which beings may be born within cyclic existence. Beings are born as *preta*s if they were greedy and spiteful in past lives. As recompense, they are born with huge bellies and tiny necks and are constantly hungry, but when they get food it appears to them to be disgusting substances such as pus and blood.

Mural depicting the sufferings of hungry ghosts (preta). *Haedongsa Monastery, North Kyŏngsang, Korea.*

Protestant Buddhism

Term coined by Gananath Obeyesekere to describe a modernist movement in THERAVĀDA countries, which developed as a Buddhist response to attacks against the tradition by Christian missionaries. According to Richard Gombrich, it has three main features: (1) a tendency toward fundamentalism; (2) it asserts that Buddhism is "rational," "scientific," and "not a religion"; and (3) it depends on English concepts, even when expressed in Asian languages.

pṛthag-jana (Pāli *puthujjana*; Tib. *so so'i skye bo*; Jpn. *bonbu*; "ordinary being")

In THERAVĀDA, this refers to beings who have worldly aspirations (*loka-dhamma*). They are contrasted with "noble persons" (*ariya-puggala*), which includes those who have attained one of the supramundane paths (from stream enterers up to ARHATS). In MAHĀYĀNA, ordinary beings are all of those who have not reached the path of seeing (DARŚAṆA-MĀRGA), and so have not directly perceived emptiness (ŚŪNYATĀ). Due to this, they assent to the false appearances of things and do not perceive them in terms of their true nature, i.e., emptiness.

Pudgala-vāda (Pāli *Puggala-vāda*; Tib. *Gang zag smra ba*; "Personalist")

A term applied to several early Indian Buddhist schools, which shared a common belief that there is a self (*pudgala*) which is the basis for KARMA and transmigration, and that this self is neither the same as, nor different from, the five aggregates (SKANDHA). The schools generally thought to have been included within this group were the Vātsiputrīyas, Saṃmatīyas, Dharmottarīyas, Ṣaṇṇagarikas, and Bhadrāyanīyas. The *pudgala* doctrine was eventually declared heretical throughout Indian Buddhism (though at one time Pudgalavādins appear to have been quite numerous), and other schools attacked them for asserting what amounted to an *ātman* (the doctrine of a permanent, partless "self" that was denied by the Buddha).

pūjā (Pāli *pūjā*; Tib. *mchod pa*; "ceremony")

A general term for Buddhist ceremonies, which covers a wide range of practices. Each country and tradition has its own ceremonies, and these may include offerings, a variety of ritual practices, chanting, etc. They may be formal and elaborate, involving large groups, or personal observances.

Pulguksa ("Buddha Land Temple")

One of the major temples of KOREAN BUDDHISM, built in 535 at the outskirts of Kyongju, capital of the Unified Silla kingdom. It was built during the reign of King Pophung (r. 514–540), the first Silla king to accept Buddhism.

Lanterns containing offerings for the deceased, Pulguksa Monastery, South Kyŏngsang, Korea.

puṇya (Pāli *puñña*; Tib. *bsod nams*; "merit")

The karmic result of the voluntary performance of virtuous actions. Such actions may include performance of PŪJĀs, prayer, or giving gifts to the monastic community (SAṂGHA). In THERAVĀDA countries, making merit is a central focus of the religious lives of laypeople, who are generally thought to be incapable of attaining the higher levels of meditative practice or NIRVĀṆA. In early Buddhism, it appears that it was assumed that merit is non-transferable, but in MAHĀYĀNA the doctrine of "transference of merit" became widespread, and is said to be one of the key virtues of a BODHISATTVA, who willingly gives away the karmic benefits of his/her good works for the benefit of others.

Pure Land

See CH'ING-T'U.

Pūrṇa (Pāli *Puṇṇa*)

One of ŚĀKYAMUNI BUDDHA's main disciples, said by the Buddha to be the most skilled in exposition of the DHARMA.

Pu-tai ("Hemp Sack")

A tenth-century Chinese Buddhist monk (whose real name was Ch'i-tz'u) popularly thought to have been a manifestation of MAITREYA (1), the future buddha. Often referred to as the "Laughing Buddha," Pu-tai is commonly depicted as a corpulent man with a bare torso and bulging belly, sitting with his right leg slightly raised. He is also represented standing up with arms above his head, palms upward; he generally has a broad smile on his face and is often surrounded by children. He was said to have carried a hemp sack from which he gave presents to children. The origin of the connection between Pu-tai and Maitreya appears to be a short poem he spoke shortly before his death, in which he implied that he was Maitreya. In Japan he is referred to as Hotai, and is one of the "seven divinities of fortune" (*shichifuku-jin*), and the connection with Maitreya is not commonly stressed.

Q

Quang-Đức, Thích

Vietnamese Buddhist monk whose public self-immolation in 1963 became one of the enduring images of the Vietnam War. He took this desperate measure in protest at the jailing of hundreds of monks and nuns by government authorities without trial, and he is widely credited with helping to restore religious freedom in Vietnam as a result of his self-sacrifice.

Questions of King Milinda

See Milinda-pañha.

R

Rāhula

Only child of SIDDHĀRTHA GAUTAMA. According to tradition, he was born on the day his father decided to leave the household life, and when his wife YAŚODHARĀ asked him what the boy should be named, he replied, "Rāhula" ("Fetter"), indicating that he perceived the child as a potential source of mundane attachment. After his awakening (BODHI), the Buddha returned to his family, and Yaśodharā sent the boy to confront him. He demanded that he be given his inheritance (Pāli *dāyajja*). The Buddha made no response, but Rāhula followed him from the palace, and he was soon ordained as a monk. When the Buddha's father ŚUDDHODANA protested, the Buddha responded by promulgating a rule that henceforth no one could be ordained without parental permission. After hearing the *Smaller Discourse Spoken to Rāhula* (*Cūla-rāhulovāda-sutta*), he became an ARHAT. He was said by the Buddha to be the foremost among his disciples in eagerness to learn (Pāli *sikkākāmānaṃ*).

Rahula, Walpola (1907–1997)

Sri Lankan THERAVĀDA monk, renowned as a scholar, who wrote a number of influential books and articles, including an introduction to Buddhism from a Theravāda perspective, entitled *What the Buddha Taught.* During the 1950s he was a research fellow at the Sorbonne, where he worked mainly on MAHĀYĀNA texts, and in 1966 he became vice-chancellor of Vidyodaya University in Sri Lanka. He later served as chancellor of Kelaniya University. During the 1980s and 1990s he generated some controversy by urging Buddhist monks to give back their vows in order to join in the government's war against Tamil militants.

rainbow body

See 'JA' LUS.

Rājagṛha (Pāli *Rājagaha*)

Capital of Magadha during ŚĀKYAMUNI BUDDHA's lifetime. Rājagṛha was an important center for Buddhist monasticism, and the Buddha is reported to have spent seven rainy season retreats there. It was also the site of a number of Buddhist monasteries, including the first reported building for monks, named Venuvana-ārāma. According to Buddhist tradition, it was the site of the "First Buddhist Council," which was convened shortly after the Buddha's death. It was sponsored by King BIMBISĀRA, who nominated the arhat KĀŚYAPA as president of the council. The intention of the gathering was to settle the SŪTRA-PIṬAKA and VINAYA-PIṬAKA, and to that end 500 arhats who had been present when the Buddha's sermons were delivered convened to recount what they had heard. UPĀLI – considered the leading expert on monastic discipline – recited the Vinaya, and ĀNANDA – who as the Buddha's personal attendant had been present at all of his sermons – recited the sūtras. At the conclusion of the council, the canon was declared to be closed.

Ral pa can (Relbachen, r. 815–836)

Third and last of the "religious kings" (*chos rgyal*) of the YAR LUNG DYNASTY of Tibet, believed by Tibetan Buddhist tradition to have been an emanation of the buddha VAJRAPĀṆI. During his reign royal patronage of Buddhism reached its apogee. He supported a wide range of Buddhist activities, and made each group of seven households responsible for the support of a monk. He was reportedly so devoted to Buddhism that during state ceremonies he would tie ribbons to his long hair, and monks would sit on them. His activities led to widespread resentment, and he was assassinated by two of his ministers in 836. This brought to an end the "first dissemination" (SNGA DAR) of Buddhism in Tibet, as his successor GLANG DAR MA (Lang Darma, r. 838–842) withdrew royal support and reportedly persecuted Buddhism.

Rāmañña Nikāya

One of the three largest monastic orders of Sri Lankan Buddhism (the others being the SIYAM NIKĀYA and the AMARAPURA NIKĀYA), which was founded in 1865.

Rampa, T. Lobsang (Cyril Hoskin, 1910–1981)

Son of a British plumber who claimed to have been possessed by a Tibetan lama and subsequently transformed into a Tibetan at the molecular level. He is best known for his book *The Third Eye*, which he claims to be his autobiography. It has been denounced by Tibetologists as a bizarre hoax, but continues to be widely popular.

rang stong (*rangdong*; "self-emptiness")

The understanding of emptiness (Tib. *stong pa nyid*; Skt. ŚŪNYATĀ) that is upheld by the DGE LUGS PA (Gelukpa) and SA SKYA PA (Sakyapa) orders of TIBETAN BUDDHISM. It follows the Indian MADHYAMAKA tradition in interpreting emptiness as a "non-affirming negative" (*med dgag*), meaning that it is a radical denial of any substantial entity or essence of phenomena (or persons) which does not imply anything in its place. Rather, all phenomena are collections of parts that are influenced by causes and conditions, constantly changing, and thus empty of inherent existence (Tib. *rang bzhin*; Skt. SVABHĀVA). This notion is opposed to the doctrine of "other-emptiness" (GZHAN STONG, *shendong*), which is held by other lineages of Tibetan Buddhism, particularly those associated with the RIS MED (Rime, "Non-Sectarian") movement. The focus of the debate is whether TATHĀGATA-GARBHA (Tib. *de bzhin gshegs pa'i snying po*, "embryo of the TATHĀGATA") should be understood as a positive reality or as a mere absence. The *rang stong* tradition interprets it in the second way and holds that it refers to the emptiness of inherent existence of the psycho-physical continuum, which is constantly changing. Because there is no fixed essence or entity, beings have the option of cultivating the qualities of buddhahood and gradually transforming themselves into buddhas. The *gzhan stong* position, by contrast, conceives of *tathāgata-garbha* as a positive, self-existent essence that is fully manifested through meditative practice.

Rangjung Rikpe Dorje (Rang 'byung rigs pa'i rdo rje, 1924–1981)

The sixteenth rGYAL BA KAR MA PA (Gyelwa Karmapa), who was one of the most influential Tibetan masters of the twentieth century. He was born in the sDe dge (Derge) region of Khams and was recognized as the reincarnation of his successor as a young child on the basis of a letter that had been written by the fifteenth rGyal ba Kar ma pa predicting the circumstances of his rebirth. At the age of seven he received ordination from T'AI SI TU RIN PO CHE (Tai Situ Rinpoche) and 'Jam mgon kong sprul (Jamgön Kongtrül), and one year later he was officially enthroned at MTSHUR PHU (Tsurpu) Monastery, the seat of the KAR MA BKA' BRGYUD PA (Karma Kagyüpa) order in Tibet. In 1957, anticipating the future devastation of Tibet by China, he began sending his followers out of the country. In 1959 he left Tibet and subsequently settled in Sikkim, where he founded Rum bteg (Rumtek) Monastery, which has become the headquarters of the order in exile. In 1974 he made a world tour, which attracted many followers from all over the world. He helped to found a number of Buddhist centers in the West and was widely recognized as one of the most charismatic lamas of his time. He died of cancer in Illinois, leaving behind a worldwide organization and a charitable trust worth an estimated $1.5 billion. The question of his successor has led to violence and acrimony among some of his followers. T'ai Si tu Rin po che and the Dalai Lama have publicly endorsed a candidate named Urgyen Tinley (U rgyan 'phrin las, b. 1985), who in 1992 was enthroned at mTshur phu, but ZHWA DMAR RIN PO CHE (Shamar Rinpoche) rejects this identification and contends that the true reincarnation is Tenzin Khyentse (bsTan 'dzin mkhyen brtse, b. 1982), who resides at the Nalanda Institute in New Delhi.

Rapten, Geshe (dGe bshes Rab brtan, 1920–1986)

Tibetan lama who entered SE RA monastic university at the age of fifteen, fled to India in 1959, and in 1963 was awarded the degree of *dge bshes lha ram pa* (*geshe lharampa*, the highest level of distinction for the DGE BSHES degree). In 1974 he made his first trip to Europe, and in 1975 became abbot of a DGE LUGS PA (Gelukpa) monastery at Rikon. In 1974 he founded the Tharpa Choeling Center for Higher Tibetan Studies at Mount Pèlerin, near Lausanne, Switzerland.

Ratna-kūṭa-sūtra (Tib. *Rin chen brtsegs pa'i mdo*; *Pile of Jewels Sūtra*)

A voluminous collection of MAHĀYĀNA texts, which comprises forty-nine independent sūtras, many of which are considered to belong to the early period of Mahāyāna literature. The entire corpus exists only in Chinese and Tibetan translations.

Ratnasaṃbhava (Tib. *Rin chen 'byung ldan*; "Jewel Born")

One of the five celestial buddhas, who presides over a "pure land" in the south. Iconographically, he is generally portrayed with golden skin and sitting in the yogic PADMĀSANA position, making the "wish-granting" gesture (*varada-mudrā*). In Tibet he is often portrayed embracing his consort Māmakī.

ratna-traya (Pāli *tiratana*; Tib. *rin chen gsum*; "three jewels")

The three objects in which Buddhists traditionally "take refuge": Buddha, DHARMA, and SAṂGHA. These are also referred to as "refuges" (ŚARAṆA), because they serve as aids for those who seek release from cyclic existence. The formal taking of refuge is generally considered to mark a person's entry into the community of Buddhists.

rdo rje

See VAJRA.

rDo rje shugs ldan (Dorje Shukden; "Powerful Vajra")

A protector deity of the DGE LUGS PA (Gelukpa) order of TIBETAN BUDDHISM, said to be the reincarnation of Grags pa rgyal mtshan (Drakpa Gyeltsen, 1618–1655). Grags pa rgyal mtshan was recognized as the third rebirth of Paṇ chen bSod nams grags pa (Panchen Sönam Drakpa, 1478–1554), the textbook writer of 'BRAS SPUNGS bLo gsal gling (Drebung Loseling) monastic college. According to the mythos of this deity, Grags pa rgyal mtshan was a rival of the fifth Dalai Lama, NGAG DBANG BLO BZANG RGYA MTSHO (Ngawang Losang Gyatso, 1617–1682), and the Dalai Lama's supporters tried to assassinate Grags pa rgyal mtshan, in addition to spreading malicious rumors about him. He eventually grew tired of this and decided to take his own life by stuffing a ceremonial scarf into his mouth and suffocating. The scarf had been given to him by the fifth Dalai Lama following a debate between the two in recognition of his victory.

Before he died he told a disciple that if the rumors about him were false a black cloud of smoke in the shape of a hand would rise from his funeral pyre. This reportedly occurred, and shortly thereafter his unquiet spirit (*rgyal po*) began terrorizing people, including the Dalai Lama. He was later persuaded, however, to become a "dharma-protector" (*chos skyong*), and his particular mission is reportedly to protect the dGe lugs pa order against its enemies. Georges Dreyfus has convincingly argued that the story of Grags pa rgyal mtshan's transformation into a vengeful spirit was probably originally a slander initiated by his enemies, but in recent times has become part of the mythology of rDo rje shugs ldan among his devotees. For several hundred years following Grags pa rgyal mtshan's death, rDo rje Shugs ldan was only a minor spirit within the dGe lugs pa pantheon, but he was elevated to the position of chief dharma protector by Pha bong ka Rin po che (Pabongka Rinpoche, 1878–1941) and his student Khri byang Rin po che (Trijang Rinpoche, 1901–1983).

He is generally depicted in a fearsome aspect, with a necklace of skulls and other terrifying ornaments, surrounded by flames. He is associated with dGe lugs pa sectarianism, and following a dream in which he saw rDo rje shugs ldan in combat with GNAS CHUNG (Nechung, the main dharma-protector of the Tibetan government) the fourteenth Dalai Lama issued a public statement urging Tibetans to cease propitiation of this deity. rDo rje shugs ldan became widely popular among dGe lugs pa lamas during the twentieth century, but following the Dalai Lama's proclamation most dGe lugs pas publicly renounced worship of this deity. The most vocal exception was Geshe Kelsang Gyatso (dGe bshes bsKal bzang rgya mtsho), the founder of the NEW KADAMPA TRADITION. He has publicly rejected the Dalai Lama's decision, and he and his followers have accused the Dalai Lama of violating their religious freedom. The dispute has precipitated a great deal of animosity and violence, and one of the Dalai Lama's most prominent supporters, Geshe Losang Gyatso (dGe bshes bLo bzang rgya mtsho, former director of the Institute of Buddhist Dialectics in Dharamsala), was brutally murdered in his residence, along with two of his students. Although supporters of rDo rje shugs ldan have publicly claimed that they had nothing to do with the killings, the leading suspects are worshipers of the deity.

rdzogs chen (*dzokchen, dzogchen;* "great perfection")

System of meditation that is particularly important in the RNYING MA PA (Nyingmapa) order of TIBETAN BUDDHISM, but which is also practiced in other orders. According to lineage histories, it originated with SAMANTABHADRA, who passed it on to VAJRASATTVA. He taught it to Dga' rab rdo rje (Garap Dorje; Skt. Surativajra). It was later transmitted to Tibet by PADMASAMBHAVA and Vimalamitra in the eighth century. Its practices aim at understanding that phenomena and emptiness interpenetrate and are inseparable. The phenomena of experience are viewed as creations of mind and as empty of inherent existence. *rDzogs chen* practice dispenses with tantric visualizations, and instead focuses on direct apprehension of the clear light nature of mind. Meditators are taught to cultivate a union of essential purity (*ka dag*) and spontaneity (*lhun grub*). "Essential purity" refers to the mode of being (*gnas lugs*), which is emptiness. Spontaneity is based on the notion that all positive qualities are already spontaneously established in the "basis-of-all" (*kun gzhi*), and so when meditators realize the innate purity of the basis-of-all, the manifold attributes of a buddha become manifest. The basic text of *rdzogs chen* is the *Fourfold Innermost Essence* (*sNying thig ya bzhi*) by KLONG CHEN RAB 'BYAMS PA (Longchen Rapjampa, 1308–1364), who is also the author of another important text, the *Seven Treasuries* (*mDzod bdun*).

Budo, a reliquary structure for the cremated remains of monks and nuns.

rebirth

The doctrine of rebirth is upheld by all traditional schools of Buddhism. According to this doctrine, sentient beings (Skt. SATTVA) are caught up in a continuous round of birth, death, and rebirth, and their present state of existence is conditioned by their past volitional actions (KARMA). Since the cycle inevitably involves suffering and death, Buddhism assumes that escape from it is a desirable goal. This is achieved by engaging in practices that serve to break the cycle, the most important of which is meditation on the nature of reality, which enables a person to recognize the mechanisms of cyclic existence and thus break their hold. The doctrine of rebirth has become problematic for many contemporary Buddhists, particularly for converts to Buddhism in Western countries whose cultural milieu does not include acceptance of this notion. It has also been questioned by some Buddhists from traditional Buddhist cultures, such as BUDDHADĀSA BHIKKHU, but is generally considered by Asian Buddhists to be an essential Buddhist doctrine. (*See also* BAR DO THOS GROL.)

refuge

See ŚARAṆA.

rGyal ba Kar ma pa (Gyelwa Karmapa)

The oldest lineage of reincarnate lamas (SPRUL SKU) in TIBETAN BUDDHISM. The rGyal ba Kar ma pas are believed to be physical emanations of the buddha AVALOKITEŚVARA, and are often referred to as the "Black Hat" (Tib. *Zhwa nag*) lamas because of the hat they wear during special ceremonies. This was given to the fifth rGyal ba Kar ma pa, De bzhin gshegs pa (Teshin Shekpa, 1384–1415), by the Chinese emperor T'ai-ming-chen and is said to have been based on a dream in which the emperor saw a black hat woven from the hair of 100,000 ḌĀKINĪS floating over De bzhin gshegs pa's head. The first rGyal ba Kar ma pa was DUS GSUM MKHYEN PA (Tüsum Khyenpa, 1110–1193). The sixteenth rGyal ba Kar ma pa, Rang 'byung rigs pa'i rdo rje (Rangjung Rikpe Dorje, 1924–1981), was one of the most influential Tibetan masters of the twentieth century. He traveled widely and established a number of centers all over the world, including the current headquarters of the order, Rum bteg (Rumtek) Monastery in Sikkim. There is currently a bitter dispute over the succession to the sixteenth rGyal ba Kar ma pa. The current ZHWA DMAR RIN PO CHE (Shamar Rinpoche) and his supporters claim that a boy named bsTan 'dzin mkhyen brtse (Tenzin Khyentse, b. 1982) is the true reincarnation, while TA'I SI TU RIN PO CHE (Tai Situ Rinpoche) and his supporters back a Tibetan child named U rgyan 'phrin las (Urgyen Tinley, b. 1985). The second claimant was officially enthroned in the monastery of MTSHUR PHU (Tsurpu) in 1992 and has been validated by the Dalai Lama, but the faction led by Zhwa mar Rin po che continues to reject his claim.

rgyud gsum (Skt. *tritantra*; "triple continuum")

One of the central notions of the SA SKYA PA (Sakyapa) order of TIBETAN BUDDHISM, which encapsulates the three primary stages of the path to buddhahood: (1) the appearance of phenomena as impure error; (2) the appearance of experience in meditation; and (3) pure appearance. The LAM 'BRAS (*lamdre*, "path and result") tradition of Sa skya asserts that all three are fundamentally the same and that their only difference lies in how they are perceived. The first refers to the perceptions of ordinary beings, which are based on afflicted mental states and lead to suffering. Because ordinary beings are subject to the operations of KARMA, this is also referred to as the "karmic appearance." The second aspect refers to people who engage in such MAHĀYĀNA practices as training in compassion (KARUṆĀ) and love (*maitrī*) or the "six perfections" (PĀRAMITĀ), etc. The central training of this level is cultivation of calming (ŚAMATHA) and higher insight (VIPAŚYANĀ). The third verse refers to buddhas, who have perfected compassion and wisdom (PRAJÑĀ), and thus perceive reality as it is. Their pure vision recognizes that all of the phenomena of cyclic existence (SAṂSĀRA) and NIRVĀṆA are the display of primordially undefiled mind. They understand that from the standpoint of ultimate reality there is really no liberation to be attained, no buddhas, and no sentient beings. (*See also* SNANG GSUM.)

Rhys Davids, Caroline Augusta Foley (1858–1942)

One of the leading figures of the PĀLI TEXT SOCIETY and wife of its founder, THOMAS W. RHYS DAVIDS. She produced a number of important translations and critical editions of Pāli texts, as well as several independent studies. Her notion that the texts of the PĀLI CANON represent a monkish alteration and corruption of the Buddha's original message has generated some controversy and is still debated by contemporary buddhologists.

Rhys Davids, Thomas William
(1843–1922)

Founder of the PĀLI TEXT SOCIETY and husband of CAROLINE A. F. RHYS DAVIDS. Originally trained as a solicitor, be became interested in Pāli literature during a court case he encountered while in the Ceylon Civil Service. He subsequently left the public service and devoted himself to the study of the PĀLI CANON. He founded the society in 1881, and in 1882 was appointed Professor of Pāli at University College, London. He produced a large volume of translations, critical editions, and independent studies.

Ri khrod ma

See ŚABARĪ.

rig pa (Skt. *vidyā*; "awareness," "knowledge")

In general, this can refer to: (1) knowledge or awareness; (2) a field of study of science; and (3) in the RDZOGS CHEN (*dzogchen*, "great perfection") lineage it refers to a primordially pure state of awareness that is the fundamental nature of mind (which is described as being of the nature of pure luminosity).

Rin chen bzang po (Rinchen Sangpo, 958–1055)

One of the great translators (Tib. *lo tsā ba*) of TIBETAN BUDDHISM, whose work marked the beginning of the translations of the "second dissemination" (PHYI DAR) of Buddhism in Tibet. He was sent to Kashmir to study by Ye shes 'od (Yeshe Ö), king of sPu hrang (Buhrang) in western Tibet, and after seventeen years there returned to Tibet, where he began translating Indian Buddhist works. He was also instrumental in re-establishing the VINAYA in Tibet. In addition, he is credited with founding several monasteries, including sTod gling (Döling) in Gu ge and Tabo in Spiti. His best-known work is entitled *Refutation of False Tantric Teachings* (*sNgags log sun 'byin*), in which he attacks tantric practices involving sexual union (*sbyor*) and "ritual slaying" (*sgrol*).

rin po che (*rinpoche*; "precious jewel")

Honorific title given to Tibetan lamas (BLA MA) in recognition of their status as teachers and exemplars of the tradition. This is most commonly used for reincarnate lamas (SPRUL SKU), but can also be used to designate any religious master.

Rinzai-shū (Chin. *Lin-chi-tsung*; Kor. *Imje-chong*; Viet. *Lâm-tế*; "Rinzai School")

One of the two main traditions of contemporary Japanese ZEN (the other being SŌTŌ). It was founded by the Chinese CH'AN master LIN-CHI I-HSÜAN (Jpn. Rinzai Gigen, d. 866) and initially brought to Japan by EISAI ZENJI (1141–1215). Eisai trained in the Huang-lung (Jpn. Ōryō) lineage in China, one of the two main schools of Lin-chi (the other being Yang-ch'i; Jpn. Yōgi). The Ōryō school did not long survive Eisai in Japan, but the Yōgi tradition continues today. It is characterized by emphasis on KŌAN practice and the use of abrupt methods to awaken students, such as shouting at them and hitting them. It claims that its methods lead to experiences of "sudden awakening," referred to as KENSHŌ or SATORI in Japanese.

Ris med ("Non-Sectarian")

Important nineteenth-century religious movement in TIBETAN BUDDHISM initiated by 'Jam dbyangs mkhyen brtse dbang po (Jamyang Khyentse Wangpo, 1820–1892) and 'JAM MGON KONG SPRUL BLO GROS MTHA' YAS (Jamgön Kongtrül Lodrö Taye, 1811–1899). It arose as a reaction to the stultifying sectarianism of Tibetan Buddhism, which had led to institutional paralysis and dogmatic adherence to tradition, as well as internecine violence. Adherents of the movement attempted to find common ground between the various traditions of Tibetan Buddhism and rejected the prevalent tendency to focus on memorization and repetition of scholastic treatises and textbooks that extrapolated from Indian sources. Ris med teachers, by contrast, required their students to study the original Indian sources of Tibetan Buddhism. The movement also had an important popular component, as Ris med teachers often adopted the themes and images of popular literature like the GE SAR epic. In addition, many Ris med teachers developed popular religious rituals, such as conferring "transference of consciousness" (*'pho ba*) initiations on groups of laypeople. Ris med has played a pivotally important role in the modern development of the SA SKYA PA, BKA' BRGYUD PA, and RNYING MA PA orders.

Risshō-koseikai ("Society for the Establishment and Enhancement of Justice and Community")

Modern Japanese movement based on the teachings of NICHIREN (1222–1282), founded in 1938 by Niwano Nikkyō (b. 1906) and Naganuma Myōkō (1889–1957). Like other Nichiren-affiliated groups, it emphasizes veneration of the *Lotus Sūtra* (Skt. SADDHARMA-PUṆḌARĪKA-SŪTRA), and the chanting of its title in Japanese ("Namu *Myōhō-renge-kyō*") is a central practice, along with veneration of ŚĀKYAMUNI BUDDHA. It also encourages veneration of ancestors and the development of one's personality through emulating the ideal of the BODHISATTVA.

Ritsu-shū (Chin. *Lü-tsung*; Kor. *Kyeyul-chong*; "Monastic Discipline School")

Japanese branch of the Vinaya school, brought to Japan by Chien-chen (Jpn. Ganjin, 688–763) in 754. It followed the tradition of the DHARMAGUPTAKA-*vinaya*, referred to in China as "the *vinaya* in four parts" (*ssu-fen lü*), which has 250 rules for monks and 348 for nuns. The tradition emphasizes strict adherence to the rules of monastic conduct, but it never gained a large following in Japan, where a married priesthood is the norm. It was considered to be one of the six main Buddhist schools of the Nara period (710–784; the others were KUSHA, HOSSŌ, JŌJITSU, SANRON, and KEGON.) Following the initiation of a "bodhisattva ordination" in the TENDAI school by Saichō (767–822), however, adherence to the letter of the *vinaya* rules came to be widely viewed as anachronistic in Japan, but the Ritsu school still continues today as a minor tradition.

rJe btsun dam pa Khutukhtu (Jetsün Dampa Hutukhtu)

The major reincarnate lama (Mon. *khubilgan*; Tib. SPRUL SKU) of MONGOLIAN BUDDHISM. The first was Ödür Gegen (1635–1723), whose monastic seat was Erdini J̌uu. *Khutukhtu* is the Mongolian equivalent of the Sanskrit term *ārya*, meaning "noble" or "wise." The traditional seat of these lamas was Da Khüree (now known as Ulan Bator). The eighth member of the lineage died in 1924 after serving as the country's temporal ruler following Mongolian independence from China, but when the Communists re-established control the lineage was banned, and so there is currently no officially recognized successor in Mongolia. Despite this, in 1991 the fourteenth DALAI LAMA publicly announced that 'Jam dpal rnam grol chos kyi rgyal mtshan (Jambel Namdröl Chögi Gyeltsen, b. 1929) is the ninth member of the lineage. He was born in Lhasa and studied with teachers from all four of the main orders of TIBETAN BUDDHISM prior to fleeing the country in 1959 following the Chinese invasion and annexation of Tibet. His identity as the *rJe btsun dam pa* was not officially announced until after the fall of the Soviet Union.

Mongolian hagiography (for example in a Chinese work entitled *Meng-ku i-shih*) traces the lineage back through fifteen incarnations prior to Ödür Gegen and claims that the first of the series lived during the time of ŚĀKYAMUNI BUDDHA. The fifteenth was the great Tibetan historian TĀRANĀTHA (1575–1634). The identification of Ödür Gegen as the reincarnation of Tāranātha was reportedly first made by the fifth Dalai Lama, NGAG DBANG BLO BZANG RGYA MTSHO (Ngawang Losang Gyatso, 1617–1682).

rnam thar (*namthar* or *namtar*; "records of liberation")

Spiritual biographies, a genre of Tibetan Buddhist writing. Often written by the disciples of a spiritual master, these texts focus on the events of a person's life that are considered to be particularly religiously significant, such as auspicious circumstances surrounding his or her birth, initiations, meetings with spiritual preceptors (BLA MA), visions, religious activities (such as building retreat centers, temples, etc.), writings, and meditative attainments. Generally hagiographical in tone, they are not critical biographies in the Western sense, but tend rather to focus on how the subject personifies core religious paradigms of TIBETAN BUDDHISM.

rNying ma pa (Nyingmapa; "Old School")

Oldest of the four orders of TIBETAN BUDDHISM. It traces itself back to PADMASAMBHAVA, the yogin who according to Tibetan tradition helped to establish Buddhism in Tibet in the eighth century. Its name is based upon the fact that its adherents rely on the "old translations" (*snga 'gyur*), made during the period of the "first dissemination" (SNGA DAR) of Buddhism to Tibet. Its highest meditative practice is RDZOGS CHEN (*dzogchen*, "great perfection"), and it is the order most closely associated with the "hidden treasure" (GTER MA) tradition. gTer ma texts are believed by rNying ma pas to have been hidden by Padmasambhava and his disciples, who placed spells on them to ensure that they would only be discovered at the proper time and by the proper "treasure discoverer" (GTER STON). The other main source of rNying ma pa doctrines and practices is the "teaching lineage" (*bka' ma*), believed to represent an unbroken line of transmission of the DHARMA from the Buddha. Unlike the other orders of Tibetan Buddhism, it never developed a centralized leadership or organized hierarchy, and generally avoided political involvements.

Robinson, Richard Hugh (1926–1970)

American scholar of Buddhism who established the first graduate degree program in Buddhist Studies in the U.S.A. at the University of Wisconsin-Madison, which has trained a number of prominent buddhologists. He is best known for his work on MADHYAMAKA, particularly his *Early Mādhyamika in India and China*.

rōhatsu sesshin

Week-long period of intensive meditation practice in Japanese ZEN monasteries, beginning on December 1 and finishing on the day of *rōhatsu* (the eighth day of the twelfth month of the lunar calendar, but in contemporary Japan it is celebrated on December 8). According to tradition, *rōhatsu* commemorates the day on which ŚĀKYAMUNI BUDDHA attained complete awakening (Skt. BODHI).

rōshi ("old master")

Japanese term for a Zen master. Generally one becomes a *rōshi* through having one's experience of awakening (KENSHŌ, SATORI) certified by an established master. A *rōshi* must also possess the maturity and wisdom needed to guide students skillfully, thus ensuring the authenticity of teaching and practice. Anyone – monk or layperson, man or woman – may become a *rōshi*, though they are most commonly older men.

Ruegg, David Seyfort

One of the twentieth century's leading scholars of Buddhism, who has published ground-breaking work on an impressive variety of subjects, including Indian Buddhist philosophy, the Pramāṇa tradition, the life of Bu ston, and Madhyamaka. His books include *Buddha-nature, Mind and the Problem of Gradualism in a Comparative Perspective* (1992) and *The Study of Indian and Tibetan Thought: Some Problems and Perspectives* (1967).

Rūpa-dhātu (Pāli *Rūpa-dhātu*; Tib. *gZugs khams*; "Form Realm")

One of the three worlds (TRILOKA) of traditional Buddhist cosmology. This realm is considered to be higher than the one in which human beings live (i.e., the "Desire Realm" or KĀMA-DHĀTU).

S

Sa skya khri 'dzin (Sakya Trindzin; "Throne Holder of Sa skya")

The head of the SA SKYA PA (Sakyapa) order of TIBETAN BUDDHISM. It is a hereditary position, which is held by a male member of the 'Khon family. The current "Throne Holder," Ngawang Günga Tekchen Belbar Sampel Wanggi Gyelpo (Ngag dbang kun dga' theg chen dpal 'bar bsam 'phel dbang gi rgyal po), was born in 1945 in southern Tibet and at the age of seven, following the death of his father, became the forty-first person to assume the position. At the age of fourteen he fled Tibet following the Chinese invasion and settled in India, where he studied with bCo brgyad khri chen Rin po che (Chogye Trichen Rinpoche, b. 1920). After completing his studies he established Sakya College in India, which has become the training center for the order.

Sa skya pa (Sakyapa; lit. "Grey Earth Order")

One of the three "new orders" (GSAR MA) of TIBETAN BUDDHISM. It traces itself back to the Indian MAHĀSIDDHA Virūpa, whom it considers to be the first human to transmit its distinctive LAM 'BRAS (*lamdre*, "path and result") teachings. The school takes its name from the place where its first monastery was established, an area called Sa skya in the province of gTsang (Tsang). It was founded in 1073 by dKon mchog rgyal po (Gönchok Gyelpo, 1034–1102), and in later centuries grew to be one of the major monastic complexes in Tibet. The central meditative practice of the tradition is *lam 'bras*, which is a comprehensive, hierarchically ordered path to buddhahood, progressing through stages, each of which requires previous successful completion of its predecessor. Its philosophy and practice is based on the HEVAJRA-TANTRA, particularly its doctrine of the inseparability of cyclic existence and *nirvāṇa* (Tib. *'khor 'das dbyer med*; Skt. *saṃsāra-nirvāṇa-abheda*). The head of the order is the SA SKYA KHRI 'DZIN (Sakya Trindzin, "Throne Holder of Sa skya"), who is always a member of the 'Khon family.

Sa skya Paṇḍita Kun dga' rgyal mtshan dpal bzang po (Sakya Pandita Günga Gyeltsen Bel Sangpo, 1182–1251)

One of the major figures of the SA SKYA PA (Sakyapa) order of TIBETAN BUDDHISM, renowned both for his scholarship and his political acumen. He is viewed by the tradition as an incarnation of MAÑJUŚRĪ. His most influential philosophical work is his *Treasury of the Knowledge of Valid Cognition* (*Tshad ma rigs pa'i gter*), which systematizes the thought of DIGNĀGA and DHARMAKĪRTI. He is also the author of two widely popular works, the *Treasury of Well-Spoken Advice* (*Legs par bshad pa rin po che'i gter*) and *Differentiation of the Three Vows* (*sDom gsum rab dbye*). The first is a collection of 457 verses containing pithy and often poetic religious and moral instructions, and the second is a discussion of the three main types of Buddhist vows in the Tibetan tradition: (1) the PRĀTIMOKṢA vows of monks and nuns; (2) BODHISATTVA vows; and (3) the vows of tantric practitioners. He played a decisive role in Tibetan history when in 1244 he accepted an invitation to travel to Mongolia to the court of Godan Khan. The mission was intended as a formal surrender of Tibet to the Mongols, but according to traditional sources the khan was so impressed by Sa skya Paṇḍita that he converted to Buddhism and made him his religious preceptor. They initiated what was called a "patron–priest" (*yon mchod*) relationship, under which the khan would protect Tibet and Buddhism and the Sa skya lamas would serve as chaplains to the Mongol court. His successor, 'PHAGS PA BLO GROS (Pakpa Lodrö, 1235–1289), inherited the role of preceptor to the Mongol court and ruler of Tibet, but Sa skya hegemony later waned along with Mongol power in the 14th century. (*See also* MONGOLIAN BUDDHISM.)

Śabarī (Tib. *Ri khrod ma*; Skt. "Variegated"; Tib. "Woman of the Mountain Ranges")

Wrathful tantric deity who is particularly associated with healing. In Tibet she is generally depicted wearing a skirt made of leaves and with a wrathful expression on her face.

Saddharma-puṇḍarīka-sūtra (Tib. *Dam pa'i chos padma dkar po'i mdo*; Chin. *Miao-fa-lien-hua-ching*; Jpn. *Myōhō-renge-kyō*; Viet. *Diệu Pháp Liên-hoa Kinh*; "*Sūtra of the Lotus of the True Doctrine*")

One of the most widely popular of Indian Buddhist MAHĀYĀNA texts, which was particularly important in East Asia. It purports to be a discourse delivered by ŚĀKYAMUNI BUDDHA on Vulture Peak (GṚDHRAKŪṬA) to a huge audience. A central focus is the notion that the many doctrines and practices taught by the Buddha are all really part of a single path (EKAYĀNA), which embraces both "HĪNAYĀNA" and "Mahāyāna." It further states that when the Buddha teaches different doctrines to different audiences he is not being deceptive; rather, this is a skillful method (UPĀYA-KAUŚALYA) that adapts the basic message to the proclivities and individual needs of each person and group. In reality, although the Buddha teaches the three vehicles (*triyāna*) of the ŚRĀVAKAS, PRATYEKA-BUDDHAS, and BODHISATTVAS, in the end all are subsumed within the "buddha-vehicle" (*buddha-yāna*), and all lead to awakening (BODHI). This idea is emphasized by the "parable of the burning house," in which a father – seeing that his three young sons are playing inside a burning house and are too distracted to notice the danger – lures them out by promising each the sort of cart he most desires. When they come out they are all given one type of cart. This is said to be skillful rather than deceitful, as the subterfuge saves their lives. The sūtra became the doctrinal basis of the Chinese T'IEN-T'AI tradition and Japanese schools that trace themselves back to NICHIREN.

sādhana (Tib. *grub thabs*; "means of accomplishment")

Tantric rituals that are central to VAJRAYĀNA Buddhism in Tibet. A *sād-*

hana is a ritual cycle which is meant to be performed by initiates. In order to begin practice of a *sādhana*, ritual empowerment by a qualified preceptor is considered necessary. A typical *sādhana* begins with recitation of a refuge prayer, followed by verses aimed at generation of BODHICITTA, and it then continues with visualization of the deities specific to the ritual cycle. There is generally a central buddha, and the *sādhana* commonly also includes a retinue. Ideally the visualization should be combined with meditation on emptiness (Skt. ŚŪNYATĀ), which allows the practitioner to generate the visualizations from the wisdom consciousness realizing emptiness, simultaneously perceiving both the deity and himself/herself as being empty of inherent existence. The core of the ritual involves imagining that the deity merges with the meditator and that the two become inseparable, with the meditator manifesting all the qualities of a buddha. After the visualization the images are dissolved into emptiness, and at the conclusion of the *sādhana* there is a prayer dedicating the merit of the practice to all sentient beings. The practice of *sādhanas* has important sociological dimensions in Tibet, as one's primary religious practice is centered on the particular *sādhanas* of one's initiational lineage, and one's group identification is largely determined by the *sādhanas* one performs.

Sahaja (also Sahajiyā; Tib. *Lhan cig*; "Innate")

Indian tantric movement whose main exponents were iconoclastic lay adepts (*siddha*) who functioned outside the monastic establishment, and whose lifestyles and practices challenged it. Although its exponents claimed great antiquity for the tradition, its literature indicates that it was in fact a relatively late phenomenon, which probably originated some time between the eighth and tenth centuries. Many of its central texts were written in Apabhrāṃśā, for example the *Dohākośa*, or in other northern Indian languages, such as Bengali (e.g. the *Caryāgīti*). The main emphasis of Sahaja is on spontaneous understanding and manifestation of awakening, which is said to be innate (*sahaja*) in all beings. The structures and rules of the monastic life are thought to be hindrances – rather than aids – to meditative progress. There is a strong emphasis on the sexual yogas of highest yoga tantra (ANUTTARA-YOGA-TANTRA), and the ideal of Sahaja is the wandering iconoclastic ascetic with his female consort (or the female master with her male consort).

Saichō (Dengyō Daishi, 767–822)

Founder of the TENDAI tradition of JAPANESE BUDDHISM, who traveled to China in 804. While there, he studied T'IEN-T'AI, as well as CH'AN and MI-TSUNG. Upon his return to Japan, he founded a small monastery on Mount Hiei, which later grew to be the headquarters of the school. His version of the tradition was more eclectic than Chinese T'ien-t'ai, and he combined elements from a number of Buddhist traditions. Like T'ien-t'ai, the Tendai tradition stresses the centrality of the *Lotus Sūtra* (Skt. SADDHARMA-PUṆḌARĪKA-SŪTRA), but Saichō also promoted the performance of tantric rituals and the practice of SHIKANTAZA meditation. He played a significant role in the history of Japanese Buddhism when he instituted the practice of conferring "bodhisattva vows" to novices, which he said superseded the "HĪNAYĀNA" vows of the PRĀTIMOKṢA that had traditionally been the primary ordination for monks and nuns. In order to counteract the potential for novices to lapse into immorality, he also required a twelve-year training regimen on Mount Hiei.

sakṛdāgamin (Pāli *sakadāgāmin*; Tib. *phyir 'ong*; "once-returner")

A person who has attained the second of the supramundane paths (ĀRYA-MĀRGA). Such a person will only be reborn once more within cyclic existence, and in the next life after that will become an ARHAT.

Śākya (Pāli *Sakka*)

The clan to which ŚĀKYAMUNI BUDDHA belonged. "Śākyamuni" means "Sage of the Śākyas." Their capital was KAPILAVASTU, and their king during the Buddha's life was his father, ŚUDDHODANA.

Sakyadhita ("Daughters of the Buddha")

International organization founded in 1987, which has been at the forefront of efforts to improve the lot of Buddhist women. It sponsors a bi-annual conference in which issues relating to women's roles in Buddhism are discussed, and it proclaims itself to be "the world's only internationally active Buddhist women's organization." It also claims that its conferences are "the only series of comprehensive international gatherings for Buddhist ordained and lay women in the 2,500-year history of Buddhism." Its conferences and seminars bring together Buddhist women from all over the world and from all Buddhist traditions to discuss matters of common concern. It has been at the forefront of efforts to introduce the full monastic ordination for women to countries in which it has died out or never existed.

Sakyapa

See SA SKYA PA.

Sakya Pandita

See SA SKYA PAṆḌITA.

Statue of Śākyamuni Buddha, dPe thub (Spitok) Monastery, Ladakh.

Śākyamuni Buddha (Pāli *Sakkamuni*; Tib. *Shā kya thub pa*; Chin. *Shih-cha-mo-ni*; Jpn. *Shaka Nyorai*; Viet. *Thích-Ca Phật-Đài*; "Sage of the Śākyas")

An epithet of the historical Buddha, who probably lived during the middle of the first millennium B.C.E. According to Buddhist tradition, he was born in the town of KAPILAVASTU and belonged to its ruling family. His name at birth was SIDDHĀRTHA GAUTAMA, and he is called Śākyamuni ("Sage of the Śākyas") because he belonged to the Śākya clan, and by this appellation he is distinguished from other buddhas.

samādhi (Pāli *samādhi*; Tib. *ting nge 'dzin*; Chin. *san-mei*; Jpn. *sanmai*; "meditative absorption")

General term for a state of meditative concentration on a single object. Buddhist meditation literature describes a plethora of such states, each of which is attained through cultivation of practices designed to lead to its actualization. *Samādhi*s are cultivated not as aims in themselves, but rather because they are believed to lead to the development of wisdom or good qualities.

Samantabhadra (Tib. *Kun tu bzang po*; Chin. *P'u-hsien*; Jpn. *Fugen*; Viet. *Phổ-hiền*; "All Good")

Important figure of the MAHĀYĀNA pantheon. As a BODHISATTVA in early Mahāyāna texts, he is said to be the protector of those who propagate the DHARMA, and he is often portrayed with VAIROCANA. Iconographically, he is often shown riding on a white elephant with six tusks, and he commonly holds a lotus, a wish-fulfilling jewel, or a scroll. In VAJRAYĀNA he is often said to be the "primordial buddha" (ĀDI-BUDDHA) and the embodiment of the "truth body" (DHARMA-KĀYA). In tantric depictions he has dark blue skin (symbolic of emptiness) and is commonly shown in sexual embrace (YAB YUM) with his consort Samantabhadrī.

śamatha (Pāli *samatha*; Tib. *zhi gnas*; Chin. *chih*; Jpn. *shi*, *sanmai*; Viet. *tam*; "calming")

A meditative state characterized by a one-pointedness of mind (*cittaikāgratā*) on an internal meditative object (*ālambana*). Theoretically, any object may serve as the focus of concentration, though virtuous objects such as the body of a buddha are said to be preferable. It is attained when the mind is able to remain upon its object one-pointedly, spontaneously and without effort (*nābhisaṃskāra*), and for as long a period of time as one wishes, without being disturbed by laxity (*laya*) or excitement (*auddhatya*). There are said to be six prerequisites for achieving *śamatha*: (1) staying in an agreeable place; (2) having few desires; (3) knowing satisfaction; (4) not having many activities; (5) pure ethics; and (6) thoroughly abandoning thoughts. It is generally considered to be a prerequisite for attainment of "higher insight" (VIPAŚYANĀ).

samaya (Tib. *dam tshig*; "vow")

A formal commitment to undertake a particular practice or set of practices. In tantric traditions, the taking of vows is generally required before any higher initiations may be conferred. These commonly involve a vow to undertake certain practices, such as daily recitation of a SĀDHANA or a promise to observe certain behaviors.

Śambhala (Tib. *Sham bha la*)

Name of a mythical kingdom described in the HEVAJRA-TANTRA, which is said to be a hidden valley protected from outsiders. Its location is cited differently in various sources, but is generally thought by Tibetan Buddhists to be somewhere in the north of the country. Śambhala has been ruled by a succession of wise Buddhist kings, and the current one is said to be the twenty-first in the lineage and to have ascended the throne in 1927. The twenty-fifth and last (who will be named Rudra) will begin his rule in 2327. He will reign for 100 years (as does every king of Śambhala). In the ninety-eighth year of his reign (i.e., 2425, which according to the calendar of the *Kāla-cakra-tantra* is 2304 years after the passing of ŚĀKYAMUNI BUDDHA), the enemies of the dharma will attack Śambhala and will be defeated, after which Buddhism will flourish for 1,000 years. In the 5140th year after Śākyamuni's passing, his period of the teaching will end.

saṃbhāra-mārga (Tib. *tshogs lam*; "path of accumulation")

First of the five paths delineated in Buddhist meditation theory, during which one amasses two "collections": the "collection of merit" (*puṇya-saṃbhāra*) and the "collection of wisdom" (*jñāna-saṃbhāra*). The first involves cultivating virtuous deeds and attitudes, which produce corresponding positive karmic results and felicitous mental states. The second collection involves cultivating wisdom for the benefit of other sentient beings. In MAHĀYĀNA meditation theory, it is said that one enters on this path with the generation of the "mind of awakening" (BODHICITTA). The training of this path leads to the next level, the "path of preparation" (PRAYOGA-MĀRGA). (*See also* AŚAIKṢA-MĀRGA; BHĀVANĀ-MĀRGA; DARŚANA-MĀRGA; MĀRGA; SAMYAK-PRAHĀṆA.)

saṃbhoga-kāya (Tib. *longs spyod pa'i sku*; "enjoyment body")

One of the three bodies of a BUDDHA, according to MAHĀYĀNA buddhology. The *saṃbhoga-kāya* is said to reside in a "pure land" and is only perceivable by advanced practitioners. In order to benefit ordinary beings, it creates physical forms called "emanation bodies" (NIRMĀṆA-KĀYA).

Saṃdhinirmocana-sūtra (Tib. *dGong pa nges par 'grel pa'i mdo*; Chin. *Chieh shen mi ching*; "*Sūtra Explaining the Thought*")

Indian MAHĀYĀNA text, probably composed some time around the third to fourth centuries, which became the main scriptural source of the YOGĀCĀRA school. It consists of ten chapters, in each of which a different interlocutor poses questions to the Buddha. It contains important discussions of the two truths, the nature of mind, Buddhist hermeneutics, and meditation. The original Sanskrit is lost, and it is only extant in Chinese and Tibetan versions.

saṃgha (Pāli *saṅgha*; Tib. *dge 'dun*; "community")

The community of Buddhists. The term can be used just to refer to monks (BHIKṢU) and nuns (BHIKṢUṆĪ), or can also include lay men (UPĀSAKA) and women (UPĀSIKĀ) who have taken the five vows of the PAÑCA-ŚĪLA (fivefold ethics). All four groups are required formally to adopt a set of rules and regulations; monastics are bound by over two hundred (the actual number varies between different VINAYA traditions). An important prerequisite for entry into any of the four categories is an initial commitment to practice of the DHARMA, which is generally expressed by "taking refuge" in the "three jewels": Buddha, dharma, and saṃgha.

saṃgraha-vastu (Pāli *sangaha-vatthu*; Tib. *bsdu ba'i dngos po*; "methods of gathering [students]")

Techniques used by teachers to attract students: (1) giving (*dāna*), which involves giving away teachings of doctrine and material goods; (2) speaking pleasantly (*priya-vādita*), or interesting them in one's teachings of doctrine through pleasant words; (3) beneficial activities (*artha-caryā*), which includes activities that accord with what trainees want; and (4) concordant function (*samanarthatā*), which involves making one's actions accord with one's words.

sampanna-krama (Tib. *rdzogs rim*; "completion stage")

Second stage of a tantric practice that begins with the "generation stage" (UTPATTI-KRAMA). In the first stage, one visualizes a vivid image of a buddha (and often a complex retinue) in front of one, and mentally imagines it to be possessed of all the ideal qualities of a buddha. After one gains mastery over this, one moves on to *sampanna-krama*, in which one invites the buddha to merge with oneself, and imagines that this occurs, with the result that one's body, speech, and mind are transformed into those of a buddha, and one is engaged in performing the compassionate activities of a buddha. The transformation is connected with the mystical physiology of highest yoga tantra (ANUTTARA-YOGA-TANTRA), which conceives of the meditator in terms of subtle energies (called winds and drops) that move through subtle energy channels. The visualization process is believed to bring about real transformation, which occurs at the level of the subtle body. (*See also*: CAKRA; SĀDHANA; TANTRA; VAJRAYĀNA.)

saṃsāra (Pāli *saṃsāra*; Tib. *'khor ba*; "cyclic existence")

The beginningless cycle of birth, death, and rebirth in which ordinary beings (PṚTHAG-JANA) are trapped. According to Buddhism, the universe is beginningless and endless, and the beings who dwell within it transmigrate from life to life in dependence upon their volitional actions (KARMA). Due to ignorance (AVIDYĀ) of the true nature of reality, they are generally predisposed toward actions and attitudes that lead to negative consequences. This process inevitably results in repeated suffering (DUḤKHA), disappointment, and death, and so the main goal of Buddhism is to extricate oneself from the cycle, which can only be done through religious practice that enables one to transform one's negative attitudes and proclivities and develop direct intuitive understanding of the nature of reality. This serves to break the cycle and can lead to full liberation (NIRVĀṆA, *mokṣa*).

saṃskāra (Pāli *saṅkhāra*; Tib. *'du byed*; "conditioning factors")

Fourth of the five aggregates (SKANDHA) and second link (NIDĀNA) in the process of dependent arising (PRATĪTYA-SAMUTPĀDA). The term refers to volitional activities – good, bad, and neutral – that produce conditions influencing one's future. In general, *saṃskāra* are the conditioning impulses that precede a volitional action, and they tend toward the formation of habits, which are said to carry over from one lifetime to the next.

saṃskṛta (Pāli *saṅkhata*; Tib. *'dus byas*; "conditioned")

Refers to phenomena that arise in dependence upon causes and conditions. It literally means "put together" or "made," and its opposite term, unconditioned (ASAṂSKṚTA), refers to whatever is not produced in dependence upon causes and conditions. Everything that is subject to arising (*utpāda*), extinction (*vyaya*), and abiding and change (*sthityanyathātva*) is conditioned.

saṃvṛti-satya (Pāli *sammuti-sacca*; Tib. *kun rdzob bden pa*; "conventional truth")

One of the "two truths" (SATYA-DVAYA), the other being ultimate truth (PARAMĀRTHA-SATYA). Conventional truths refer to things that are true on the level of ordinary perceptions and phenomenal reality. Thus, a table may be said to be a conventional truth, because conventionally it is able to perform the functions of a table. This perception is superseded, however, at the level of ultimate truth, in which the table is seen as a collection of parts brought together due to causes and conditions, and thus empty of inherent existence (SVABHĀVA).

samyak-prahāṇa (Pāli *samma-pahāna*; Tib. *yang dag par spong ba*; "thorough abandonings")

Four factors that are developed through meditation and moral training: (1) abandoning of non-virtuous phenomena already generated (*utpannākuśala-dharma-prahāṇa*); (2) non-generation of non-virtuous phenomena not yet generated (*anutpannākuśala-dharmāropaṇa*); (3) increasing of virtuous phenomena already generated (*utpanna-kuśala-dharma-vṛddhi*); and (4) generation of virtuous phenomena not yet generated (*anutpanna-kuśala-dharma-ropaṇa*). These are attained during the path of accumulation (SAṂBHĀRA-MĀRGA).

One of the four stone gateways (toraṇa) *of the Great Stūpa of Sāñcī.*

samyak-sambuddha (Pāli *sammā-sambuddha*; Tib. *yang dag par rdzogs pa'i sangs rgyas*; "completely, perfectly awakened")

An epithet of buddhas, which distinguishes them from other beings who have attained release from cyclic existence (i.e., ARHATS and PRATYEKABUDDHAS). Buddhas train for longer than *arhats* and *pratyekabuddhas*, and so they reach a higher level of perfection of good qualities and deeper wisdom. In MAHĀYĀNA, buddhas are said to be distinguished by having attained omniscience (*sarvajñātā*) and the ten powers (BALA), both of which are exclusive to *samyak-sambuddhas*.

Samye

See BSAM YAS.

Saṃyutta nikāya ("Connected Discourses")

Third of the five collections of discourses (Pāli *sutta*; Skt. SŪTRA) in the Sutta-piṭaka (SŪTRA-PIṬAKA) of the PĀLI CANON, which corresponds to the Saṃyuktāgama of the Sanskrit TRIPIṬAKA. It contains fifty-six groups of *suttas*, which are arranged according to subject matter.

San Francisco Zen Center

SŌTŌ center founded by SHUNRYU SUZUKI RŌSHI in 1961. It is one of the oldest and most influential ZEN centers in North America.

Sāñcī

Site in central India that contains some of the most significant examples of early Indian Buddhist art and architecture, generally dated between the third and first centuries B.C.E. The most impressive of these is the "Great Stūpa of Sāñcī."

saṅgha

See SAṂGHA.

Sangharakshita (Dennis Longwood, b. 1925)

British-born monk who founded the FRIENDS OF THE WESTERN BUDDHIST ORDER (FWBO), a non-sectarian worldwide organization. He served in the British army in India during World War II and deserted his unit when he was about to be sent home. After a period of several years as a wandering mendicant he met some Buddhist monks and was ordained in 1950 by a THERAVĀDA preceptor. For the next decade he studied with a variety of teachers, both Theravāda monks and lamas from various Tibetan traditions. In 1976 he founded the FWBO, which was dedicated to a non-sectarian vision of Buddhism in which all Buddhist traditions would be equally respected.

San-lun (Jpn. *Sanron*; Kor. *Sammon*; "Three Treatises School")

Tradition founded by KUMĀRAJĪVA (344–413), a Kushan monk who traveled to Ch'ang-an in 401 and set up a translation group. The San-lun school is derived from the Indian MADHYAMAKA tradition, and focuses on three central texts: (1) NĀGĀRJUNA's *Fundamental Verses on the Middle Way* (Skt. MŪLAMADHYAMAKA-KĀRIKĀ; Chin. *Chung-lun*); (2) ĀRYADEVA's *Treatise in One Hundred Verses* (Skt. *Śata-śāstra*; Chin. *Po-lun*); and (3) the *Twelve Gate Treatise* (Chin. *Shih-erh-men lun*; Skt. *Dvādaśa-dvara-śāstra*, attributed to Nāgārjuna in China but extant only in Chinese). The school was influential during Kumārajīva's life and enjoyed renewed popularity after being revived by CHI-TSANG (549–623), but did not survive for long as a separate school after his death.

Sanron (Chin. *San-lun*; Kor. *Sammon*; "Three Treatises School")

Japanese version of SAN-LUN, brought to Japan in 625 by Ekwan, a Korean student of CHI-TSANG. It became one of the six main Buddhist schools of the Nara period (710–784; the others were: HOSSŌ, JŌJITSU, KEGON, KUSHA AND RITSU.)

Sanskrit (Skt. *Saṃskṛta*; "Perfected," "Cultured")

The ancient sacred language of India, which for millennia served as the *lingua franca* of scholars and authors of literary and religious works. The classical language was codified in the sixth century B.C.E. by the great grammarian Pāṇinī, author of the monumental grammatical treatise *Aṣṭādhyāyī*.

Śāntarakṣita (Tib. Zhi ba 'tsho, ca. 680–740; "Protector of Peace")

Indian Buddhist philosopher, whose best-known work is the *Compendium of Truth* (*Tattva-saṃgraha*). He is credited in Tibetan tradition with having been one of the three people who helped to establish Buddhism in the Land of Snows. Together with KHRI SRONG LDE BRTSAN (Trisong Detsen) and PADMASAMBHAVA, he established the first monastery in Tibet, named BSAM YAS (Samye).

Santi Asoke

Thai Buddhist reform movement initiated by a monk named Bodhiraksa. In 1975 he officially resigned from the state monastic hierarchy because he believed the Thai SAṂGHA to be corrupt and lax in its observance of monastic discipline. He and his followers eat only one vegetarian meal per day, do not wear shoes, and do not have buddha statues in their temples. Because of their uncompromising ascetic lifestyle and criticism of the mainstream *saṃgha* and the government, they have encountered significant opposition from civil and monastic authorities. In 1989 the group's leaders were detained by police and accused of falsely claiming to be Buddhists, and they were subsequently banned from preaching. In 1995 some of its members were given a suspended sentence of two years following a trial by opponents who wanted to have their activities and teachings declared illegal.

Śāntideva (Tib. *Zhi ba lha*, ca. 650–750; "Lord of Peace")

Indian Buddhist philosopher associated with the MADHYAMAKA school, best known for two works, *Entering the Path to Awakening* (*Bodhicaryāvatāra*) and *Compendium of Studies* (*Śikṣā-samuccaya*).

sanzen ("going to Zen")

General term for receiving instruction from a ZEN master (RŌSHI). In RINZAI, this is associated with DOKUSAN, private meetings between students and teachers, and in SŌTŌ it means the correct practice of Zen.

śaraṇa (Pāli *saraṇa*; Tib. *skyabs*; "refuge")

In Buddhism, a refuge is something on which one can rely for support and guidance. In most Buddhist traditions, "going for refuge" in the "three refuges" (or "three jewels": Buddha, DHARMA, and SAṂGHA) is considered to be the central act that establishes a person as a Buddhist. Going for refuge is an acknowledgment that one requires aid and instruction and that one has decided that one is committed to following the Buddhist path. The Buddha is one who has successfully found the path to liberation, and he teaches it to others through his instructions on dharma. The *saṃgha*, or monastic community, consists of people who have dedicated their lives to this practice and teaching, and so are a source of instruction and role models. The standard refuge prayer is:

I go for refuge in the Buddha.
I go for refuge in the dharma.
I go for refuge in the *saṃgha*.

In tantric traditions, initiates often have additional refuges, such as the GURU and ḌĀKINĪS.

Śāriputra (Pāli *Sāriputta*)

The chief disciple (Pāli *agga-sāvaka*) of ŚĀKYAMUNI BUDDHA, also referred to as Upatissa. Born into a brahman family, he joined the Buddhist order along with his friend MAUDGALYĀYANA shortly after hearing a dharma discourse by the monk Assaji (Skt. *Aśvajit*, one of the first five disciples of the Buddha). He attained arhathood fifteen days later after hearing the Buddha expound the *Dīghanakhasutta*. He was declared by the Buddha to be the foremost of his disciples in attainment of wisdom (*etadaggaṃ mahāpaññānaṃ*). He was so highly regarded that there are a number of discourses in the PĀLI CANON spoken by him, and a declaration by the Buddha that Śāriputra's words fully accord with his own doctrine.

śarīra (Pāli *sarīra*; Tib. *ring bsrel*; "relics")

Relics of a deceased buddha or revered teacher, generally the result of cremation of the body. The cult of relics has played an important role in Buddhism, and probably began shortly after the death of ŚĀKYAMUNI BUDDHA.

Sārnāth

Town near Vārāṇasī in which is located the Deer Park, where, according to Buddhist tradition, ŚĀKYAMUNI BUDDHA preached his first sermon shortly after becoming awakened. The spot is marked with the Dhamek Stūpa, said to have been built some time around the fourth to sixth centuries around a smaller STŪPA erected during the time of AŚOKA.

Nearby is a modern sculpture depicting the Buddha surrounded by the five ascetics who constituted the audience of the sermon.

Sarvāstivāda (Tib. *Thams cad yod par smra ba*; "Everything Exists School")

Indian Buddhist school that split off from the Sthaviravāda sometime around the mid-third century B.C.E. The name of the school derives from its realistic and pluralistic doctrines, according to which the basic building-blocks of the universe are simple reals called DHARMAS, which exist during the three times: past, future, and present. The phenomena of experience are composed of these dharmas, and are regarded as momentary (*kṣaṇika*) by Sarvāstivāda, each combination of dharmas coming into being in dependence upon causes and conditions, enduring for only a moment, and then passing away. In the Sarvāstivāda system, there are seventy-five dharmas, seventy-two of which are conditioned (SAṂSKṚTA), and three of which are unconditioned (ASAṂSKṚTA). The best-known works of the school are two scholastic treatises: VASUBANDHU's *Treasury of Higher Doctrine* (ABHIDHARMA-KOŚA) and the *Great Book of Alternatives* (MAHĀVIBHĀṢĀ).

Sarvodaya Shramadāna

Movement founded by the Sri Lankan lay Buddhist social activist A. T. Ariyaratne in 1958. From modest beginnings, it has grown into one of the world's largest and most celebrated "Engaged Buddhist" movements. It represents a Buddhist response to the often-repeated criticism that Buddhism is "other-worldly" and not concerned with social problems. Sarvodaya Shramadāna incorporates Buddhist principles into its philosophy, but also is connected with Mahatma Gandhi's Sarvodaya movement. It is a lay organization that emphasizes the notions that laypeople can – and should – attain liberation and that this is best achieved not through quietistic withdrawal from the world, but rather by working for the benefit of others. The movement mainly focuses on improving conditions in Sri Lanka's villages, and is currently active in over eight thousand throughout the country. Its main activity is referred to as *shramadāna* ("donation of work"), in which volunteers work together with villagers on projects designed to improve the lives of local people. These may include digging wells, building roads, establishing vocational training centers, improving farming, founding preschools, etc. Each day of work begins with a "family gathering," during which Buddhist concepts are discussed and the day's work is planned. During the project, all participants are expected to adhere to the four "bases of kindness" (*sangaha vatthumi*): (1) generosity (*dāna*); (2) kind speech (*peyya-vajja*); (3) useful work (*attha-cariya*); and (4) equality (*samamattata*). Ariyaratne contends that these are in fact the basic principles of traditional Sri Lankan village life and that they are the antithesis of modern urban societies. The movement idealizes these traditional values and considers modern society to be corrupt and materialistic.

Sasaki, Ruth Fuller (1885–1967)

One of the early pioneers of ZEN study in the U.S.A. She traveled to Japan in the 1930s and studied ZAZEN at Nanzen-ji in Kyōto. In 1938 she moved to New York City and later married Sokei-an Sasaki. In 1949 she returned to Japan and studied at Daitoku-ji with Zuigan Rōshi. In 1958 she was ordained as a Zen priest. She wrote a number of books, including *Zen Dust* and *The Zen Koan*.

sāsana (Skt. *śāsana*; "teaching")

The most common term by which Buddhism is referred to in contemporary THERAVĀDA countries. It designates Buddhism in general, including its doctrines and meditational techniques, as well as rules of conduct and rituals, all of which are thought to derive from ŚĀKYAMUNI BUDDHA. Its textual basis is the PĀLI CANON, which Theravāda tradition asserts is the only authentic collection of the Buddha's teachings.

śāstra (Pāli *sattha*; Tib. *bstan bcos*; "treatise")

In Buddhism this generally refers to a treatise by a Buddhist author other than the Buddha. They are often philosophical texts that discuss Buddhist doctrines and practices or commentaries on other works.

Satipaṭṭhāna-sutta (*Discourse on the Foundations of Mindfulness*)

Discourse attributed to ŚĀKYAMUNI BUDDHA, which exists in two versions in the PĀLI CANON (one in the MAJJHIMA NIKĀYA and another in the DĪGHA NIKĀYA). It focuses on one of the most important meditational practices of THERAVĀDA Buddhism, cultivating mindfulness of the body, feelings, mind, and mental objects. This meditational technique is said to be conducive to attainment of calming (Pāli *samatha*; Skt. ŚAMATHA), and eventually to *nibbāna* (Skt. NIRVĀṆA). (*See also* SMṚTYUPASTHĀNA.)

satori (Chin. *wu*; "awakening")

Derived from the Japanese word *satoru*, "to know," in ZEN this refers to non-conceptual, direct apprehension of the nature of reality, which is said to transcend words and concepts. It is often equated with another term, KENSHŌ (Chin. *chien-hsing*), both of which signify the experience of awakening to truth, but which are not considered to be the end of the path; rather, the experience must be deepened by further training.

sattva (Pāli *satta*; Tib. *sems can*; "sentient being")

In Buddhist philosophy, a sentient being is one who has a mind, that is, something that is aware of its surroundings and is capable of volitional activity. In Buddhist psychological literature, the minimum necessary requirements for something to be a sentient being are the five "omnipresent mental factors" (*sarvatraga*): (1) feeling (*vedanā*); (2) discrimination (*saṃjñā*); (3) intention (*cetanā*); (4) mental activity (*manasikāra*); and (5) contact (*sparśa*).

satya-dvaya (Tib. *bden pa gnyis*; "two truths")

Two levels of reality, or two ways in which phenomena may be perceived: (1) conventional truths (SAṂVṚTI-SATYA); and (2) ultimate truths (PARAMĀRTHA-SATYA). The first refers to the way in which phenomena are viewed by ordinary beings, and are said to be true on the conventional level. A car, for example, is a conventional truth, because it is able to perform the functions of a car, even though from the point of view of ultimate analysis it is perceived as a collection of parts, constructed as a result of causes and conditions, and constantly changing. When one searches to find a truly existent car, what one finds instead is just this collection of parts, none of which can function as a car. Thus from the point of view of ultimate truth, the car is empty of inherent existence. The ultimate truth is emptiness (ŚŪNYATĀ), which is only perceived by sages (ĀRYA).

Satyasiddhi (Chin. *Ch'eng-shih*; Jpn. *Jōjitsu*; "Establishment of Truth")

Philosophical tradition imported to East Asia, based on Harivarman's *Satyasiddhi-śāstra* (Chin. *Ch'eng-shih lun*; Jpn. *Jōjitsuron*). It is generally classified as a MAHĀYĀNA school because it held that all phenomena – both persons and DHARMAS

– are empty. Unlike most Mahāyāna schools, however, this negation is reached by breaking objects down into smaller and smaller parts, until all that remains is emptiness (ŚŪNYATĀ). (*See also* JŌJITSU.)

Sautrāntika (Tib. *mDo sde pa*; "Sūtra Only School")

Indian Buddhist school that developed from the SARVĀSTIVĀDA, probably some time around 150 C.E. As the name suggests, this tradition bases itself on the SŪTRAs, rather than on ABHIDHARMA texts.

sayādaw ("teacher")

Burmese term for a Buddhist monk. Technically, it is used for the abbot of a monastery, but in current usage may designate other highly revered teachers.

Schwezigon Pagoda

The most revered pagoda in Burma, the construction of which was begun by King Anawrathā (Anuruddha, 1040–1077) and probably completed by his successor Kyanzittha (fl. ca. 1084–1113) to house three relics of the Buddha: a collarbone, a frontlet bone, and a tooth.

Se ra (Sera)

One of the three major monasteries of the DGE LUGS PA (Gelukpa) order of TIBETAN BUDDHISM, located near Lhasa. It contains two colleges, Se ra rje (Seraje) and Se ra smad (Serame). Following the invasion and annexation of Tibet by China in the 1950s, the leading teachers of the monastery escaped to India and built a new Se ra in Karnataka state.

second dissemination

See PHYI DAR.

secret autobiography

See GSANG BA'I RANG RNAM.

selflessness

See ANĀTMAN.

sesshin ("collecting the mind")

Japanese ZEN term referring to periods of intense ZAZEN meditation. During most of the year, residents of Zen monasteries carry on a number of activities, such as work, chanting, etc., but during *sesshin* these are kept to a minimum in order to emphasize meditation.

sesshin rōhatsu

See RŌHATSU SESSHIN.

Seung Sahn Sunin (b. 1927)

Korean Sŏn monk, ordained in 1948, following which he began an intensive meditation retreat. During the Korean war he served in the army for five years, following which he returned to the monastic life. He was the first Korean master to teach in America. In 1972 he traveled to the U.S.A., and at first worked in a laundry in Providence, RI, but began to attract a circle of students. He founded the Providence Zen Center, which now has affiliated centers around the country. He has written several books, including *Bone of Space: Zen Poems* and *Dropping Ashes on the Buddha.*

sGam po pa bSod nams rin chen (Gampopa Sönam Rinchen, 1079–1153; "Man of sGampo")

Student of MI LA RAS PA (Milarepa), who became a monk following the death of his wife. The name "sGam po pa" is a reference to the area of sGam po, where he practiced meditation for a number of years. He is also referred to as "The Doctor of Takpo" (Dwags po lha rje). Originally ordained as a monk in the BKA' GDAMS PA (Kadampa) tradition, he studied with a number of teachers, including Mi la ras pa. From him he received instructions in the "six dharmas of Nāropa" (NĀ RO CHOS DRUG) and MAHĀMUDRĀ. Unlike Mi la ras pa, however, he remained a monk, and following his teacher's death he began to reorganize the BKA' BRGYUD PA (Kagyüpa) tradition, developing a monastic component to what had previously been mainly a lineage of lay tantrics. His best-known work is the *Jewel Ornament of Liberation* (*Thar pa rin po che'i rgyan*), which synthesizes the teachings of bKa' gdams pa and bKa' brgyud pa.

shakubuku ("break and subdue")

A technique advocated by NICHIREN (1222–1282), based on his conviction that only the *Lotus Sūtra* (Skt. SADDHARMA-PUṆḌARĪKA-SŪTRA) can lead to salvation during the "final dharma age" (MAPPŌ). Thus the *Lotus* is true (*jitsu*), and all other teachings are provisional (*gon*), but in the present age people are no longer able to derive any benefit from the latter, and so Nichiren felt that provisional teachings must be suppressed, by force if necessary. His practice of *shakubuku* involved debating the proponents of other schools and submitting memorials to government officials in which he attacked his rivals, using arguments and quotations from Buddhist scriptures to argue that their teachings were both false and harmful to the nation. In the modern period *shakubuku* has been developed into a confrontational method of conversion, which has been used mainly by the SŌKA GAKKAI. In 1951 its second president, JŌSEI TODA, officially launched a program called the "great march of *shakubuku*" (*shakubuku no daikōshin*), the goal of which was to convert 750,000 families by aggressive proselytizing. The main format for this was small neighborhood discussion groups (*zadankai*), in which potential converts were pressured to join the organization. The campaign brought in more converts than the target number, but also drew public criticism for the methods used. Aggressive *shakubuku* has been de-emphasized in recent years.

Shamar Rinpoche

See ZHWA DMAR RIN PO CHE.

Shambhala

See ŚAMBHALA.

Shan-tao (Jpn. *Zendō*, 613–681)

Regarded by the Pure Land (Chin. CH'ING-T'U; Jpn. *Jōdō*) tradition as its third Chinese patriarch. He wrote an influential commentary on the *Amitāyurdhyāna-sūtra*, which emphasized the practice of chanting the *nien-fo* (Jpn. NEMBUTSU; Kor. *yŏmbul*; Viet. *niệm-phật*), "Na mo A-mi-t'o-fo" (Jpn. "*Namu Amida Butsu*"; Viet. "*Nam-mô A-Di-Đà Phật*"; "Praise to AMITĀBHA BUDDHA"), which he believed to be the most effective means to ensure rebirth in Amitābha's "Pure Land" of SUKHĀVATĪ.

Shao-lin-ssu (Jpn. *Shōrin-ji*)

Chinese monastery on Mount Sung, built in 477 by Emperor Hsiao-wen of the Northern Wei dynasty. According to Ch'an/Zen tradition, after BODHIDHARMA (ca. 470–543) arrived in China, he decided that the country was not yet ready for his teachings, and so he went to Shao-lin, where he meditated facing a wall for nine years until his eventual disciple HUI-K'O convinced him to accept him as a student. In a popular American television show, it was portrayed as a training center for kung-fu, a martial art which according to tradition was developed there.

Shen-hsiu (Jpn. *Jinshū*, 606–706)

Considered by the CH'AN tradition to be the founder of the "Northern School" (Pei-tsung). He was one of the main disciples of the fifth patriarch, HUNG-

JEN, but he was passed over as his successor in favor of HUI-NENG. This occurred as a result of a competition between Hung-jen's students, who were asked to compose verses indicating their level of understanding. Hui-neng was adjudged the winner, but Shen-hsiu later claimed to be the true successor and established his own lineage. Because he was mostly active in Lo-yang and Ch'ang-an, his tradition was labeled the "Northern School," while Hui-neng's lineage was called the "Southern School." Although the Northern School was widely influential during his lifetime, it declined within a few generations. (*See also* NAN-TSUNG-CH'AN.)

Shibayama Zenkai (1894–1975)

One of the most influential ZEN masters (RŌSHI) of modern Japan. He belonged to the RINZAI tradition, and received his certification of awakening (INKA-SHŌMEI) from Bukai Kono. He was a professor at Ōtani University and Hanazono University, and from 1946 to 1967 was abbot of Nanzen-ji. In 1959 he was appointed head of the entire Nanzen-ji tradition. He is best known in the West for two books that were translated into English, *Zen Comments on the Mumonkan* and *A Flower Does Not Talk*.

shikantaza (Chin. *chih-kuan-ta-tso*; "just sitting")

Japanese term for meditative practice that does not rely on techniques such as KŌAN practice, but instead involves the entire person in sitting meditation. According to DŌGEN ZENJI, it is a state of lucid concentration in which there is no content and in which one is not striving to attain anything at all. Rather, the practice itself is to be viewed as the actualization of one's innate buddha-nature.

Shin Arahan (ca. eleventh century)

Theravāda monk from Thaton who converted King Anawrahtā of Pagān. The king made him leader of the *saṃgha* in unified Burma. (*See also* BURMESE BUDDHISM.)

Shingon (Chin. Chen-yen, Skt. Mantra; "True Word School")

Japanese tradition of esoteric Buddhism (Jpn. *mikkyō*), brought from China by KŪKAI (774–835), who traveled there in 804 and studied with Hui-kuo (Jpn. *Keika*). In 816 he founded a monastery on Mount Kōya, which today remains the headquarters of the order. Shingon is a tantric tradition, which emphasizes the use of rituals, MANTRAS, MUDRĀS, MAṆḌALAS, and other symbolism. Its main scripture is the *Dainichi-kyō* (Skt. *Mahāvairocana-sūtra*), which describes VAIROCANA (Jpn. *Dainichi Nyorai*) as the DHARMA-KĀYA (Jpn. *hosshin*). Shingon draws a distinction between the teachings of esoteric and exoteric Buddhism: The latter is taught by "emanation body" (Skt. NIRMĀṆA-KĀYA; Jpn. *ōshin*) buddhas like ŚĀKYAMUNI and adapted to the capacities of their audiences, while the former is taught by the *dharma-kāya* to his own retinue for his own enjoyment. Because esoteric teachings are more profound than exoteric, they provide a faster path to buddhahood. Shingon practice focuses on the "three mysteries" (Jpn. *sammitsu*; Skt. *triguhya*) of body, speech, and mind, and its rituals are said to attune the practitioner's three mysteries to those of the *dharma-kāya*. Thus, by making *mudrā*s with the body, chanting mantras, and focusing the mind on a single object of observation such as a *maṇḍala* one realizes that one's body, speech, and mind are of one essence with those of the *dharma-kāya*. These practices are based on the notion that all beings are already primordially buddhas (Jpn. *sokushin-jōbutsu*). The two most important *maṇḍala*s (Jpn. *mandara*) for Shingon are the *garbha-dhātu-maṇḍala* (Jpn. *taizōkai-mandara*, "womb realm *maṇḍala*") and the *vajra-dhātu maṇḍala* (Jpn. *kongōkai-mandara*, "*vajra* realm *maṇḍala*"). The former depicts Vairocana in the center, seated on a red lotus, and on each of its eight petals are buddhas and bodhisattvas. It is said to represent the static aspect of reality, the suchness (TATHATĀ; Jpn. *shinnyo*) that characterizes all things. The second *maṇḍala* portrays Vairocana seated on a white lotus throne, surrounded by the four transcendent buddhas. It represents the dynamic aspect of reality, the wisdom of Vairocana, which manifests throughout the cosmos. According to Shingon, both aspects interpenetrate and are inseparable.

shinjin-datsuraku (Chin. *shen-hsin-t'o-lo*; "casting off body and mind")

A central doctrine of DŌGEN ZENJI's meditation philosophy. According to traditional biographies, his great awakening experience was precipitated by hearing his Chinese master Ju-ching admonish a monk who had fallen asleep with the words, "In ZEN, body and mind are cast off; why do you sleep?" Although Dōgen later came to see this idea as the cornerstone of the meditation system of SŌTŌ-SHŪ (Chin. TS'AO-TUNG-TSUNG), it is interesting that the expression "casting off body and mind" does not appear in Ju-ching's surviving writings. There is, however, one instance of the expression "casting off the dust of the mind" (Chin. *hsin-chen-t'o-lo*). The similarity in the two expressions may indicate that Dōgen simply misunderstood what Ju-ching said, or it may be a case of scribal error. In Dōgen's interpretation, "casting off body and mind" refers to the state of pure concentration in ZAZEN, in which one is fully immersed in the experience of meditation.

Shinran (1173–1262)

Founder of JŌDŌ SHINSHŪ, who claimed that the saving power of AMITĀBHA (Jpn. Amida) is so great that it can save even the most depraved of sinners. All that is needed for salvation, according to Shinran, is a single moment of "believing mind" (Jpn. *shinjin*). If for one moment of one's life one experiences sincere faith in Amitābha, one is assured of rebirth in his "pure land" of SUKHĀVATĪ. For Shinran – unlike his predecessor HŌNEN – chanting the NEMBUTSU ("Namu Amida Butsu," "Praise to Amitābha Buddha") is not a means for the attainment of salvation, but rather an expression of gratitude in recognition of one's conviction that salvation is already assured. Shinran taught that in the "final dharma age" (Jpn. MAPPŌ) there is no possibility of attaining salvation through one's own power (Jpn. JIRIKI). Instead, one must rely on the "other power" (Jpn. TARIKI) of Amitābha, which fortunately is specifically effective for the sinners of the present age. The tradition he founded is a lay movement which sees no need for ordination, since the taking of vows implies that it is possible to engage in actions that might contribute to salvation. Though ordained as a monk, Shinran married and fathered a number of children, for which he was expelled from the monastic order. His teachings were collected by his student Yuiembō in a work entitled *Tannishō*.

shin-shūkyō (or *shinkō-shūkyō*; "new religions")

Japanese term used to denote modern religious groups, which often differ significantly from the mainstream traditions of Buddhism and Shintō in terms of doctrines and practices. They are often founded by – and centered on – a charismatic founder, and generally emphasize the notion that followers will accrue tangible worldly benefits. Examples are AGONSHŪ and SŌKA GAKKAI.

Shōbōgenzō (*Treasury of Knowledge of the True Dharma*)

Major work of Dōgen Zenji (1200–1253), a voluminous treatise that discusses all aspects of Buddhist life and practice, from meditation to details concerning personal hygiene.

Shōmu (724–748)

Japanese emperor who was influential in the early spread of Buddhism in Japan. He patronized the new religion and is said to have sponsored the construction of several temples, including the Tōdai-ji in Nara (built in 728). In 741 he issued an official decree that a network of state-subsidized temples (*kokubunji*) would be built throughout the country in order to protect it.

Shōtoku Taishi (574–622)

First major royal patron of Buddhism in Japan, credited with sponsoring the construction of the Horyū-ji near Nara (the oldest Buddhist structure in Japan) and with writing a seventeen-article constitution based on Buddhist and Confucian principles. He is also said to have written commentaries on several Buddhist texts, including the Vimalakīrti-nirdeśa-sūtra. His activities on behalf of Buddhism opened up Japan to Chinese Buddhism, and to Chinese culture in general. (*See also* Japanese Buddhism.)

Siddhārtha Gautama (Pāli Siddhattha Gotama)

According to Buddhist tradition, this is the given name of Śākyamuni Buddha. He was the son of Śuddhodana, king of Kapilavastu, and his wife Māyā. According to legends of his life, his father kept him insulated from the harsh realities of worldly life, fearing that exposure to them would prompt him to leave the home life and seek liberation from cyclic existence. This plan failed, however, and

Siddhārtha Gautama announcing to his wife, Yaśodharā, and his son, Rāhula, his decision to renounce the world. Wall carving at Ellora caves, Mahārāṣṭra.

Siddhārtha left his wife Yaśodharā shortly after she gave birth to their son Rāhula. After leaving his father's palace, Siddhārtha spent six years pursuing liberation, studying with several teachers, practicing ascetic austerities, and finally discovering the key to nirvāṇa through introspective meditation. After the attainment of awakening (bodhi) under the Bodhi Tree in Bodhgayā, he is said to have become a buddha. He is referred to in Buddhist tradition as Śākyamuni ("Sage of the Śākyas") Buddha to distinguish him from other buddhas. Following his awakening, he began to attract followers, and soon instituted a monastic order. According to Buddhist tradition, he traveled all over India for the next forty years and died at the age of eighty.

siddhi (Tib. *dngos grub*; "magical power")

Supranormal abilities, which in Tibetan Buddhism are divided into two types:

(1) supreme accomplishments (*mchog gi dngos grub*, such as the attainment of buddhahood and associated qualities like omniscience); and (2) mundane accomplishments (*thun mong gi dngos grub*), such as clairvoyance or clairaudience, which are said to result from the practice of meditation. Although the latter type are often impressive, Buddhism generally discourages practitioners from cultivating or valuing them, as they often prove to be distractions. They are often more highly valued in tantric traditions, however, where they are sometimes viewed as signs of progress. Eight types of *siddhi* are commonly enumerated in tantric literature: (1) the power to walk through the earth without obstruction (*sa 'og gi dngos grub*); (2) the power of creating an eye ointment that can extend vision (*mig sman gyi dngos grub*); (3) the power to create pills that can keep one alive for long periods of time without solid food (*ril bu'i dngos grub*); (4) the power to cure illness (*nad 'joms pa'i dngos grub*); (5) the power to extend one's life indefinitely (*'chi ba med pa'i dngos grub*); (6) the power to fly through the air on a sword (*ral gri'i dngos grub*); (7) the power of flight (*phur ba'i dngos grub*); and (8) the power of invisibility (*mi snang ba'i dngos grub*).

signlessness

See ANIMITTA.

śīla (Pāli *sīla*; Tib. *tshul khrims*; "ethics," "precepts")

A general term for moral behavior and attitudes. In MAHĀYĀNA, it is the second of the "perfections" (PĀRAMITĀ) that a BODHISATTVA cultivates on the path to buddhahood. It involves developing perfect ethical behavior and a mind that is free from immoral tendencies. It is cultivated on the second bodhisattva level (BHŪMI). *Śīla* is codified as two sets of rules, one for laypeople and another for monks and nuns. The five precepts for laypeople involve avoiding: (1) killing; (2) stealing; (3) sexual misconduct; (4) false speech; and (5) intoxicants. The monastic precepts include these five, and add: (6) not eating after noon; (7) avoiding music, dance, and theatrical performances; (8) avoiding perfumes, unguents, and other physical adornments; (9) not sleeping on high beds; and (10) not handling gold or silver.

sikkhamat (lit. "studying mothers")

Thai term for female renunciants who take lay precepts but adopt elements of the monastic lifestyle, such as celibacy. Because the full ordination lineage for nuns died out long ago in THERAVĀDA countries, women who wish to pursue a monastic lifestyle may take *sikkhamat* vows, but they are not regarded as full monastics by most monks.

silmātā

See DASA SILMĀTĀ.

Sivaraksa, Sulak (b. 1933)

Thai social activist, one of the leading theorizers of "ENGAGED BUDDHISM." Beginning in the 1960s, he became a trenchant critic of the country's dictators and military, and in 1984 he was arrested for *lèse-majesté* (defamation of the monarchy), but was later released, largely due to an international campaign on his behalf. He is the founder of an impressive number of activist organizations and NGOs, including the INTERNATIONAL NETWORK OF ENGAGED BUDDHISTS (INEB). He has been active in working for democracy and human rights, peace and non-violence, rural and urban community development projects, workers' rights, improving the lives of women, and promoting appropriate technology. Sivaraksa takes the Buddha and the early SAṂGHA as models for personal conduct and social organization. Both represent the cultivation of wisdom and the practice of morality, and Sivaraksa considers the *saṃgha* to be a community of religious practitioners that embraces the ideals of economic simplicity, non-attachment, and commitment to religious practice. He has published numerous books and articles, both in Thai and English, including *Seeds of Peace* (1992) and *A Socially Engaged Buddhism* (1988).

six dharmas of Nāropa

See NĀ RO CHOS DRUG.

Siyam Nikāya

The largest monastic NIKĀYA (2) in Sri Lanka today. Over half of the monks on the island belong to this tradition. It was brought to Sri Lanka from Thailand in 1753 to revive the SAṂGHA, which had declined to the point where there were not enough monks to hold a valid ordination. The Siyam Nikāya traces itself back to Phra Upāli, who led the delegation of monks from Thailand.

skandha (Pāli *khandha*; Tib. *phung po*; "aggregate")

The five components of the psycho-physical personality, and the factors on the basis of which ordinary beings impute the false notion of a "self" (*ātman*): (1) form *(rūpa)*; (2) feelings (*vedanā*); (3) discrimination (*saṃjñā*); (4) compositional factors (SAṂSKĀRA); and (5) consciousness (VIJÑĀNA). Because these components are constantly changing, beings who attempt to cling to the "self" are subject to suffering. These factors are often referred to as the "aggregates of attachment" (*upādāna-skandha*) because, although they are impermanent and changing, ordinary beings (that is, those who have not attained the awareness of ARHATS and BUDDHAS) develop desire for them.

skill in means

See UPĀYA-KAUŚALYA.

skyabs mgon (*kyabgön*; "refuge and protector")

Honorific title given to revered teachers in TIBETAN BUDDHISM.

skyabs rje (*kyabje*; "glorious refuge")

Honorific title given to revered teachers in TIBETAN BUDDHISM.

sMin grol gling (Mindroling)

One of the major monasteries of the RNYING MA PA (Nyingmapa) order of TIBETAN BUDDHISM, founded in the seventeenth century by the "treasure-discoverer" (GTER STON) gTer bdag gling pa (Terdak Lingpa, 1646–1714) in the Lho kha (Hlokha) region of Tibet. It suffered extensive damage during the early Chinese invasion and annexation of Tibet, but is now being restored. Another sMin grol gling has also been established in Dehra Dun, India by Tibetan refugees.

sMon lam chen mo (Mönlam Chenmo; "Great Prayer Festival")

One of the most important annual festivals of TIBETAN BUDDHISM, instituted by TSONG KHA PA (Tsong Khapa) in 1409. It is celebrated annually, and begins at the Tibetan New Year (Lo gsar). It involves both monks and laypeople, and encompasses a plethora of religious activities, such as prayer, prostrations, and public lectures by Buddhist teachers.

smṛti (Pāli *sati*; Tib. *dran pa*; "mindfulness")

One of the focal points of meditative practice in Buddhism, which involves cultivating awareness of one's body, actions, and thoughts in order to become consciously aware of what one does and one's motivations. It is the seventh part of the eightfold noble path (ĀRYĀṢṬĀNGA-MĀRGA), and it leads to direct understanding of the transitory, conditioned nature of all existence. (*See also* BALA.)

smṛtyupasthāna (Pāli *sati-paṭṭhāna*; Tib. *dran pa nye bar gzhag pa*; "establishments of mindfulness")

These are establishment in mindfulness of: (1) body (*kāya*); (2) feelings (*vedanā*) (3) mind (CITTA); and (4) phenomena (DHARMA). They are said to be attained during the path of accumulation (SAṂBHĀRA-MĀRGA). Mindfulness of the body involves cultivating awareness of inhalation and exhalation, physical postures such as walking, sitting, etc., awareness of bodily activities and functions, contemplation of the various parts of the body (traditionally enumerated as thirty-eight), and analysis of the elements that make up the body. Mindfulness of feelings refers to cultivating awareness of feelings as pleasant, unpleasant, and neutral, and recognizing their transitory nature. The training in mindfulness of mind consists in becoming aware of the arising and passing away of thoughts and categorizing them as deluded or non-deluded, afflicted or non-afflicted. The final element refers to cultivating awareness of the nature of the phenomena of experience, how they arise and pass away, and understanding that they are composite. In MAHĀYĀNA, mindfulness of body, feelings, mind, and phenomena is combined with meditation that perceives them as being empty of inherent existence.

snang gsum (Skt. *tryavabhāsa*; "triple vision")

A doctrine that is fundamental to the tantric system of the SA SKYA PA (Sakyapa) order of TIBETAN BUDDHISM. The three components are: (1) basis (Tib. *gzhi*; Skt. *ādhāra*); (2) path (Tib. *lam*; Skt. *mārga*); and (3) result (Tib. *'bras bu*; Skt. *phala*). They are said to be fundamentally undifferentiable, as all discriminations are merely creations of mind. They are only divided for the purpose of making Buddhist practice conceptually graspable for ordinary beings. The basis is the two truths (Tib. *bden pa gnyis*; Skt. SATYA-DVAYA, i.e., conventional truths and ultimate truths). The path consists of the cultivation of method (Tib. *thabs*; Skt. *upāya*), which involves training in compassion (Tib. *snying rje*; Skt. KARUṆĀ) and wisdom (Tib. SHES RAB; Skt. PRAJÑĀ, which focuses on meditation on emptiness). The result is the attainment of the pure vision (Tib. *dag snang*), which is the way in which buddhas perceive reality. (*See also* RGYUD GSUM.)

snga dar (*ngadar*; "first dissemination")

The first period of the transmission of Buddhism to Tibet, which began with the arrival of PADMASAMBHAVA and ŚĀNTARAKṢITA during the reign of KHRI SRONG LDE BRTSAN (Trisong Detsen, ca. 740–798). The three founded the first Buddhist monastery in the country, called BSAM YAS (Samye). As Buddhism gained popularity, increasing numbers of Tibetans traveled to India to study, and more Indian Buddhist teachers were brought to Tibet. Translation bureaus were established, and the government began sponsoring Buddhist activities. The period of the first dissemination ended when king RAL PA CAN (Relbachen, r. 815–836) was assassinated and GLANG DAR MA (Lang Darma, r. 838–842) ascended the throne. He instituted a persecution of Buddhism and withdrew government funding for Buddhist teachers and projects, but was soon assassinated by a disaffected Buddhist monk named dPal gyi rdo rje (Belgi Dorje). This brought the YAR LUNG DYNASTY to an end, and Buddhism went into decline. This ended with the start of the "second dissemination" (PHYI DAR) when ATIŚA arrived in Tibet in 1042.

sngags pa (*ngakpa*; Skt. *mantrin*)

Tibetan term that refers to tantric practitioners in general, but most commonly designates lay practitioners who are recognized as adepts. They often adopt a particular way of dress that includes long hair piled up on top of their heads.

sngon 'gro (Skt. *pūrvaṃ-gama*; Tib. *ngöndro*; "preliminary practices")

A set of practices that must generally be performed before one may receive tantric initiations in TIBETAN BUDDHISM. They combine physical movements with visualizations, and are said to prepare one for further training by removing the negative conditioning of past afflicted actions and thoughts. In the rNYING MA PA (Nyingmapa), bKA' BRGYUD PA (Kagyüpa), and SA SKYA PA (Sakyapa) orders, most teachers will not give tantric initiations or higher instructions to students who have not completed the preliminary practices, but in the dGE LUGS PA (Gelukpa) order some teachers will, the reasoning being that for one to have interest in tantric practice and to seek out a lama for training, one must have completed the preliminary practices in a previous life. They are: (1) taking refuge and manifesting BODHICITTA (*byang chub kyiems*); (2) prostration (*phyag 'tshal*); (3) visualization of VAJRASATTVA and recitation of his 100-syllable MANTRA (*rdor sems bsgom bzlas*); (4) MAṆḌALA offering (*maṇḍal 'bul*); and (5) GURU YOGA (*bla ma'i rnal 'byor*). These are commonly referred to as the "five one hundred thousands," because each is performed 100,000 times.

Snow Lion Publications

Leading publisher of books on Buddhism. It was founded in the 1970s as an outlet for translations of oral teachings by Tibetan teachers and translations of Tibetan Buddhist texts, but later expanded its offerings. Today it has a large catalog of books on a broad spectrum of Buddhist Studies, and it also distributes books by other publishers.

sōbei ("warrior monks")

A class of monks in medieval Japanese monasteries, who formed military units that both protected monasteries from their enemies and also fought against other monasteries. Records of the time indicate that the purpose of these monks was to protect their monasteries' property and power and to seize the property of other monasteries. By the twelfth century, most Buddhist monasteries had their own monk-armies, which in many cases exerted considerable power. There are, for example, accounts of fighting monks storming the capital and forcing the court to grant their demands. They would often carry icons (*mikoshi*) believed to enshrine a Shintō deity (*kami*). The purpose of this was to dissuade government troops from fighting with them, since damaging the icons would anger the *kami*.

Sogyal Rinpoche (bSod nams rgyal mtshan Rin po che, b. 1945)

Reincarnate lama (SPRUL SKU) of the rNYING MA PA (Nyingmapa) lineage, student of 'JAM DBYANGS MKHYEN BRTSE CHOS KYI BLO GROS (Jamyang Khyentse Chögi Lodrö, 1896–1969), who recognized him as the reincarnation of gTer ston bSod rgyal (Tertön Sögyel, 1826–1926). He also studied with bDud 'jom Rin po che 'Jigs 'bral ye shes rdo rje (DUDJOM RINPOCHE JIKDREL YESHE DORJE, 1904–1987) and DIL MGO MKHYEN BRTSE RIN PO CHE (Dingo Khyentse Rinpoche, 1910–1991). In 1971 he traveled to England, where he studied Comparative Religions at Cambridge University. In 1974 he began teaching meditation. He became increasingly popular in Western countries, and his Rigpa Foundation has centers all over the world. His *Tibetan Book of Living and Dying* has become a best-seller.

Sōji-ji

One of the two main temples of the Japanese Sōtō school of Zen (the other being Eihei-ji). It was founded by Gyōgi in the eighth century as a Hossō monastery. After Keizan Jōkin (1268–1325) was appointed abbot in 1321, it became a Zen monastery. It was destroyed by fire in 1898, and rebuilt in Yokohama.

Sōka Gakkai ("Value Creation Society")

One of the two main contemporary organizations (along with Nichiren Shōshū) that trace themselves back to Nichiren (1222–1282). The Nichiren Shōshū Sōkagakkai ("Nichiren Value Creation Society") was founded in 1930 by Tsunesaburō Makiguchi and further expanded by his disciple Jōsei Toda (1900–1958). It was formally incorporated in 1937, and in 1951 adopted the name Nichiren Shōshū Sōkagakkai. After an acrimonious battle between the priesthood and the lay leadership, in 1991 the high priest of Nichiren Shōshū, Nikken Abe, officially excommunicated the lay Sōka Gakkai organization. He declared that only the priesthood of the Nichiren Shōshū represented the true tradition of Nichiren, and further claimed that only its gohonzon (a scroll inscribed by Nichiren with the Chinese characters of the daimoku) is an authentic basis for chanting and worship. The Sōka Gakkai reject this claim and assert that their *gohonzon* is equally effective.

Sokkuram

A grotto near the crest of Mount Jinhyundong in Kyongsangbukdo Province, Korea, which houses a stone buddha statue that is widely regarded as one of the great religious treasures of Korean Buddhism. It was carved during the Unified Silla period (668–918), commissioned by Kim Tae-song. It was constructed some time around 751.

sokushin jōbutsu ("becoming a buddha in this very body")

Central notion of the Japanese Shingon tradition, according to which one does not need to abandon the body to become a buddha because the "three mysteries" (*sammitsu*) of body, speech, and mind can be progressively identified with those of Vairocana (Jpn. *Dainichi Nyorai*). Through ritual practices and visualizations, one actualizes the state of Vairocana.

Sŏn (Chin. *Ch'an*; Jpn. *Zen*; Viet. *Thiền*)

The Korean tradition of Ch'an (Jpn. Zen), which according to traditional accounts was introduced to Korea by the Silla monk Pŏmnang (Chin. Fa-lang, fl. 632–646). He traveled to China, where he studied with the fourth Chinese patriarch of the tradition, Tao-hsin (580–646). The earliest established Sŏn school in Korea was Hŭiyang-san, and during the eighth and ninth centuries Koreans who traveled to China to study founded eight Sŏn monasteries, which together with Hŭiyang-san became known as the "Nine Mountains" (Kusan Sŏnmun) tradition. Seven of these derived from the Hung-chou school of Chinese Ch'an, and the Sumi-san school derived from the Ch'an master Ch'ing-yüan Hsing-ssu (d. 740), whose lineage later developed into the Ts'ao-tung school.

Sönam Gyatso

See bSod nams rgya mtsho.

Songgwangsa ("Spreading Pine Temple")

One of Korea's "three jewels" temples, representing the saṃgha (the others are Haeinsa, representing the dharma, and Tongdosa, representing the Buddha). It is located on Mount Chogye, named after the mountain in China on which HUI-NENG lived. It was originally founded by CHINUL (1158–1210) as a meditation retreat, but later grew to be one of Korea's largest temples.

Sŏnjong ("Meditation School")

During the reign of King Sejong (r. 1418–1450) of the Chosŏn dynasty, the number of Buddhist schools in Korea was reduced to two. Sŏnjong combined the Kyeyul (Chin. LÜ-TSUNG; Skt. Vinaya), Chŏnt'ae (Chin. T'IEN-T'AI), and SŎN (Chin. CH'AN) traditions, while the KYO-JONG ("Textual") school brought together elements of the Hwaŏm (Chin. HUA-YEN), Pŏpsang (Chin. FA-HSIANG), and Sammon (Chin. SAN-LUN) traditions. These two remained the only official schools of Buddhism in Korea until 1935.

Sopa, Geshe Lhundrup (dGe bshes Lhun grub bzod pa, b. 1923)

DGE LUGS PA (Gelukpa) scholar, born in the gTsang (Tsang) province of Tibet. He joined SE RA (Sera) monastery at the age of eighteen and in 1961 earned the DGE BSHES (*geshe*) degree with highest distinction (*lha ram pa*). In 1967 he accepted an offer from Professor RICHARD ROBINSON to join the faculty of the University of Wisconsin-Madison, which had the first Ph.D. program in Buddhist Studies in North America. During his career there, he trained a number of students, many of whom have themselves become prominent scholars.

Sōtō-shū (Chin. Ts'ao-tung-tsung; Viet. Tào-Động)

One of the two main lineages of Japanese ZEN today (the other being RINZAI). It was founded by DŌGEN ZENJI (1200–1253), who traveled to China in 1223 and studied with T'ien-t'ung Ju-ching (1163–1228). The tradition stresses *mokushō* Zen (Chin. *mo-chao* Ch'an), "the Zen of silent awakening," so called because it is based on *zazen* practice that does not rely on verbal instructions or KŌAN training. *Kōan*s are used in Sōtō, but are not assigned the same centrality as in Rinzai. The main meditative practice of Sōtō is SHIKANTAZA ("just sitting"), in which one becomes totally involved in the practice of zazen without relying on supports such as focusing on the breath or *kōan*s. According to this system, the practice of *zazen* itself is the actualization of buddhahood (which is inherent in all beings), rather than a means for attaining it.

Southern School of Ch'an

See NAN-TSUNG-CH'AN.

sprul sku (*tülku*; Skt. *nirmāṇa-kāya*; Mon. *khubilgan*; "emanation body")

Tibetan term for a reincarnate lama (BLA MA). According to Tibetan tradition, advanced practitioners acquire the ability to choose their rebirth situations consciously, and other advanced masters are able to identify them (magical methods such as divination and consultation with mediums are also often utilized). These reincarnations are said to occur in an unbroken series (referred to in TIBETAN BUDDHISM as *sku 'phreng*, "rosary of bodies"). The idea of *tülku*s developed gradually in Tibetan Buddhism, and the earliest figure who was officially considered to be a reincarnation of his predecessor was the third RGYAL BA KAR MA PA, Rang 'byung rdo rje (Gyelwa Karmapa Rangjung Dorje, 1284–1330). Today there are hundreds of reincarnational lineages in Tibetan Buddhism, the most prominent of which are the DALAI LAMAS. (*See also* NIRMĀṆA-KĀYA.)

sPyan ras gzigs dbang phyug

See AVALOKITEŚVARA.

śraddhā (Pāli *saddhā*; Tib. *dad pa*; Chin. *hsin*; Jpn. *shin*; "faith")

An attitude of belief in the Buddha and his teachings, coupled with devotion toward them. Ideally, this should be based on conviction that grows out of one's own direct experience of the truth of the teachings, but Buddhist scriptures commonly indicate that simple faith is also highly efficacious. Faith is classified as one of the eleven virtuous mental factors (*eka-daśa-kuśala*) because it predisposes one to practice Buddhism with diligence and conviction, which in turn leads to the development of virtuous qualities and wisdom.

śrāmaṇera (Pāli *sāmaṇera*; Tib. *dge tshul*; "novice monk")

A male member of the monastic community (SAṂGHA) who has taken the novice vows. In most traditions, the minimum age for this ordination is seven, but it is not uncommon for much younger children to be ordained. The novice ordination includes a formal ceremony which contains recitation of the refuge prayer and an agreement to uphold the "ten precepts" (*daśa-śīla*), following which the novice is assigned a "teacher" (*ācārya*) and a "preceptor" (*upādhyāya*). The novice's head is shaved, and he is given three robes and a begging-bowl. The full ordination of a BHIKṢU is generally reserved for men who are at least twenty years of age. (*See also* ŚĪLA.)

śrāmaṇerī (Pāli *sāmaṇerī*; Tib. *dge tshul ma*; "novice nun")

A female member of the SAṂGHA, whose ordination follows the outlines of the ŚRĀMAṆERA described above.

śrāvaka (Pāli *sāvaka*; Tib. *nyan thos*; "hearer")

Disciples of ŚĀKYAMUNI BUDDHA who heard his words and practiced them in accordance with their capacities. They include such notable figures as ŚĀRIPUTRA, MAUDGALYĀYANA, and RĀHULA. According to MAHĀYĀNA, they constitute one of the three main types of Buddhist

Young bKa' brgyud pa (Kagyupa) monks at Spyi dbang (Phyang) Monastery, Ladakh.

practitioners, the others being PRATYEKABUDDHAS and BODHISATTVAS. In Mahāyāna, they are characterized as "Hīnayānists" because they seek a personal NIRVĀṆA as ARHATS. (*See also* HĪNAYĀNA.)

Sri Lankan Buddhism

According to traditional chronicles, Buddhism was first brought to Sri Lanka by MAHINDA, a monk who was sent as a missionary by his father, the Mauryan ruler AŚOKA, some time around 240 B.C.E. He converted the king of the island, DEVĀNAMPIYA TISSA (r. 247–207 B.C.E.). The king subsequently donated a tract of land near the capital, ANURĀDHAPURA, where a monastery named the MAHĀVIHĀRA was built. Shortly after this, the first Buddhist monks on the island were ordained, prompting the king to ask Mahinda if Buddhism was now established in Sri Lanka. In response, Mahinda is reported to have replied that this would not occur until an ordination place (*sīmā*) had been established and a man born in Sri Lanka to Sri Lankan parents was ordained as a monk in Sri Lanka. This happened soon afterwards, and Buddhism quickly spread throughout the island. An order of nuns was also established at the time by Mahinda's sister Saṃghamittā, a Buddhist nun who brought both the *bhikkhunī* (Skt. BHIKṢUṆĪ) ordination and a cutting from the Bodhi Tree to Sri Lanka. The cutting was planted at the site of the Mahāvihāra and served as a symbol of Buddhism's establishment there.

Although Theravāda became the dominant tradition early in Sri Lanka's history, in later centuries Mahāyāna and tantric missionaries also came to the island. In addition, there were periods during which the tradition was disrupted by outside invasions. During the reign of DUṬṬHAGĀMAṆI (r. 101–77 B.C.E.), the Coḷa ruler Eḷāra was defeated, ending forty-four years of rule by the south Indian Damiḷas (Tamils). A century later, another wave of Tamil invaders conquered and ruled the island until they were defeated by Vaṭṭagāmaṇi (r. 29–17 B.C.E.). During his reign, the PĀLI CANON was written down on palm leaves, and a number of commentaries in Sinhalese were translated into Pāli. He also founded the ABHAYAGIRI monastery, which later became the main rival to the Mahāvihāra.

Buddha imagery, Negombo, Sri Lanka.

Some time around the fourth to fifth century C.E., BUDDHAGHOSA, widely regarded as the greatest scholar of the Theravāda tradition, composed some of its most influential commentarial works. His *magnum opus* is his *Path of Purification* (VISUDDHIMAGGA), which summarizes the meditation philosophy of the Mahāvihāra NIKĀYA (2). During the fourth century, Mahāyāna competed with Theravāda and enjoyed royal patronage from King MAHĀSENA (r. 334–362), who built the monastery of JETAVANA (2) for Mahāyāna monks. Royal sponsorship of Mahāyāna was

Buddhist nuns near the holy Bodhi Tree in Anurādhapura.

short-lived, however, and his son Śrīmeghavaṇṇa restored the Mahāvihāra and reinstated Theravāda as the dominant Buddhist tradition. In later centuries, there was continual squabbling between the main monasteries on the island, as well as foreign invasions, and by the eleventh century the SAṂGHA had declined to such an extent that it was necessary to restore it by bringing monks from Burma to create a new ordination lineage. During this period the order of nuns died out in Sri Lanka, and has not yet been restored (though there is a movement to import the lineage from East Asia). In the sixteenth century, the Portugese conquered Sri Lanka, and ruled from 1505 to 1658. They were followed by the Dutch, who controlled the island from 1658 until 1753, but in turn were supplanted by the British, who ruled until Sri Lanka gained its independence in 1948. As a result of the disruptions of the colonial period, the *saṃgha* again declined, and the Theravāda ordination lineage was again imported, this time from Thailand. During the twentieth century, Buddhism in Sri Lanka experienced a revival, and is now the religion of the overwhelming majority of Sinhalas. There is a downside to Buddhism's popularity, however: Buddhist triumphalism has contributed to the tensions that resulted in civil war between the majority Sinhalas and minority Tamils. Under the governments of S. W. R. D. Bandaranaike and his wife Sirimavo, Buddhist chauvinism was enshrined in the constitution, along with a number of laws that marginalized the Tamils. In addition, members of the *saṃgha*, such as the late WALPOLA RAHULA, have publicly urged Sinhalas to fight against the Tamils in a "holy war" that some compare to the campaigns of Duṭṭhagāmaṇi and Vaṭṭagāmaṇi.

S. W. R. D. Bandaranaike was elected in 1956 after conducting a campaign that explicitly appealed to Buddhist conservatives. He was the first Sri Lankan politician to publicly endorse the so-called "Ten Commandments" set by the *saṃgha* for politicians, which

Renovated stupas at Mihintale, a place of pilgrimage linked with the beginnings of Buddhism in Sri Lanka.

included following Buddhist lay precepts and safeguarding the role of Buddhism as the sole legitimate religion of the country. He publicly declared that Sri Lanka had always been Sinhalese and Buddhist, and further claimed that the end of Sri Lanka's "golden age" was caused by invasions of Tamils from India. Their descendants were characterized as aliens whose very presence threatened security and religious–ethnic identity. Ironically, Bandaranaike himself fell victim to the very ethnonationalism he had helped propagate when he was assassinated in 1959 by a Buddhist monk who felt that he was making too many concessions to Tamils. Since then successive governments have also appealed to Buddhist chauvinism and have enshrined persecution of religious and ethnic minorities in the country's laws and constitution. Sinhalese Buddhists constitute over seventy percent of the population, and Buddhism is well established on the island, but the rise of ethnonationalist Buddhist chauvinism has contributed to a bloody civil war that impoverishes the country both financially and morally.

Srong btsan sgam po (Songsen Gampo, ca. 618–650)

Considered by TIBETAN BUDDHISM to be the first of the three "religious kings" (*chos rgyal*, the others being KHRI SRONG LDE BRTSAN and RAL PA CAN). He is thought to have been a physical manifestation of AVALOKITEŚVARA. He married two Buddhist wives: (1) a Nepalese princess (referred to as Khri btsun [Tritsün] or Bal bza' [Pelsa] in Tibetan chronicles, who is believed by tradition to be an emanation of Bhṛkutī; she is said to have brought an image of AKṢOBHYA BUDDHA with her to Tibet, which was housed in the Ra mo che Temple); and (2) a Chinese princess named Wen-cheng, who brought an image of ŚĀKYAMUNI BUDDHA as a young prince. This was housed in the Jo khang Temple in Lhasa and is today the holiest image in Tibet (referred to as "Jo bo rin po che" [Jowo Rinpoche] by Tibetans). Both women are regarded by Tibetan tradition as emanations of the buddha TĀRĀ. Although records of the time do not indicate that the king was particularly devoted to Buddhism, he is regarded by the later tradition as an ardent promoter of the dharma who firmly established it in Tibet.

srotāpanna (Pāli *sotāpanna*; Tib. *rgyun zhugs*; "stream enterer")

A person who has entered the first of the four "supramundane paths" (ĀRYA-MĀRGA). One attains this level through developing a firm conviction in the DHARMA – and at this point is said to be firmly established in the Buddhist path – but one has not yet eliminated the afflictions (KLEŚA). A *srotāpanna* may be reborn as many as seven more times, but will eventually attain the level of "once-returner" (Skt. SAKṚDĀGAMIN), and will later become a "non-returner" (ANĀGAMIN).

stabilizing meditation

See ŚAMATHA.

Stcherbatsky, Fedor Ippolitovich (1866–1942)

Russian scholar best known for his work on Buddhist logic. He also published important studies in a number of other areas and was involved in a famous dispute with LOUIS DE LA VALLÉE POUSSIN that centered on the nature of NIRVĀṆA.

Steinkellner, Ernst (b. 1937)

Eminent Austrian buddhologist, best known for his work on the Epistemological tradition (PRAMĀṆA-VĀDA). His books include *Texte der erkenntnistheoretischen Schule des Buddhismus* (1995) and *Dharmakīrti's Pramāṇaviniścayaḥ: zweites Kapitel* (1973–1979).

Sthavira (Pāli *Thera*; "Elder")

One of the two groups involved in the first Buddhist schism (the other being the MAHĀSĀṂGHIKAS). The Sthaviras claimed to uphold the orthodox scriptural and disciplinary tradition of ŚĀKYAMUNI BUDDHA, and they branded their opponents (who appear to have constituted a majority) as heretics. The present-day THERAVĀDA NIKĀYA claims descent from the Sthaviras, although there is no historical basis for the assertion. Theravāda arose at least two centuries later.

storehouse consciousness

See ĀLAYA-VIJÑĀNA.

stūpa (Pāli *thūpa*; Tib. *mchod rten*; "relic shrine"; lit. "heap," "pile")

Monuments that often house the relics (ŚARĪRA) of a deceased teacher or sacred objects such as texts or statues. The *stūpa* was probably the earliest distinctively Buddhist structure, and the first ones were reportedly built to house the relics of ŚĀKYAMUNI BUDDHA. As Gregory Schopen has pointed out, they were the

Dhamek Stūpa, Deer Park, Sārnāth, with the ruins of a monastery in the foreground.

Mural depicting people entering Amitābha's paradise of Sukhāvatī. Ch'ŏngnyangsa Monastery, South Kyŏngsang, Korea,

focus of a number of important early Buddhist cults, and today are important focal points for veneration throughout the Buddhist world. They are associated with numerous merit-making activities, the most common of which is circumambulation (Skt. PRADAKṢIṆA). (*See also* ART.)

Śubhākarasiṃha (Chin. *Shan-wu-wei*, 637–735)

One of the three Indian tantric masters credited with bringing esoteric Buddhism (MI-TSUNG) to China (the other two were Vajrabodhi and Amoghavajra). He translated the most important scripture of the tradition, the *Mahāvairocana-sūtra*, into Chinese.

Subhūti (Pāli *Subhūti*; Tib. *Rab 'byor*)

One of the main disciples of ŚĀKYAMUNI BUDDHA, said by the Buddha to be the foremost of his followers in dwelling in remoteness and peace (*araṇa-vihārinaṃ aggo*). He is also declared to be the best expounder of the dharma and the foremost among those worthy of alms (*dakkhiṇeyyānaṃ aggo*). He is a minor figure in the PĀLI CANON, but became an important interlocutor in a number of MAHĀYĀNA sūtras. This is probably because the Buddha declared him to be the foremost among his disciples in the practice of the concentration on emptiness (Skt. *śūnyatā-samādhi*; Pāli *suññatā-samādhi*). A famous story on this point states that when the Buddha returned from TRĀYASTRIṂŚA heaven his disciples went to meet him, but Subhūti remained in meditation in RĀJAGṚHA, figuring that this was the best way to honor the Buddha. When he arrived, the Buddha declared that Subhūti was the first to greet him.

Śuddhodana (Pāli *Suddhodana*)

Father of ŚĀKYAMUNI BUDDHA, king of the ŚĀKYA clan, whose capital city was KAPILAVASTU. According to Buddhist tradition, he tried to prevent his son from becoming aware of the harsh realities of life, hoping thereby to keep him attached to worldly concerns, so that he would follow in his footsteps and become a king. After his son became a buddha and returned to his home, however, Śuddhodana took ordination as a monk, and eventually became an ARHAT.

suffering

See DUḤKHA.

Sukhāvatī (Tib. *bDe ba can*; Chin. *Ch'ing-t'u*; Jpn. *Jōdō*; Kor. *Chŏngt'o*; Viet. *Đạo Trang*; "Joyous Land")

The heaven of AMITĀBHA BUDDHA, said to be located in the west. It is the central focus of the religious practice of the "Pure Land" (Chin. CH'ING-T'U; Jpn. *Jōdō*) traditions of East Asia, which believe that it is a place in which the conditions are optimal for the attainment of buddhahood. This idea is connected with the prevalent notion that this is the final age of the degeneration of the dharma (Chin. *mo-fa*; Jpn. MAPPŌ), in which the capacities of humans have degenerated to such an extent that it is no longer possible to gain salvation through one's own effort. Thus, the wisest course of action is to work toward rebirth in Sukhāvatī, so that one may attain buddhahood in one's next lifetime. The wondrous qualities of this paradise are described in several texts, most popularly the Larger and Smaller SUKHĀVATĪ-VYŪHA-SŪTRA and the *Amitāyur-dhyāna-sūtra*.

Sukhāvatī-vyūha-sūtra (Tib. *bDe ba can gyi bkod pa'i mdo*; Chin. *Wu liang ch'ing ching p'ing teng chiao ching*; *Sūtra of the Array of the Joyous Land*)

Indian Buddhist text in two versions, generally referred to respectively as the Larger *Sukhāvatī-vyūha-sūtra* and the Smaller *Sukhāvatī-vyūha-sūtra*. The first became the doctrinal basis of the East Asian "Pure Land" (Chin. CH'ING-T'U; Jpn. *Jōdō*; Kor. *Chŏngt'o*) traditions, which base their practices on the forty-eight vows made by AMITĀBHA BUDDHA in a past life as the monk Dharmākara. The most important of these (the eighteenth) promises that anyone who invokes Amitābha's name ten times (or desires rebirth in SUKHĀVATĪ ten times) will surely be reborn there. The Larger *Sukhāvatī-vyūha-sūtra* is set on Vulture Peak, where ŚĀKYAMUNI BUDDHA tells ĀNANDA the story of Amitābha's past vows and his subsequent practice, which culminated in his attainment of buddhahood and led to his establishment of the paradise of Sukhāvatī, in which the conditions are optimal for Buddhist practice. The Smaller *Sukhāvatī-vyūha-sūtra* does not mention rebirth in Sukhāvatī at all, but rather emphasizes its unique characteristics, including the fact that in Sukhāvatī all the sounds – even the wind whistling through the leaves – constitute DHARMA teachings.

śūnyatā (Pāli *suññatā*; Tib. *stong pa nyid*; Chin. *k'ung*; Jpn. *kū*; Kor. *kong*; Viet. *không*; "emptiness")

The notion that all phenomena lack an essence or self, are dependent upon causes and conditions, and so lack inherent existence (SVABHĀVA). Thus persons (Skt. *pudgala*) are said to be empty of being a "self" (Skt. *ātman*) because they are composed of parts that are constantly changing and dependent upon causes and conditions. In MAHĀYĀNA the concept of emptiness is predicated of all phenomena (DHARMA), which are said to be empty because they are dependent arisings (PRATĪTYA-SAMUTPĀDA). Although often characterized by its critics as a nihilistic doctrine, the concept of emptiness is viewed by Buddhists as a positive perspective on reality, because it implies that everything is constantly changing, and is thus open toward the future. If things possessed an unchanging essence, real change would be impossible, and so all beings would be stuck in their present situations. Because everything is empty, however, it is possible for beings to take control of the process of change and to move their respective psycho-physical continuums in the direction of greater wisdom and compassion, the development of positive qualities, and even to the state of buddhahood. In Mahāyāna, the direct realization of emptiness is the focus of the "perfection of wisdom"

(PRAJÑĀ-PĀRAMITĀ), one of the primary qualities in which BODHISATTVAS train.

superior

See ĀRYA.

supernatural abilities

See ABHIJÑĀ.

sūtra (Pāli *sutta*; Tib. *mdo*; Jpn. *kyō*; "discourse")

Sermons attributed to ŚĀKYAMUNI BUDDHA (and less commonly to one of his immediate disciples). They begin with the formula, "Thus have I heard at one time" (Skt. EVAṂ MAYĀ ŚRUTAM EKASMIN SAMAYE), which according to tradition was adopted at the "first Buddhist council" at RĀJAGṚHA, when 500 ARHATS gathered to recite the discourses of the Buddha. These discourses are collected in the SŪTRA-PIṬAKA (Pāli *Sutta-piṭaka*) section of Indian Buddhist canons. There is also a huge corpus of Mahāyāna sūtras, which generally differ markedly in terms of contents, participants, and form from those of the PĀLI CANON. They did not begin to appear in India until around the first century B.C.E. (several centuries after the death of Śākyamuni). The temporal discrepancy is explained by their adherents as being due to their being hidden from the masses and only passed on to advanced practitioners. The THERAVĀDA school rejects the Mahāyāna sūtras as forgeries that could not have been spoken by Śākyamuni, but adherents of Mahāyāna assert that their texts are advanced teachings, while the SUTTAS of the Pāli canon were spoken for followers of lesser capacities.

Sūtra-piṭaka (Pāli *Sutta-piṭaka*; Tib. *mDo sde snod*; "Basket of Discourses")

The section of the Buddhist canon (TRIPIṬAKA; Pāli *tipiṭaka*) that contains sermons attributed to ŚĀKYAMUNI BUDDHA (and less commonly to his immediate disciples). The PĀLI CANON divides them into five sections: (1) DĪGHA NIKĀYA ("Long Discourses," which corresponds to the Dīrghāgama of the Sanskrit Buddhist canon); (2) MAJJHIMA NIKĀYA ("Middle Length Discourses," which corresponds to the Madhyamāgama); (3) SAṂYUTTA NIKĀYA ("Connected Discourses," which corresponds to the Saṃyuktāgama); (4) AṄGUTTARA NIKĀYA ("Increased-by-one Discourses," which corresponds to the Ekotarikāgama); and (5) KHUDDAKA NIKĀYA ("Lesser Discourses," which does not, despite its title, correspond to the Kṣudrakāgama).

Suzuki, Daisetz Teitaro (1870–1966)

Japanese scholar of Buddhism who studied with the RINZAI master Shaku Sōen and reportedly had an experience of KENSHŌ while meditating on the MU KŌAN. He traveled to the U.S.A. and worked with Paul Carus from 1897 to 1909, after which he returned to Japan. In 1911 he married Beatrice Lane, and returned to the U.S.A. briefly in 1936. He lived in Japan during World War II, and again returned to America from 1950 to 1958. He published a number of influential books, and played an important role in the popularization of ZEN in the West.

Suzuki, Shunryu (1904–1971)

Japanese SŌTŌ master, a student of Kishizawa Rōshi, who was the son of a Sōtō ZEN priest. He traveled to the U.S.A. in 1958, following which he founded several Zen centers, including the SAN FRANCISCO ZEN CENTER and the Zen Mountain Center in Tassajara, CA, which was the first Sōtō monastery in the West. His book *Zen Mind, Beginner's Mind* is one of the most popular books on Zen in English.

svabhāva (Pāli *sabhāva*; Tib. *rang bzhin*; "own-being," "inherent existence")

Refers to an essence or inherent quality. In ABHIDHARMA, *svabhāva* is said to be the defining character of a DHARMA. Thus hardness, for example, is the defining characteristic of earth. In *abhidharma*, only dharmas – the ultimate simple reals that are the constituents of complex phenomena – are said to have an essence. Any sort of essence – either for simple atomic elements or complex wholes – is denied in MADHYAMAKA, which extends the logic of selflessness (ANĀTMAN) to all phenomena. All things without exception are said to lack any enduring essence or self. Because things are collections of parts and are produced in dependence upon causes and conditions, they do not exist by way of their own nature, but rather only exist conventionally. Thus their final nature is emptiness (ŚŪNYATĀ). This does not mean, however, that things do not exist; rather, they do not exist in the way that they appear to the cognitions of deluded beings.

svastika (Tib. *g.yung drung*, *geg gsangs*; Chin. *wan-tzu*; Jpn. *manji*)

An ancient solar symbol of well-being and good fortune. It is often found on Buddhist monasteries and temples. The term *svastika* derives from the Sanskrit prefix *su*, meaning "good, well" and the verb asti, "to be." In INDIAN BUDDHISM it is sometimes associated with the wheel of DHARMA, and in ZEN symbolizes the "seal of the buddha-mind" (*busshin-in*), the direct realization of truth that is passed on from master to student.

Svātantrika-madhyamaka (Tib. *Rang rgyud dbu ma pa'i lugs*; "Middle Way Autonomy School")

One of the two main divisions of the MADHYAMAKA tradition, according to Tibetan doxographers (the other being PRĀSAṄGIKA). Its founder is considered by tradition to have been BHAVYA (ca. 490–570), who is said to have favored the use of autonomous (*svatantra*) syllogisms in addition to the *reductio ad absurdum* (*prasaṅga*) dialectic of NĀGĀRJUNA and BUDDHAPĀLITA. According to Tibetan exegetes, he claimed that a Madhyamaka philosopher should be able to formulate a thesis and develop an epistemology. TSONG KHA PA contends that a key difference between the two divisions of Madhyamaka is that the Svātantrikas accept inherent existence (Skt. *svabhāva*) conventionally, but Prāsaṅgikas deny it both ultimately and conventionally.

Swearer, Donald K. (b. 1934)

American buddhologist, one of the leading authorities on Theravāda Buddhism in Southeast Asia. He received his Ph.D. from Princeton University in 1967, and is currently the McDowell Professor of Religion at Swarthmore College in Pennsylvania. His publications include studies of classical Theravāda, cross-cultural studies, and contemporary Buddhist movements in Southeast Asia.

T

T'ai-hsü (1899–1947)

Chinese Buddhist monk who founded the Chinese Buddhist Society in 1929. He also formed the Institute of Buddhist Studies in 1922, which played an important role in the revival of the FA-HSIANG tradition in China. As part of his campaign to modernize Buddhism, he argued that the doctrines of Fa-hsiang are compatible with modern science. He also emphasized the essential harmony of various Chinese Buddhist traditions. He was an important figure in the revitalization of Buddhism in China in the early part of the twentieth century, but his efforts were effectively ended when the Communists came to power in 1947.

Taishō Shinshū Daizōkyō

A compilation of the Chinese Buddhist canon, published in Tokyo between 1924 and 1929, comprising 55 volumes with 2,184 texts. There is also a supplement comprising 45 additional volumes.

Ta'i si tu Rin po che (Tai Situ Rinpoche)

One of the main reincarnational lineages of the KAR MA BKA' BRGYUD PA (Karma Kagyüpa) order of TIBETAN BUDDHISM; these lamas are considered by the tradition to be emanations of MAITREYA (1). The twelfth member of the series, Padma don ngag snying bshad (Bema Tönngak Nyingshe), was born in 1954 in dPal yul (Beyül) in Sde dge (Derge), eastern Tibet. He was enthroned at the age of eighteen months by the sixteenth RGYAL BA KAR MA PA (Gyelwa Karmapa), and fled the country at the age of six following the Chinese invasion of Tibet. After a period of illness, he settled at Rum bteg (Rumtek) Monastery in Sikkim. He has traveled extensively in the West, and in 1984 he visited Tibet.

Tanjur

See BSTAN 'GYUR.

T'an-luan (Jpn. *Donran*, 476–542)

The first Chinese patriarch of the "Pure Land" (Chin. CH'ING-T'U; Jpn. *Jōdō*; Kor. *Chŏngt'o*; Viet. *Đạo Trang*) tradition. He is said to have embraced Pure Land practice after meeting the Indian missionary monk Bodhiruci (Jpn. *Bodairushi*). He was the first to divide Buddhist practices into two types, the "easy" and the "difficult." The former is the "path of the sages" (*sheng tao*), which refers to the meditative practices and monastic rules taught by the Buddha. T'an-luan felt that such practices are ineffective and inappropriate in the "final dharma age" (Chin. *mo-fa*; Jpn. MAPPŌ), and he initiated the practice of chanting the *nien-fo* (Jpn. NEMBUTSU; Kor. *yŏmbul*; Viet. niệm-phật), "Na mo A-mi-t'o-fo"

(Jpn. "*Namu Amida Butsu*"; Viet. "*Nam mô A-Di-Đà Phật*"; "Praise to AMITĀBHA BUDDHA"). This practice was combined with prostrations, visualizations of the Pure Land of SUKHĀVATĪ, and making vows to be reborn there.

tantra (Tib. *rgyud*; "continuum," "thread")

Discourses attributed to ŚĀKYAMUNI BUDDHA that appeared some time around the seventh century in India. They adopted the same basic narrative structure as the MAHĀYĀNA sūtras, but taught a number of very different practices (though the basic outline of the BODHISATTVA path and the primary goal of the attainment of buddhahood for the benefit of others were retained). These texts emphasize the use of rituals, symbols, MANTRAS, and visualizations, and are the basic textual sources of VAJRAYĀNA Buddhism. Tibetan doxographers divide these texts into four classes: (1) action tantras (Skt. KRIYĀ-TANTRA; Tib. *bya rgyud*); (2) performance tantras (Skt. CARYĀ-TANTRA; Tib. *spyod rgyud*); (3) yoga tantras (Skt. YOGA-TANTRA; Tib. *rnal 'byor rgyud*); and (4) highest yoga tantras (Skt. ANUTTARA-YOGA-TANTRA; Tib. *rnal 'byor bla na med kyi rgyud*).

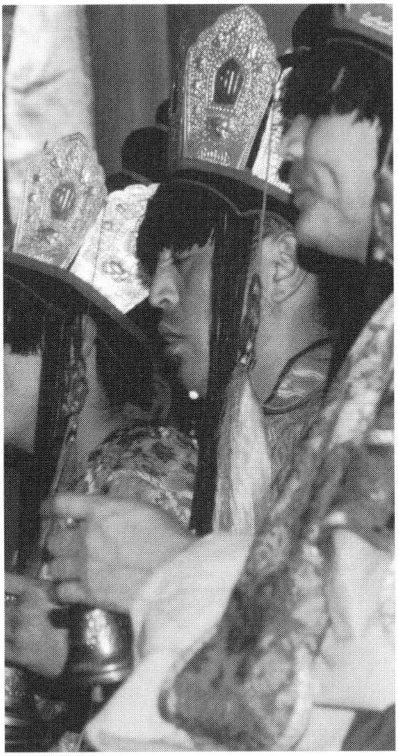

Monks from Gyuto Tantric Monastery (rGyud stod grwa tshang) chanting.

Tao-an (312–385)

One of the most influential figures in the early period of Buddhism in China. He compiled a catalogue of sūtras that were available in translation in China at that time, and also developed a set of rules for monks. This activity was prompted by his realization that China lacked a complete VINAYA at that time. He is also credited with initiating the cult of MAITREYA (1) in East Asia.

Tao-sheng (360–434)

Important figure of the Nirvāṇa school in China, which was based on the Mahāyāna MAHĀPARINIRVĀṆA-SŪTRA. He worked with KUMĀRAJĪVA on the translation of several important texts, including the VIMALAKĪRTI-NIRDEŚA-SŪTRA and the SADDHARMA-PUṆḌARĪKA-SŪTRA. He had a significant impact on the future development of Buddhism in China, mainly due to his formulation of several new doctrines, such as his assertion that all beings, without exception, possess the buddha-nature and so are capable of becoming buddhas. He also advocated the notion of sudden awakening, which held that buddhahood is attained all at once in a sudden flash of realization.

Tārā (Tib. *Grol ma*; Chin. *T'o-lo*; Jpn. *Tarani*; Mon. *Dara eke*; "Savioress")

One of the most popular buddhas in TIBETAN BUDDHISM. According to legend, she was born from tears shed by AVALOKITEŚVARA, who was saddened by the sufferings of sentient beings. In a past life she is said to have declared that there are many buddhas who manifest in male form, but few in female form. Thus – although she realized that gender distinctions only operate on the conventional level – she vowed always to appear in female form because that would be particularly beneficial to women. There are twenty-one main forms of Tārā, each of which has different colors and other iconographic features. In Tibetan Buddhism the most popular forms are White Tārā, Green Tārā, and Red Tārā.

Tāranātha (Tib. *Tā ra nā tha*, 1575–1634)

Scholar and historian of the JO NANG PA lineage of TIBETAN BUDDHISM, which was suppressed as heretical by the fifth Dalai Lama, NGAG DBANG BLO BZANG RGYA MTSHO (Ngawang Losang Gyatso, 1617–1682). His best-known work is entitled *History of Buddhism in India* (*Rgya gar chos 'byung*).

tariki (Chin. *t'o-li*; "other power")

Japanese term particularly associated with "Pure Land" (Jpn. *Jōdō*; Chin. CH'ING-T'U) traditions, which is based on the notion that in the "final dharma age" (Jpn. MAPPŌ; Chin. *mo-fa*) people are no longer capable of bringing about their own salvations, and so must rely on the saving grace of AMITĀBHA (Jpn. *Amida*; Chin. *A-mi-t'o*). *Tariki* is commonly opposed to JIRIKI (Chin. *tzu-li*, "own power"), which involves engaging in meditation and other practices aimed at the attainment of liberation. *Tariki* is said by Pure Land traditions to be an "easy path," since one is saved by someone else, while *jiriki* is a "difficult path" because it relies on personal striving.

Tarthang Tulku (Dar thang sprul sku, b. 1935)

A reincarnate lama (SPRUL SKU) who fled Tibet in 1959. He was appointed by the DALAI LAMA as a teacher of RNYING MA PA (Nyingmapa) studies at the Central Institute of Higher Tibetan Studies in Sārnāth in 1962. He traveled to America in 1968 after giving up his monastic ordination, and subsequently established the Nyingma Meditation Center, the Nyingma Institute, and DHARMA PUBLISHING, all of which are located in Berkeley, CA.

Ta-sheng-ch'i-hsin-lun (Jpn. *Daijō-kishinron*; Kor. *Taesŭng-kisimnon*; Skt. *Mahāyāna-śraddhotpāda-śāstra*; *Treatise on the Awakening of Faith in the Great Vehicle*)

A work attributed by East Asian Buddhist tradition to AŚVAGHOṢA, but extant only in Chinese. It is one of the seminal texts for the TATHĀGATA-GARBHA (Chin. *ju-lai-tsang*) doctrine in East Asia. The text claims that all beings are primordially awakened, and this basic nature is referred to as "essence" (Chin. *t'i*). It is prevented from manifesting due to ignorance (Chin. *wu-ming*; Skt. AVIDYĀ), and once this is removed one actualizes the basic potential of buddhahood.

Tashilhunpo

See BKRA SHIS LHUN PO.

tathāgata (Pāli *tathāgata*; Tib. *de bzhin gshegs pa*; "thus-gone-one")

An epithet of buddhas, which signifies their attainment of awakening (BODHI), a transcendental state that surpasses all mundane attainments.

tathāgata-garbha (Tib. *de bzhin gshegs pa'i snying po*; Chin. *ju-lai-tsang*; "embryo of the *tathāgata*")

Sanskrit term for the innate potential for buddhahood that is present in all beings. In some texts this is equated with emptiness (ŚŪNYATĀ) and is based on the notion that since beings lack inherent existence (SVABHĀVA) and are constantly changing in dependence upon causes and conditions there is no fixed essence, and so it is possible to move the psycho-physical continuum in the direction of buddhahood. According to this interpretation, one gradually cultivates the qualities of a buddha – such as compassion and wisdom – to their highest level, at which point one becomes a buddha. In other sources, however, *tathāgata-garbha* is presented as a substantially existent essence that pervades all of reality. According to this interpretation, buddhahood is not something that is developed through meditation, but rather is one's most basic nature, which is simply made manifest through removing the veils of ignorance that obscure it. The earliest known exponent of the second position was Sāramati, who wrote a commentary on the *Discrimination of the Precious Lineage* (*Ratna-gotra-vibhāga*), in which he contended that buddhahood is innate and merely becomes manifest through religious practice. The potential for buddhahood is referred to as "lineage" (Skt. *gotra*), and is said to be present in all beings.

tathatā (Pāli *tathatā*; Tib. *de bzhin nyid*; Chin. *chen-ju*; Jpn. *shinnyo*; "suchness")

Sanskrit term that refers to the final nature of reality, and which is commonly equated with such terms as emptiness (ŚŪNYATĀ), truth body (DHARMA-KĀYA), and reality limit (*bhūta-koṭi*). It is unchanging, immutable, and beyond the range of conceptual thought.

Tendai (Chin. *T'ien-t'ai*; Kor. *Chŏn-t'ae*)

Japanese lineage of the Chinese T'IEN-T'AI school, brought to Japan by SAICHŌ (767–822). He built a monastery on Mount Hiei, which later grew to be one of the major Buddhist centers in Japan. It remains the seat of the order today. Tendai has been more eclectic than its Chinese predecessor, following the approach of Saichō, who incorporated elements of esoteric Buddhism (Jpn. *mikkyō*) and CH'AN (Jpn. ZEN), while maintaining T'ien-t'ai's emphasis on the *Lotus Sūtra* (Skt. SADDHARMA-PUṆḌARĪKA-SŪTRA).

Tenzin Gyatso (bsTan 'dzin rgya mtsho, b. 1935)

The fourteenth DALAI LAMA, and the first to travel extensively outside Tibet. Born in a small village in eastern Tibet on July 6, 1935, he was officially recognized at the age of six as the reincarnation of THUB BSTAN RGYA MTSHO (Tupden Gyatso, 1876–1933), the thirteenth Dalai Lama. Forced to flee his homeland in 1959 following the Chinese invasion of Tibet, he formed a government-in-exile in the north Indian hill station of Dharamsala. In 1989 he was awarded the Nobel Peace Prize in recognition of his efforts to bring about a peaceful solution to the "Tibet Question," and in recent years has emerged as one of the most influential theoreticians of "ENGAGED BUDDHISM."

terma

See GTER MA.

tertön

See GTER STON.

Thai Buddhism

The area of modern-day Thailand was originally inhabited by the Mons, who were conquered by Khmers during the reign of King Sūryavarman of Angkor (1001–1050); they in turn were displaced by the Thais about two centuries later. Following Khubilai Khan's (r. 1260–1294) conquest of Nan-chao in 1254, increasing numbers of Thais migrated from southern China into the hills east of the Irawaddy River, the upper Manam Plain, and east to the Nam U. As they moved into the lowlands – which were controlled by the Khmers – they came into contact with MAHĀYĀNA Buddhism. Around 1260, the kingdom of Sukhothai (Pāli Sukhodaya) freed itself from Khmer domination, and shortly thereafter King Rama Khamheng (1275–1317) established THERAVĀDA as the state religion. His grandson, Lü Thai (who ascended the throne in 1347), invited monks from Sri Lanka to increase the purity of the Thai SAṂGHA. During this time Sinhala Buddhism became normative among the Thais, and the *Jīnakālamāli* reports that a monk from Sukhothai received ordination from a Sinhala MAHĀTHERA named Udumbara Mahāsāma. He returned to Sukhothai and established the Sāhaḷa Saṅgha, and this order spread throughout the region. It was brought to Chiangmai by Sumana Mahāthera in 1369, and King Küna (1355–1385) is reported to have actively patronized it. He built Wat Suan Doc to house a Buddha relic that had been brought by Sumana, and royal support continued during the reigns of Tilokarāja and Phra Mu'ang Kaew (1495–1526).

After Sukhothai was overthrown in 1492, it was replaced by the kingdom of Ayudhya, which ruled from 1350 to 1767. Several of the Ayudhya rulers were personally concerned with fostering the purity of the Thai *saṃgha*, which came to be viewed as an important duty of the sovereign. One such ruler was Songdharm (1610–1628), who worked to purify the *saṃgha* and sponsored an edition of the PĀLI CANON. A high point in the development of Thai Buddhism was the reign of King Maha Dhammarāja II (1733–1758), during which monks from Sri Lanka were sent to Ayudhya to receive ordination. Songdharm in turn sent a group of monks led by Phra Upāli to Sri Lanka. They remained there for three years and in 1753 ordained a group of monks who would later found the SIYAM NIKĀYA. Ayudhya was conquered by invaders from Burma in 1767, but King Taksin (1767–1782) regained his kingdom's independence. He moved the capital to Thonburi, but was overthrown by Rāma I (1782–1809), who became the first king of the Chakri dynasty.

Rāma I moved the capital to Bangkok, and like his predecessors devoted himself to "purification of the teaching" (Pāli *sāsana-visodhana*; Skt. *śāsana-viśodhana*). This concern continued with Rāma IV (MONGKUT, r. 1851–1868), who had been a monk for twenty-five years before ascending the throne. While he was still ordained, he formed a reformist group in the *saṃgha* named the Thammayut (Pāli *Dhammayuttika*) Nikāya. This sect emphasized stricter adherence to the rules of the VINAYA than the rest of the Thai *saṃgha*, which belonged to the Mahānikāya. After he became king, he decreed that the Mahānikāya must also adopt his reform measures. His reign continued a long tradition of royal involvement in the affairs of the *saṃgha*, which was carried on by his successors. In 1902 Rāma V (Chulalongkorn, 1868–1910) issued the Buddhist Order Act, which explicitly stated that the business of the *saṃgha* was also the business of the government and that the government should oversee the *saṃgha*. A hierarchy of religious positions was created, with the supreme patriarch (*sangha-rāja*) at the top. He is the final authority in monastic affairs, but is appointed by the king.

Under the leadership of Rāma V and Vajiravudh (1910–1925), Thailand was able to avoid becoming a European colony like most of its neighbors, and in 1932 the country became a constitutional democracy. Today Buddhism influences all strata of Thai society, and is actively promoted by the government, which links Buddhist piety with Thai nationalism and patriotism. It is common for young Thai men to take monastic ordination during a three-month rainy-season retreat, and although most subsequently return to lay life, many find the monastic lifestyle attractive and remain for longer periods of time. Monks are highly revered in Thai society, but like other Theravāda countries contemporary Thailand is also witnessing a surge of lay involvement in Buddhism. SULAK SIVARAKSA, for example, is one of the leading exponents of "ENGAGED BUDDHISM," and he has founded a number of organizations that aim to incorporate Buddhist principles in daily life, including the INTERNATIONAL NETWORK OF ENGAGED BUDDHISTS.

thang ka (*tanka*)

Scroll paintings found throughout the Tibetan cultural area, generally goache on linen base, using vegetable- and mineral-based pigments. They often depict buddhas, Buddhist luminaries, *maṇḍalas*, or artistic motifs like the "wheel of becoming" (Tib. *srid pa'i 'khor lo*; Skt. BHAVA-CAKRA). They are commonly used at initiation ceremonies, and are often combined with SĀDHANA (Tib. *grub thabs*) practice, in which they serve as aids for visualization. Although from the viewpoint of TIBETAN BUDDHISM they are religious objects – and not art for display – they have become popular souvenirs for tourists in the shops of Kathmandu and Leh, and many old and valuable *thang kas* (mostly looted from Tibetan monasteries by the Chinese) have appeared in auctions in Western countries in recent decades.

thera (Skt. *sthavira*; "elder")

Pāli term for a senior THERAVĀDA monk (*bhikkhu*) who has distinguished himself in learning, meditative attainments, and comportment.

Theragātha (*Verses of the Male Elders*)

Collection of writings of the elder monks of the early Buddhist community, contained in the KHUDDHAKA NIKĀYA of the PĀLI CANON. There are 264 poems attributed to 259 monks that mostly describe their meditative attainments and religious lives.

Theravāda Nikāya ("Order of the Teachings of the Elders")

The only surviving tradition of the collection of schools referred to collectively as "HĪNAYĀNA" by their MAHĀYĀNA opponents (and as "NIKĀYA BUDDHISM" in this encyclopedia). It is the dominant Buddhist tradition in Southeast Asia, and

Theravāda temple, Ko Samui, Thailand.

is particularly strong in Thailand, Sri Lanka, Burma, Laos, and Cambodia. Although there is no historical basis for the claim, modern Theravāda traces itself back to the STHAVIRA tradition in India. Its origins in Southeast Asia are traced back to MAHINDA, the son of King AŚOKA who became a Buddhist monk and led a mission to Sri Lanka. From this base it later spread throughout the region, and in recent decades has attracted increasing numbers of students in Europe and North America. It prides itself on being a deeply conservative school of Buddhism and bases its teachings and practices on the PĀLI CANON, which it considers to be the only authentic Buddhist canon.

Therīgātha (*Verses of the Female Elders*)

Collection of writings of the elder nuns of the early Buddhist community, contained in the KHUDDHAKA NIKĀYA of the PĀLI CANON. There are seventy-three poems attributed to seventy-one nuns that mostly describe their meditative attainments and religious lives.

Thich Nhat Hanh

See NHAT HANH, THICH.

Thiền

See CH'AN; VIETNAMESE BUDDHISM; ZEN.

Thiên-ân, Thich (1926–1980)

Vietnamese Thiền (Chin. CH'AN) monk who trained in the Lâm-tế (Chin. LIN-CHI) tradition, but later adopted an ecumenical approach. He traveled to the U.S.A. in 1966, and founded the International Buddhist Meditation Centre and the University of Oriental Studies in Los Angeles, CA.

thilashin (lit. "bearers of morality")

Burmese term for female renunciants, who follow the rules for novice nuns but do not receive official ordination because the tradition of monastic ordination for women died out in THERAVĀDA countries centuries ago. Unlike female renunciants in other Theravāda countries, they enjoy a high social status and command a level of respect from the laity that is nearly equal to that of monks. Like monks, they often make daily alms rounds, and many engage in advanced scriptural studies.

Third Buddhist Council

See PĀṬALIPUTRA.

three jewels

See RATNA-TRAYA.

three refuges

See ŚARAṆA.

Thub bstan rgya mtsho (Tupden Gyatso, 1876–1933)

The thirteenth DALAI LAMA, who was born into a peasant family and officially recognized in 1878 as the reincarnation of 'Phrin las rgya mtsho (Trinle Gyatso, d.1875), the twelfth Dalai Lama. His reign was a time of increasing turmoil for Tibet, mainly due to external forces. The first of these was a British expedition led by Col. Francis Younghusband, which entered Tibet with the intention of opening it to trade. After encountering resistance from poorly armed Tibetans, the soldiers of the expedition opened fire, killing scores of Tibetans. After this altercation they marched unopposed to Lhasa, where they forced the government to sign a trade treaty. This highlighted the military weakness of Tibet and prompted the Dalai Lama to attempt to modernize Tibet's army and to institute a number of other reforms. These were, however, scuttled by the monasteries and the aristocracy after he died, because they feared that reforms might threaten their power. China was in the throes of civil war, and he warned in a prophetic statement that Tibet's huge neighbor stood poised to engulf it, which would lead to immense suffering. The fulfillment of the prophecy came in the 1950s, when the People's Liberation Army invaded and annexed Tibet, leading to an estimated 1.2 million deaths in the following decades.

thudong (Pāli *dhutaṅga*; "asceticism")

Thai term for ascetic practices in general (thirteen are mentioned in works on monastic discipline), but today it is most commonly used to refer to monks who leave their monasteries and travel on foot on a pilgrimage. During the period of pilgrimage, it is common to adhere to the VINAYA rules strictly, and monks often only eat one meal per day (and eat it directly from the alms bowl) and sleep on the ground in a shelter called a *krot*, which is covered by a mosquito net. This practice is often undertaken by two or three monks traveling together, but they are supposed to avoid conversation as much as possible.

Thurman, Robert A. F. (b. 1941)

American scholar of Tibetan Buddhism and prominent activist for Tibet-related causes. He received his Ph.D. from Harvard University in 1972, and subsequently traveled to India, where he studied with several Tibetan teachers. He was the first Westerner to be ordained as a Tibetan Buddhist monk, and he has written extensively on Tibetan Buddhism and social issues. Thurman is the first Jey Tsong Khapa Chair of Tibetan Buddhist Studies at Columbia University.

Thus have I heard at one time

See EVAṂ MAYĀ ŚRUTAM EKASMIN SAMAYE.

Tibetan Book of the Dead

See BAR DO THOS GROL.

Tibetan Buddhism

In traditional Tibetan histories, the introduction of Buddhism to the "Land of Snows" is believed to have been accomplished by the efforts of various buddhas and bodhisattvas, who first prepared the populace for the DHARMA and then assumed human forms in order to propagate it. The central figure in this mythical drama was AVALOKITEŚVARA (Tib. *sPyan ras gzigs dbang phyug*), who worked behind the scenes for centuries before incarnating as the Tibetan king Srong btsan sgam po (ca. 618–650). He is considered to be the first of the three "religious kings" (*chos rgyal*) of the YAR LUNG DYNASTY (so called because its capital was in the Yar lung valley). Two of his wives, a Nepalese princess (referred to as Khri btsun [Tritsün] or Bal bza' [Belsa] in Tibetan chronicles) and the Chinese princess Wen-cheng, are considered to be emanations of the buddha TĀRĀ (the Nepalese wife is thought to be an emanation of Bhṛkutī, a manifestation of Tārā). Although the two wives appear to have been Buddhists, there is little evidence in records of the time that the king had any interest in Buddhism. There is no mention of Buddhism in contemporary sources, and the king was buried in the traditional way, with BON priests performing rituals associated with the royal cult.

The evidence is clearer with respect to the second "religious king," KHRI SRONG LDE BRTSAN (Trisong Detsen, ca. 740–798), believed by tradition to have been an incarnation of MAÑJUŚRĪ. He reportedly invited the Indian scholar-monk ŚĀNTARAKṢITA to Tibet, but upon his arrival he met with opposition from adherents of Tibet's traditional religion and had to return to India almost immediately. Before he left, however, he advised the king to invite PADMA-

Khrig rtse (Tikse) Monastery, Ladakh.

SAMBHAVA, a tantric master renowned for his magical powers. The king did so, but when Padmasambhava reached the border he encountered opposition from Tibet's demons, who attempted to drive him back in order to preserve traditional religious practices. He was able to defeat them with powerful spells, and one by one they "offered up their life-force." He allowed them to live in return for promises that henceforth they would be protectors of the dharma.

The king and court were reportedly impressed by this display of magical power, and subsequently Śāntarakṣita was invited back to Tibet. Together with the king and Padmasambhava, he established the first monastery in the country, called BSAM YAS (Samye). It was probably consecrated around 767.

The apogee of royal patronage for Buddhism in this period came during the reign of the third "religious king," RAL PA CAN (Relbachen, r. 815–836), said to be an emanation of VAJRAPĀṆI. He spent large amounts of money on the construction of Buddhist monasteries and temples, sponsored Tibetan monks to study in India, and brought Indian scholars to Tibet. As a sign of his submission to the SAṂGHA, he reportedly tied ribbons to his long braids and had monks sit on them during state ceremonies. These practices led to increasing opposition, and he was assassinated in 836. He was succeeded by GLANG DAR MA (Lang darma, r. 838–842), who supported the traditional royal cult and withdrew government sponsorship for Buddhism. Monasteries were closed, and many monks and nuns were forced to return to lay life, but although traditional sources report that he actively persecuted Buddhism, there is little contemporary evidence for this. His anti-Buddhist measures led to his assassination by a Buddhist monk named dPal gyi rdo rje (Belgi Dorje), and his death signaled the end of the dynasty. It was also the beginning of an interregnum period of over a hundred years during which no person or group had sufficient power to unite the country under a single rule.

Ral pa can's death marks the end of the "first dissemination" (SNGA DAR) of Buddhism to Tibet in traditional histories. Buddhism declined after that, but was revived by Atiśa (Dīpaṃkara Śrījñāna, 982–1054), who traveled to Tibet at the behest of the rulers of the kingdom of sPu hrangs (Buhrang) in western Tibet. His arrival in 1042 is viewed as the beginning of the "second dissemination" (phyi dar) of Buddhism. He championed the Indian Mahāyāna gradualist paradigm and stressed the importance of intensive study and strict adherence to the vinaya. He attracted a number of Tibetan disciples, including 'Brom ston (Dromdön, 1008–1064), who is considered to be the founder of Tibet's first order, the bKa' gdams pa (Kadampa). At the same time, a very different form of Buddhism was brought to Tibet from Bihār and Bengal. This was the tradition of the tantric mahāsiddhas, a group of enigmatic figures who rejected the constraints of the monastic establishments and who were credited with miraculous powers. The most influential early exponent of this tradition was Mar pa (Marpa, 1012–1097), who traveled to Bihār and studied with Nāropa (Nāḍapāda, 1016–1100). Following this, he returned to Lho brag (Hlodrak) in Tibet and became outwardly a translator (*lo tsā ba*) and local hegemon, but to his disciples he was really a tantric master who transmitted the esoteric tradition of Nāropa. The most famous of his disciples was Mi la ras pa (Milarepa, 1040–1123), whose biography is one of the most popular pieces of literature in the Tibetan cultural area. Mi la ras pa's disciple sGam po pa (Gampopa, 1079–1153) initiated a monastic order in what had previously been mainly a tradition of lay tantric masters. This grew into one of the four main orders of Tibetan Buddhism, the bKa' brgyud pa (Kagyüpa). During the second dissemination, two other orders appeared, the Sa skya pa (Sakyapa), founded by dKon mchog rgyal po (Gönchok Gyelpo, 1034–1102), and the dGe lugs pa (Gelukpa), founded by Tsong kha pa (Tsong Khapa, 1357–1419). These three sects are referred to collectively as the "new schools" (gsar ma) because they favor translations of tantras prepared during the second dissemination. The other order of Tibetan Buddhism, the rNying ma pa (Nyingmapa, "Old School"), relies mainly on translations produced during the first dissemination.

The Sa skya pas became rulers of the whole of Tibet when Sa skya Paṇḍita (Sakya Pandita, 1182–1251) was appointed regent by the Mongol ruler Godan in 1244. Sa skya pa hegemony continued with his nephew and successor 'Phags pa blo gros (Pakpa Lodrö, 1235–1289), who also played a major role in converting the Mongols to Buddhism.

In the seventeenth century the dGe lugs pas became rulers of Tibet with Mongol help. The fifth Dalai Lama, Ngag dbang blo bzang rgya mtsho (Ngawang Losang Gyatso, 1617–1682), became the first Dalai Lama to rule Tibet, a tradition that continued until the fourteenth Dalai Lama, bsTan 'dzin rgya mtsho (Tenzin Gyatso, b. 1935), fled to India in 1959 following the Chinese invasion and annexation of his country. After consolidating control over Tibet, the Chinese attempted to eradicate traditional religion and culture, viewing them as vestiges of the old "feudal" society that needed to be destroyed in order for Tibet to fully embrace Maoist socialism. Most of Tibet's monasteries were destroyed, monks and nuns were executed, and the Tibetan government-in-exile estimates that approximately 1.2 million people were killed during the invasion and the period of the Cultural Revolution. As a result of the invasion and subsequent repression, tens of thousands of Tibetans fled to India and other neighboring countries. Most prominent religious teachers also fled, and they soon began to establish Buddhist centers in India and elsewhere. A number of

Tibetan lamas began to attract Western students, and there are now Tibetan Buddhist centers all over the world. Tibetan Buddhism is flourishing in exile and in Western countries, but at the same time it is being systematically eradicated in the land of its origin. After the repression of the 1960s and 1970s, the Chinese government initiated a period of relative lessening of religious persecution in 1979, but Buddhism in Tibet is still strictly controlled, and monks are not allowed to engage in the intensive study that formed the bedrock of traditional Tibetan Buddhism. They are still allowed (and even encouraged) to enact colorful ceremonies for the benefit of tourists who bring in foreign currency, but except in isolated pockets Tibetan Buddhism in Tibet today is a hollow shell, and only its outward vestiges are allowed to continue under the suspicious gaze of the Chinese authorities. (*See also* MONGOLIAN BUDDHISM; SAHAJA.)

T'ien-t'ai (Jpn. *Tendai*; Kor. *Chŏnt'ae*; "Heavenly Platform School")

One of the major traditions of Chinese Buddhism, founded by Hui-ssu (515–576) and systematically reformulated by CHIH-I (538–597). It derives its name from Mount T'ien-t'ai, and its main scriptural source is the *Lotus Sūtra* (Chin. *Miao-fa lien-hua ching*; Skt. SADDHARMA-PUṆḌARĪKA-SŪTRA). The three major texts of the tradition were lectures given by Chih-i and transcribed by his disciple Kuan-ting (561–632): (1) *The Profound Meaning of the Lotus Sūtra* (*Miao-fa lien-hua ching hsüan-i*); (2) *Textual Commentaries on the Lotus Sūtra* (*Miao-fa lien-hua ching wen-chü*); and (3) *The Great Calming and Insight* (*Mo-ho chih-kuan*). (*See also* TENDAI.)

Tilopa (988–1069)

Indian MAHĀSIDDHA whose name derives from his reported occupation of pressing sesame seeds to extract their oil. According to BKA' BRGYUD PA (Kagyüpa) tradition, he received teachings directly from the buddha VAJRADHARA and later transmitted them to NĀROPA, his main student.

tīrthika (Pāli *titthaya*; Tib. *mu stegs can*; "non-Buddhist"; lit. "forder")

A Sanskrit term that refers to non-Buddhist schools in general. According to Tibetan etymologies, they are called "forders" because their treatises set forth paths leading to high status within cyclic existence or purport to outline ways of crossing over (or fording) the river of cyclic existence altogether.

tiryak (Pāli *tiriyan*; Tib. *dud 'gro*; "animal")

One of the six possible destinies (GATI) into which beings may be born within cyclic existence. It is considered to be one of the three "bad destinies" (along with hungry ghosts and hell beings) because animals inevitably experience great suffering and their minds are too clouded for them to be able to attain liberation.

Toda, Jōsei (1900–1958)

Second president of SŌKA GAKKAI, who succeeded the founder of the organization, TSUNESABURŌ MAKIGUCHI. He is generally credited with spearheading its phenomenal early growth, which was largely the result of an aggressive method of proselytizing called SHAKUBUKU. (*See also* NICHIREN; NICHIREN SHŌSHŪ.)

Tōdaiji

See DAIBUTSU.

t'ong pulgyo ("interpenetrated Buddhism")

Doctrinal concept formulated by WŎNHYO (617–686), according to which the various teachings of different Buddhist schools are all fundamentally compatible. All are said to flow from the same primordial source, the fundamental nature of reality. This was connected to his notion of the "harmonization of disputes" (Kor. *hwa-jaeng*), in which the doctrinal debates between different Buddhist traditions are viewed as misguided, since all of them participate in the single, unmanifest reality underlying all phenomena. He summarized this idea in the final sentence of his *Essentials of the Nirvāṇa-sūtra* (*Yŏlban-gyŏng Chong-gyo*): "It should be known that the Buddha's meaning is deep and profound, with no limitations. Thus, for those who wish to divide the meanings of scriptures into four teachings or limit the Buddha's intent with five periods, this would be like using a snail's shell to scoop out the ocean or trying to see the heavens through a narrow tube." (*See also* P'AN-CHIAO.)

Tongdosa ("Entry into Awakening Temple")

The largest Buddhist temple in Korea, originally built in 646 during the reign of Queen Sondok by the monk Chajang. It is one of Korea's "three jewels temples," and represents the Buddha (the others are HAEINSA, representing the DHARMA, and SONGGWANGSA, representing the SAṂGHA). This identification is probably due to the fact that it has a relic of the Buddha in its main temple. It houses about 220 monks and 200 nuns and has 65 buildings in the main complex.

tonglen

See GTONG LEN.

tongo (Chin. *tun-wu*; Kor. *ton'gyo*; "sudden teachings")

Japanese term that refers to the notion that awakening (KENSHŌ, SATORI) must be attained all at once, in a sudden flash of realization. This is a key tenet of the so-called "Southern School of CH'AN" (Chin. NAN-TSUNG-CH'AN) and is contrasted with "gradual awakening" (ZENGO), in which one progresses by stages. *Zengo* is associated with the "Northern School" (Pei-tsung).

Trailokya Bauddha Mahasangha Sahayaka Gana (TBMSG, "Association of Friends of the Buddhist Order of the Three Realms")

Organization founded in 1979 by SANGHARAKSHITA, the main aim of which is to provide Buddhist education and training for the former Untouchables of India who followed B. R. AMBEDKAR in converting to Buddhism. It sponsors a range of activities, including day-care centers, kindergartens, health-care programs for mothers and children, and vocational training. It is a branch of the FRIENDS OF THE WESTERN BUDDHIST ORDER (FWBO), and if current trends continue will soon constitute the majority of its members.

Trāyastriṃśa (Pāli *Tāvatiṃsa*; Tib. *Sum cu rtsa gsum pa*; Jpn. *Tōriten*; "Heaven of the Thirty-Three Gods")

One of the six worlds of gods (*deva-loka*). ŚĀKYAMUNI BUDDHA is said to have visited it for three months during the seventh year after his awakening in order to preach the ABHIDHARMA to his mother, who had been reborn there. It is said to be located at the top of Mount Meru (Pāli *Sineru*), and its king is Śakra. It gets its name because it has thirty-three gods as inhabitants; they are said to live for 30,000,000 years.

trikāya (Tib. *sku gsum*; "three bodies")

MAHĀYĀNA doctrine that buddhas have three bodies: (1) truth body (DHARMAKĀYA); (2) enjoyment body (SAṂBHOGAKĀYA); and (3) emanation bodies (NIR-

MĀṆA-KĀYA). The first is said to be identical to the final nature of reality, i.e., emptiness (ŚŪNYATĀ) and represents a buddha's full realization of – and identification with – ultimate reality. The second is a subtle body that resides in "pure lands" and is only perceivable by advanced practitioners. The third refers to the multiple forms that buddhas are said to create for the benefit of sentient beings. Emanation bodies are the physical forms of buddhas and other teachers who appear in human form, such as ŚĀKYAMUNI BUDDHA.

trilakṣaṇa (Pāli *tilakkhana*; Tib. *mtshan nyid gsum*; "three characteristics")

These are the characteristics that the Buddha declared are common to all phenomena: (1) selflessness (ANĀTMAN); (2) impermanence (ANITYA); and (3) unsatisfactoriness or suffering (DUḤKHA).

triloka (Pāli *tiloka*; Tib. *khams gsum*; "three worlds")

The three realms within cyclic existence (SAṂSĀRA) in which sentient beings are born: (1) the Desire Realm (KĀMA-DHĀTU); (2) the Form Realm (RŪPA-DHĀTU); and (3) the Formless Realm (ĀRŪPYA-DHĀTU). The first is so named because desire is the predominant emotion there. Its inhabitants are humans, animals, hell beings, demi-gods, and six classes of gods. The Form Realm is a sphere in which there is corporeality but no desire. Its inhabitants live blissful lives; rebirth in this realm is a result of successfully attaining meditative states (DHYĀNA). The Formless Realm comprises four heavens in which beings are born as a result of cultivating the four "formless absorptions" (ĀRŪPYA-SAMĀPATTI).

tripiṭaka (Pāli *tipiṭaka*; Tib. *sde snod gsum*; "three baskets")

The Buddhist canon. The three baskets are: (1) SŪTRA-PIṬAKA (Pāli *Sutta-piṭaka*, "Basket of Discourses"); (2) VINAYA-PIṬAKA ("Basket of Monastic Discipline"); and (3) ABHIDHARMA-PIṬAKA (Pāli *Abhidhamma-piṭaka*, "Basket of Higher Doctrine"). The first contains sermons attributed to ŚĀKYAMUNI BUDDHA, and sometimes his immediate disciples (who speak with his permission and approval). The second includes texts that focus on monastic discipline. The third section consists of scholastic treatises that systematize the doctrines found in the other sections, particularly the first. The focus is on psychology and systematic philosophy. It appears that a number of Indian schools had their own canonical collections, but the only complete extant one in an Indic language is the PĀLI CANON of the THERAVĀDA NIKĀYA. Parts of other canons exist in scattered Sanskrit texts, and large sections of several canons exist in Chinese.

triple continuum

See RGYUD GSUM.

triple vision

See SNANG GSUM

triratna (Pāli *tiratana*; Tib. *rin chen gsum*; Chin. *san-pao*; Jpn. *sambō*; "three jewels")

Also referred to as the "three refuges" (Skt. *triśaraṇa*), these are the three things to which Buddhists "go for refuge" (Skt. *śaraṇa-gamana*): (1) Buddha; (2) DHARMA; and (3) SAṂGHA. The Buddha is an object of veneration and a source of refuge because he has found the path to liberation and taught it to others. The dharma, his teaching, is a source of refuge because it outlines the path and the means to traverse it successfully. The *saṃgha* is a source of inspiration and of refuge because it comprises people who have dedicated their lives to following the dharma and are able to teach it to others.

Trisong Detsen

See KHRI SRONG LDE BRTSAN.

tṛṣṇā (Pāli *taṇhā*; Tib. *sred pa*; "thirst," "craving")

Second of the four "noble truths" (ĀRYA-SATYA). It refers to afflicted desire and is said to arise from the contact of a sense organ and an object. It is divided into three types: (1) craving for sensual pleasures (*kāma-tṛṣṇā*); (2) craving for continued existence (*bhava-tṛṣṇā*); and (3) craving for non-existence (*vibhava-tṛṣṇā*). This is one of the root problems identified by the Buddha, since it inevitably leads to loss, disappointment, and suffering (DUḤKHA). In the schema of the twelve links (*nidāna*) of dependent arising (PRATĪTYA-SAMUTPĀDA), it is said to be conditioned by feelings (*vedanā*), and in turn it conditions the appropriation (*upādāna*) of a new body.

Trúc Lâm ("Bamboo Grove School")

One of the earliest CH'AN (Viet. *Thiền*) schools in Vietnam. It was founded by Trân Nhân Tông, the third king of the Trân dynasty (1225–1400). It was a LIN-CHI (Viet. *Lâm-tế*) tradition, and probably the first distinctively Vietnamese tradition of Thiền. It only survived as a distinguishable lineage until the death of its third patriarch, Huyền Quang.

Trungpa Rinpoche, Chögyam (Chos kyi rgya mtsho drung pa Rin po che, 1940–1987)

Reincarnate lama (SPRUL SKU) of the BKA' BRGYUD PA (Kagyüpa) order of TIBETAN BUDDHISM recognized in 1941 as the eleventh Drung pa. He fled Tibet in 1959 following the Chinese invasion, and in 1963 he was awarded a fellowship to study at Oxford. In 1970 he traveled to America, where he established the VAJRADHATU FOUNDATION (1973), which later grew to be one of the largest Buddhist organizations in the country. In 1974 he founded the Nalanda Foundation, and in 1976 passed on the leadership of the organization to his "Vajra Regent" Ösel Tenzin (Thomas Rich). He was the author of a number of popular books, including *Cutting through Spiritual Materialism* and *Shambhala: Sacred Path of the Warrior.*

truth

See SATYA-DVAYA.

Tsangnyön Heruka

See GTSANG SMYON HE RU KA.

Ts'ao-tung-tsung (Jpn. *Sōtō-shū*)

Chinese CH'AN tradition founded by TUNG-SHAN LIANG-CHIEH (Jpn. *Tōzan Ryōkai*, 807–869) and his student Ts'ao-shan Pen-chi (Jpn. *Sōzan Honjaku*, 840–901). The name of the school derives from the first Chinese characters of their names. It was one of the "five houses" (Jpn. GOKE-SHICHISHŪ) of Ch'an.

Tshar pa Sa skya pa (Tsarpa Sakyapa)

One of the two main branches of the SA SKYA PA (Sakyapa) order of TIBETAN BUDDHISM (the other being the NGOR PA). Its headquarters is Nalendra Monastery, built by the VAJRAYOGINĪ master Tshar chen bLo gsal rgya mtsho (Tsarchen Losel Gyatso, 1502–1556) in the area of Phan yul (Penyül) in dBu (Ü) Province.

Tsomo, Karma Lekshe (b. 1944)

American-born nun ordained in the Tibetan tradition, who lived for a number of years in Tibetan communities in India. She is one of the founders of

SAKYADHITA and has been a leading advocate and activist regarding women's issues in Buddhism. She has been at the forefront of efforts to establish the full BHIKṢUṆĪ ordination in traditions in which it does not exist.

Tsong kha pa bLo bzang grags pa (Tsong Khapa Losang Drakpa, 1357–1419)

Founder of the DGE LUGS PA (Gelukpa) order of TIBETAN BUDDHISM, born in the Tsong kha Valley in A mdo. He was ordained by the fourth RGYAL BA KAR MA PA, Rol pa'i rdo rje (Gyelwa Karmapa Rolpe Dorje, 1340–1383), at the age of three. At the age of seven he received novice vows and was given the name bLo bzang grags pa. For most of his life he traveled all over the country, studying with teachers from various traditions, focusing both on the philosophical traditions that Tibet inherited from India and on tantric literature and practice. He is renowned throughout the Tibetan cultural region as one of its most eminent scholars, meditators, and philosophers. His written works fill twelve volumes in the Tibetan canon. His three most influential works are: (1) *Great Exposition of the Stages of the Path* (*Lam rim chen mo*, a comprehensive treatment of the traditional MAHĀYĀNA Buddhist path to buddhahood); (2) *Great Exposition of Secret Mantra* (*sNgags rim chen mo*, which presents a similarly graduated tantric path to buddhahood); and (3) *The Essence of Good Explanations* (*Legs bshad snying po*, a discussion of Buddhist hermeneutics in accordance with the Indian YOGĀCĀRA and MADHYAMAKA schools). In addition, he wrote numerous other texts, which have become the basis of training in the dGe lugs pa tradition. He was one of Tibet's great reformers, and the structure of the dGe lugs pa order reflects this orientation. The order's emphasis is on extensive study supplemented with oral debate, combined with strict adherence to the rules of monastic discipline (Tib. *'dul ba*; Skt. VINAYA). According to dGe lugs pa tradition, he was able to accomplish so much because he was a physical manifestation of MAÑJUŚRĪ, the buddha of wisdom, and he reportedly was able to meet with Mañjuśrī and receive instructions directly from him. In the dGe lugs pa tradition, he is credited with four great actions: (1) establishing the annual "Great Prayer Festival" (SMON LAM CHEN MO); (2) restoring an important statue of MAITREYA (1); (3) championing strict observance of monastic discipline; and (4) construction of several major monasteries.

tsung (Jpn. *shū*; Kor. *chong*; "doctrine," "system")

Chinese term that can refer to a doctrine or thesis, as well as to a system of doctrines and practices. In the second sense, such systems generally have a coherent set of teachings and practices and trace themselves back to a particular founder or patriarch whose tradition has been passed on through a series of successors who consider themselves to belong to that particular lineage (or at least are reported in traditional sources as thinking this).

Tsung-mi (780–841)

Fifth and last patriarch of the Chinese HUA-YEN tradition, who developed a syncretic version of Hua-yen that incorporated CH'AN meditation. His best-known work is *The Original Nature of Humans* (*Yuan-jen lun*), which is still studied today in Japan. The Hua-yen school did not long survive his death, however, largely due to the anti-Buddhist persecutions that began in 845.

Tucci, Giuseppe (1894–1984)

Pioneering Italian scholar of Buddhism, who published a number of ground-breaking studies of Tibetan religion, history, art, and culture. He was one of the first Western scholars to travel extensively in Tibet and surrounding areas, and his publications are often notable for both their content and the author's adventures during the course of his research.

tülku

See SPRUL SKU.

Tung-shan Liang-chieh (Jpn. *Tōzan Ryōkai*, 807–869)

Chinese master of the TS'AO-TUNG (Jpn. *Sōtō*) tradition of CH'AN, best known for developing a five-fold classification scheme of levels of spiritual attainment (GO-I). He was one of the most influential Ch'an masters of the T'ang dynasty, and together with Ts'ao-shan Pen-chi (Jpn. *Sōzan Honjaku*, 840–901) is credited with founding the Ts'ao-tung tradition (which derives its name from the first characters of their names).

Tun-huang

Central Asian oasis town in the province of Kansu in northwestern China, where the ancient northern and southern routes through Central Asia converged. It has the largest complex of Buddhist caves in the world (referred to in Chinese as Mo-kao-k'u). The earliest of these date back to the fourth century, but they were neglected for centuries until rediscovered by a local farmer around 1900. They were visited by Sir Aurel Stein in 1907 and by Paul Pelliot in 1908 and were found to be a repository of ancient Buddhist and Taoist texts, artwork, and other archeological treasures. To date 492 intact caves have been found, which contain thousands of manuscripts (many of which were transported to Europe in the early part of the twentieth century), 2,400 statues, and 45,000 square meters of wall paintings.

Tu-shun (557–640)

First patriarch of the HUA-YEN school in China. His successor was Chih-yen (602–668), who in turn was the teacher of FA-TSANG (643–712), the tradition's most influential thinker.

Tuṣita (Pāli *Tusita*; Tib. *dGa' ldan*; "Joyous Realm")

One of the major Buddhist heavens, said to be the abode of those BODHISATTVAS who will become buddhas in their next lifetimes. Thus it was the residence of ŚĀKYAMUNI BUDDHA before his decision to begin his final rebirth, and is currently the abode of MAITREYA (1), the future buddha.

two truths

See SATYA-DVAYA.

t'zu-li

See JIRIKI.

U

Ŭisang (625–702)

One of the most influential figures of the Unified Silla period in Korea (668–918). He traveled to China and studied with the second HUA-YEN (Kor. *Hwaŏm*) patriarch, Chih-yen (600–669). He spent twenty years in China, and after his return to Korea, Hua-yen became one of the dominant philosophical traditions in KOREAN BUDDHISM (although it disappeared as a distinct scholastic tradition during the late Koryŏ period (918–1392).

Ullambana (Chin. *Yu-lan*; Jpn. *Obon*; Viet. *An-cu'*)

Sanskrit term for the festival of the hungry ghosts (Skt. PRETA), which is traditionally celebrated on the fifteenth day of the seventh month. It involves giving offerings of food, money, clothing, and prayers for the hungry ghosts and hell beings and is particularly important in East Asian traditions. It was first celebrated in 538, and it is said to have derived from a story in which MAUDGALYĀYANA, through his use of the "divine eye" (Skt. *deva-cakṣus*), realized that his mother had been reborn as a hungry ghost. He subsequently made offerings to help ease her torment. In East Asia, the rite is based on the *Ullambana-sūtra*, which appears to have originated in India and been augmented in China. (*See also* OBON.)

ultimate [truth]

See PARAMĀRTHA[-SATYA].

unsui ("novice")

A novice in a ZEN monastery (also sometimes referred to as *unnō*).

Upāli (Pāli *Upāli*)

One of the ten main disciples of ŚĀKYAMUNI BUDDHA, said by him to have been the foremost of the "guardians of the VINAYA" (Pāli *aggo vinaya-dharānaṃ*). Before joining the Buddhist order, he is said to have been a barber who served the ŚĀKYA clan, and after his ordination he specialized in study of the *vinaya* rules. After the Buddha's death he became the chief *vinaya* master (*vinaya-pāmokkha*) of the order, and he is said to have been one of the 500 ARHATS who attended the "first Buddhist council" at RĀJAGṚHA, where he was responsible for reciting the *vinaya*.

upāsaka (Pāli *upāsaka*; Tib. *dge bsnyen*); "layman")

A Buddhist layman, who is accorded this status by formally "going for refuge" (*śaraṇa-gamana*) in the "three jewels" (TRIRATNA: Buddha, DHARMA, and SAṂGHA) and by pledging to uphold the five lay precepts (PAÑCA-ŚĪLA), which involve avoiding: (1) killing living beings; (2) taking what is not given; (3) sexual misconduct; (4) harmful and false speech; and (5) intoxicants. In THERAVĀDA, laypeople are generally considered to be unable to attain NIRVĀṆA due to being involved in worldly affairs (though there are some examples in the PĀLI CANON of lay disciples attaining *nirvāṇa*), and so their adoption of these precepts is designed to generate merit (Pāli *puñña*; Skt. PUṆYA), which might lead to a better rebirth, in which they might perhaps become monks or nuns. Another important function of the laity is to give alms to the *saṃgha*, which also brings merit. In MAHĀYĀNA, the role of laypeople is more elevated, and buddhahood is thought to be a possibility for everyone, and not just monks and nuns.

upāsikā (Pāli *upāsikā*; Tib. *dge bsnyen ma*; "laywoman")

A Buddhist laywoman, who takes the same vows as laymen (UPĀSAKA), and like laymen primarily works to generate merit through the performance of meritorious actions.

Upatissa (ca. first–second century C.E.)

Author of the *Path to Liberation* (*Vimutti-magga*), an influential discussion of the path to awakening that is generally believed to have been the basis of BUDDHAGHOSA's monumental *Path of Purification* (VISUDDHIMAGGA). The text exists in Pāli, Sinhalese, and Chinese versions.

upāya-kauśalya (Pāli *upāya-kosalla*; Tib. *thabs la mkhas pa*; Chin. *fang-pien*; Jpn. *hōben*; "skill in means")

The ability to adapt Buddhist teachings and practices to the level of understanding of one's audience. This is particularly important in MAHĀYĀNA, where it is said to be one of the most important abilities developed by BODHISATTVAS. It is the seventh in the tenfold list of perfections (PĀRAMITĀ) and is cultivated on the seventh bodhisattva "level" (BHŪMI).

uposatha

See POṢADHA.

uṣṇīṣa (Pāli *uṇhīsa*; Tib. *gtsug tor*; "topknot")

A protuberance on the top of a buddha's head, one of the thirty-two major marks (DVĀTRIṂŚADVARA-LAKṢAṆA) that distinguish them physically.

utpatti-krama (Tib. *bskyed rim*; "generation stage")

Tantric practice involving generating a vivid image of a buddha (and often a surrounding retinue), who embodies the good qualities and realizations to which one aspires. This practice is particularly important in highest yoga tantra (ANUTTARA-YOGA-TANTRA). After one is able to sustain the image for extended periods of time with a high level of clarity, one may then (if one has received the proper initiations) proceed to the "completion stage" (SAMPANNA-KRAMA), in which one invites the buddha to enter and merge with oneself and imagines that this actually occurs. Following this one visualizes oneself as having the body, speech, and mind of a buddha and as performing a buddha's compassionate activities. There are three primary prerequisites for entering the generation stage: (1) previous practice of paths common to both the MAHĀYĀNA bodhisattva path and TANTRA; (2) initiation into the practice of the relevant tantra; and (3) taking on tantric pledges and vows.

Uttarakuru (Pāli *Uttarakuru*; Tib. *Byang gi sgra mi snyan*)

One of the nine divisions of the world in traditional Indian cosmology. This is the country of the northern Kurus, situated to the north of JAMBUDVĪPA, and described as a country of eternal beatitude. It is said to be square, measuring 20,000 YOJANAs per side, and the beings who live there have lifespans of 1,000 years. In addition to their long lifespans, the inhabitants are said to have exceptionally pleasant lives and to be naturally virtuous.

V

Vaibhāṣika (Tib. *Bye brag smra ba*; "Great Book of Alternatives School")

Indian scholastic tradition of the SARVĀSTIVĀDA school that was based on the *Great Book of Alternatives* (MAHĀVIBHĀṢĀ). It is classified by Tibetan doxographers as one of the two "HĪNAYĀNA" schools (the other being SAUTRĀNTIKA), and according to this classification scheme its proponents are distinguished by asserting that past, present, and future phenomena (DHARMA) exist as substantial entities (*dravya*).

vaipulya-sūtra (Tib. *shin tu rgyas pa'i mdo*; "extensive discourses")

Term for large MAHĀYĀNA sūtras – and often large collections of independent works – such as the PRAJÑĀ-PĀRAMITĀ SŪTRAs, the AVATAṂSAKA-SŪTRA, and the RATNA-KŪṬA-SŪTRA.

Vairocana (Mahāvairocana; Tib. *rNam par snang mdzad*; Chin. *Ba-lu-shih-na*, *P'i-lo fo*; Jpn. *Birushana*, *Dainichi Nyorai*; Kor. *Pirosana*; Viet. *Tỳ-lô Giá-na Phật*)

One of the five transcendent buddhas in the MAHĀYĀNA tradition, often depicted iconographically with white skin and making the MUDRĀ of "supreme wisdom." He is commonly associated with SAMANTABHADRA, and one of his symbols is the "wheel of doctrine" (DHARMA-CAKRA). In East Asian traditions, this buddha is often referred to as the

Images of the five celestial Buddhas at Nan Tien Temple, Woolongong, New South Wales, Australia. Vairocana is in the center.

"original buddha" (Skt. ĀDI-BUDDHA), meaning that he has always been awakened. He represents the "truth body" (Skt. DHARMA-KĀYA), and he is said to preside over the "Flower Treasury World."

Vaiśālī (Pāli *Vesāli*)

Town located about 40 kilometers northwest of modern Patna in the Indian state of Bihār. During ŚĀKYAMUNI BUDDHA's lifetime, it was the capital of the Licchavis, who belonged to the Vṛji republic. It was the site of the Ambapālīvana, one of the rainy-season retreats of the early SAṂGHA, which was donated by the courtesan Ambapālī. It was also the venue for the "second Buddhist council," reportedly held 100 years after the Buddha's death and prompted by a complaint by the monk Yaśas concerning the conduct of monks who lived in the area. During a visit to Vaiśālī, he found that the local monks were engaging in behavior that was forbidden in the VINAYA. After he brought the offenses to the monks' attention, they gathered as a community and unanimously voted against his complaint – and also required that he publicly apologize to them. He refused to do so and went on to Kauśāmbī to enlist the support of other monks. Shortly after this, a council (*saṃgīti* or *saṃghāyanā*) was held to resolve the dispute, which was attended by 700 monks and presided over by a senior monk named Revata. Another senior monk named Sarvagāmin was asked for his opinion regarding the conduct of the Vaiśālī monks, and he ruled against every article.

vajra (Tib. *rdo rje*)

An important symbol in tantric Buddhism: a five-pronged scepter, the two ends of which are said to represent wisdom and compassion, the two primary qualities that characterize buddhas. The *vajra* as a whole represents an

indissoluble union of wisdom and compassion, which is said to be indestructible (and so one meaning of *vajra* is "adamantine").

Vajracchedikā-prajñā-pāramitā-sūtra (Tib. *rDo rje gcod pa'i mdo*; Chin. *Chin-kang [po-jo] ching*; Jpn. *Kongōkyō*; Viet. *Kim-cang*; *Sūtra of the Cutting Diamond of the Perfection of Wisdom*)

One of the most influential texts of the MAHĀYĀNA "Perfection of Wisdom" (PRAJÑĀ-PĀRAMITĀ) literature. Consisting of thirty-two chapters, it is purportedly a dialogue between ŚĀKYAMUNI BUDDHA and his disciple SUBHŪTI, focusing on emptiness (ŚŪNYATĀ), which is said to be the final nature of all phenomena. A central theme is the idea that all reality is a projection of mind, and so is insubstantial and deceptive.

Statue of Vajradhara surrounded by luminaries of the bKa' brgyud pa lineage. He mis (He mis) Monastery, Ladakh.

Vajradhara (Tib. *rDo rje 'chang*; Mon. *Ochirdara*; "Vajra Holder")

One of the most important buddhas in Tibetan tantric traditions, in which he is commonly conceived as the primordial buddha (Skt. ĀDI-BUDDHA). Iconographically, he is generally depicted with dark blue skin, his arms crossed on his chest, holding a VAJRA and bell in his hands. He is often shown in sexual embrace (YAB YUM) with his consort Prajñāpāramitā.

Vajradhatu Foundation

Tibetan Buddhist organization founded in 1973 by CHÖGYAM TRUNGPA, the headquarters of which is in Halifax, Nova Scotia. It has more than one hundred local centers and claims 5,500 members worldwide, making it one of the largest Buddhist organizations in the West.

Vajrapāṇi (Tib. *Phyag na rdo rje*; "Vajra Hand")

Wrathful tantric buddha, classified as a "knowledge-holder" (Skt. *vidyā-dhara*; Tib. *rig 'dzin*). Iconographically, he is often depicted wearing a tiger skin around his waist and with long hair. He generally has blue skin and either two or four arms. In the four-armed version, two of his hands make a threatening gesture (Skt. MUDRĀ) that overcomes obstacles, and the other two hold a VAJRA and a lasso respectively. In some texts – for example the *Sūtra of Golden Light* (*Suvarṇa-prabhāsa-sūtra*) – he is described as merely a YAKṢA (or as lord of *yakṣas*), and in the *Lotus Sūtra* (SADDHARMA-PUṆḌARĪKA-SŪTRA) he is said to be an emanation of AVALOKITEŚVARA, but in TIBETAN BUDDHISM he becomes one of the most important wrathful buddhas. He is said to have played a crucial role in the establishment of Buddhism in Tibet when PADMASAMBHAVA, after being attacked by the country's demons upon his arrival, grew angry and subsequently meditated on Vajrapāṇi, which caused the demons to become frightened and submit to him. In Tibetan Buddhism, he is said to personify the power of all the buddhas and to overcome obstacles. In some traditions it is said that he will become the final buddha of the present era.

Vajrasattva (Tib. *rDo rje sems dpa'*; Chin. *Wo-tzu-lo-sa-tsui*; Jpn. *Kongōsatta*; "Vajra Being")

One of the most important buddhas in Tibetan tantric Buddhism, particularly associated with mental purification. Iconographically, he generally holds a VAJRA in his right hand and a bell in his left. The former symbolizes compassion, and the latter wisdom. In Tibetan art, he is often depicted in sexual embrace (YAB YUM) with his consort Ghaṇṭāpaṇī. His importance in tantric traditions is evidenced by the fact that beginning tantric students are generally required to recite his 100-syllable mantra 100,000 times as the first of the "preliminary practices" (SNGON 'GRO).

Vajrayāna (Tib. *rDo rje theg pa*; "Vajra Vehicle")

One of the terms used to designate tantric Buddhism. The scriptural basis for the tradition is a disparate collection of texts called TANTRAS, which were probably composed in India some time between the sixth–seventh and tenth centuries, but which are claimed to have been spoken by ŚĀKYAMUNI BUDDHA (and sometimes by other buddhas). Vajrayāna followed the basic BODHISATTVA path of MAHĀYĀNA Buddhism, but taught new techniques that it claimed could greatly shorten the time required to attain buddhahood, including rituals and the use of hand symbols (MUDRĀ), MAṆḌALAS, and visualizations. A central practice is "deity yoga" (Skt. DEVATĀ-YOGA), in which the meditator visualizes him- or herself as a buddha, possessing all the perfected qualities of a buddha, and engaging in compassionate activities. The tradition emphasizes the secrecy and efficacy of its practices, and generally requires that one receive initiation from a qualified GURU before one enters onto the tantric path. Vajrayāna became the dominant meditative tradition in Tibet and Mongolia, and is also found in East Asia in the schools of esoteric Buddhism, including the Chinese Chen-yen school and the Japanese SHINGON tradition.

Vajrayoginī (Tib. *rDo rje rnal 'byor ma*)

Tantric buddha who is particularly associated with the BKA' BRGYUD PA (Kagyüpa), SA SKYA PA (Sakyapa), and DGE LUGS PA (Gelukpa) orders of Tibetan Buddhism. She is generally depicted with red skin and wearing a necklace of skulls. She is also generally naked, symbolizing her non-attachment to material things.

Vạn-Hạn Buddhist University

Vietnam's major academic Buddhist institution, founded in Saigon in 1964 by Dr. Thích Minh-châu, Thích Nhất-Hạnh (THICH NHAT HANH), and Dr. Thích Thiên-ân.

vassa (Skt. *varṣa*; "rains")

The traditional rainy-season retreat for monks, which according to tradition was instituted by ŚĀKYAMUNI BUDDHA. He dictated that Buddhist monks should wander from place to place, having no fixed abode, but that they should remain in retreat for the three months of the rainy season (June–October).

Vasubandhu (Tib. *dbYigs gnyen*, ca. 330–400; "Excellent Kinsman")

Indian Buddhist philosopher, who along with his older brother ASAṄGA is considered to be one of the two main figures in the early development of the YOGĀCĀRA tradition. According to traditional accounts of his life, after joining the Buddhist order he studied in the SARVĀSTIVĀDA tradition, but later became dissatisfied with key elements of its philosophical system. This process is reflected in the *Treasury of Higher Doctrine* (ABHIDHARMA-KOŚA), which consists of a root text written from the

Sarvāstivāda perspective and a commentary that criticizes it from a SAUTRĀNTIKA perspective. He reportedly was later converted to MAHĀYĀNA by Asaṅga, after which he composed some of the most influential Yogācāra treatises, including the *Twenty Verses* (*Viṃśatikā*), the *Thirty Verses* (*Triṃśikā*), and the *Commentary on the Differentiation of the Middle and the Extremes* (*Madhyānta-vibhāga-bhāṣya*).

Vasumitra ("Excellent Friend")

Indian monk who according to tradition presided over the "Fourth Buddhist Council" sponsored by KANIṢKA I and held in GANDHĀRA around 100 C.E.

Vātsīputrīya

Indian Buddhist tradition that is considered to be one of the main branches of a group of schools collectively referred to as "PUDGALA-VĀDA" ("Personalists") because they espoused the notion that there is a person (*pudgala*) that is the bearer of KARMA and that is the basis of transmigration from life to life. The Vātsīputrīyas held that the *pudgala* is neither the same as the collection of the five aggregates (SKANDHA) nor different from it, but its position was trenchantly criticized by other Buddhist sects, who accused them of positing what effectively amounted to an enduring "self" (*ātman*), which had been denied by the Buddha. The school takes its name from its founder, Vātsīputra.

Vaṭṭagāmaṇi (fl. ca. first century B.C.E.)

Sri Lankan king who ascended the throne in 43 B.C.E. but was deposed soon after. He regained power again, and ruled from 29 to 17. After returning to the throne, he built the ABHAYAGIRI Monastery in ANURĀDHAPURA. During his reign the PĀLI CANON was written down for the first time.

vegetarianism

See MEAT EATING.

Vesak (Thai *Visākhā Pūjā*)

One of the major festivals of the THERAVĀDA Buddhist religious calendar, which celebrates the day on which, according to tradition, ŚĀKYAMUNI BUDDHA was born, attained awakening, and passed into final *nirvāṇa* (PARINIRVĀṆA). It is celebrated on the full-moon day of the month of Visākhā (April–May).

Vessantara Jātaka

One of the most popular canonical texts in contemporary THERAVĀDA Buddhist countries, which tells the story of Prince Vessantara ("Ideal Action") of Sivi, who in his next rebirth became ŚĀKYAMUNI BUDDHA. In his penultimate lifetime before the attainment of buddhahood, Vessantara perfected the quality of generosity (DĀNA). The text begins with his gift of a royal elephant with magical rain-making powers to a neighboring kingdom that is caught in a drought. Following this, his subjects expel him from the kingdom, and he goes into the wilderness with his faithful wife and two children. After they build a simple jungle hut, Indra appears in disguise and requests his wife, and he gives her up. After this a greedy brahman named Jūjaka asks that he give his children to be his servants, and he agrees to this also. When he has given up everything, the gods intervene and his possessions, family, and kingdom are restored to him. The story is thought to provide a heroic paradigm of generosity perfected to its highest degree, and it is performed all over the Theravāda world every year.

Vetter, Tilmann (b. 1937)

German buddhologist who has published a number of influential studies on the Epistemological tradition and on early Buddhism. He is a professor of Buddhology, Indian Philosophy, and Tibetology at Leiden University. His works include *Erkenntnisprobleme bei Dharmakīrti* (1964) and *The Ideas and Meditative Practices of Early Buddhism* (1988).

Vietnamese Buddhism

Because of its location at the edge of Southeast Asia and bordering on China, Vietnam has been influenced by both Theravāda and Chinese forms of Buddhism. Buddhism (Viet. Phật Giáo) came to Vietnam from a variety of quarters, including China, Funan, the Khmers of present-day Cambodia, and the kingdom of Campā. Until the eleventh century, present-day Vietnam was effectively under Chinese control, and even after the Lý dynasty (1010–1225) carved out an independent territory China continued to exert considerable influence. Early chronicles report that the rulers of southern Annan (part of modern-day Vietnam) patronized Buddhism, and the Chinese pilgrim I-ching (635–713) wrote that the dominant school during his visit was the Āryasammatīya *nikāya*. Buddha images in the style of Amarāvatī dating to the ninth century have been found in Quang Nam province, and inscriptions from the same period from An-Thai indicate that Mahāyāna (Viet. Bắc-Tông) images were constructed there. The dominant forms of Buddhism were the Chinese traditions of Ch'an (Viet. Thiền) and Pure Land (Chin. Ch'ing-t'u; Viet. Đạo Trang), which later melded into a syncretic tradition. A central doctrine of this tradition is "the union of Ch'an and Pure Land" (Viet. Thiền-tịnh Nhất-trí). The inclusivist philosophy of T'ien-t'ai has also been influential in the history of Vietnamese Buddhism. According to early chronicles, Ch'an was first introduced to Vietnam in 580 by the Indian master Vinītaruci (Viet. Tỳ-Ni-Đa-Lu'u-Chi; Chin. Ti-ni-da-lu-chi). His lineage continued until the fourteenth century, but another Ch'an tradition was later established by the Chinese master Wu-yen-tung (Viet. Vô Ngôn Thông, d. 826). The Lâm-tế (Chin. Lin-chi; Jpn. Rinzai) school of Thiền was introduced to Vietnam in the seventeenth century by Nguyên-Thiều (d. 1712), and today it is the largest Buddhist order in the country.

Buddha at Vinh Trang Pagoda, near Saigon.

The first significant period of royal patronage came during the reign of King Đinh Tiên Hoàng (968–979), who provided government support for Buddhism, a policy that was continued during the Early Lê dynasty (980–1009). Royal patronage reached its apogee with the Lý dynasty, during which the government sponsored the building of pagodas and financially supported the saṃgha. During the reign of emperor Lý Anh-tông (1138–1175), Buddhism became the state religion, and by the eleventh century it was established among all strata of the society.

During this time Buddhism became mingled with Taoism and Confucianism, as well as with indigenous beliefs and practices.

The rulers of the Trần dynasty (1225–1400) continued to support Buddhism, but it also experienced increasing competition from Confucians, who gradually replaced Buddhists within the mandarin corps. Support for Confucianism was accelerated as a result of Chinese invasions in 1414, but the rulers of the Nguyễn dynasty reversed this trend and supported Buddhism. In 1601, Nguyễn Hoàng sponsored the construction of the famous Thiên Mụ Pagoda in Huế. In later centuries Buddhism steadily declined, both as a result of laxity within the *saṃgha* and dilution of the tradition due to the incorporation of folk religious practices.

Buddhism remained popular among the masses, however, but encountered another setback during the age of European colonialism. In the nineteenth century the French established protectorates over Annan, Tonkin, Cochin, and Cambodia, which together were amalgamated into the Union Indochinoise in 1887. The French were only expelled in the twentieth century. In the 1920s, there was a Buddhist revival in Vietnam, and beginning in 1931 a number of new Buddhist organizations were founded throughout the country. The power of the Vietnamese *saṃgha* was demonstrated by the decisive role it played in bringing down the repressive Diệm regime in 1963. In 1958 a notable attempt was made to bring unity to the Buddhist community in the Fourth Buddhist Congress, held in Hanoi, and the Unified Buddhist Church of Vietnam, founded in 1964, has continued this initiative. A number of other influential Buddhist organizations formed during the 1960s, such as the United Buddhist Association, led by Thích Thiên Minh and Thích Trí Quang, and the School of Youth for Social Service, led by Thích Nhất Hạnh (THICH NHAT HANH). This grew into a huge and effective volunteer organization based on Buddhist principles. At its peak, it had over ten thousand volunteers, mostly working in rural villages. Despite the role of monks in opposing the Diệm regime, the Communists saw Buddhism as a threat and as a vestige of the old "feudal" order, and they worked to eradicate it. They closed temples and monasteries throughout the country, and they continue to undermine it in various ways. Despite the government's opposition, Buddhism remains deeply rooted in Vietnam, and official persecution has done little to weaken public support.

Thien Mu pagoda, near Hue.

The canonical literature of Vietnamese Buddhism comes mainly from China, and although many scriptures have been translated into Vietnamese, they contain a plethora of Sinitic technical terms, which renders them unintelligible to most laypeople, as well as most monks. Despite this, chanting of sūtras is one of the most widespread religious practices of Vietnamese Buddhism. The most popular sūtras in Vietnamese Buddhism include the SADDHARMA-PUṆḌARĪKA-SŪTRA, the VIMALAKĪRTI-NIRDEŚA-SŪTRA, the ŚŪRAṄGAMA-SAMĀDHI-SŪTRA, and the MAHĀPARINIRVĀṆA-SŪTRA. The main VINAYA lineage in Vietnam is the DHARMAGUPTAKA, and the BODHISATTVA precepts derive from T'ien-t'ai. These are supplemented by the Ch'an monastic rules. Among the laity, practices designed to accumulate merit are the main forms of religiosity. These include chanting the names of buddhas (most commonly AMITĀBHA and AVALOKITEŚVARA) and praying for rebirth in Amitābha's "Pure Land." It is generally assumed by laypeople that the attainment of liberation is not a realistic possibility, and so their religious practice is primarily designed to result in a better rebirth. In Vietnam today, Thiền is the dominant tradition of Buddhism, but in the ten southern delta provinces Theravāda predominates, the main sect being the disciplinary school (Viet. *Luật-Tông*). It is mainly practiced by Khmers.

vihāra (Pāli *vihāra*; Tib. *gnas pa*; "monastery")

A Buddhist monastery. In the early Buddhist community these were individual huts that were mainly used by monks and nuns during the rainy-season retreat, but as Buddhism grew monastic complexes developed. As part of this process, monasteries created administrative structures, and many became large and wealthy. Over time the eremitical ideal of a community of wandering ascetics largely disappeared and was replaced by settled monastic establishments.

Entrance to Sambulsa (Three Buddhas) Monastery at the base of Mount Namsan near Kyongju.

vijñāna (Pāli *viññāna*; Tib. *rnam par shes pa*; "consciousness")

Sanskrit term generally translated as "consciousness," but which includes mental phenomena that are considered to be part of the subconscious in Western psychology, such as unconscious motivations. Etymologically, it is comprised of the Sanskrit prefix *vi* plus the root jñā, "to know." Buddhist scholastic philosophy generally enumerates six types of consciousness: eye consciousness, ear consciousness, nose consciousness, tongue consciousness, bodily consciousness, and mental consciousness. It is the fifth aggregate (SKANDHA) and the third link in the chain of dependent arising (PRATĪTYA-SAMUTPĀDA).

Vijñāna-vāda

See YOGĀCĀRA.

vijñapti-mātra (Chin. *wei-shih*; Jpn. *yuishiki*; Kor. *yusiki*; "cognition-only")

Central doctrine of the YOGĀCĀRA tradition, according to which all of the phenomena of experience are merely products of mind. This has been interpreted in two main ways by modern buddhologists: (1) as a statement of universal idealism, meaning that every perception is generated by mind and has no basis in external reality; and (2) as a phenomenological stance that "brackets" the question of the status of external objects and focuses instead on how knowledge operates. This second position is based on the fact that every experience is a mental event and is interpreted by mind, and so every phenomenon is always already conditioned by consciousness and cannot be known apart from it.

Vikramaśīla Monastic University

One of the two great ancient Buddhist monastic universities of north India. The other was NĀLANDĀ, which was eclipsed by Vikramaśīla in the eleventh century as the major center of Buddhist learning in India. Vikramaśīla was founded around 800 and supported by the rulers of the Pala dynasty.

Vimalakīrti-nirdeśa-sūtra (Tib. *Dri ma med par grangs pas bstan pa'i mdo*; Chin. *Wei-mo-ching*; Jpn. *Yuimagyō*; *Sūtra Spoken by Vimalakīrti*)

One of the most popular MAHĀYĀNA sūtras, particularly in East Asia. Its core is a dharma discourse between the lay BODHISATTVA Vimalakīrti and MAÑJUŚRĪ, which focuses on the "perfection of wisdom" (PRAJÑĀ-PĀRAMITĀ). It begins when the Buddha perceives that Vimalakīrti is pretending to be sick, and so he asks a number of his disciples to go and inquire after his health. One by one they confess that they are intimidated by Vimalakīrti's great wisdom, and recount stories of how he made them feel inadequate. Finally Mañjuśrī agrees to pay a visit, and all of the disciples follow along in anticipation of a clash between two great bodhisattvas. The climax of the sūtra comes when thirty-one bodhisattvas give their respective answers to the question of how a bodhisattva enters "the dharma-door of non-duality." Each successive answer is more sophisticated than the one preceding it, but each exhibits some lingering attachment to duality. Finally Mañjuśrī enunciates what appears to be the last word, but when he turns to Vimalakīrti for his response, he answers by saying nothing. The sūtra is particularly popular because its central character is a layman with a family who manages to surpass all of the other characters in his grasp of the perfection of wisdom.

vinaya (Pāli *vinaya*; Tib. *'dul ba*; "monastic discipline")

General term for the rules and regulations governing the conduct of Buddhist monks and nuns, derived from the VINAYA-PIṬAKA.

Vinaya School

See LÜ-TSUNG; RITSU-SHU.

Vinaya-piṭaka (Pāli *Vinaya-piṭaka*; Tib. *'Dul ba'i sde snod*; "Basket of Monastic Discipline")

One of the "three baskets" (TRIPIṬAKA) of the Buddhist canon, which contains rules and regulations for the conduct of Buddhist monks and nuns. It is divided into three parts: (1) *Sūtra-vibhaṅga*; (2) *Skandhaka*; and (3) *Parivāra*. The first contains specific rules, followed generally by stories regarding their initial promulgation, and it also includes details on their scope and application. The second section focuses on regulations for the

SAṂGHA as a whole, discussing such topics as the POṢADHA, the rainy-season retreat, etc. The third section deals with procedural matters, including details relating to admission to the order, the *poṣadha*, and monastic conduct during the rainy-season retreat. There are several extant Vinayas, but only the THERAVĀDA school's Pāli version survives in its original language. The Vinayas of the SARVĀSTIVĀDA and DHARMAGUPTAKA schools, among others, are extant in Sanskrit fragments and in Chinese and/or Tibetan translations.

Vinītaruci (Viet. *Tỳ-Ni-Đa-Lu'u-Chi*; Chin. *Ti-ni-da-lu-chi*, ca. sixth century)

Indian monk who according to Vietnamese tradition arrived in China in 574, but soon left because of anti-Buddhist persecutions. He reportedly met the third CH'AN patriarch, Seng-ts'an (Jpn. *Sōsan*, d. 606), and in 580 traveled to Vietnam. There he founded a Ch'an lineage (the Vinītaruci School), which according to traditional records had an emphasis on ritualism and asceticism and engaged in public works. Its center was the Pháp Vân Temple in Long Biên province. The tradition lasted for over six hundred years, but died out after its nineteenth patriarch, Y So'n (d. 1213). Although traditional accounts describe it as a Ch'an tradition, there is little to support this idea, and its doctrines and practices appear to have little connection with Ch'an.

vipassanā

See VIPAŚYANĀ.

vipaśyanā (Pāli *vipassanā*; Tib. *lhag mthong*; Chin. *kuan*; Jpn. *kan*; Viet. *quán*; "higher insight")

Sanskrit term for a meditative practice involving analysis of a meditative object (*ālambana*), which aims at directly realizing its final nature. In THERAVĀDA meditation theory, this involves becoming aware of the object as being characterized by the "three characteristics" (Pāli *tilakkhana*; Skt. TRILAKṢAṆA): selflessness (Pāli *anattā*; Skt. ANĀTMAN), impermanence (Pāli *anicca*; Skt. ANITYA), and suffering (Pāli *dukkha*; Skt. DUḤKHA). In MAHĀYĀNA, it refers to a mind that is characterized by analyzing its object with clarity and intensity, which perceives its emptiness (ŚŪNYATĀ) of inherent existence (SVABHĀVA). It is generally held that the attainment of *vipaśyanā* is preceded by calming (Skt. ŚAMATHA; Pāli *samatha*), the ability to remain internally focused on the object without being disturbed by laxity or excitement.

vīrya (Pāli *viriya*: Tib. *brtson 'grus*; "effort")

In general, this refers to an attitude of sustained enthusiasm for religious practice. In MAHĀYĀNA, it is the fourth of the "perfections" (PĀRAMITĀ) that a BODHISATTVA cultivates on the path to buddhahood. It is perfected on the fourth bodhisattva "level" (BHŪMI).

Visākhā Pūjā

See VESAK.

Visuddhimagga (*Path of Purification*)

Postcanonical Pāli text by the THERAVĀDA scholar BUDDHAGHOSA (ca. fourth–fifth century), consisting of twenty-three chapters, outlining the Buddhist path according to the system of the MAHĀVIHĀRA *nikāya*. It is divided into three parts: (1) ethics (*sīla*; Skt. ŚĪLA); (2) meditative absorption (Skt. and Pāli SAMĀDHI); and (3) wisdom (Pāli *paññā*; Skt. PRAJÑĀ). The first part comprises two chapters, which focus on the practice of morality. The next eleven chapters outline the path to liberation, with particular emphasis on meditative practice. The final ten chapters focus on the fruits of practice.

Vô Ngôn Thông (Chin. *Wu-yen-tung*, d. 826)

Chinese CH'AN master who traveled to Vietnam and settled at Kiên So Temple in Tiên Du prefecture. He is said to have been an enigmatic figure who sat in meditation facing a wall (Viet. *bích-quán*; Chin. *pi-kuan*) for many years, as did BODHIDHARMA. He is considered to be the founder of the Vô Ngôn Thông school of Thiền (Chin. *Ch'an*), which emphasized meditative practice in which one overcomes random and discursive thoughts and abides in the state of "no-thought." The order reportedly continued for forty generations. Its last recorded patriarch was a layman named Ú'ng-Vu'o'ng, who lived in the thirteenth century.

Vulture Peak

See GṚDHRAKŪṬA.

W

Wangyal, Geshe Ngawang

(dGe bshes dBang rgyal, 1901–1983)

Kalmyk Mongolian of the dGe lugs pa (Gelukpa) order, whose main teacher was the Buryat lama Agvan Dorjiev (1854–1938). He fled Tibet in 1951 following the Chinese invasion of Khams. In 1955 he moved to the U.S.A. to minister to a small Kalmyk community. He subsequently founded the first Tibetan monastery in North America, called the Lamaist Buddhist Monastery of North America, in Freewood Acres, NJ. His students included Robert Thurman and Jeffrey Hopkins.

war

Although modernist Buddhists often proclaim that Buddhism eschews war and that fighting in the name of religion is unknown in Buddhism, there are numerous counter-examples. These can be found in most Buddhist countries and in most traditions, despite the first precept prohibiting killing. In both Tibet and Japan, for example, many monasteries had warrior monks (*ldob ldob* in Tibetan, sōbei in Japanese), who fought with other monks and with civil authorities. Records from Tibet and Japan indicate that the battles in which monks engaged were mainly concerned with money and power, and not with matters of doctrine or practice. In Korea, Buddhist monks were at the forefront of nationalist struggles against Japanese invaders, and in China there were well-established martial arts traditions among monks. Perhaps the clearest examples of Buddhist notions of "holy war" can be found in both traditional Sri Lankan chronicles (the Mahāvaṃsa and Dīpavaṃsa) and in the rhetoric of some contemporary Theravāda monks. The early chronicles describe the heroic battles of kings such as Duṭṭhagāmaṇi against the Damiḷas (Tamils), who are characterized as subhuman non-Buddhist foreign invaders whose very presence on the island threatens Buddhism. When the kings express concern regarding the karmic consequences of killing them, monks assure them that killing Damiḷas should not be seen as equivalent to killing humans, and the kings are further told that they accrue great merit from fighting. In modern times, a number of senior monks, for instance the late Walpola Rahula, adopted the same rhetoric with respect to the civil war between Hindu and Muslim Tamils and the Sinhala Buddhist-dominated government. Rahula even went so far as to describe the conflict as a righteous battle between dharma and its enemies, and he urged young monks to disrobe in order to join the fight. Similarly, the Thai monk Kitthiwuttho has often called on devout Buddhists to kill Communists, for example in a speech entitled "Killing Communists is not Demeritorious." He argues that because Communists threaten the nation and Buddhism they are subhuman, and killing them is morally equivalent to killing MĀRA. Moreover, he contends that Buddhists who kill Communists gain merit by protecting the country and Buddhism. As he has developed this idea, he asserts that some people are so depraved that killing them is equivalent to killing affliction (*kilesa*; Skt. KLEŚA) itself, and so fighting them is similar to the practice of taking medicine in order to rid the body of disease. Similar examples of Buddhists advocating war and violence abound throughout the Buddhist world, and although it should be added that such sentiments are often condemned by other Buddhists as a violation of Buddhist precepts and beliefs, the examples given above indicate that many Buddhists do not consider Buddhism and war to be antithetical.

Warren, Henry Clarke (1854–1899)

American scholar who studied Sanskrit with Charles Lanman at Johns Hopkins University, and with Lanman began the Harvard Oriental Series. He published a number of influential translations of Sanskrit and Pāli texts, including *Buddhism in Translation.*

wat

Term used in THERAVĀDA countries for a Buddhist monastery or temple.

Wat Dhammakāya

Popular Thai Buddhist movement, founded in the 1970s by Chaiyaboon Sitthiphon (Phra Dhammajayo) and Phadet Phongasawad (Phra Dattajīvo). They established a Buddhist center at Pathum Thani (near Bangkok), which has grown into a huge complex. The movement has

Wat Arun ("Temple of the Dawn"), Bangkok, Thailand.

become the controlling force in the Buddhist Associations of most major Thai universities and has attracted the support of the royal family and powerful segments of the military. Its main stated goal is to restore Thai Buddhist civil religion, but its critics contend that it is mainly interested in amassing money and attracting members.

wato ("the point")

Japanese term for the point of a KŌAN, which sums up the intent of the apparent paradox that it poses.

Watts, Alan (1915–1971)

British popularizer of Buddhism, especially ZEN. He lacked an academic background in the field and had no knowledge of Asian languages, but was able to convey difficult and abstruse ideas in ways that appealed to a general readership. His first book was *The Spirit of Zen* (1936). He became deeply involved in the counter-culture during the 1960s, and is the basis for the character Arthur Whane in Jack Kerouac's *Dharma Bums*. Although generally dismissed by academic specialists as superficial and inaccurate, his works still have a wide popular appeal.

Wayman, Alex

American scholar of Buddhism, who spent most of his career at Columbia University. He has published prolifically on a range of topics, most significantly on Tibetan Buddhism and Yogācāra.

wen-ta

See MONDŌ.

wheel of becoming

See BHAVA-CAKRA.

White Lotus Society

See PAI-LIEN-TSUNG.

Williams, Paul Martin (b. 1950)

British buddhologist, best known for his work on Madhyamaka. He received a D.Phil. degree from Oxford University in Madhyamaka Philosophy in 1978 and has spent most of his academic career at University of Bristol, where he is a professor and co-director of the Centre for Buddhist Studies in the Department of Theology and Religious Studies. He has published a number of influential books and articles, including *Mahāyāna Buddhism: The Doctrinal Foundations* (1989) and *The Reflexive Nature of Awareness: A Tibetan Madhyamaka Defence* (1997).

wisdom

See PRAJÑĀ.

Wisdom Publications

Publisher of books on Buddhism, founded in London as a charitable organization called Wisdom Communications Ltd. in the early 1980s. Its original purpose was to provide an outlet for books of teachings by LAMA YESHE and LAMA ZOPA. In 1988 it moved its headquarters to Boston, MA, U.S.A., and since that time has greatly expanded its catalog. It now publishes books on a wide spectrum of Buddhist Studies, including translations, oral teachings, and academic works.

Wŏn

A school of KOREAN BUDDHISM founded in 1916 by Chung-bin Pak (1891–1943, referred to his followers as Sot'aesan), which combined Buddhist doctrines with elements from Confucianism, Taoism, Tonghak, and Christianity. The founder is regarded by the tradition as a living buddha, one whose teachings are particularly appropriate to the present age, which it characterizes as one in which materialism is engulfing the world and suppressing the human spirit. The term "*wŏn*" means "circular," and the school is symbolized by a black circle that represents the DHARMA-KĀYA, which is said to be the source of all beings, the original mind of all sentient beings, and the enlightened mind of all buddhas. Its main scripture is the *Chong-jon*, written by the founder. It has about four hundred temples in Korea and about thirty in other countries. Its temples are very austere, with no images of buddhas or bodhisattvas; the only decoration is the circle.

Wŏnch'ŭk (Chin. *Yüan-tse*, 631–696)

Korean scholar-monk of the Unified Silla period (668–918). He traveled to Chang-an in China, where he studied with HSÜAN-TSANG (596–664) and became one of his main disciples. His best-known work is his *Commentary on the Saṃdhinirmocana-sūtra* (*Chieh-shen-mi-ching shu*) in ten sections.

Wŏnhyo (617–686)

One of the great figures of the Unified Silla period of KOREAN BUDDHISM (668–916), founder of the Pŏpsang (Skt. *Dharma-lakṣaṇa*; Chin. FA-HSIANG) tradition in Korea. His main concern was to find ways of harmonizing the disparate – and often contradictory – doctrines of the Korean Buddhist schools of his day. He was widely influential both as a scholar and as a propagator of Buddhism among the masses. He wrote numerous scholarly works that covered a wide spectrum of Buddhist topics, and at the same time lived and worked among the masses. He is credited with writing more than eighty separate works in 240 fascicles, of which twenty works in twenty-two fascicles are still extant. (See also T'ONG-PULGYO.)

World Fellowship of Buddhists

Organization founded in 1950 by G. P. Malalasekhera, a Sri Lankan scholar. The aims of the organization are to promote Buddhism worldwide and to seek reconciliation between Buddhist traditions.

wu-hsin (Jpn. *mushin*; Kor. *musin*; "no-mind")

Considered to be the ideal state of awareness in the CH'AN (Jpn. ZEN; Kor. SŎN) tradition, in which all dualistic thoughts are eliminated and one attains a state of mental equanimity. In this state one fully actualizes one's "buddha-nature" (Jpn. *busshō*; Skt. BUDDHATĀ), which is the essence of all reality.

Wu-men Hui-k'ai (Jpn. *Mumon Ekai*, 1183–1260)

Chinese CH'AN master of the Yang-ch'i (Jpn. *Yōgi*) lineage of LIN-CHI (Jpn. RINZAI), best known for his work *The Gateless Barrier* (WU-MEN-KUAN; Jpn. *Mumonkan*), a collection of forty-eight *kung-an* (Jpn. KŌAN), along with commentaries and "praises" (Jpn. *ju*) on them.

Wu-men-kuan (Jpn. *Mumonkan*; *The Gateless Barrier*)

Along with the PI-YEN-LU (Jpn. *Hekigan-roku*), one of the two most influential collections of *kung-an*s (Jpn. KŌAN) and commentaries. Composed in 1229 by WU-MEN HUI-K'AI (Jpn. *Mumon Ekai*, 1183–1260), it includes forty-eight *kung-an*, along with commentaries and "praises" (Jpn. *ju*). It begins with the MU KŌAN, the one that led to Wu-men's own first awakening experience. The text was brought to Japan by his student and dharma-successor (Jpn. HASSU) Kakushin in 1254, and it became one of the main texts of the RINZAI tradition.

wu-nien (Jpn. *munen*; "no-thought")

CH'AN concept closely related to "no-mind" (Chin. WU-HSIN; Jpn. *mushin*); it is a state of awareness in which one is no longer attached to some thoughts and averse to others. Attachment to one thought is said to lead to attachment to a series of thoughts, and this situation is the state of bondage, according to Ch'an. When one cuts off attachment to thoughts, the mind flows freely, not privileging some thoughts and rejecting others. According to HUI-NENG's *Platform Sūtra* (LIU-TSU-TA-SHIH FA-PAO-T'AN-CHING), "No-thought is not thinking even when involved in thought." As he explains this idea, thought *per se* is not the issue, but rather whether or not one is attached to it. Attachment is based on the mistaken notion that the concept of a thing is the thing itself, but when one realizes that the things one desires are only fleeting mental events, attachment vanishes.

Wu-tai shan ("Five Terrace Mountain")

Mountain in Shanshi province in China, believed by Chinese tradition to be the abode of MAÑJUŚRĪ (Chin. *Wen-shu*). It is one of China's most important pilgrimage sites, and in the sixth century it had over two hundred monasteries (only around fifty-five are preserved today).

Wu-tsung (814–846)

Chinese emperor of the T'ang dynasty, a fervent Taoist who in 842 initiated a massive anti-Buddhist persecution, which reached its peak in 845. Reportedly 260,000 monks and nuns were forced to return to lay life, and 4,000 Buddhist monasteries were looted. It was the harshest persecution of Buddhism in China until the Cultural Revolution in the 1960s.

Y

yab yum (lit. "father–mother")

A common iconographic theme in VAJRAYĀNA art, in which a male and female buddha are depicted in sexual embrace. In this motif, the two represent respectively compassion and wisdom, the two primary qualities that are perfected by buddhas, and their union represents an indissoluble union of the two.

yakṣa (Pāli *yakkha*; Tib. *gnod sbyin*)

The eight attendants of Kubera (or Viṣṇu), as well as a class of beings who live in the earth, air, lower heavens, and forests. They are endowed with supernatural powers and are sometimes beneficent and sometimes malignant and violent, while others (mainly the females, called *yakṣiṇī*) are devourers of human flesh. They are often said to be present at the preaching of Buddhist sūtras.

Yama (Pāli *Yama*; Tib. *gShin rje*; Chin. *Yen-man*; Jpn. *Enna*)

The god of death in Buddhist mythology, who rules over the Buddhist hells. He is also said to be responsible for judging the dead and deciding which of them merit rebirth in a hell.

Yamāntaka (Tib. *gShin rje gshed*; Chin. *Yen-man-te-chia*; Jpn. *Daitoku Myō-ō*; Mon. *Erlig-jin Jarghagchi*; "Subduer of Yama")

Wrathful manifestation of MAÑJUŚRĪ, the buddha of wisdom. In this form he appears with the head of a raging bull, surrounded by flames. He is one of the most important dharma-protectors (Skt. DHARMA-PĀLA; Tib. *chos skyong*) in TIBETAN BUDDHISM, particularly for the dGE LUGS PA (Gelukpa) order.

yāna (Pāli *yāna*; Tib. *theg pa*; "vehicle")

A path to salvation, which is internally consistent and which encompasses a particular complex of doctrines and practices. Buddhism is claimed by its adherents to encompass many vehicles, each of which is said to have been articulated by the Buddha due to the varying capacities and proclivities of different beings. This notion becomes particularly important with the development of Buddhist sectarianism, with newly emerging traditions often developing categorization schemas that label their opponents as belonging to an inferior "vehicle," while they adhere to the supreme one. Thus the emerging MAHĀYĀNA movement termed itself the

"Great Vehicle" (the literal meaning of Mahāyāna), and labeled its opponents as the "Lesser Vehicle" (HĪNAYĀNA). When tantric Buddhism emerged in India, it distinguished itself from mainstream Mahāyāna with such terms as "Vajra Vehicle" (VAJRAYĀNA) and "Mantra Vehicle" (Mantrayāna).

Yang-shan Hui-chi (807–883)

CH'AN master who along with his teacher KUEI-SHAN LING-YU (Jpn. *Kyōzan Ejaku*, 771–853) co-founded the Kuei-yang (Jpn. Igyō) school, one of the "five houses" of Ch'an.

Yar lung dynasty (also spelled Yar klungs)

The ruling dynasty of Tibet prior to and during the "first dissemination" (SNGA DAR) of Buddhism. Its main power base was the Yar lung valley in central Tibet, and during the eighth–ninth centuries it became a major military power and even conquered parts of China. It came to an end with the assassination of GLANG DAR MA (Lang Darma, r. 838–842).

Yaśodharā (Pāli Yasodharā; Tib. Grags 'dzin ma)

The wife of SIDDHĀRTHA GAUTAMA before he left her and his newborn son RĀHULA to pursue liberation. She is also referred to in Pāli literature as Rāhulamātā and Bimbā.

Yasutani Rōshi, Hakuun Ryōko (1885–1973)

Influential modern Japanese ZEN master who entered a SŌTŌ temple at the age of thirteen and later studied at a teachers' college, after which he became a schoolteacher in Tokyo for sixteen years. He married at thirty and had five children. At forty he began meditation training with SOGAKU HARADA RŌSHI, and became a temple priest at Hosshin-ji, where he soon experienced awakening (KENSHŌ) while concentrating on the MU KŌAN. At fifty-eight he received a certification of awakening (INKA-SHŌMEI) from Harada Rōshi, and later became his dharma-successor (HASSU). As a teacher, he emphasized both SHIKANTAZA ("just sitting") and KŌAN training. From 1962 to 1969 he visited the U.S.A., and subsequently traveled to England, Germany, and France. He was a prolific writer, best known for his commentaries on several of the great kōan collections, including the WU-MEN-KUAN (Jpn. *Mumonkan*), PI-YEN-LU (Jpn. *Hekiganroku*), and *Ts'ung-jung-lu* (Jpn. *Shōyōroku*).

Ye shes mtsho rgyal (Yeshe Tsogyel, ca. 757–817)

Consort and main disciple of PADMASAMBHAVA, considered by tradition to be the first Tibetan to fulfill the tantric ideal of attainment of buddhahood in one lifetime. She was born into an aristocratic family, but when her father arranged for her to be married she escaped in order to engage in religious practice. The culmination of her training was her attainment of the "rainbow body" (Tib. 'JA' LUS), symbolizing that she had become a buddha. She is credited with concealing teachings of Padmasambhava called "hidden treasures" (GTER MA), many of which have become highly influential in TIBETAN BUDDHISM, particularly in the RNYING MA PA (Nyingmapa) tradition (in which she is considered to be a ḌĀKINĪ).

Yeshe, Lama Tupden (bLa ma Thub bstan ye shes, 1935–1984)

DGE LUGS PA (Gelukpa) lama who studied at SE RA Monastery, where he followed the standard scholastic curriculum until he fled to Nepal in 1959 following the Chinese invasion of Tibet. Together with LAMA TUPDEN ZOPA (bLa ma Thub bstan bzod pa), he established Kopan Monastery as a meditation center for Westerners. He attracted a large number of students, and in 1975 founded the FOUNDATION FOR THE PRESERVATION OF THE MAHAYANA TRADITION (FPMT), which has grown into one of the largest Tibetan Buddhist organizations in the world, with 110 centers.

yi dam (Skt. *iṣṭa-devatā*; "tutelary deity")

Tibetan term for buddhas who are the focus of tantric visualization practices. They are archetypal, in that they often represent ideal qualities such as compassion or wisdom, but are also considered to be real entities, which exist as "enjoyment bodies" (Skt. SAṂBHOGA-KĀYA; Tib. *longs spyod pa'i sku*) residing in the Buddhist heavens. In deity yoga (Skt. DEVATĀ-YOGA; Tib. *lha'i rnal 'byor*) practice, meditators create a vivid image of a particular *yi dam* and imagine that it possesses all the ideal qualities of a buddha. This is called the "generation stage" (Skt. UTPATTI-KRAMA; Tib. *bskyed rim*); it is followed by the "completion stage" (Skt. SAMPANNA-KRAMA; Tib. *rdzogs rim*), in which one imagines that the buddha merges with oneself and that one becomes indistinguishable from the *yi dam*. The visualized image is referred to as the "pledge being" (Tib. *dam tshigs sems dpa'*; Skt. *samaya-sattva*), and the actual entity that is being summoned in the visualization practice is called the "wisdom being" (Tib. *ye shes sems dpa'*; Skt. *jñāna-sattva*). This practice requires that one obtain the requisite initiation from a qualified GURU, and the actual visualization is guided by his or her oral instructions.

yin-k'o

See INKA-SHŌMEI.

yoga (Pāli *yoga*; Tib. *rnal 'byor*; "discipline")

A term that can refer to any physical and/or mental discipline. It is common to both Hinduism and Buddhism (as well as other Indic traditions), and each religion's yogic practices involve training in the development of physical and mental states that are valued by it.

yoga-tantra (Tib. *rnal 'byor rgyud*)

One of the four classes of tantras, according to Tibetan doxographers. These tantras emphasize internal yogas in which one visualizes oneself and an archetypal deity (Skt. *iṣṭa-devatā*; Tib. YI DAM) as separate beings and then causes the deity to enter oneself. The practitioners of this type of TANTRA are supposed to visualize all phenomena as being primordially free from the signs of mental projection and as manifestations of luminosity and emptiness. (*See also* ANUTTARA-YOGA-TANTRA; CARYĀ-TANTRA; KRIYĀ-TANTRA.)

Yogācāra (also Vijñāna-vāda; Tib. *rNal 'byor spyod pa*; "Yogic Practice School")

School of INDIAN BUDDHISM whose main early exponents were the brothers ASAṄGA and VASUBANDHU (ca. fourth century), the primary focus of which was psychology and epistemology. The term "Yogic Practice School" may have been an implied rejection of the emphasis on dialectic and debate found in other Indian Buddhist traditions, particularly the MADHYAMAKA. Meditation practice and analysis of the workings of the mind are central concerns of Yogācāra, as reflected in the voluminous literature it produced on these subjects. One of its central doctrines is "cognition-only" (VIJÑAPTI-MĀTRA), according to which all phenomena are essentially products of mind. This has been interpreted in two main ways: (1) as a statement of universal idealism, according to which external objects do not exist and all the phenomena of experience are simply mental projections; and (2) as a phenomenological stance, which brackets the question of the existence of external objects and instead focuses on the process of how they are revealed to our awareness. Tibetan doxographers interpret it in the first way, and thus refer to the school as "Mind-Only" (Tib. *Sems tsam*; Skt. *Citta-mātra*). Yogācāra also developed a distinctive eightfold schema of consciousness, which included the traditional six consciousnesses and added "sentience" (MANAS) and "basis-consciousness" (ĀLAYA-VIJÑĀNA). Along with Madhyamaka, it became one of the two most important philosophical traditions of Indian Buddhism, and also was highly influential in East Asia. (*See also* FA-HSIANG; HOSSŌ; HSÜAN-TSANG; SAṂDHINIRMOCANA-SŪTRA.)

yogin (Tib. *rnal 'byor ba*; female: *yoginī*; Tib. *rnal 'byor ma*; "practitioner of yoga")

Sanskrit term for someone who engages in yogic practice. In Tibetan tantric Buddhism it commonly refers to practitioners who are engaged in intensive meditative practice, generally conducted in solitary retreat or in small communities that tend to exist outside the monastic establishment (but are often associated with a monastery).

yojana (Tib. *dpag tshad*)

A measure of distance in ancient India, said to be the distance that one can travel on horseback between harnessing and unharnessing a horse. There are various estimates of how far this is, ranging from four to thirteen kilometers.

Yon tan rgya mtsho (Yönden Gyatso, 1589–1617)

The fourth DALAI LAMA, a great-grandson of the Mongol leader ALTAN KHAN, whose recognition as Dalai Lama was an important factor in creating close ties between the Mongols and the DGE LUGS PA (Gelukpa) order. This led in 1642 to the elevation of the fifth Dalai Lama, NGAG DBANG BLO BZANG RGYA MTSHO (Ngawang Losang Gyatso, 1617–1682), to the position of ruler of Tibet, which was achieved with the help of Mongol troops.

Young Men's Buddhist Association (YMBA)

Organization founded in Colombo in 1898 by C. S. Dissanayake, a Sri Lankan Buddhist who converted from Christianity. It was modeled on the Young Men's Christian Association, and its members played crucial roles in the politics of a number of Southeast Asian countries in the early decades of the twentieth century.

Yun-kang ("Cloud Hill")

A complex of grottoes in the Shansi province of China, near the city of Ta-t'ung, built between 460 and 540 and housing some of the finest examples of early Chinese Buddhist art. The impetus for its construction was the destruction wrought during the anti-Buddhist persecutions of 446 by Emperor Wu, during which many wood and metal statues were destroyed. Concerned with the fragility of such images, the monk T'an-yao decided to have buddha images carved out of rock to ensure their longevity. The project was financed by the emperor's successor, who patronized Buddhism and who indicated his regret for the previous destruction in inscriptions preserved in the caves. Today fifty-three caves are extant, spanning an area of one kilometer and containing 50,000 images.

Yün-men Wen-yen (Jpn. *Ummon Bun'en*, 864–949)

One of the greatest Chinese CH'AN masters, particularly famous for his abrupt and confrontational methods, such as shouting at students, hitting them with sticks, etc. He appears in numerous places in the great *kung-an* (Jpn. KŌAN) collections, particularly the WU-MEN-KUAN (Jpn. *Mumonkan*) and the PI-YEN-LU (Jpn. *Hekigan-roku*). In many of the entries about him he is said to have altered the wording of the traditional stories, substituting his own words or phrases. He is also famous for his use of "one word barriers" (Jpn. *ichiji-kan*), one-word *kōan*s that were abrupt and generally apparently nonsensical answers to students' questions. Despite his skill in the use of language, he reportedly had a profound distrust of its ability to distort one's intentions, and so he forbade his students to write down his words. Despite the ban, however, one of his followers wore a paper robe on which he wrote Yun-men's sayings, and these constitute the bulk of the anecdotes about his teachings that survive.

Z

zabuton ("sitting-mat")

Japanese term for a square meditation mat, generally filled with kapon and covered with blue cloth, used for seated meditation (ZAZEN) practice.

zafu ("sitting-cushion")

A round meditation cushion, generally stuffed with kapok and covered with blue cloth.

zazen (Chin. *tso-ch'an*; "sitting meditation")

Japanese term for the practice of seated meditation, which is the main religious practice in all ZEN traditions. It is considered to be the primary means by which students attain realization (KENSHŌ or SATORI), and in most Zen monasteries it is practiced for several hours every day. Ideally *zazen* is practiced in a state of mind free from grasping or striving, with the mind intensely focused, but not on any particular object (this state is referred to as SHIKANTAZA, "just sitting"). The practice is based on the notion that all beings are already buddhas, and so during the practice of *zazen* one attempts to drop off accumulated conceptions and analytical thinking in order to allow this fundamental buddha-nature (Jpn. *busshō*; Chin. *fo-hsin*; Skt. BUDDHATĀ) to manifest spontaneously.

Zen (Chin. *Ch'an*; Kor. *Sŏn*; Viet. *Thiền*; Skt. *Dhyāna*; "Meditation School")

Short for *zenna*, a Japanese term for a tradition that was brought from China which emphasizes the centrality of meditative practice. Zen is the Japanese pronunciation of the Chinese word CH'AN (short for *ch'an-na*), which in turn is the Chinese pronunciation of the Sanskrit technical term DHYĀNA, meaning "meditation." There are a number of different Zen lineages in Japan, each of which has its own practices and histories, but all see themselves as belonging to a tradition that began with ŚĀKYAMUNI BUDDHA. Zen histories claim that the lineage began when the Buddha passed on the essence of his awakened mind to his disciple KĀŚYAPA, who in turn transmitted it to his successor. The process continued through a series of twenty-eight Indian "patriarchs" (Jpn. *soshigata*) to BODHIDHARMA, who transmitted it to China. Although Zen tacitly acknowledges that its doctrines and practices are very different from what is reported in Indian Buddhist sources, it claims that it has maintained the essence of the Buddha's awakened realization and that the words of Buddhist scriptures are at best a pale reflection (and at worst a complete distortion) of this. Thus Zen is often said by its adherents to be "a special transmission outside the scriptures" (Chin. *chiao-*

Zen Buddhist monk.

wai pieh chuan; Jpn. *kyōge-betsuden*) that "does not rely on words" (Chin. *pu li wen-tzu*; Jpn. *furyū-monji*) and that "directly points to the human heart" (*jikishi-ninshin*). Despite this assertion, contemporary scholars generally consider its significant differences from INDIAN BUDDHISM to be mainly due to changes that arose as a result of the influence of Chinese (and later Japanese) culture, which began when early translators opted to use indigenous Chinese terms (mainly from Taoism) to translate Sanskrit technical terms that had no real equivalents in Chinese. One important result of this was that Taoist concepts became intermingled with Buddhist notions, leading to East Asian traditions that combined Buddhism and Taoism. Among other things, this led to a widespread acceptance of substantialist notions like "buddha-nature" (Chin. *fo-hsing*; Jpn. *busshō*; Skt. *buddhatā*), which are thought by contemporary proponents of "Critical Buddhism" (HIHAN BUKKYŌ) to be fundamentally antithetical to the central tenets of Indian Buddhism as reported in the PĀLI CANON and early MAHĀYĀNA literature. In addition, the Zen lineage history is considered by modern scholars to be a fabrication, as there is no historical evidence to support it. (*See also* HUI-NENG; ISHIN-DENSHIN; KO-I.)

zendō ("meditation hall")

Japanese term for a place in which meditation is practiced. In most ZEN monasteries it is sparsely furnished, with few if any decorations or adornments. This austerity is thought to be conducive to meditation because there is little to distract students from their practice.

zengo (Chin. *chien-wu*; "gradual teachings")

Japanese term that refers to the notion that awakening is attained through a program of gradual training. It is associated with the "Northern School" (Pei-tsung) of Chinese CH'AN and is contrasted with the doctrine of TONGO ("sudden teachings"), which holds that awakening must be attained all at once, in a sudden flash of realization. The latter notion is associated with the "Southern School" (Chin. NAN-TSUNG).

zenji (Chin. *ch'an-shih*; "Zen master")

Honorific title for masters of the ZEN (Chin. CH'AN) tradition.

Zhwa dmar Rin po che (Shamar Rinpoche)

The "Red Hat Lama," one of the main reincarnational lineages of the KAR MA BKA' BRGYUD PA (Karma Kagyüpa) order of TIBETAN BUDDHISM. The lineage originated with Grags pa seng ge (Drakpa Sengge, 1283–1345), but ran afoul of the Tibetan government when the eighth Zhwa dmar Rin po che was found guilty of plotting with a Gurkha army that invaded Tibet and sacked BKRA SHIS LHUN PO (Tashilhünpo) Monastery. He committed suicide in 1792 (or was murdered by the government but made to look like a suicide), and was subsequently officially forbidden to reincarnate. Despite this ban, members of the lineage were recognized in secret until it was safe for them to go public. The thirteenth incarnation was born in 1952 in sDe dge

(Derge) in the Khams province of Tibet. He was recognized at the age of nine by the sixteenth RGYAL BA KAR MA PA (Gyelwa Karmapa) and the fourteenth DALAI LAMA and enthroned in 1964 in Rum bteg (Rumtek) Monastery in Sikkim. Like his predecessor, he has been at odds with the Tibetan government-in-exile (and with other lamas in his lineage), most prominently over the question of the succession to the sixteenth rGyal ba Kar ma pa. The present Zhwa dmar Rin po che supports a candidate who resides in his center in New Delhi, but the other hierarchs of the lineage, as well as the Dalai Lama, support another candidate, who escaped from MTSHUR PHU (Tsurpu) Monastery in Tibet in January 2000 in order to pursue his studies in India.

Zopa, Lama Tupden (bLa ma Thub bstan bzod pa Rin po che, b. 1946)

DGE LUGS PA lama who together with LAMA TUPDEN YESHE (bLa ma Thub bstan ye shes, 1935–1981) established the FOUNDATION FOR THE PRESERVATION OF THE MAHAYANA TRADITION (FPMT), which has grown into one of the largest Tibetan Buddhist organizations in the world.

Chronology

563–483 B.C.E.	Life of Śākyamuni Buddha
483	First Buddhist Council at Rājagṛha
383	Second Buddhist Council at Vaiśalī
327–325	Alexander the Great invades India
322–298	Reign of Candragupta Maurya
272–236	Reign of Aśoka
247	Mahinda's mission to Sri Lanka
240	Third Buddhist Council at Pāṭaliputra
200	Beginnings of Mahāyāna Buddhism
200 B.C.E.–100 C.E.	Invasions of Indian subcontinent by Śuṅgas, Iranians, Śakas, and Kuśānas
101–77 B.C.E.	Reign of Duṭṭhagāmaṇi Abhaya in Sri Lanka; establishment of Buddhism as state religion
25–17 B.C.E.	Pāli canon written down in Sri Lanka
100 C.E.	Reign of Kaniṣka I; Fourth Buddhist Council in Gandhāra
1st century C.E.	Buddhism enters Central Asia and China
148	An Shih-kao arrives in China and establishes first translation bureau
150–250	Life of Nāgārjuna
2nd century	Founding of Nālandā
3rd century	Buddhism transmitted to Burma, Cambodia, Laos, Indonesia
4th century	Life of Asaṅga and Vasubandhu
334–416	Life of Hui-yüan
344–413	Life of Kumārajīva
4th–5th centuries	Life of Buddhaghosa
372	Buddhism transmitted to Korea
414	Fa-hsien travels to India
520	Bodhidharma arrives in China
530–600	Life of Dharmakīrti; flourishing of Epistemological tradition
538–597	Life of Chih-i; development of T'ien-t'ai school
552	Buddhism enters Japan from Korea
6th century	Development of Hua-yen, T'ien-t'ai, Ch'an, Ch'ing-t'u schools in China
574–622	Prince Shōtoku patronizes Buddhism in Japan
589–617	Chinese Sui dynasty
618–906	Chinese T'ang dynasty; apogee of Buddhism in China

629–645	Hsüan-tsang travels to India
638–713	Life of Hui-neng; split of Ch'an into Northern and Southern schools
668–918	Unified Silla Period in Korea; flourishing of Buddhism
710–784	Nara period in Japan; establishment of Sanron, Hossō, Jōjitsu, Kusha, Ritsu, and Kegon schools
760	Padmasambhava arrives in Tibet; beginning of first dissemination of Buddhism to Tibet
767	Consecration of bSam yas in Tibet
767–822	Life of Saichō; founding of Tendai
774–835	Life of Kūkai; founding of Shingon
792	Council of Lhasa (?)
794–1185	Heian period in Japan
800–1250	Coḷa dynasty in Tamil Nadu
838–842	Reign of gLang dar ma; end of first dissemination of Buddhism to Tibet
845	Persecution of Buddhism in China
960–1279	Sung dynasty in China
983	First printing of Chinese Buddhist canon
999–1026	Mahmud Ghorī attacks northern India
1009–1224	Lý dynasty in Vietnam
1012–1097	Life of Mar pa; beginnings of bKa' brgyud pa order
1016–1100	Life of Nāropa
1040–1123	Life of Mi la ras pa
1042	Atiśa arrives in Tibet; beginning of second dissemination of Buddhism
1073	Sa skya pa order of Tibetan Buddhism founded by dKon mchog rgyal po
1079–1153	Life of sGam po pa; establishment of a monastic order in bKa' brgyud pa
1133–1212	Life of Hōnen; establishment of Japanese Jōdō-shū school
1141–1215	Life of Eisai; Rinzai Zen brought to Japan
1158–1210	Life of Chinul; development of Sŏn in Korea
1173–1262	Life of Shinran; founding of Jōdō-shinshū in Japan
1192–1338	Kamakura Period in Japan
1200	Destruction of Nālandā Monastic University
1200–1253	Life of Dōgen Zenji; Sōtō Zen established in Japan
1222–1282	Life of Nichiren
1235	Tibetan pilgrim Dharmasvāmin visits north India; Buddhism dies out in India after this time
1244	Sa skya Paṇḍita travels to Mongolia; conversion of Mongols begins
1290–1364	Life of Bu ston; Tibetan canon compiled by 1334
1327	King Jayavarman Parameśvara ascends the throne and establishes Theravāda in Cambodia
1357–1419	Life of Tsong kha pa; dGe lugs pa order founded in Tibet
1360	Theravāda becomes state religion of Thailand
1368–1644	Ming dynasty in China
1543–1588	Life of bSod nams rgya mtsho, third Dalai Lama; beginning of Dalai Lama lineage

1603–1867	Buddhism becomes state religion in Japan during Tokugawa period
1617–1682	Life of fifth Dalai Lama, Ngag dbang blo bzang rgya mtsho; beginning of rule of Tibet by Dalai Lamas
1644–1912	Ch'ing dynasty in China
1749	Mongolian Buddhist canon completed
1813–1899	Life of 'Jam mgon kong sprul; beginning of Ris med movement in Tibet
1851–1868	Reign of Rāma IV in Thailand; reform of Thai *saṃgha*
1853–1878	King Mindon works to revive Buddhism in Burma
1868–1912	Meiji period in Japan; Buddhism supplanted by State Shintō as state religion
1881	Pali Text Society founded by T. R. W. Rhys Davids
1891–1956	Life of B. R. Ambedkar; mass conversion of former Untouchables in India
1893	French colonial rule established over Cambodia, Laos, and Vietnam
1910–1945	Japanese occupation of Korea
1924–1929	Compilation of Chinese canon (Taishō Shinshū Daizōkyō) in Japan
1947	Founding of Nichiren Shōshū Sōkagakkai
1950	People's Liberation Army enters Tibet
1954–1956	Council of Rangoon
1959	Fourteenth Dalai Lama forced to flee to India; persecution of Buddhism in Tibet by Chinese
1975	Khmer Rouge begin "killing fields" period; Buddhism decimated in Cambodia

Thematic Bibliography

Buddhism general

Bareau, André. *Recherches sur la biographie du Buddha*. Paris, 1995

Bechert, Heinz and Gombrich, Richard. *The World of Buddhism*. New York: Thames & Hudson, 1984

Beyer, Steven. *The Buddhist Experience: Sources and Interpretations*. Encino, CA: Dickenson, 1974

Harvey, Peter. *The Selfless Mind: Personality, Consciousness and Nirvana in Early Buddhism*. Surrey: Curzon Press, 1995

Kalupahana, David J. *Buddhist Philosophy: A Historical Analysis*. Honolulu: University of Hawaii Press, 1976

Kitagawa, Joseph and Cummings, Mark D., eds. *Buddhism and Asian History*. New York: Macmillan, 1987

Paul, Diana. *Women in Buddhism: Images of the Feminine in Mahāyāna Tradition*. Berkeley: Asian Humanities Press, 1979

Prebish, Charles S. *Historical Dictionary of Buddhism*. Metuchen: Scarecrow Press, 1993

Prebish, Charles S. *A Survey of Vinaya Literature*. Richmond: Curzon Press, 1994

Rahula, Walpola. *What the Buddha Taught*. New York: Grove Press, 1959

Robinson, Richard H. and Johnson, Willard L. *The Buddhist Religion*. 3rd edition. Belmont, CA: Wadsworth Publishing, 1982

Snelling, John. *The Buddhist Handbook: A Complete Guide to Buddhist Schools, Teaching, Practice, and History*. Rochester, VT: Inner Traditions, 1991

Strong, John S. *The Experience of Buddhism*. Belmont, CA: Wadsworth, 1994

Williams, Paul. *Mahāyāna Buddhism: The Doctrinal Foundations*. London and New York: Routledge, 1989

Indian Buddhism

Bareau, André. *Les premiers conciles bouddhiques*. Paris: Presses Universitaires, 1955

Dutt, Sukumar. *Early Buddhist Monachism*. New Delhi: Munshiram Manoharlal, 1984

Hirakawa, Akira. *A History of Indian Buddhism: From Śākyamuni to Early Mahāyāna*. Paul Groner, tr. Honolulu: University of Hawaii Press, 1990

Lamotte, Etienne. *History of Indian Buddhism*. Sara Boin-Webb, tr. Louvain: Peeters Press, 1988

Murcott, Susan. *The First Buddhist Women: Translations and Commentary on the Therigatha*. Berkeley: Parallax Press, 1991
Nakamura, Hajime. *Indian Buddhism: A Survey with Bibliographical Notes*. Delhi: Motilal Banarsidass, 1987
Norman, K. R. *Pāli Literature*. Wiesbaden: Otto Harrassowitz, 1983
Schopen, Gregory. *Bones, Stones, and Buddhist Monks: Collected Papers on the Archaeology, Epigraphy, and Texts of Monastic Buddhism in India*. Honolulu: University of Hawaii Press, 1997
Warder, A. K. *Indian Buddhism*. Delhi: Motilal Banarsidass, 1980

Buddhism in Southeast Asia

Adikaram, E. W. *Early History of Buddhism in Ceylon*. 2nd edition. Colombo: M. D. Gunasena, 1953
Bond, George D. *The Word of the Buddha: The Tipiṭaka and its Interpretation in Theravāda Buddhism*. Colombo: Gunasena, 1982.
Gard, Richard. *The Role of Thailand in World Buddhism*. Bangkok: World Fellowship of Buddhists, 1971
Gombrich, Richard F. *Precept and Practice: Traditional Buddhism in the Rural Highlands of Ceylon*. Oxford: Clarendon Press, 1971
Gombrich, Richard F. *Theravāda Buddhism: A Social History from Ancient Benares to Modern Colombo*. London: Routledge & Kegan Paul, 1988
Gombrich, Richard and Obeyesekere, Gananath. *Buddhism Transformed: Religious Change in Sri Lanka*. Princeton: Princeton University Press, 1988
Law, Bimala Churn. *The Life and Work of Buddhaghosa*. Calcutta: Thacker, Spink, 1923
Law, Bimala Churn. *The Chronicle of the Island of Ceylon, or the Dīpavaṃsa, a Historical Poem of the 4th Century* A.D. Ceylon: Saman Press, 1959
Leclere, Adhemard. *Le Bouddhisme au Cambodge*. Paris: E. Leroux, 1899
Malalasekera, George Peiris. *The Pāli Literature of Ceylon*. London: Royal Asiatic Society of Great Britain and Ireland, 1928
Malalgoda, Kitsiri. *Buddhism in Sinhalese Society*. Berkeley: University of California Press, 1976
Mendelson, E. Michael. *Saṃgha and State in Burma: A Study of Monastic Sectarianism and Leadership*. Ithaca: Cornell University Press, 1975
Rahula, Walpola. *History of Buddhism in Ceylon: The Anurādhapura Period, 3rd Century* B.C.–*19th Century* A.D. 2nd edition. Colombo: M. D. Gunasena & Co., 1966
Sarkisyanz, Emanuel. *Buddhist Backgrounds of the Burmese Revolution*. The Hague: M. Nijhoff, 1965
Swearer, Donald K. *The Buddhist World of Southeast Asia*. Albany: State University of New York Press, 1995
Wells, Kenneth E. *Thai Buddhism: Its Rites and Activities*. Bangkok: The Christian Bookstore, 1960

Chinese Buddhism

Bush, Richard C. *Religion in Communist China*. New York: Abingdon, 1970
Ch'en, Kenneth. *Buddhism in China: A Historical Survey*. Princeton: Princeton University Press, 1984
Gimello, Robert M. and Gregory, Peter N., eds. *Studies in Ch'an and Hua-yen*. Honolulu: University of Hawaii Press, 1983

Gregory, Peter N., ed. *Sudden and Gradual: Approaches to Enlightenment in Chinese Thought*. Honolulu: University of Hawaii Press, 1987
Gregory, Peter N., ed. *Traditions of Meditation in Chinese Buddhism*. Honolulu: University of Hawaii Press, 1986
Gregory, Peter N. *Tsung-mi and the Sinification of Buddhism*. Princeton: Princeton University Press, 1991
Lai, Whalen and Lancaster, Lewis R., eds. *Early Ch'an in China and Tibet*. Berkeley: Asian Humanities Press, 1983
McRae, John R. *The Northern School and the Formation of Early Ch'an Buddhism*. Honolulu: University of Hawaii Press, 1986
Thompson, Laurence G. *Chinese Religion in Western Languages*. Tucson: University of Arizona Press, 1985
Weinstein, Stanley. *Buddhism under the T'ang*. Cambridge: Cambridge University Press, 1987
Wright, Arthur F. *Buddhism in Chinese History*. Stanford: Stanford University Press, 1959
Yampolsky, Philip, ed. and tr. *The Platform Sūtra*. New York: Columbia University Press, 1967

Japanese Buddhism

Bellah, Robert. *Tokugawa Religion: The Cultural Roots of Modern Japan*. New York: Free Press, 1957
Bielfeldt, Carl, tr. *Dōgen's Manuals of Zen Meditation*. Berkeley: University of California Press, 1988
Bloom, Alfred. *The Life of Shinran Shonin: The Journey of Self-Acceptance*. Leiden: E. J. Brill, 1968
Dumoulin, Heinrich. *Zen Buddhism: A History*. New York: Macmillan, 1988 (2 vols.)
Earhart, H. Byron. *Japanese Religion: Unity and Diversity*. Belmont, CA: Wadsworth, 1982
Kapleau, Philip. *The Three Pillars of Zen: Teaching, Practice, Enlightenment*. Boston: Beacon Press, 1967
Kasulis, T. P. *Zen Action/Zen Person*. Honolulu: University of Hawaii Press, 1981
Kitagawa, Joseph M. *Religion in Japanese History*. New York: Columbia University Press, 1966
Matsunaga, Daigan and Alicia. *Foundation of Japanese Buddhism*. Los Angeles: Buddhist Books International, 1974 (2 vols.)
Reader, Ian. *Religion in Contemporary Japan*. Honolulu: University of Hawaii Press, 1991

Korean Buddhism

Buswell, Robert E., Jr. *The Korean Approach to Zen: The Collected Works of Chinul*. Honolulu: University of Hawaii Press, 1983
Chun, Shin-yong, ed. *Buddhist Culture in Korea*. Seoul: International Cultural Foundation, 1974
Clark, Charles Allen. *Religions of Old Korea*. New York: E. H. Eevell, 1932
Cleary, Thomas, tr. *A Buddha From Korea: The Zen Teachings of T'aego*. Boston: Shambhala, 1988
Lancaster, Lewis R. and Yu, C. S., eds. *Assimilation of Buddhism in Korea: Religious*

Maturity and Innovation in the Silla Dynasty. Berkeley: Asian Humanities Press, 1991
Lancaster, Lewis R. and Yu, C. S., eds. *Introduction of Buddhism to Korea*. Berkeley: Asian Humanities Press, 1989
Starr, Frederick. *Korean Buddhism: History, Condition, Art*. Boston: Marshall Jones, 1918

Vietnamese Buddhism

Buttinger, Joseph. *Vietnam: A Political History*. New York: Praeger, 1968
Chi, Minh. *Le Bouddhisme au Vietnam*. Hanoi: The Gioi, 1993
Nhat Hanh, Thich. *Vietnam: Lotus in a Sea of Fire*. New York: Hill & Wang, 1967
Nhat Hanh, Thich. *Zen Keys: A Zen Monk Examines the Vietnamese Tradition*. New York: Anchor, 1974
Revertegat, Bruno. *Le Bouddhisme traditionnel au Sud-Vietnam*. Vichy: Wallon, 1974
Thien An, Thich. *Buddhism and Zen in Vietnam in relation to the development of Buddhism in Asia* (ed., annotated, and developed by C. Smith). Los Angeles: College of Oriental Studies, Graduate School, 1975

Tibetan Buddhism

Beyer, Stephan. *The Cult of Tārā: Magic and Ritual in Tibet*. Berkeley: University of California Press, 1978
Coleman, Graham. *A Handbook of Tibetan Culture: A Guide to Tibetan Centres and Resources throughout the World*. London: Rider, 1993
Dudjom Rinpoche. *The Nyingma School of Tibetan Buddhism*. London: Wisdom, 1991 (2 vols.)
Guenther, Herbert V. *The Life and Teachings of Naropa*. London: Oxford University Press, 1963
Gyaltsen, Khenpo Könchog. *The Garland of Mahamudra Practices*. Ithaca: Snow Lion, 1986
Gyatso, Tenzin (fourteenth Dalai Lama). *Kindness, Clarity and Insight*. Jeffrey Hopkins, tr. Ithaca: Snow Lion, 1984
Gyatso, Tenzin. *Path to Bliss: A Practical Guide to Stages of Meditation*. Ithaca: Snow Lion, 1991
Hookham, Susan K. *The Buddha Within: Tathāgatagarbha Doctrine According to the Shentong Interpretation of the Ratnagotravibhāga*. Albany: State University of New York Press, 1991
Hopkins, Jeffrey. *Meditation on Emptiness*. London: Wisdom, 1983
Jackson, David. *Enlightenment by a Single Means*. Wien: Verlag der Österreichischen Akademie der Wissenschaften, 1994
Karmay, Samten. *The Great Perfection (Rdzogs Chen): A Philosophical and Meditative Training in Tibetan Buddhism*. Leiden: E. J. Brill, 1988
Klein, Anne C. *Meeting the Great Bliss Queen: Buddhists, Feminists, and the Art of the Self*. Boston: Beacon Press, 1995
Lama Yeshe. *Introduction to Tantra: A Vision of Totality*. London: Wisdom, 1987
Powers, John. *Introduction to Tibetan Buddhism*. Ithaca: Snow Lion, 1995
Samuel, Geoffrey. *Civilized Shamans: Buddhism in Tibetan Societies*. Washington, D.C.: Smithsonian Institution Press, 1993
Snellgrove, David and Richardson, Hugh. *A Cultural History of Tibet*. New York: Frederick A. Praeger, 1968

Mongolian Buddhism

Bawden, C. R. *The Jebtsundamba Khutukhtus of Urga*. Wiesbaden: Otto Harrassowitz, 1961

Heissig, Walther. *The Religions of Mongolia*. Los Angeles: University of California Press, 1980

Hyer, Paul. *A Mongolian Living Buddha*. Albany: State University of New York Press, 1983

Moses, Larry William. *The Political Role of Mongol Buddhism*. Bloomington, IN: Asian Studies Research Institute, Indiana University, 1977

Moses, Larry William, and Halkovic, Stephen. *Introduction to Mongolian History and Culture*. Bloomington, IN: Research Institute for Inner Asian Studies, 1985

Western Buddhism

Almond, Philip C. *The British Discovery of Buddhism*. Cambridge: Cambridge University Press, 1988

de Jong, Jan Willem. *A Brief History of Buddhist Studies in Europe and America*. 2nd edition. Delhi: Sri Satguru, 1986

Fields, Rick. *How the Swans Came to the Lake: A Narrative History of Buddhism in America*. Boston: Shambhala, 1992

Friedman, Lenore. *Meeting with Remarkable Women: Buddhist Teachers in America*. Boston: Shambhala, 1987

Hunter, Louise. *Buddhism in Hawaii: Its Impact on a Yankee Community*. Honolulu: University of Hawaii Press, 1971

Kashima, Tetsuden. *Buddhism in America: The Social Organization of an Ethnic Religious Institution*. Westport, CT: Greenwood Press, 1977

Morreale, Don, ed. *Buddhist America: Centers, Retreats, Practices*. Santa Fe, NM: John Muir Publications, 1988

Prebish, Charles S. *Luminous Passage: The Practice and Study of Buddhism in America*. Berkeley: University of California Press, 1999

Prebish, Charles S. and Tanaka, Kenneth, eds. *The Faces of Buddhism in America*. Berkeley: University of California Press, 1999

Tweed, Thomas A. *The American Encounter with Buddhism, 1844–1912*. Bloomington: Indiana University Press, 1992

Art, architecture, and iconography

Frédéric, Louis. *Buddhism: Flammarion Iconographic Guides*. Paris: Flammarion, 1995

Landaw, Jonathan and Weber, Andy. *Images of Enlightenment: Tibetan Art in Practice*. Ithaca: Snow Lion, 1993

Pal, Pratapaditya. *A Buddhist Paradise: The Murals of Alchi, Western Himalayas*. New Delhi: Ravi Kumar, 1982

Pal, Pratapaditya. *Tibetan Paintings*. London: Ravi Kumar, 1984

Reynolds, Valrae. *Tibet: A Lost World*. New York: American Federation of Arts, 1978

Rhie, Marylin and Thurman, Robert. *Wisdom and Compassion: The Sacred Art of Tibet*. New York: Harry N. Abrams, 1991

Ricca, Franco and Lo Bue, Erberto. *The Great Stupa of Gyantse*. London: Serindia, 1993

Saso, Michael. *Tantric Art and Meditation*. Honolulu: Tendai Educational Foundation, 1990
Snodgrass, Adrian. *The Matrix and Diamond World Maṇḍalas in Shingon Buddhism*. Delhi: Aditya Prakashan, 1988
Tucci, Giuseppe. *Tibetan Painted Scrolls*. Rome: ISmeo, 1949 (2 vols.)

Buddhist philosophy

Anacker, Stefan. *Seven Works of Vasubandhu*. Delhi: Motilal Banarsidass, 1984
Boisvert, Mathieu. *The Five Aggregates: Understanding Theravāda Psychology and Soteriology*. Waterloo: Wilfrid Laurier Press, 1995
Collins, Steven. *Nirvana and Other Buddhist Felicities*. Cambridge: Cambridge University Press, 1998
Collins, Steven. *Selfless Persons: Imagery and Thought in Theravāda Buddhism*. Cambridge: Cambridge University Press, 1982
Griffiths, Paul J. *On Being Buddha: The Classical Doctrine of Buddhahood*. Albany: State University of New York Press, 1994
Griffiths, Paul J. *On Being Mindless: Buddhist Meditation and the Mind–Body Problem*. La Salle, IL: Open Court, 1986
Hayes, Richard. *Dignāga on Interpretation*. Dordrecht: Kluwer Academic, 1988
Huntington, C. W. *The Emptiness of Emptiness: An Introduction to Early Indian Mādhyamika*. Honolulu: University of Hawaii Press, 1989
Nagao, Gadjin. *Madhyamika and Yogācāra*. Leslie Kawamura, tr. Albany: State University of New York Press, 1991
Powers, John. *Hermeneutics and Tradition in the Saṃdhinirmocana-sūtra*. Leiden: E. J. Brill, 1993
Ruegg, David S. *The Literature of the Madhyamaka School of Philosophy in India*. Wiesbaden: Otto Harrassowitz, 1981
Schmithausen, Lambert. *Ālayavijñāna: On the Origin and the Early Development of a Central Concept of Yogācāra Philosophy*. Tokyo: International Institute for Buddhist Studies, 1987 (2 vols.)

Contemporary Buddhist issues

Badiner, Allan Hunt. *Dharma Gaia: A Harvest of Essays in Buddhism and Ecology*. Berkeley: Parallax Press, 1990
Batchelor, Martine and Brown, Kerry. *Buddhism and Ecology*. London: Cassell, 1992
Boucher, Sandy. *Turning the Wheel: American Women Creating the New Buddhism*. San Francisco: Harper & Row, 1985
Gross, Rita M. *Buddhism after Patriarchy*. Albany: State University of New York Press, 1993
Queen, Christopher S. and King, Sallie B. *Engaged Buddhism: Buddhist Liberation Movements in Asia*. Albany: State University of New York Press, 1996

Thematic Index

The Principal figures and periods of Buddhist history

PEOPLE

Indian Buddhism

Ajātaśatru
Ambedkar, Dr. Bhimrao Ramji
Ānanda
Anāthapiṇḍika
Anuruddha (1)
Āryadeva
Asaṅga
Aśoka
Aśvaghoṣa
Bhavya
Bimbisāra
Buddhapālita
Candrakīrti
Devadatta
Dharmakīrti
Dharmapāla
Dignāga
Jñānagarbha
Kamalaśīla
Kaniṣka I
Kāśyapa
Mahāprajāpatī
Maitreya (2)
Maudgalyāyana
Māyā
Nāgārjuna
Nāropa
Paramārtha
Pūrṇa
Rāhula
Śākya
Śākyamuni Buddha
Śāntarakṣita
Śāntideva
Śāriputra
Siddhārtha Gautama
Subhūti
Śuuddhodana
Tilopa
Upāli
Vasubandhu
Vasumitra
Yaśodharā

East Asian Buddhism

An Shih-kao
Bankei Eitaku
Bassui Zenji
Bodhidharma
Buddhabhadra
Ch'an-ch'ing Hui-leng
Chao-chou Ts'ung-shen
Chih-i
Chinul
Chi-tsang
Dōgen Zenji
Dōshō
Eisai Zenji
Ennin
Fa-hsien

Southeast Asian Buddhism

Evans-Wentz, Walter Yeeling
Frauwallner, Erich
Gombrich, Richard F.
Guenther, Herbert V.
Hayes, Richard Philip
Herrigel, Eugen
Hirakawa, Akira
Hopkins, P. Jeffrey
Horner, Isabelle Blew
Humphreys, Travers Christmas
Korösi, Csoma Sándor
la Vallée Poussin, Louis de
Lamotte, Étienne
Lindtner, Christian
Nagatomi, Masatoshi
Nakamura, Hajime
Oldenberg, Hermann
Prebish, Charles S.
Rhys Davids, Caroline Augusta Foley
Rhys Davids, Thomas William
Robinson, Richard Hugh
Ruegg, David Seyfort
Stcherbatsky, Fedor Ippolitovich
Steinkellner, Ernst
Swearer, Donald K.
Thurman, Robert A. F.
Tucci, Giuseppe
Vetter, Tilmann
Warren, Henry Clarke
Wayman, Alex
Williams, Paul Martin

PLACES

India

Ajaṇṭā
Bodhgayā
Bodhi-vṛkṣa
Ellora
Gandhāra
Gṛdhrakūṭa
Kapilavastu
Kuśinagara
Lumbinī
Nālandā Monastic University
Pāṭaliputra
Rājagṛha
Sāñcī
Sārnāth
Vaiśālī
Vikramaśīla Monastic University

East Asia

Chogyesa
Daitoku-ji
Eihei-ji
Engaku-ji
Fo Kuang Shan
Haeinsa
Hieizan
Lung-men
Pai-ma-ssu
Pulguksa
Shao-lin-ssu
Sōji-ji
Songgwangsa
Tongdosa
Tun-huang
Wu-tai shan
Yun-kang

Southeast Asia

Abhayagiri
Angkor Wat
Anurādhapura
Borobudur
Jetavana (1)
Jetavana (2)
Mahāvihāra
Schwezigon Pagoda

Tibet, Himalayas, and Mongolia

bKra shis lhun po
'Bras spungs
bSam yas
dGa' ldan
Gandan Monastery
Ivolginsky Monastery
Kailāsa

animitta
anitya
anuyoga
ārya-satya
asaṃskṛta
avidyā
avyākṛta
āyatana
bala
bar do
blo rigs
bodhi
buddha-dharma
buddhatā
catur-mudrā
catur-nimitta
citta
citta-mātra
dauṣṭhulya-bandhana
dharma
dharma-cakra
dharma-kāya
dṛṣṭi
duḥkha
ekayāna
evil
fugyō-ni-gyō
fukasetsu
gedatsu
go-i
goke-shichishū
goseki
gzhan stong
haibutsu-kishaku
hannya
hongaku
honrai-no-memoku
icchantika
ishin-denshin
'ja' lus
jiriki
jñāna
kāma
karma
karuṇā
kleśa
ko-i
kṣānti
madhyama-pratipad
manas
mappō
mārga
meat eating
nāma-rūpa
nirmāṇa-kāya
nirvāṇa
pañca-mahābhaya
p'an-chiao
paramārtha[-satya]
pāramitā
parinirvāṇa
prabhāsvara-citta
prajñā
pratītya-samutpāda
pṛthag-jana
puṇya
rang stong
ratna-traya
rebirth
rgyud gsum
rig pa
saṃbhoga-kāya
saṃskāra
saṃskṛta
saṃvṛti-satya
samyak-prahāṇa
śaraṇa
sāsana
sattva
satya-dvaya
skandha
snang gsum
sokushin jōbutsu
śraddhā
śūnyatā
svabhāva
tariki
tathāgata-garbha
tathatā
t'ong pulgyo

Meditation: theory and practice

mahāthera
mKhan zur Rin po che
Paṇ chen bLa ma
phra
pratyeka-buddha
rGyal ba Kar ma pa
rin po che
rJe btsun dam pa Khutukhtu
rōshi
Sa skya khri 'dzin
samyak-sambuddha
sayādaw
sikkhamat
skyabs mgon
skyabs rje
sngags pa
sprul sku
śrāmaṇera
śrāmaṇerī
śrāvaka
srotāpanna
Ta'i si tu Rin po che
tathāgata
thera
thilashin
tīrthika
unsui
upāsaka
upāsikā
yogin
zenji
Zhwa dmar Rin po che

LITERATURE

India

Abhidharma-kósa
Abhidharma-piṭaka
Abhidharma-samuccaya
Abhisamayālaṃkāra
āgama
Aṅguttara Nikāya
anuttara-yoga-tantra
Aṣṭa-sāhasrikā-prajñā-pāramitā-sūtra
Avataṃsaka-sūtra
Bhāvanākrama
Bodhicaryāvatāra
Bodhipatha-pradīpa
Bodhisattva-bhūmi
Buddhacarita
caryā-tantra
Dásabhūmika-sūtra
Dhammapada
Dharma-cakra-pravartana-sūtra
Dīgha Nikāya
Dīpavaṃsa
Evaṃ mayā śrutam ekasmin samaye
Gaṇḍavyūha-sūtra
Guhyasamāja-tantra
Hevajra-tantra
Jātaka
Kālacakra-tantra
Khuddaka Nikāya
kriyā-tantra
Lalitavistara
Laṅkāvatāra-sūtra
Mahāparinibbāna-sutta
Mahaparinirvana-sutra
Mahāvaṃsa
Mahāvastu
Mahāvibhāṣā
Mahāyāna-śraddhotpāda-śāstra
Majjhima Nikāya
Milindapañha
Mūlamadhyamakārikā
nikāya (1)
Pāli canon
prajñā-pāramitā sūtras
Prajñā-pāramitā-hṛdaya-sūtra
Ratna-kūṭa-sūtra
Saddharma-puṇḍarīka-sūtra
Saṃdhinirmocana-sūtra
Saṃyutta Nikāya
Sanskrit
sāstra
Satipaṭṭhāna-sutta
Sukhāvatī-vyūha-sūtra
sūtra
Sūtra-piṭaka
tantra

Theragātha
Therīgātha
tripiṭaka
vaipulya-sūtra
Vajracchedika-prajñā-pāramitā-sūtra
Vessantara Jātaka
Vimalakīrti-nirdeśa-sūtra
Vinaya-piṭaka
Visuddhimagga
yoga-tantra

East Asia

Ching-te ch'uan-teng-lu
Denkō-roku
Genjō-kōan
hua-t'ou
Liu-tsu-ta-shih fa-pao-t'an-ching
Pi-yen-lu
Shōbōgenzō
Taishō Shinshū Daizōkyō
Ta-sheng-ch'i-hsin-lun
Wu-men-kuan

Tibet

bKa' 'gyur
Bar do thos grol
bsTan 'gyur
gsang ba'i rang rnam
gter ma
gter ston
kLong chen snying thig
rnam thar

Western languages

Journal of Buddhist Ethics
Journal of the International Association of Buddhist Studies

Acknowledgments

The publisher and author would like to thank the following people for assistance and permission to produce the following pictures:

Dr Elizabeth J. Harris (pp. 104, 105, 106, 207, 208); Mr David Rose (pp. 206, 238, 239).